ASSOCIATIONAL LIFE AND FREEDOM

What is the reality of what it is to participate in associations, such as sports clubs, charities, trade unions, or political parties? This book explores the complexities surrounding the right of association from a legal and philosophical perspective.

Legal chapters explore how the right is protected in jurisdictions as diverse as Chile, Germany, Indonesia, Kenya, Slovenia, Türkiye and the United Kingdom, alongside thematic chapters on judicial review, associational schism and the lived experience of associational participation. Philosophical chapters employ social ontology to illuminate the nature of group interaction and the reality of associational life.

Offering the first interdisciplinary examination of freedom of association, this collection contributes significantly to our understanding of this fundamental right.

Volume 32: Human Rights Law in Perspective

Human Rights Law in Perspective

General Editor: Colin Harvey
Professor of Human Rights Law
School of Law
Queen's University Belfast

The language of human rights figures prominently in legal and political debates at the national, regional and international levels. In the UK the Human Rights Act 1998 has generated considerable interest in the law of human rights. It will continue to provoke much debate in the legal community and the search for original insights and new materials will intensify.

The aim of this series is to provide a forum for scholarly reflection on all aspects of the law of human rights. The series will encourage work which engages with the theoretical, comparative and international dimensions of human rights law. The primary aim is to publish over time books which offer an insight into human rights law in its contextual setting. The objective is to promote an understanding of the nature and impact of human rights law. The series is inclusive, in the sense that all perspectives in legal scholarship are welcome. It will incorporate the work of new and established scholars.

Human Rights Law in Perspective is not confined to consideration of the UK. It will strive to reflect comparative, regional and international perspectives. Work which focuses on human rights law in other states will therefore be included in this series. The intention is to offer an inclusive intellectual home for significant scholarly contributions to human rights law.

Recent titles in this series

Social Rights and the Constitutional Moment: Learning from Chile and International Experiences
Edited by Koldo Casla, Magdalena Sepúlveda, Vicente Silva, and Valentina Contreras

Article 8 ECHR, Family Reunification and the UK's Supreme Court: Family Matters?
Helena Wray

Rethinking Human Rights: Critical Insights from Palestinian Youth
Erika Jiménez

Immediate and Progressive Realisation in International Human Rights Law
Tobias Wirthle

Associational Life and Freedom: Insights from Philosophy and Law
Edited by Maria Cahill and Giulia Lasagni

For the complete list of titles in this series, see 'Human Rights Law in Perspective' link at www.bloomsbury.com/uk/series/human-rights-law-in-perspective/

Associational Life and Freedom

Insights from Philosophy and Law

Edited by
Maria Cahill
and
Giulia Lasagni

•HART•
OXFORD • LONDON • NEW YORK • NEW DELHI • SYDNEY

HART PUBLISHING

Bloomsbury Publishing Plc

Kemp House, Chawley Park, Cumnor Hill, Oxford, OX2 9PH, UK

1385 Broadway, New York, NY 10018, USA

Bloomsbury Publishing Ireland Limited, 29 Earlsfort Terrace, Dublin 2, D02 AY28, Ireland

HART PUBLISHING, the Hart/Stag logo, BLOOMSBURY and the Diana logo are trademarks of Bloomsbury Publishing Plc

First published in Great Britain 2026

A catalogue record for this book is available from the British Library.

A catalogue record for this book is available from the Library of Congress.

ISBN: HB: 978-1-50998-669-9
ePDF: 978-1-50998-671-2
ePub: 978-1-50998-670-5

Typeset by Compuscript Ltd, Shannon

For product safety related questions contact productsafety@bloomsbury.com

To find out more about our authors and books visit www.hartpublishing.co.uk. Here you will find extracts, author information, details of forthcoming events and the option to sign up for our newsletters.

Table of Contents

List of Contributors .... *vii*

Introduction: Comparative and Interdisciplinary Interfaces of Associational Life and Freedom *1*
Maria Cahill

PART I
THE LAW OF ASSOCIATIONAL FREEDOM

1. *Freedom of Association and the Law in the United Kingdom* *21*
   Julian Rivers
2. *Freedom of Association in Chile* *41*
   Sebastian Soto
3. *Unfolding Pluralism: Freedom of Association in Slovenia's Constitutional Democracy* *61*
   Katarina Vatovec
4. *Freedom of Association in Germany* *81*
   Leannán Martan O'Grady
5. *Freedom of Association in Türkiye* *103*
   Fatih Öztürk
6. *Freedom of Association and its Restrictions in Indonesia* *115*
   Inna Junaenah
7. *Freedom of Association in Kenya: Constitutional Foundations, Judicial Reasoning, and Democratic Tensions* *135*
   Njoki Mboce
8. *Judicial Review of Associative Agreements: Insights from a Civil Law Perspective* *151*
   José Juan Anzures Gurría
9. *Schisms and Internal Disputes within Religious Associations under the European Convention on Human Rights* *167*
   Nicholas McMurry
10. *Portraits of Associational Participation: Exploring Personal Narratives* *181*
    Erin Jackson

PART II
PHILOSOPHICAL PERSPECTIVES ON ASSOCIATIONAL FREEDOM

11. *Social Ontology and Collective Intentionality: A Philosophical Perspective on Human Association* 197
Giulia Lasagni

12. *Associating on Familiar Grounds: A Habitual Perspective on the Freedom of Association* 213
Judith H Martens

13. *The Right to be We: The Case of Associations* 229
Michael Schmitz

14. *Recognising Associations: A Social Ontology Perspective* 245
Valeria Martino

15. *The Good of Association and the Freedom that We Share* 259
Hans Bernhard Schmid

16. *The Nature, Ground, and Legal Expression of a Right to Freedom of Association* 277
Kirk Ludwig

Index 295

List of Contributors

José Juan Anzures Gurría is Professor and Researcher at the School of Law, Universidad Panamericana, Mexico; PhD; janzures@up.edu.mx.

Maria Cahill is Professor of Law at the School of Law, University College Cork, Ireland; LLB, LLM, PhD; maria.cahill@ucc.ie.

Erin Jackson is Assistant Professor at the School of Law, Utrecht University, the Netherlands; BJ, LLM, PhD; e.e.jackson@uu.nl.

Inna Junaenah is Senior Lecturer at the Department of Constitutional Law (Hukum Tata Negara) and Researcher at the Centre for State Policy Studies, Universitas Padjadjaran, Indonesia; SH, MH, PhD; inna.junaenah@unpad.ac.id.

Giulia Lasagni is Senior Postdoctoral Researcher at the School of Law, University College Cork, Ireland; BA, MA, PhD; glasagni@ucc.ie.

Kirk Ludwig is Ruth N Halls Professor of Philosophy and Cognitive Science at Indiana University, Bloomington, USA; BS, PhD; ludwig@iu.edu.

Nicholas McMurry is Lecturer and Programme Director in Law, Griffith College Cork, Ireland; MA, MPhil, LLM, PhD; nicholas.mcmurry@griffith.ie.

Fatih Öztürk is Professor of Constitutional Law at the Faculty of Law, Istanbul University, Türkiye; LLB, LLM, PhD; fatih.ozturk@istanbul.edu.tr, attorney33@hotmail.com.

Leannán Martan O'Grady is a PhD candidate at Scuola Superiore Sant'Anna, Institute of Law, Politics and Development, Pisa, Italy; BA, MA, LLM; leannan.ogrady@santannapisa.it.

Judith H Martens is Assistant Professor at the Centre for Philosophical Psychology, University of Antwerp, Belgium; BA, BSc, MA, MSc, PhD; judith.martens@uantwerpen.be.

Valeria Martino is Postdoctoral Research Fellow at the Department of Philosophy and Education Sciences, University of Turin, Italy; BA, MA, PhD; valeria.martino@unito.it.

Njoki Mboce is Lecturer of Law at the School of Law, University of Nairobi, Kenya; LLB, LLM, PhD; njokimboce@uonbi.ac.ke.

Julian Rivers is Professor of Jurisprudence at the School of Law, University of Bristol, United Kingdom; MA, LLM, MJur, PhD; julian.rivers@bristol.ac.uk.

Hans Bernhard Schmid is Professor of Political and Social Philosophy, University of Vienna, Austria; PhD, Hab.; hans.bernhard.schmid@univie.ac.at.

Michael Schmitz is Senior Researcher at the Central European University, Philosophy Department, and Privatdozent, University of Vienna, Austria; MA, PhD, Hab.; Michael.Schmitz@univie.ac.at.

Sebastian Soto is Associate Professor at the Law School, Pontificia Universidad Católica de Chile, Chile; LLB, LLM, PhD; jssoto@uc.cl.

Katarina Vatovec is Assistant Professor at the European Faculty of Law, New University, Slovenia; LLB, LLM, PhD; katarina.vatovec@epf.nova-uni.si.

Introduction

Comparative and Interdisciplinary Interfaces of Associational Life and Freedom

MARIA CAHILL

ASSOCIATIONAL LIFE AND *Freedom: Insights from Philosophy and Law* is an edited volume focusing on the lived and legal reality of what it is to participate in associations, whether they be sports clubs, charities, trade unions or political parties, or indeed student, cultural, minority or religious associations. Although freedom of association is a fundamental human right protected in legal systems around the world, to date, scholarly inquiry into what it protects and why it offers that protection has not kept pace with that explicating other rights. Its most compelling feature is that freedom of association protects individuals in their sociality, in the collaborative context of their relationships with others, the nuances of which make the work of judicially interpreting its nature and scope quite complex. This collection, the first interdisciplinary effort to illuminate the complexities of associational life and freedom, is an output of a Laureate project funded by Research Ireland entitled 'Societās: Exploring the Value of Freedom of Association' IRCLA/2022/3860, led by Professor Maria Cahill as Principal Investigator at the School of Law, University College Cork, Ireland, and running from 2022 until 2026. The project has two principal dimensions: first, it investigates how the right to freedom of association is enshrined, interpreted and vindicated in the diverse cultural and political contexts of jurisdictions around the world, and second, it considers how this right might be more fully understood and protected, including by reference to interdisciplinary perspectives. The former entails an extensive comparative study, expanding beyond the scope of this present work,[1] involving dozens of scholars from different jurisdictions, some of whom are writing the first piece of legal scholarship on how this particular right is protected in their jurisdiction. The

[1] See 'Global Perspectives on Freedom of Association' (2025) 12 (1 & 2) *European Journal of Comparative Law and Governance*, a double special issue emanating from the Societās project, edited by Maria Cahill, Dwight Newman and Seán Ó Conaill, and featuring 20 articles examining the right to freedom of association in Australia, Canada, China, Egypt, Ethiopia, Finland, France, Ireland, Italy, Japan, Mexico, Nigeria, Peru, Poland, South Africa, Spain, the United States, as well as international human rights systems such as the Council of Europe, the Inter-American System of Human Rights and the United Nations.

latter entails cross-disciplinary conversation with scholars, mostly philosophers, whose research on the social dimension of the human experience helps to inspire greater sensitivity to the contours and the importance of the right within law. To promote the cross- and inter-disciplinary aims of the project, Dr Giulia Lasagni (a philosopher with expertise in the field of social ontology) was appointed as Senior Postdoctoral Researcher on the Societās project team.

The comparative and the interdisciplinary dimensions of the Societās are brought together in this collection. Part I, 'The Law of Associational Freedom', comprises ten chapters, seven of which examine how freedom of association is protected in Chile, Germany, Indonesia, Kenya, Slovenia, Türkiye and the United Kingdom, while the remaining three consider associational freedom in the light of associational experience, associational schism and judicial review of associative agreements. Part II, 'Philosophical Perspectives on Associational Freedom', comprises six chapters, the first of which is written by Giulia Lasagni and introduces social ontology (and in particular the concept of collective intentionality) before contextualising the remainder of the chapters and the ways in which they illuminate associational experience from a philosophical perspective. Meanwhile, this introduction proceeds as follows: in Part I, there is a reflection on the principled importance of freedom of association; in Part II, there follows an overview of the landscape of doctrinal protection of the right, which also presents and introduces the legal chapters in this volume: and in Part III, attention is drawn to two pressure points that can arise in the effort to interpret and vindicate freedom of association in detail, which pressure points can usefully be engaged from an interdisciplinary perspective. The philosophy chapters in this volume emerged from a webinar and a two-day workshop on the theme of 'Exploring Associational Life: From Social Ontology to Law and Back Again' which took place at the School of Law at University College Cork on 25–26 April 2024, organised by Dr Lasagni and Professor Cahill, and also received some support from a National University of Ireland grant. The legal chapters in this volume were prepared for an online workshop on the theme of 'Comparative Insights on Freedom of Association', which took place on 30 January 2025. Thanks to the generous funding for the Societās project provided by Research Ireland, it has been possible to spark the valuable comparative and interdisciplinary conversations that have led to the reflections that follow in the pages of this collection.

I. THE IMPORTANCE OF ASSOCIATIONAL LIFE

When a particular dimension of the human experience is identified and protected as a human right, we must start with the assumption that something important is in play. Freedom of association protects the right to form and to join and to internally organise groups that are oriented towards a particular goal or purpose, and by corollary the rights to leave and refuse to join particular associations. Although members of an association are working together in pursuit of the same goals, associational interaction is different from the kinds of collegial relationships we have at work, since the latter are generally contractual and paid while the former are generally voluntary and unpaid. Although members of an association may be inspired by civic-minded purposes to create change and have an impact for good in local or wider communities, associational involvement is not the same as ordinary civic interaction since citizenship does not necessitate the level of interpersonal engagement and practical effort that associational involvement involves. And although members of an association may be or become friends and family members, associational relationships are not coextensive with familial or romantic relationships or friendships because associational relationships are developed in the common pursuit of identified purposes rather than for their own sake. In other words, associations are not only about the goal to be pursued, and they are not only about the relationships between the members: the relationships exist because of the orientation towards a shared goal, and the goal can be pursued only because of the voluntary commitment and collaboration of the members. In short, it is the hybridity of associations as spaces of *interpersonal connection* in the *voluntary pursuit of identified purposes* that is particular to them and special about them.

Recognising and enshrining a right to freedom of association affirms that there is something about this hybridity that is important to the human experience. Perhaps we intuitively know that from our own life experience. It might be clear to us that involvement in a sports club or a student society or a charity has had a decisive impact for good in our lives, whether by allowing us to participate in something bigger than ourselves or by offering us a lived example of what sustainable cooperation looks like, all the while shaping us to be the people that we are. More often than not, though, we take the legacy of associational involvement in our lives for granted. Perhaps it is not fully clear to us, then, why freedom of association deserves recognition as a human right. Although it has been recognised in most jurisdictions of the world and over the course of many decades as a fundamental right, it may still seem necessary to reflect on why it matters. Within legal contexts, there are two major justifications offered for the right to freedom of association: that freedom of association protects individual liberty and that it safeguards democracy. A more tentatively expressed position is that freedom of association is important because it supports self-development and promotes personal flourishing. Each of these is considered below.

The first justification for freedom of association is that it protects the right of people to live their lives as they decide.[2] Within this broadly liberal vision, freedom of association sits alongside freedom of conscience and the right to privacy, emphasising the importance of allowing individuals to live their lives as they

[2] See, eg, the work of Chandran Kukathas and William Galston which advocate robust protection for freedom of association as a protection of liberty: C Kukathas, *The Liberal Archipelago: A Theory of Diversity and Freedom* (Oxford, Oxford University Press, 2003); W Galston, *Liberal Pluralism: The Implications of Value Pluralism for Political Theory and Practice* (Cambridge, Cambridge University Press, 2002).

choose. While freedom of conscience and privacy safeguard the rights of individuals to pursue their own goals and to live their lives as they please alone and within the inner sanctuary of personal and family relationships, freedom of association contemplates that the individual will also want to join together with others in the pursuit of certain goals and purposes that are shared. Freedom of association thus protects that broader collective aspect of doing things together, which might be represented by membership of a sports club or a student society or a residents' association or a charity. On this view, the importance of the right is grounded in the freedom that it protects, and therefore all kinds of associations deserve protection in principle, and none of them is especially privileged. Understood in this way, freedom of association sits in partnership with freedom of expression and freedom of assembly, the former protecting the right of people to cooperate in *doing* something, while the latter protect the rights of people in *expressing* something. Freedom of association can also partner with freedom of religion, protecting the associational aspects of that right. Freedom of association is supportive of these other rights, but it is also a fundamental right on its own terms. On this liberal view, freedom of association is the right that provides for the living out of people's different ideas of the good life and is therefore the fundamental principle – arguably the *only* fundamental principle[3] – of a free society which safeguards against a monolithic state-centred polity. A liberal justification of freedom of association makes sense of the right to form and the right to join associations as being consequent on the importance of people being free to live their lives as they see fit. It justifies the right to leave and to refuse to join associations, perhaps even as an 'inalienable' right,[4] in defence of the same freedom. Moreover, it justifies the right of associations to be self-organising and free from unwarranted outside interference on the basis that associations are allowed to pursue independent (non-criminal) purposes rather than being required to align with state goals. In some sense, the liberal vision of freedom of association presents itself as a right antecedent to law: it almost goes without saying, although it is expressly enshrined in constitutions and human rights treaties, that persons should be allowed to live their lives as they see fit, including by collaborating and cooperating with others when purposes or circumstances favour consolidation.

The second justification for freedom of association proposed by courts and commentators is that it protects the right of people to participate in the wider project of self-government for the sake of a vibrant participatory democracy.[5] Within this broadly republican vision, freedom of association sits alongside the right to vote, the right to stand for political office, the principle of representation

[3] Kukathas (n 2) 4, 5.

[4] ibid 3.

[5] See, A de Tocqueville, *Democracy in America* (HC. Mansfield & D Winthrop (eds), Chicago, University of Chicago Press, 2000). This view finds legal expression in the work of the European Court of Human Rights and the United Nations. See M Cahill, 'Freedom of Association at the ECHR: A Right in Service of Democracy' (2025) 12 (1&2) *European Journal of Comparative Law and Governance* 124; M Cahill and R McIntyre, 'Freedom of Association under the Treaties of the United Nations' (2025) 12 (1&2) *European Journal of Comparative Law and Governance* 342.

and the principle of freedom to participate in public affairs. In some jurisdictions, in fact, freedom of association is expressly protected as a political right[6] (rather than a human right), and in other jurisdictions it is interpreted in that way.[7] The central argument is that associations support a vibrant democracy by relativising the place of the extant political majority, allowing alternative and minority perspectives to be galvanised through collaboration and cooperation, thus promoting a healthy pattern of democracy over time. Alexis de Tocqueville famously made this point when he argued that associations provide opportunities for individuals to 'learn the art of uniting with those like them' to defend their freedom and goals, and thus 'to weaken the moral empire of the majority'.[8] Understood as a political right and/or within a republican vision, associations that are especially facilitative of political engagement can take on a deeper significance than they would under a broadly liberal vision: political parties and trade unions could be seen as exemplar associations because they are most closely connected with the political sphere and most readily vivify the importance of freedom of association as a civil and political right. Non-governmental associations and minority associations can also make a claim to be higher-status associations, on this view, given that they seek to participate in decision-making and/or influence policy and/or raise consciousness in respect of specific issues and concerns. Freedom of association still sits alongside freedom of expression and freedom of assembly within this vision, because all three create space for political engagement: freedom of expression protects the right to present a message, and freedom of assembly protects the right to congregate in the articulation of that message, while freedom of association protects the more sustained and stable but still voluntary form of collective action in pursuit of chosen goals. The importance of freedom of association as a civil and political right arguably deserves more emphasis at this particular moment in history, especially in places where there is increasing multiculturalism and/or where there are weakened democracies and diminished public institutions, with a consequent need to foster sites of sustainable cooperation and encourage patterns of mutual understanding among and between existing majorities and (new) minorities.

Beyond these two major justifications of freedom of association that stress its importance in terms of freedom and democracy, a third option might emphasise the importance of freedom of association in terms of its capacity to support self-development and promote human flourishing.[9] At a very human level,

[6] See, eg, KK Negesse, 'The Purpose and Potential of Freedom of Association in Ethiopia' (2025) 12 (1&2) *European Journal of Comparative Law and Governance* 244.

[7] V Barbé, 'Freedom of Association in France: A Freedom in Danger' (2025) 12 (1&2) *European Journal of Comparative Law and Governance* 322; S Zhu, 'Freedom of Association in Contemporary China' (2025) 12 (1&2) *European Journal of Comparative Law and Governance* 92.

[8] Tocqueville (n 5) 489, 185.

[9] See, eg, M Monti, 'Freedom of Association in Italy: Genesis, Evolution and Limits of Protections of Associations in the Italian Legal System' (2025) 12 (1&2) *European Journal of Comparative Law and Governance* 39; MO Silva, 'Freedom of Association in Peru' (2025) 12 (1&2) *European Journal of Comparative Law and Governance* 288. See also, N Rosenblum, *Membership and Morals: The Personal Uses of Pluralism in America* (Princeton, Princeton University Press, 2000).

associations offer us opportunities to pursue something that we are interested in, creating bonds and developing character under the protective cover of that shared passion. That is not to say that associational involvement is always easy or that it only leaves a positive legacy in our lives. But in a context where social connectedness is a recognised predictor of health outcomes,[10] where 'social prescribing' is becoming increasingly important within health care contexts,[11] and where some parts of the world are experiencing 'an epidemic of loneliness',[12] perhaps it is this justification for freedom of association that will become the most significant in the years to come. To fully understand the connection between associational freedom and human flourishing would require further interdisciplinary research and conversation with expert colleagues from the fields of psychology, sociology and public health. To start to intuit what might be at stake here, we would do well to build patterns of reflection and conversation on our own experiences of associational involvement and the legacy that they have left in our lives.

That freedom of association is protected as a human right signifies that there is something fundamentally important about associational life, even if it has been undermined in some parts of the world and forgotten in others. It seems to me that all three of these justifications for freedom of association – emphasising its importance by reference to freedom, to democracy and to flourishing – deserve to be taken seriously, deeply considered and further researched. In support of that larger purpose, the legal chapters in this volume tell the story of how freedom of association is currently regulated and interpreted in specific jurisdictions, both against the backdrop of their particular political, legal, social and cultural histories and in the context of current challenges. Even when we agree *that* freedom of association is important, and even if we were to reach consensus on *why* freedom of association is important, there is still a lot of work to be done in figuring out *how* it should be vindicated.

II. THE LANDSCAPE OF LEGAL PROTECTION

Although law may – and should – be idealistic, especially when it comes to protecting human rights, it does not have the luxury of remaining abstract.

[10] Report of the WHO Commission on Social Connection, *From Loneliness to Social Connection: Charting a Path to Healthier Societies* 30 June 2025 Available at: www.who.int/publications/i/item/978240112360, last accessed 28 August 2025.

[11] D Morse, S Sandhu, K Mulligan, S Tierney, M Polley, BC Giurca, et al., 'Global Developments in Social Prescribing' (2022) 7(5) *British Medical Journal of Global Health* Available at: doi.org/10.1136/bmjgh-2022-008524, last accessed 28 August 2025.

[12] See, eg, D Surkalim, M Luo, R Eres, K Gebel, J van Buskirk, A Bauman and D Ding, 'The Prevalence of Loneliness across 113 Countries: Systematic Review and Meta-Analysis' [2022] *British Medical Journal* 9 February 2022 doi.org/10.1136/bmj-2021-067068 last accessed 28 August 2025; US Department of Health and Human Services, *Our Epidemic of Loneliness and Isolation: The US Surgeon General's Advisory on the Healing Effects of Social Connection and Community* Washington, DC 2023, Available at: pubmed.ncbi.nlm.nih.gov/37792968/, last accessed 28 August 2025.

It must stipulate something specific, recognise that those stipulations will create concrete effects in people's lives, bear with the fact that legitimate challenges may arise, be attentive to the ways they are adjudicated, and find a new practical solution whenever it is established that the current stipulation is out of alignment with the normative ideal as it is currently understood. In functioning legal systems, law actually courts its own self-correction, creating opportunities for its deficiencies to come to the surface. It is neither only pure ideal nor merely gritty reality: it is ideal worked through in the context of gritty reality.

Constitutions and international treaties enshrine freedom of association as a fundamental human right, and the legal reality of the scope of that right is given through legislative and regulatory frameworks that stipulate what it means in practical terms. A regulatory rule may stipulate, for example, that 'to be recognised as an association, it is necessary to satisfy criteria A and B and C and to fulfil obligations X and Y and Z', thereby defining associations as a matter of law. Any stipulation offers a kind of certainty, which by itself is helpful, insofar as it offers a degree of stability and predictability: we know how to become legally recognised as an association now, even if we privately think that C is too restrictive and Z is too onerous. However, within functioning legal systems, as Neil MacCormick neatly expresses it, the certainty that it offers is only 'defeasible certainty': it can be defeated by a better argument.[13] We can publicly argue that C is too restrictive and Z is too onerous, and therefore, at least in principle, we can participate in helping law to arrive at a new certainty. That new certainty is also a new defeasible certainty, capable of being defeated by better arguments still to come. The dual orientation of law towards normativity and towards lived reality creates the central animating tension within our discipline. Resolution of that tension is the mark of its success. The dogged, determined, iterative effort to resolve that tension over time is the evidence of its nobility. To more fully understand why associations are important and how they function is not only an interesting intellectual endeavour, therefore, but also a weighty obligation undertaken in service of that iterative effort to achieve a more fully just vindication of the right.

This animating tension is neither created nor resolved in the abstract. The original stipulation is made in the context of a particular legal system, informed by specific historical, political, cultural and social contexts that shape understandings of what the right means and why it is important in that specific place and time. Any challenges that need to be made to the justice of what is being stipulated have to be argued in particular courts by reference to particular laws before particular judges who have been educated and appointed within those same contexts. At one end of the spectrum, those contexts can be surprisingly open and conducive to the generation of better and better defeasible certainties.

[13] N MacCormick, *Rhetoric and the Rule of Law: A Theory of Legal Reasoning* (Oxford, Oxford University Press, 2005) 28.

At the other end of the spectrum, those contexts can become so corrupted and totalising that they have a stranglehold on the legal system, stymieing the process of self-correction in practice if not also in principle. Cross-disciplinary perspectives can serve as lamps to our feet, offering contributions to evidence and argument that can serve as illumination at whichever point along the spectrum we find ourselves. Comparative perspectives on the nature and scope of a right are another valuable resource, both where there is a systemic openness and where there is a systemic shutdown, not only in creating understanding about its nature and scope but also in spotlighting dark corners and offering non-hypothetical examples of alternative approaches.

There are seven jurisdictional chapters in this collection, which examine how the right to freedom of association is protected in Chile, Germany, Indonesia, Kenya, Slovenia, Türkiye and the United Kingdom. The range of these jurisdictions offers perspective from the global north and the global south, from common law and civil law systems, from jurisdictions with a long-standing tradition of rights protection and jurisdictions with a recently renewed commitment to constitutional rights and democracy, from jurisdictions with a constitutional commitment to secularity and jurisdictions with a constitutional commitment to an established religion, and from jurisdictions with relatively low rates of government corruption and jurisdictions with comparatively higher rates of corruption or abuse of power. The contributors themselves are also a motley crew, including professors who are leading figures in their discipline, mid-career academics consolidating their place in the academy and early-career researchers building their profile and expertise. In some cases, the authors can rely on and respond to some existing scholarship on the right to freedom of association in their jurisdiction, but in most cases the contributor has been ploughing a new field, piecing together how the right to freedom of association is articulated and interpreted through consideration of the legislative frameworks, administrative implementation and judicial decisions that exist in their jurisdiction. The global research network of freedom of association scholars created by the Societās project, and within it this list of contributors, is inclusive and committed to giving a voice to scholars at different stages of their careers, from diverse jurisdictions and from varying cultural, religious and ethnic backgrounds. To maximise opportunities for informed cross-fertilisation, contributors were requested to write their chapters from their position as jurisdictional experts in conversation with a global network of freedom of association scholars, meaning that their chapters are both doctrinally rich and comparatively aware.

Julian Rivers' chapter, '*Freedom of Association and the Law in the United Kingdom*', opens the collection with a rich insight into how freedom of association was and is protected under the common law as a civil liberty constituted by the absence of legal restraints. Even though that common law position has since been supplemented by the Human Rights Act 1998 and at least to some extent supplanted by increasing regulatory intervention, it still carries an important affirmation of the vision for freedom of association as a liberty that is ultimately antecedent to law. From a jurisdiction without a formal written constitution, we turn next to one which has been preoccupied with constitutional reform. Sebastian Soto's chapter, '*Freedom of Association in Chile*', explains how attraction to freedom of association has ebbed and flowed in Chilean political history, with the 1980 Constitution affirming in particular the right to associate 'without prior permission', the right not to be forced to belong to an association, and the right of intermediate groups to 'adequate autonomy to fulfil their own specific purposes'. The meaning and extent of associational autonomy, as well as its relationship to the principle of subsidiarity and institutional conscientious objection, have been the subject of recent debate and dispute. Although the United Kingdom is a common law jurisdiction and Chile is a civil law jurisdiction chapters one and two both seem to affirm the importance of the broadly liberal vision for freedom of association as the right of people to live their lives without undue interference from the state.

By contrast, the following chapters three and four, exploring the nature of freedom of association in Slovenia and Germany, seem to put the emphasis on the value of freedom of association from a democratic perspective. Katarina Vatovec's chapter '*Unfolding Pluralism: Freedom of Association in Slovenia's Constitutional Democracy*' offers a picture of how, against a particular historical background, freedom of association can be interpreted in a way that emphasises its vital role in sustaining a multi-party political system and avoiding a slide towards totalitarianism. This chapter also points out that freedom of association is implicated, even when it is not expressly invoked, in constitutional challenges brought against Covid-19 measures restricting movement or gatherings and through litigation seeking to expand the *locus standi* of NGOs in the context of environmental litigation. Meanwhile, in '*Freedom of Association in Germany*', Leannán Martan O'Grady reflects on the historical restoration of freedom of association under the 1949 Constitution and its purpose in guarding against totalitarianism by enabling a free, pluralistic and democratic state. In the light of recent restrictions and prohibitions on associations as well as ongoing challenges, the complex inter-relationship between associational freedom and a healthy democracy is usefully illuminated.

While these two jurisdictions stress the democratic importance of freedom of association and its capacity to support the structures of the state, there is a risk that such a vision can become corrupted. Sometimes, associations are not only facilitated to participate in the functioning of the state, but also financially incentivised or even legally required to align their goals and values with those of the state. In chapter five, '*Freedom of Association in Türkiye*', Fatih Öztürk notes that excessive oversight and bureaucracy, such as a recent amendment requiring that membership admissions and resignations be reported in writing to the local authority, indirectly restrict freedom of association. Although the Constitutional Court has upheld the right to freedom of association in significant cases, still the lived reality of that freedom is compromised in Türkiye both by excessive administrative burdens and the related failure to fully protect freedom of expression. Meanwhile, in chapter six, '*Freedom of Association and its Restrictions in Indonesia*', Inna Junaenah reflects on the fact that although freedom of association is constitutionally protected, its practical regulation is governed by the provisions of the Civil Society Organisations Act 2013, as amended in 2017. This legislative framework encourages associations to align themselves with the primary purposes of the state and provides that associations which have fallen out of obedience can be restricted and even banned by executive action with no judicial oversight. Although this may increase the level of proximity and apparent influence that civil society associations have vis-à-vis the state, it comes at the cost of their independence, the democratic credibility of the state and the very freedom that freedom of association purports to protect. On a more positive note, in chapter seven, '*Freedom of Association in Kenya: Constitutional Foundations, Judicial Reasoning and Democratic Tensions*', Njoki Mboce outlines how the 2010 Constitution of Kenya has rehabilitated not only the right to freedom of association but also political rights that depend on the right to freedom of association. This constitutional protection is realised also through the 2011 Political Parties Act, which reinforces the democratic credibility of political parties and secures the multi-party system. While there is still more work to be done, legislative and judicial developments seem promising.

Each of these jurisdictional chapters tells the story of a nation's effort to vindicate freedom of association not only in the abstract provisions of a constitution, but also in the gritty detail of particular circumstances and particular associations. We might be tempted to rush to judgement: to conclude, for example, that the democratic importance of freedom of association outweighs the importance of freedom of association in protecting liberty or promoting flourishing, or vice versa. A more measured approach might simply be to be attentive to the differences, to allow comparative reflection to offer perspective between jurisdictions and to seek to understand the tensions that are in play and the compromises that have been made against the background pull of both competing visions on the importance of the right and of different priorities in terms of its practical vindication. How can the importance of the right be more compellingly presented in situations where the right seems not to be taken seriously? How can the harmful effects of excessive regulation be more fully explained in situations where such regulation is commonplace? There is no jurisdiction that would not profit from serious reflection on those questions. Each jurisdiction faces some pressure points, and even though the particularity of those pressure points may vary, there are certain common features, too, as we shall see in the next section.

Following the jurisdictional chapters, we have two chapters reflecting in a more focused way on what happens, from a legal perspective, when there are internal disputes within associations and on the possible terms of engagement when courts are dealing with a legal challenge taken by a member (or a former member or putative member) to an association's own constitution or internal rules. At one extreme, obviously, a court could decline to decide the matter at all, considering that it does not have jurisdiction to interpret, let alone determine, the internal rules of the association. At the other extreme, a court could decide that it has the authority to resolve the dispute by finally interpreting the rules, even if that interpretation is not in line with how the association understands and interprets its own rules. In chapter eight, '*Judicial Review of Associative Agreements: Insights from a Civil Law Perspective*', José Juan Anzures Gurría provides a helpful overview of how courts in civil law countries engage with these kinds of disputes. Anzures Gurría draws attention to the space between the two extremes, reflecting on the legitimacy of judicial review in light of considerations such as the type of association involved, its position vis-à-vis the state, its dominance in the field, its own democratic pedigree and the nature of the internal agreement. In chapter nine, Nicholas McMurry examines more advanced cases of associational breakdown. '*Schisms and Internal Disputes within Religious Associations under the European Court of Human Rights*' focuses on 'deep division' within associations, particularly religious associations, and therefore involves the right to freedom of religion, too. The Court in these cases is sometimes called upon to determine the level or nature of associational breakdown: whether it should be characterised as dissent or whether it has reached the point of schism. Moreover, it may need to determine and examine the practical implications of associational breakdown in disputes about access to and control of property held by the association.

Although law is most often trying to pick up the pieces when something has gone wrong, and courtrooms are the hospitals of relational breakdown of various kinds, we conclude the legal part of this volume with a palate cleanser which helps to return our focus to a reflection on the reasons why associational life is important from a human perspective. Chapter ten, written by Erin Jackson, entitled '*Portraits of Association Participation: Exploring Personal Narratives*', reflects on first-person accounts of the importance of associational involvement, based on a set of interviews conducted as part of a pilot study under the auspices of the Societās project. Jackson reflects on the participants' own narratives, revealing themes of connection, purpose, friendship and fulfilment, as participants reflect on their motivations for associational involvement, the positive aspects of associational experience, the frustrations and challenges of associational life, and the legacy it leaves or has left in their lives.

Before going further, I would like to pay tribute to these lawyers for their independence of thought, for their magnanimity and moral courage in identifying problematic aspects of how law regulates associations in their jurisdictions, and for the lively spirit of collaboration that has pervaded their engagement with the Societās project and this collection. I am also grateful to Aoife Nazneen Kharsi for language and editorial support in the preparation of final drafts.

III. FREEDOM OF ASSOCIATION AT THE PRESSURE POINTS

Amidst all the variation in context and legal rules around the world, there are two major pressure points that create legal disputes invoking freedom of association. The first of these relates to legislative and regulatory frameworks: the specificity of the conditions and restrictions that are imposed on the freedom to form and run an association. There are many jurisdictions that explicitly protect the right to form and participate in unincorporated associations, meaning that the state does not have a right to regulate every form of associational involvement.[14] There are other jurisdictions in which legislation lays down a regulatory framework in respect of specific types of associations eg, political parties or trade unions or other categories of associations.[15] Some such regulation can be helpful in establishing legal clarity for associations and setting expectations for internal governance and finance arrangements. But it can certainly go too far.[16] The first pressure point is a kind of external pressure on associations, created by regulation of associational autonomy, which can stymie the freedom and vitality of associational life. Even when the principle of associational autonomy is officially protected, and regardless of whether regulators intend or do not intend to violate freedom of association, they can be insufficiently attentive to its delicacy in a way that has a chilling effect on associational life and freedom.

The second pressure point relates to internal pressure on associations which emerges from internal or quasi-internal conflict when the views and entitlements of certain members are out of step with the official position taken by the association. This could happen when an existing member wishes, say, to assume a leadership position or not to be removed from leadership or not to be expelled from the association, and their wishes are out of line with the internal rules of the association. It could also happen when an aspiring member wishes to join the association even though they do not meet the membership criteria. One person's right to join a particular association, for example, might

[14] Certain jurisdictions specifically recognise the right to associate 'in the wild', as it were, prior to any interaction with and in the absence of any formal recognition by the state. See, M Monti, 'Freedom of Association in Italy: Genesis, Evolution and Limits of Protections of Associations in the Italian Legal System' (2025) 12 (1&2) *European Journal of Comparative Law and Governance* 39, at 43; R Neuvonen, 'Freedom of Association Doctrine in Finland' (2025) 12 (1&2) *European Journal of Comparative Law and Governance* 226, at 227; MO Silva, 'Freedom of Association in Peru' (2025) 12 (1&2) *European Journal of Comparative Law and Governance* 288, at 292.

[15] See, JJA Gurría, 'Freedom of Association in Mexico' (2025) 12 (1&2) *European Journal of Comparative Law and Governance* 177, at 179; F Amao, 'Freedom of Association in Nigeria: A Cacophony of Constellations' (2025) 12 (1&2) *European Journal of Comparative Law and Governance* 304, at 309.

[16] See, V Barbé, 'Freedom of Association in France: A Freedom in Danger' (2025) 12 (1&2) *European Journal of Comparative Law and Governance* 322; S Zhu, 'Freedom of Association in Contemporary China' (2025) 12 (1&2) *European Journal of Comparative Law and Governance* 92; EM Rashwan, 'The Constitutional Framework and Legislative Regulation of the Right to Freedom of Association in Egypt after 2013' (2025) 12 (1&2) *European Journal of Comparative Law and Governance* 58; KK Negesse, 'The Purpose and Potential of Freedom of Association in Ethiopia' (2025) 12 (1&2) *European Journal of Comparative Law and Governance* 244.

come into conflict with existing members' right to define the association as they choose. This pressure point arises because the individual dimension of freedom of association – the right to join and to continue to be a member of an association – has come into tension with the collective dimension of freedom of association – the right of the members to define and internally regulate the association as they choose. On one hand, the associational rights of the individuals concerned need to be respected. On the other, associational rights include the right of the association to be able to define itself on its own terms and create the sense of identity, coherence and authority needed for it to perdure. Even when everybody is acting in good faith, these kinds of disputes also create internal pressure points that have a chilling effect on associational life and freedom.

Much of the time, these pressure points will be dealt with without making their way into a court. External pressure from regulations may be resolved in the sense that the relevant associations find ways to meet regulatory obligations or else fade out of existence for lack of capacity and/or willingness to do so. Internal disputes may become resolved either in the sense that collaboration and shared purpose are renewed over time or else in the sense that disaffected members leave to form new associations under different conditions. When these kinds of disputes arrive in court, though, and when we resolve them there, we are not only addressing the specific circumstances and the particular effects that the pressure points have on the lives of the disputants, we are also fine-tuning what freedom of association means and why it matters to us.

A Societās webinar held on 3 November 2023 entitled 'First Conversation between Law and Social Ontology on Freedom of Association' sought to bring philosophers working in the field of social ontology into dialogue with freedom of association scholars through a shared focus on these pressure points. A further two-day workshop, 'Exploring Associational Life: From Social Ontology to Law and Back Again', hosted at the School of Law at University College Cork on 25–26 April 2024, explored these conversations in greater depth, as philosophers not only shared their presentations, which were interspersed with snapshots of jurisdictional reports graciously provided by my colleagues from the School of Law, Professor Femi Amao, Dr Nicholas McMurry, Dr Sahara Nankan, Dr Seán Ó Conaill, Dr Shaoming Zhu and Mr Ruairí McIntyre, but they also participated in two moot court exercises focused on the pressure points. To facilitate engagement with the pressure points, I developed and presented moot court scenarios that could act as proxies for the disputes that happen at the pressure points. There were three reasons for this. The first was that it offered an opportunity to facilitate philosophers engaging directly with the issues raised by the relevant caselaw without requiring them to immerse themselves in lengthy judicial decisions. The second was that it offered an entry point into the conversation which would not unnecessarily target specific jurisdictions or cultural contexts. And the third reason was that it provided a mechanism by which philosophers could begin to find a space for themselves inside law's animating tension between the normative ideal and the gritty detailed reality, rather than remaining outside of that tension in a more abstract, detached consideration of the issues. This creative approach to workshop design seemed to work well, thanks to the enthusiasm with which all participants took to the process, and it certainly made for a memorable and enjoyable experience.

The two moot scenarios that animated our interdisciplinary dialogue at the Societās workshop and provided a point of reference not only for the philosophical chapters presented in Part II of this collection but also for José Juan Anzures Gurría's chapter on judicial review of associative agreements in Part I are provided for reference in the pages immediately following this Introduction. These moot scenarios are adaptations of real events. The first scenario of the Cairde ar son Cairdre Soup Kitchen is based on a newspaper report from 17 February 2024 detailing the experience of Glenda Harrington, founder of Friends helping Friends (in the Irish language translated as '*Cairde ar son Cairdre*') an outdoor soup kitchen which offered food to 300 people per week in an economically deprived area of Dublin and was facing scrutiny from the Charities Regulator and pressure to become legally registered.[17] The second scenario is conceptually based on a dispute that played out over time in the Irish courts, eventually making its way to the Irish Supreme Court, on the question of whether women should be admitted as members to a particular golf club.[18] The idea of moot scenarios, of course, is that they should be designed so that there are good arguments to be made on both sides and it is arguable that either side should win. By using these calibrated mooting scenarios as a starting point for reflection and dialogue on the tension between normative ideal and gritty reality, we hope that we can both provide and inspire further reflection within, between and beyond the disciplines of philosophy and law on the scope and importance of associational life and freedom.

Still, cross-disciplinary and interdisciplinary research entails considerable challenges. There is the obvious linguistic barrier to overcome, since we describe similar or adjacent concepts in different ways. This is redolent of a deeper disparity: we are attentive to different elements within those concepts and find them to be worthy of inquiry for different reasons. More deeply still, we engage in scholarly inquiry using fundamentally different methodologies; in each case deploying a methodology that has become so deeply instilled in us that it has become the air that we breathe, difficult to do without. These disciplinary differences surfaced during the workshop and remain to a greater or lesser extent in the various philosophical chapters presented in this collection.

[17] 'Founder of Dublin soup run feeding the homeless says she has 'no intention' of becoming a registered charity' Irish Independent, 17 February 2024, available at: m.independent.ie/regionals/dublin/dublin-news/founder-of-dublin-soup-run-feeding-the-homeless-says-she-has-no-intention-of-becoming-a-registered-charity/a760526930.html?fbclid=IwAR3SFcFawJlxCHgsLsbnm34BDcVMhWY6reBOv86PBBLITFqJYw0jxmjd_hM (last accessed 22 August 2025).

[18] *Equality Authority v Portmarnock Golf Club and Others and Cuddy & Keane v Equality Authority and Others* [2009] IESC 73.

At the linguistic level, there can be a tendency to see marriage or personal relationships as a proxy for associational involvement in a way that might at first sight seem strange to lawyers because those rights are not typically seen as analogous to each other. Conversely, the idea that the individual and collective dimensions of freedom of association could be in conflict may seem strange to a social ontologist when considered abstractly. In terms of scholarly focus, there may be a preference among social ontologists to describe associational life and clarify its terms while remaining conscientiously neutral on the question of whether associations are a good thing, a position that may be difficult to align with law's normative endorsement of associational freedom. And in terms of methodology, of course, philosophy is generally committed to achieving valuable clarity in the relatively more abstract expression of the nature of the material under consideration rather than to participating in an iterative process of reconciling a tension between ideal and reality. All of this means that the effort it takes for philosophers to genuinely engage in cross-disciplinary and interdisciplinary research on associational freedom in a spirit of humility and service to another discipline is very significant. In the chapters of this collection, they have engaged concepts from their own discipline in the effort to offer a perspective on the moot scenarios that were examined at the workshop. In doing so, they have reached beyond their comfort zones and sought to make a contribution in an arena in which they would not necessarily choose to find themselves and in which they do not necessarily feel at home. I hope that they have found it to be an intellectually interesting and worthwhile experience. I want to pay tribute to them also for their disciplinary humility, their creativity and their intellectual courage in stepping into a new space as conversation partners for legal scholars and lawyers engaged in the deliberative iterative process of understanding more deeply and explaining more fully, amidst the gritty reality of our lived experiences, why and how freedom of association deserves protection as a fundamental human right.

IV. MOOT SCENARIO 1: 'CAIRDE AR SON CAIRDRE' SOUP KITCHEN

Together with a few friends, Gráinne has been running an outdoor soup kitchen called Cairde ar son Cairdre (*phonetically: car-ja air son car-ja*) in her local area for more than ten years. She receives leftover food from local grocery shops, and a local butcher's shop has an account that allows people to donate money indirectly. Whenever possible, they also provide sleeping bags, underwear, socks, toiletries and period products. Gráinne founded the group and has always been involved at the helm of the initiative. Three of her neighbours and friends, Aisling, Bláithín, and Clodagh, initially volunteered alongside her, but Aisling of these has since moved to another city, and Bláithín has stepped back from Cairde to care for her three small children. Clodagh still helps out every week and is the head chef of the group. Deirdre and Eithne have joined the organisation in the last five years and are very dedicated to its work. Deirdre takes the lead on getting in food supplies and helps Gráinne with serving and hosting, while Eithne sources the personal provisions and discreetly makes them available to clients when needed.

Cairde ar son Cairde is not a registered charity. It does not have a bank account or a bookkeeper. It does not have a formal organisational structure or a constitution. None of the volunteers have formal training in finance, and they don't want to have to use their small funds to pay for a bookkeeper. In any case, Gráinne always has to keep a more informal feel to the organisation. The volunteers are all good friends, and she wants her guests to feel like they are being invited to a dinner with people they know, rather than receiving an impersonal handout from people who don't care. When provoked to say something, all of the group are very critical of the failures of local and national government to address problems of homelessness and cycles of deprivation, but most of the time they just focus on what they can do to help.

Cairde ar son Cairde is in violation of the Charities Acts for not having proper accounts and for not registering as a charity. The Charities Regulator has made several attempts to encourage Gráinne to register, but she is determined not to. The Charities Regulator then approached the butcher and told him that what he is doing is illegal. Eventually, Gráinne may be prosecuted for failure to comply with the Charities Acts. The Charities Regulator defends its actions on the grounds that all charities must be subject to the same legal standards so that members of the public can be assured that charities are operating with financial integrity as they pursue their charitable purposes. Gráinne challenges the actions of the Charities Regulator for being a disproportionate violation of her right to freedom of association. The Supreme Court of Bureaucratlandia finds in favour of the Regulator.

V. MOOT SCENARIO 2: RÓISÍN'S GOLFING AMBITIONS

The Kilmartin Golf Club was created more than 40 years ago by a group of local businessmen as a way of building connections and networking informally. Over the decades, many good things have happened on the course: ideas have been brainstormed, friendships have been made and strengthened, and disputes have been avoided or resolved, all of which also coincides with the fact that the local economy has continued to thrive and remain vibrant despite various pressures of economic crises, rising costs of living and globalisation.

Women are not welcome as members of the club. Even though this is not a formal rule, it is club convention that somebody could only become a member having been nominated by an existing member, and no women have been nominated.

Róisín is a very accomplished amateur golfer as well as the owner of a local restaurant. She golfs four mornings a week in the Kilgallen Golf Club, which is based in the same town, half a mile from the Kilmartin Club, and which has an open membership policy.

Róisín would be very keen to build her connections in and contribute more to the local community. She believes that she could do this more effectively if she were allowed to become a member of the Kilmartin Golf Club.

Is it a violation of her right to freedom of association not to be able to participate in the Kilmartin Golf Club?

Does the Kilmartin Golf Club have a right to determine its own membership policy, even if that membership policy effectively discriminates against women?

If a new golf club, the Kilbrigid Golf Club, were established by and for local businesswomen, which operated a nomination-based membership policy that effectively excluded men, would that violate the right to freedom of association of men in the local area?

If the Kilbrigid Golf Club adopted a formal women-only membership policy, would that violate the right to freedom of association of men in the local area?

If the Kilgallen Golf Club were to change its membership policy so as to exclude business owners, on the grounds that they want the club to be a social space that is open to everyone rather than a spillover chamber of commerce, would that violate Róisín's right to freedom of association?

Part I

The Law of Associational Freedom

1

*Freedom of Association and the Law in the United Kingdom**

JULIAN RIVERS**

I. INTRODUCTION: A NEGATIVE AND A POSITIVE RIGHT

IF THERE IS one feature of the British Constitution which is generally well-known, apart, that is, from the existence of a monarchy, it is the fact that it is 'unwritten'. Having escaped major political turmoil since the revolution of 1688–89, it has evolved incrementally rather than experienced processes of wholesale codification. The highest form of law within the United Kingdom is an Act of Parliament, a piece of primary legislation, almost always promoted by the government of the day, and approved by both Houses. But 'Parliament does not legislate in a vacuum. Parliament legislates for a European liberal democracy founded on the principles and traditions of the common law, and courts may approach legislation on this initial assumption.'[1] The common law provides a rich and complex legal context within which legislation takes its effect, somewhat as the conventions of language shape the possibilities of intelligible speech. The political context is further stabilised by constitutional conventions. These are normative practices which modify political powers in line with modern principles of governance. For example, by convention the monarch appoints as Prime Minister that person best able to command the support of a majority of the House of Commons, and by convention the monarch assents to any legislation which passes both houses. In this way traditional forms of rule are made responsive to democratic principles.

* The United Kingdom contains three main legal systems: England & Wales, Scotland and Northern Ireland. Scottish law differs in important respects from the law of the other two jurisdictions. However, laws relating specifically to freedom of association are substantially similar throughout the United Kingdom.

** I am particularly grateful to my colleague Matthew Burton for his assistance in preparing this chapter; also to Maria Cahill and Giulia Lasagni for their comments on an earlier draft.

[1] *R v Secretary of State for the Home Department, ex p. Pierson* [1998] AC 539, per Lord Steyn at 587.

The sources of the British Constitution may thus be found in statute, the common law and political convention, a feature which gives it both resilience and flexibility. It also makes it distinctively open to competing interpretations, lacking as it does a single canonical text to act as a fixed point of constitutional debate. One of the most enduring accounts was provided by the constitutional theorist and Oxford professor, Albert Venn Dicey (1835–1922). He reduced the Constitution to three main elements: a sovereign Parliament, the rule of law, and constitutional conventions, at the same time providing a gloss on those elements which reflected his hostility to the increasing role of the state. He was also sceptical of the value of codified fundamental rights, emphasising instead the practical effectiveness of historic legal processes such as the writ of habeas corpus against executive detention.

Dicey's account of the place of fundamental rights within the British Constitution continues to influence the assumptions of many English lawyers.[2] In his main treatment, the closest he gets to discussing the topic of freedom of association addresses the 'Right of Public Meeting'. He states this:

> The right of assembling is nothing more than a result of the view taken by the Courts as to individual liberty of person and individual liberty of speech. There is no special law allowing A, B, and C to meet together either in the open air or elsewhere for a lawful purpose, but the right of A to go where he pleases so that he does not commit a trespass, and to say what he likes to B so that his talk is not libellous or seditious, the right of B to do the like, and the existence of the same rights of C, D, E, and F, and so on *ad infinitum*, lead to the consequence that A, B, C, D, and a thousand or ten thousand other persons, may (as a general rule) meet together in any place where otherwise they each have a right to be for a lawful purpose and in a lawful manner.[3]

Historically, the most frequent forms of legal intervention on the activities of groups have focused on constraining the potentially disruptive consequence of public gatherings, particularly those with express or covert intent to bring about political change. But by focusing on restrictions of the manifestation of group life – on what we would now call freedom of assembly, rather than the freedom of association as such – Dicey's account tended to render the constitutional place of social groups invisible. In themselves, crowds have no distinct legal form. These assumptions coloured even his account of associations. In an article published in 1904, he reflected further on the nature of the 'right of association', describing it as 'nothing more than the right of two or more citizens, X, Y, and Z, to combine together by agreement among themselves for the attainment of a common purpose'.[4] His subsequent discussion of laws relating to early trade unions was framed as a tension between people exercising their normal individual liberties in concert and various attempts by the legislature to

[2] AV Dicey, *Introduction to the Study of the Constitution*, 8th edn (London, Macmillan, 1915).

[3] ibid 170.

[4] AV Dicey, 'Combination Laws as Illustrating the Relation between Law and Opinion in England During the Nineteenth Century', (1903–1904) 17 *Harvard Law Review* 511–532, 512.

prevent these collective exercises of social power from having what were considered to be anti-social effects.

While Dicey was entirely correct to emphasise the importance of embedding abstract claims of fundamental right within the doctrine and practice of courts, not least in informing judicial approaches to the interpretation of statutory entrenchments upon basic rights, his conception of the content of such rights was *negative* in two important ways. It was negative, first, in its assumption that civil liberty is legally residual; it is part of the sphere of freedom left to people once one has subtracted all the legal limits, whether civil or criminal, on their actions. It was negative, secondly, in its assumption that liberty is most completely constituted by the absence of law and that law can only ever restrict the freedom of the individual rather than acting as a source of empowerment. This can perhaps best be explained as a reflection of the way Dicey emphasised parliamentary legislative supremacy. Even today, this dual negativity can lead to programmatic claims, seen often enough in contemporary treatments, that there is no positive right of association in English law.[5] This then leads to the further claim that the Human Rights Act 1998 – which undoubtedly gives effect to a positive right – represents a major shift in constitutional thought.

Historically, the two main examples of restrictive intervention by Parliament were the attempts to suppress 'conventicles' and 'combinations'. The Clarendon Code of legislation passed in the first decade after the restoration of the monarchy in 1660 sought to impose a policy of religious uniformity within England.[6] In particular, the Conventicles Act 1670 made it an offence to be present at an assembly of five or more adults for religious worship apart from the established Church of England. Relief came – at least for Trinitarian Protestant dissenters – in the form of the Toleration Act 1689, which established a system of registration and licensing for places of worship, ministers and schoolmasters. Over the centuries that followed, toleration was expanded, and processes of registration rationalised, although the obligation to register groups of 20 or more meeting for religious worship, even on private premises, was not technically repealed until the 1970s. By then, registration had long become a means of obtaining benefits such as relief from local taxation and the capacity to conduct weddings, as it still is today.

The other main historical example – and the one which Dicey considered in his article – was the attempt to suppress 'combinations' of workers seeking to improve the conditions of organised labour in the wake of the Industrial Revolution.[7] The highly restrictive, even draconian, Combination Act of 1800 criminalised strikes and the support of strikers, and the history of trade union

[5] R Clayton and H Tomlinson, *The Law of Human Rights*, 2nd edn (Oxford, Oxford University Press, 2009) para 16.49.

[6] J Rivers, *The Law of Organized Religions* (Oxford, Oxford University Press, 2010) 13–20.

[7] JV Orth, *Combination and Conspiracy: A Legal History of Trade Unionism 1721–1906* (Oxford, Oxford University Press, 1991).

law is one of gradual but uneven amelioration as the widening of the franchise generated political parties more sympathetic to the interests of labour. But there is an important difference between these two examples in respect of judicial attitudes. In the case of dissenting religious groups, the courts were broadly supportive of a policy of widening toleration. Once Parliament had removed the taint of illegality from non-Anglican religion, they were willing enough to craft private law remedies which gave minority religious groups a secure and permanent legal existence. In the case of trade unions, the judiciary tended to use their creativity in more restrictive ways, as seen in the case-law on both the crime and, later, the tort of conspiracy. Even Dicey's choice of example is loaded.

Focusing on statutory restriction and administrative regulation can divert attention from the more fundamental ways in which the common law has long facilitated the legal expression of associational life. Although the common law contains no general means of acquiring legal personality, which was treated as a privilege to be granted by Royal Charter or Act of Parliament, lawyers managed to craft a series of rules and remedies which secured practical solutions to typical problems. As Maitland said, commenting on continental European debates about the theoretical foundations of collective legal personality in the light of English common law:

> … what for the civilians was a question of life and death was often in England a question of mere convenience and expense, so wide was that blessed back-stair. The trust deed might be long; the lawyer's bill might be longer; new trustees would be wanted from time to time; and now and again an awkward obstacle would require ingenious evasion; but the organized group could live and prosper, and be all the more autonomous because it fell under no solemn legal rubric.[8]

Maitland was drawing attention here to a major point of difference between legal systems based upon the English common law and those influenced primarily by the continental European reception of Roman law. The device of the trust divides the ownership of property into two parts: legal title and benefit or enjoyment. In this way, the legal owners come to have duties to deal with 'their' property for the benefit of others. Maitland's reference is most readily understandable in the case of charitable trusts. A trust of property for purposes which the law recognises as conferring a public benefit may exist in perpetuity for the fulfilment of those purposes. Trustees (legal owners) are subject to a regime of powers and duties to apply the property to those purposes, which is treated as a fund distinct from their own personal property. The fund becomes a quasi-person in itself. But even in the case of private (non-charitable) trusts – such as the ownership of the premises of a private members' club – the trust can be embedded in the group's constitution.[9] If the trust deed is well drafted,

[8] FW Maitland, 'Translator's Introduction' to *Otto v. Gierke, Political Theories of the Middle Ages* (Cambridge, Cambridge University Press, 1900) 31.

[9] See, generally, Stewart et al.

the property, which belongs beneficially to the members collectively, can only be applied in accordance with the terms of association.[10] Although the association is unincorporated, officers of the association may generally sue or be sued in a representative capacity.[11] In this way, English common law has for a long time offered techniques for the private legal ordering of collective action sustained over time. This was not a foregone conclusion; as Maitland's reference to 'ingenious evasion' hints, some of the older cases were clearly driven less by legal logic than by the pragmatic need to craft a suitable remedy.[12] Yet by one route or another, English law protects and regulates the existence of unincorporated groups, as if they were for almost all practical purposes incorporated.[13] In this respect, the general statutory presumption that the use of the word 'person' in statute law includes 'a body of persons corporate or unincorporate' is entirely understandable.[14]

If we are to think about freedom of association within law, it is not sufficient to focus, as Dicey did, merely on the history and current state of legal restrictions on associational life. Instead, we must take as our starting-point the capacity within the law for individuals, through private initiative and without public administrative authorisation, to form themselves effectively into legally-recognised groups. A legitimate public policy concern for the anti-social potential of organised humanity still remains, but this is reflected less in outright restrictions on groups formed for unlawful purposes and more in administrative regulation. The private capacity to create, operate and dissolve associations within the common law has been modified and supplemented by a range of statutory regimes for specific types of association. The hallmark of the modern law is increasing public differentiation and intervention, as different types of association come under public scrutiny. And the problems of associational liberty are problems of balancing a deep-rooted constitutional commitment to positive associational freedom with relevant public policy considerations such as legality of purpose, public benefit and financial transparency.

Against this background we can consider in more detail the problem of the relationship between private law and liberty, sketching in the ways in which the law now has specific legal regimes for different types of social groups, prohibiting some which are anti-social. We then consider the impact of the Human Rights Act 1998 and Equality Act 2010 on this right.

[10] Jean Warburton states that the common form is, 'upon trust for the members of the association according to the rules thereof': J Warburton, *Unincorporated Associations: Law and Practice*, 2nd edn (London, Sweet & Maxwell, 1992) 45.

[11] There are also statutes empowering particular types of association to sue in their own name. See Stewart et al ch 9.

[12] See, eg, Lord Eldon's reasoning in *Lloyd v Loaring* (1802) 6 Ves. J. 773 on the right of a majority of members to recover their society's property from a member who was holding it to ransom.

[13] See SJ Stoljar, *Groups and Entities: An Enquiry into Corporate Theory* (Canberra, Australian National University Press, 1973), 59: '... the voluntary association emerges as a corporate body in virtually all but name.'

[14] Interpretation Act 1978, s 5 and Sch 1, para 1.

II. LAW AND LIBERTY IN ASSOCIATION

Considered more closely, the law of unincorporated associations reveals an important doctrinal disagreement about the basis for the court's jurisdiction to regulate the internal life of groups. The origins of this jurisdiction lie in a branch of law called 'equity', which in this context does not mean 'fairness' but is the name given to the body of legal rules and principles developed by the Court of Chancery to protect property and provide redress for misappropriation. On this basis, the internal rules of a private association were of no inherent legal significance, being a purely private matter between the members who could continue to act by majority with complete freedom. 'Save for the due disposal and administration of property, there is no authority in the Courts either of England or Scotland to take cognizance of the rules of a voluntary society entered into merely for the regulation of its own affairs.'[15] New individuals could join according to the rules, which is to say, with the consent of existing members, and individual members could leave at any time without such consent, since their right to dissociate was inalienable.[16] The principle of majority rule flowed naturally from this individualistic foundation. However, the courts would intervene to protect proprietary interests, and at this point any formal rules adopted by the group would become relevant in working out what the nature of the member's interest was.[17] The effect of this approach, which we can call the proprietary model, was to deny a remedy to a member who had suffered under a breach of the association's rules if their personal stake was not recognised by the courts as sufficiently akin to a property interest, such as an interest in a personal financial benefit or exclusive occupation of premises.

However, over time, courts throughout the United Kingdom became increasingly willing to remedy breaches of internal rules and other improper action by officers and members of associations, without paying much attention to the nature of the property interest at stake. The effect of this development is that associations are now considered primarily in terms of contract. A modern exposition would be likely to start with a definition offered by Lawton LJ. An unincorporated association consists of:

> two or more persons bound together for one or more common purposes, not being business purposes, by mutual undertakings, each having mutual duties and obligations, in an organisation which has rules which identify in whom control of it and its funds rests and upon what terms and which can be joined or left at will. The bond of union between the members of an unincorporated association has to be contractual.[18]

[15] *Forbes v Eden* (1867) LR1 Sc 568.
[16] *Finch v Oake* [1896] 1 Ch. 409.
[17] See, eg, *Hopkinson v Marquis of Exeter* (1867) LR 5 Eq 63; *Rigby v Connol* (1880) 14 ChD 482.
[18] *Conservative and Unionist Central Office v Burrell* [1982] 1 WLR 522 at 525.

This shifts the legal focus of attention from the individual's stake in the material basis of the group towards the terms on which a group of people have agreed to collaborate. Of course, there is still a threshold question of whether the relationships within the group are sufficiently formal to constitute even a contract. On the facts of the case from which that quotation is drawn, the Court of Appeal held that the Central Office of the Conservative Party was simply an informal coordinating body, not contractually and directly linked to the large number of local party associations which select candidates to contest General Elections. Perhaps surprisingly, the central institution of the world's oldest political party does not, in law, exist.

The contractual model suffers from substantial doctrinal weaknesses,[19] leading the Australian High Court in an important case to reject it in favour of the older proprietary model.[20] However, as far as the laws applied in the United Kingdom are concerned, the contractual model seems now to be very firmly embedded. To take just one recent example, the English High Court issued a declaration that elections of an executive committee of an Islamic association were conducted unconstitutionally and gave orders curing that illegality.[21] No consideration was given to the question of the litigants' proprietary or other personal interests in the matter. The mere fact that the group had a constitution was a sufficient basis for the court to provide an authoritative ruling – as if that were an entirely legitimate judicial undertaking. This approach is reinforced by the social expectations of those involved in voluntary collective action that any group beyond the merely temporary needs, sooner or later, to be 'properly' constituted. And 'properly' for these purposes means according to some fairly standard rules which are legally intelligible and enforceable.[22] The enforceable legal requirement that the principles of natural justice will be observed in internal proceedings is also consistent with these expectations.[23]

To some extent, the older proprietary model was motivated not merely by concerns of doctrinal purity but also by a sense that judicial interference in the internal affairs of a private association is, generally speaking, inappropriate. A recent manifestation of the same concern can be found in a line of cases concerning the justiciability of internal disputes. This arises most naturally in the context of religious groups, in which it is plausible enough – as a general proposition – that judges are not competent to resolve disputed matters of religious belief, although the same point could be made about many other dimensions of social life. This argument from non-justiciability recently started to get some traction, leading the Court of Appeal in 2012 to strike out an action

[19] See SJ Stoljar, *Groups and Entities: An Enquiry into Corporate Theory* (Canberra, Australian National University Press, 1973) 38–63.

[20] *Cameron v Hogan* [1934] HCA 24; (1934) 51 CLR 358.

[21] *Mohammed v Patel* [2024] EWHC 2581 (Ch).

[22] See, eg, Warburton (n 10), who in a lengthy Appendix provides a familiar set of model rules, notices, deeds of appointment, etc.

[23] *Lee v Showmen's Guild of Great Britain* [1952] 2 QB 329; *John v Rees* [1970] Ch 345.

arising from litigation over the control of two Sikh gurdwaras.[24] The case turned on whether one of the parties had been validly dismissed and another appointed as trustee of the property. This depended on whether the individual purporting to make these decisions was, in line with the trust deed's conditions, the true successor of the Second Holy Saint. And that was a matter of hot dispute between the factions struggling to control the gurdwaras. Although the court insisted that it would not refuse to determine civil rights even if that raised in the process 'controversial and profound' religious questions, in this case the court was being asked to pronounce on matters of religious doctrine and practice, matters which it was incompetent to address.

Even on the older proprietary model, the decision was puzzling. It seemed to establish an unsustainable dichotomy between two issues – control of the property and succession to the first Holy Saint – which were in fact intertwined. The Supreme Court reasserted legal orthodoxy by drawing a distinction between two types of justiciability.[25] Some matters are 'forbidden areas', such as political questions under the separation of powers; others, however, are only non-justiciable in the sense that courts will not entertain actions to resolve them *in the abstract*. But the court has to address religious questions if they arise in the course of resolving private rights and obligations, such as contractual rights of members of a community against others, or to ensure that trust property is applied according to its lawful purposes. The court could not avoid interpreting the trust deed to determine who had the power to appoint trustees, and so, inevitably, the underlying religious dispute had to be resolved as best as possible, taking expert evidence if necessary.

The difference between the proprietary and the contractual models correlates to different understandings of the relationship between law and associative liberty. Under the older, proprietary model, the freedom of the individual remains paramount and is expressed in the unwillingness of the court to intervene in the internal life of groups, except to protect an individual's proprietary interest in the group. Freedom of association is here conceived as an individual right held and exercised in common. This also fits the Diceyan notion of freedom of association as an essentially negative right. The contractual view shifts the focus towards the constitution of the group itself as a living and purposive entity. Individual members have a stake in this entity – a stake in which participation in the social purpose of the group may well be more significant than any financial or proprietary benefit – but they are subject to its rules for the duration of their membership.[26] In this way, freedom of association becomes a collective right, rather than merely a right held in common.[27]

[24] *Khaira v Shergill* [2012] EWCA Civ 983.

[25] *Khaira v Shergill* [2014] UKSC 33.

[26] See *Andrews v Mitchell* [1905] AC 78.

[27] For an extended version of this point in the context of religious groups, see J Rivers, 'Religious Liberty as a Collective Right' in R O'Dair and A Lewis (eds), *Law and Religion* (Oxford, Oxford University Press, 2001).

It also implies a positive right: a legal power on the part of individuals to form social groups which can then take on a legal life of their own.

III. PROHIBITION AND REGULATION

As has already been indicated, the central constitutional principle for the protection of civil liberty within the constitutional framework of the United Kingdom remains the principle of legality.[28] According to this principle, the common law – understood as the guarantor of an ordered liberty – provides the presumptive foundation onto which is grafted a series of statutory limitations and modifications for a wide range of public purposes. The legitimacy of these legislative interventions is provided by Parliament, which is taken to represent the consent of the people to the abridgement of their legal rights. Freedom of association has been substantially shaped by such interventions.

Even apart from the principle of legality, the common law sets limits to associative freedom. While it is true that a group of people may constitute themselves into an association for any lawful purpose, the meaning of 'lawful' has changed over time. Until the early twentieth century, it excluded purposes considered hostile to law, state and society generally, as seen most clearly in the cases involving groups established for 'superstitious' or 'irreligious' purposes.[29] Even though the parties concerned were not guilty of any criminal offence, they would struggle to enforce their civil rights against others: 'An act may be illegal in the sense that it will not be recognised by the law as capable of being the foundation of any legal right, or that it may even deprive what it accompanies of that capacity, although it is followed by no penalty.'[30] This whole line of cases was formally overruled by a majority of the House of Lords in *Bowman v Secular Society*.[31] As Lord Dunedin put it, 'I cannot bring myself to believe that there is still a terra media of things illegal, which are not criminal, not directly prohibited, not *contra bonos mores*, and not against public policy.'[32] The latter terms, while still flexible, are fairly narrow in scope, covering agreements which are evidently immoral or which require the law to condone illegality.[33]

[28] *R v Secretary of State for the Home Department ex parte Leech (no. 2)* [1994] QB 198; *R v Secretary of State for the Home Department ex parte Pierson* [1998] AC 539; *R v Secretary of State for the Home Department ex parte Simms* [2000] 2 AC 115. JNE Varuhas, 'The Principle of Legality' (2020) 79(3) *Cambridge Law Journal* 578–614.

[29] eg, *Cary v Abbott* (1802) 7 Ves 490, 32 ER 198; *West v Shuttleworth* (1835) 2 My & K 684, 39 ER 1106 both involving Roman Catholic groups. *Cowan v Milbourn* (1867) LR 2 Ex 23 concerned a secular society.

[30] Bramwell B in *Cowan v Milbourn* (1867) LR 2 Ex 230, 233.

[31] *Bowman v Secular Society* [1917] AC 406.

[32] ibid 434.

[33] For a modern discussion, see *Patel v Mirza* [2016] UKSC 42.

In practice, there are very few restrictions on the purposes for which a group may be established. Conspiracy to commit a crime is itself a crime, but since the objects of any formally constituted group are likely to be couched in positive and at least superficially lawful terms, the effect is that while the law may restrict some of the ways in which a group promotes its objects, the groups themselves are rarely unlawful. It was this basic assumption which led the English Court of Appeal to dismiss the claim of the Countryside Alliance that the prohibition on hunting foxes contained in the Hunting Act 2004 interfered with their right to assembly and association. The Court approved the following statement of the Scottish Inner House:

> [T]here is a material distinction, in our opinion, between a restriction which compels an individual to join an association or prohibits him from joining it, or penalises him in either event … and a restriction that, without reference to any association, merely prohibits a particular activity with the indirect result that persons cannot associate for the purpose of carrying it out. A restriction of the former kind is capable of engaging article 11; but a restriction of the latter kind is not. If it were otherwise, the prohibition of any activity would infringe article 11.[34]

This draws the scope of Article 11 of the European Convention on Human Rights too narrowly,[35] but its distinction between the existence of an association and its ability to conduct certain activities expresses well the basic assumptions of English law.

We turn now to the statutory restrictions. The Public Order Act 1936 contains a statutory prohibition on quasi-military political organisations. It was passed to deal with fascist groups in the years preceding the Second World War, and the provisions have also been used against members of the Irish Republican Army.[36] Section 1 deals with the problem in typical fashion by making it a criminal offence to wear a uniform in public which signifies association with any political organisation or the promotion of any political object. Here, the target is the individual wrongdoer, not the group. However, section 2 targets the group itself by making it a criminal offence to be involved in controlling or managing a group which organises, trains or equips members to usurp the functions of the police or the armed forces, or enables them to use or display physical force in promoting any political object.[37] The law is designed to deal with the militarisation of political action. In the context of political parties more generally, it is worth noting that a system of registration was only introduced for the first time in 2000. Political parties who wish to field candidates at general or local elections must register with the Electoral Commission, and a party can

[34] *Adams v Scottish Ministers* 2004 SC 665 at [82] cited in *R (Countryside Alliance) v Attorney General* [2006] EWCA Civ 817, [2007] QB 305 at [106].

[35] The scope of European Convention on Human Rights 1950, art 11, is outlined below.

[36] *R v Fell* [1974] Crim LR 673.

[37] See *R v Jordan and Tyndall* [1963] Crim LR 123.

only be removed from the register at its own request or for failure to comply with formalities.[38] Parties are subject to a regime of financial accountability, and there are restrictions and reporting obligations in respect of donations, but there is no mechanism for outright prohibition. For all its flaws, the British electoral system, which requires candidates as individuals to stand and win the largest share of the vote in one of 650 constituencies to gain a seat in the House of Commons, has so far proved remarkably effective at inhibiting the rise of populist leaders and extremist parties.

The most significant modern limit on associative freedom arises from the Terrorism Act 2000. This includes a process for proscribing organisations concerned with terrorism, empowering the Secretary of State to add to, and remove from, the list.[39] The list appears in a statutory schedule which has been updated more or less annually.[40] There is a statutory process for applying for deproscription, and an appeal can be made on standard judicial review grounds to a public body, the Proscribed Organisations Appeal Commission, appointed by the Lord Chancellor. The chair is a judge (usually the chair of the Special Immigration Appeals Panel), and the other members are a mix of legal and lay members. It is a criminal offence to belong, or profess to belong, to a proscribed organisation, to invite support (whether financial or otherwise), or to arrange or manage a meeting to support the organisation or further its activities.[41] There are also extensive provisions empowering the government to freeze and confiscate terrorist property.[42]

Outright prohibition is a peripheral feature of the law. Far more common is a set of gradually increasing regulatory regimes in which certain benefits (such as public visibility and reputation, incorporation and tax advantages) are offered in return for public registration and financial accountability. This approach creates strong incentives, both negative and positive, towards social conformity and responsibility. Before the advent of general statutory regimes, organisations could seek to incorporate their trustees – although not typically the entire enterprise – by Royal Charter or, more commonly, private Act of Parliament. The latter might well include a basic constitution for the organisation. This was as true for joint stock companies established for profit as it was for local public enterprises and other large social or religious organisations. We can trace the advent of modern generic regimes of registration to the Friendly Societies Act 1793, which used local magistrates to review the rules and oversee the operations of the large numbers of mutual aid associations which developed

[38] Political Parties, Elections and Referendums Act 2000, s 33.

[39] Terrorism Act 2000, ss 3–10.

[40] Sch 2 currently includes the names of about 100 organisations. Eight of them are Irish nationalist or loyalist groups; the rest operate principally overseas.

[41] ss 11–13.

[42] ss 14–23B.

in the later eighteenth century. Today, there are several such general statutory frameworks:

> Limited liability companies are primarily profit-making enterprises with a shareholding established for commercial purposes, although there is nothing to stop a company being limited by guarantee and being a non-profit-making enterprise for any lawful purpose, whether charitable or purely private. In the case of charities, this has the disadvantage of subjecting the organisation to two parallel regulatory systems, both Companies House and the Charity Commission. Once incorporated and registered under the Companies Acts, they are subject to a regime of transparency and financial accountability.
>
> Trade unions are subject to a complex and distinctive body of law which has varied over the years depending on the economic and industrial labour policy of the Government. The law regulating both trade unions and commercial enterprises is now highly developed and specific to each type of group, reflecting distinct policy imperatives.[43]
>
> Friendly Societies are mutual associations, typically providing financial assurance or other social welfare provision for their members, who were typically poorer wage-earners. Legislative intervention started in the late 18th century, with a system of registration and regulation, which has expanded over the years. A wide range of societies may register, including benevolent societies, working men's clubs and old people's homes. Under the Friendly Societies Act 1992, friendly societies which offer insurance on a range of typical life events may incorporate. Industrial and provident societies, which are essentially incorporated co-operatives of workers in any trade or handicraft, were originally registered as Friendly Societies, but after 1852 they had their own statutory regime. The law here has recently been consolidated by the Cooperative and Community Benefit Societies Act 2023.
>
> Charities are associations exclusively directed towards public benefit purposes, which include a wide range of activities such as relief of poverty, advancement of education or religion, health, the arts, culture, sport, environmental protection and animal welfare. With some exceptions they are required to register with the Charity Commission, and subject to transparency and financial accountability requirements. Although subject to lower levels of regulation than commercial companies, there is also a growing body of 'soft law' policy guidance on their operation. Charities may now incorporate without recourse to company law under a new vehicle, the Charitable Incorporated Organisation, which offers the advantages of separate legal personality under the single regulatory oversight of the Charity Commission.[44]

These are the main types of social groups recognised by statute law and subject to public regulation. However, they are all grafted onto the set of legal background assumptions about the legal formation of associations sketched out in the previous sections. These background assumptions shape the interpretation

[43] A Bogg, 'Freedom of Association' in G Davidoff et al. (eds), *The Oxford Handbook of the Law of Work* (Oxford, Oxford University Press, 2024).

[44] Introduced by the Charities Act 2006; see now Charities Act 2011, ss 204–250.

of legislative material, fill gaps, and provide an independent means for the creation of wholly private associations.

IV. THE HUMAN RIGHTS ACT 1998

Until relatively recently, the scepticism voiced by Dicey as to the practical value of codified and legally enforceable fundamental rights was widely shared by the major British political parties. Caution about the language of rights and judicial enforcement can be based upon conservative, utilitarian or socialist foundations. However, what the United Kingdom was unwilling to countenance domestically, it was ready enough to approve at an international level and even in respect of the new constitutions of its former colonies. As in the case of other similar international instruments, the UK was an original signatory to the European Convention on Human Rights 1950, ratifying it in 1952, and in 1966 conferring on citizens the right of individual petition. Thereafter, the Convention had a small but gradually increasing indirect influence on English law. Long-standing political opposition to 'Bills of Rights' was finally overcome in the constitutional reform programme of Prime Minister Tony Blair's 'New Labour' government after 1997, and the domestic significance of the ECHR was formalised and strengthened from 2000 when the Human Rights Act 1998 came into force. This statute obligates courts to interpret law where possible in conformity with the Convention,[45] and creates a separate cause of action against public bodies which violate Convention rights.[46] It also authorises courts to issue declarations of incompatibility in the case of primary legislation,[47] which triggers a fast-track, albeit political, remedial process.[48] In this way, the strict primacy of Acts of Parliament is preserved. In developing case-law, courts are under obligation to take into account the relevant case-law of the European Court,[49] and as a result, domestic law is now closely aligned to that of the European Court. However, British judges have on occasion consciously departed from European case-law in the name of 'judicial dialogue' with their European partners.[50]

Article 11 of the ECHR protects the right of each person to 'freedom of association with others, including the right to form and to join trade unions for the protection of his interests'. The European case-law under Article 11 tends to fall

[45] Human Rights Act 1998, s 3.
[46] s 6.
[47] s 4.
[48] s 10.
[49] s 2.
[50] *R (Ullah) v Special Adjudicator* [2004] UKHL 26. L Graham, 'The Modern Mirror Principle' [2021] *Public Law* 523–541; J Letwin, 'Strasbourg's Views on the Modern Mirror Principle: Shattering the Mirror?' [2023] *Public Law* 628–649.

into three groups.[51] First there are cases involving public assemblies, demonstrations and protests. These may also be considered as infringements of Article 10, freedom of expression. They are not the concern of this chapter, although it is worth noting in passing that the principal impact of Article 11 in domestic law under the Human Rights Act 1998 has also been in precisely this area of public protest. The second group concerns trade union activity, as suggested by the express wording of the article. Here, the European Court is in a subordinate position vis-à-vis other international bodies such as the International Labour Organisation. Nevertheless, it has upheld certain minimum protections for trade union registration, membership, collective bargaining and strike action. Most of the cases in which the United Kingdom has been found to have violated Article 11 fall into this group.[52] Finally, there is a group of cases involving denials of registration or access via public registration to differential regimes of legal privilege. Such systems of regulatory restriction are foreign to the laws of the United Kingdom, which, as we have seen, enable groups to function effectively in law without any such status and even makes the corporate form relatively easily accessible.

In practice then, and apart from the notable exception of trade union activity, there has been very little British-origin litigation before the European Court on freedom of association. Perhaps the most notable exception is *Redfearn v United Kingdom*, in which the United Kingdom was found to have violated its positive obligation to secure effective protection of the right to associate freely.[53] An otherwise exemplary employee who had been dismissed on account of his membership of the British National Party – a far-right, albeit lawful, political party – lacked a legal remedy against his employer. Unfair dismissal was not available to an employee who had only been employed for a short period of time, and although he would have qualified in principle to bring an action based on religion or belief discrimination, the courts have not extended this concept to party political membership as opposed to the holding of comprehensive political ideologies.[54] After the finding of a violation, the law was amended to introduce a specific protection against dismissal on grounds of political opinions or affiliation for all employees.[55]

In general, the domestic impact of Article 11, via the Human Rights Act 1998, has followed similar contours to the European case-law. The largest group of cases in which the right has clearly affected judicial reasoning involves trade unions. In *Wandsworth LBC v Vining*, the Court of Appeal decided that a rule

[51] See B Rainey, P McCormick and C Ovey, *Jacobs White and Ovey: The European Convention on Human Rights*, 8th edn (Oxford, Oxford University Press, 2021) ch 19.

[52] *Young, James and Webster v UK* (1981) Series A No 44 (1982) 4 EHRR 38; *Wilson and the National Union of Journalists v UK* (2002) 35 EHRR 523; *ASLEF v UK* (2007) 45 EHRR 34.

[53] *Redfearn v United Kingdom* (47335/06) (2013) 57 EHRR 2.

[54] *Olivier v Department of Work and Pensions* UKET 1701407/2013; *McEleny v Ministry of Defence* [2018] UKET S/4105347/2017.

[55] Employment Rights Act 1996, s 108(4).

preventing two local authority parks police officers from joining a trade union was a breach of Article 11 and unlawful.[56] In 2021, the Court of Appeal again reversed the Employment Appeal Tribunal to find a breach of Article 11 in the refusal to register a trade union for foster carers – this had been refused on the grounds that as independent contractors with local authorities, foster carers are not in a qualifying employment relation to have a union.[57] On the other side of that problem lies the Supreme Court decision in *R (Independent Workers Union) v Central Arbitration Committee*.[58] Here the Committee was found to be right to refuse recognition of a trade union for delivery riders, as not falling within the scope of an employment relationship for Article 11 purposes. Finally, in *Kostal v Dunkley*, Article 11 played a central role in the Supreme Court's reasoning, finding that offers made by an employer during a collective bargaining process were unlawful financial inducements undermining the process.[59] In these and other cases, Article 11 forms part of the legal background to the interpretation and application of domestic law.

Apart from the trade union cases, there are very few involving claims based on freedom of association, and where it is even pleaded, it seems to have little impact. Judicial review of the process for challenging listing as a proscribed organisation under the anti-terrorist legislation has – perhaps unsurprisingly – been unsuccessful.[60] Article 11 was hovering somewhere in the background of this case, but it was not clearly considered. Similarly, differential tax treatment of donations to political parties depending on whether they have an elected MP has survived judicial scrutiny.[61] In the context of a claim based on Article 14 in connection with Article 11, the court accepted a fairly low bar of rationality.

One exception in which Article 11 litigation has clearly raised problems of associative freedom is *Royal Society for the Prevention of Cruelty to Animals v Attorney General*.[62] The RSPCA sought guidance from the court as to whether it could exclude from membership those who wished to change its long-standing policy of opposition to hunting with dogs. In relation to Article 11, Lightman J made several points: The RSPCA is not a public authority bound directly by Convention rights. Although the RSPCA is incorporated by private Act of Parliament, it would be hard to treat their rules as 'subordinate legislation'. In any case, Article 11 allows a society to exclude from membership, although this needs to be through a managed process of amending the application form to gather the data allowing for an objective consideration of whether a potential

[56] *Wandsworth LBC v Vining* [2017] EWCA Civ 1092. The illegality was remedied by a constructive interpretation of the Trade Union and Labour Relations (Consolidation) Act 1992, s 280.

[57] *National Union of Professional Foster Carers v Certification Officer* [2021] EWCA Civ 548.

[58] *R (Independent Workers Union) v Central Arbitration Committee* [2023] UKSC 43.

[59] *Kostal UK Ltd v Dunkley* [2021] UKSC 47.

[60] *R (Kurdistan Workers Party) v Secretary of the Home Department* [2002] EWHC 644 (Admin).

[61] *Banks v Revenue and Customs Commissioners* [2012] EWCA Civ 1439.

[62] *Royal Society for the Prevention of Cruelty to Animals v Attorney General* [2002] 1 WLR 448, ChD.

member had disqualified themselves by their active opposition to the society's policy.

The case illustrates nicely the difficulties of applying Article 11 within domestic law. Freedom of association as a Convention right attaches itself most readily to restrictions on the existence of certain types of group (eg, undesirable political parties) or on differential access to legal privileges (eg, historic religious denominations). As we have seen, English law has very few of either of these types of legal provision. Grounds for banning groups barely extend beyond those engaging in criminal activities, and there are few legal regimes of differential access, whether political, cultural or religious. The relevant categories, such as 'charity', are extremely broad. Tensions internal to groups may arise, but these raise the more limited positive obligation to secure effective protection of freedom of association against third parties. In any case, the right applies to both sides of the dispute, and the group takes priority over the individual. The European case-law on Article 11 provides little if any guidance on more subtle questions of the nature of associative freedom in its relation to state legal facilitation and regulation outlined in earlier sections of this chapter.

V. GROUP RECOGNITION UNDER THE EQUALITY ACT 2010

More notable than the Human Rights Act 1998, in terms of recent development, has been the rise in constitutional status of 'equality law'. Bob Hepple argues that the Equality Act 2010 'mark[s] a decisive shift from the politics and law of single identities … towards the politics and law of fundamental human rights'.[63] The Act is the culmination of several decades of equality-related legislation, combining several statutes into a single coherent code. What started life in the 1960s as a series of discrete policy interventions to address race relations at points of particular social hostility and discrimination has become a wide-ranging and effective legal regime. Although the more recent impetus for reform has been provided by European Union initiatives, these have survived 'Brexit' and been fully assimilated into domestic law. The Equality Act both restricts the scope of associative freedom and provides legal protection for the activities of certain groups.

In brief, the Equality Act 2010 identifies nine 'protected characteristics': age, disability, gender reassignment, marriage and civil partnership, race, religion or belief, sex, sexual orientation, and pregnancy and maternity.[64] It prohibits four kinds of conduct in relation to those characteristics: direct discrimination,[65]

[63] B Hepple, *Equality: the legal framework*, 2nd edn (Oxford, Hart Publishing, 2014) 1.
[64] Equality Act 2010, s 4 and Ch 1.
[65] s 13.

indirect discrimination,[66] harassment,[67] and victimisation.[68] It makes such discriminatory conduct unlawful if it takes place in a wide range of public-facing contexts. Associations, whether incorporated or unincorporated, are thus bound to legal equality obligations in the same way as any other legal person, in their capacity as employers, providers of goods and services to the public, occupants of premises, and so on. In spite of the technical lack of legal personality of unincorporated associations, the courts have shown procedural flexibility in allowing discrimination claims to be brought directly against associations.[69]

The Act also applies to associations as such.[70] These have a specific meaning under the Act: associations to which this part of the Act applies must contain at least 25 members and operate admission according to a set of rules and a process of selection.[71] With the exception of marriage or civil partnership,[72] such associations may not discriminate against proposed members on the basis of a protected characteristic,[73] nor can they apply membership terms differently to members on the basis of a protected characteristic.[74] The Act also prohibits associations from harassing or victimising members,[75] and their obligations extend to associates and guests of an association.[76]

The basic equality obligations contained in the Equality Act 2010 are subject to a vast number of exceptions and adjustments specific to different characteristics and situations. For the most part, these adjust non-discrimination expectations to accommodate socially acceptable forms of collective identity and practice. However, some groups have found that their freedom to continue existing practices has been abridged. For example, the law protects the existence of many single-sex spaces. Single-sex services can be provided to people of a particular sex as long as certain conditions are met, such as that 'the service would be insufficiently effective if it were only to be provided jointly', and that it 'is a proportionate means of achieving a legitimate aim'.[77] This exception means that single-sex schools, hospital wards or women-only crisis shelters are not unlawful. Yet a male-only golf club would be.

There are protections generally for single-characteristic associations, meaning that a Muslim walking group that restricts membership to Muslims would not be unlawful.[78] However, 'colour' is an exception to this: no association may

[66] s 19.
[67] s 26.
[68] s 27.
[69] *Affleck v Newcastle Mind* [1999] ICR 852; *Nazir v Asim* [2010] ICR 1225.
[70] Part 7.
[71] s 107(2).
[72] s 100(1).
[73] s 101(1). See, eg, *Sivagurunathan v Tamils Forum UK Ltd* [2018] 12 WLUK 653.
[74] s 101(2).
[75] ss 101(4)–(7).
[76] ss 107(6) and 102 respectively.
[77] Sch 3, para 27.
[78] Sch 16, para 1(1).

operate a colour-bar.[79] There is also protection for religious and philosophical groups who wish to restrict involvement in their activities to those who share their beliefs and lifestyle. Where an organisation has the purpose of practicing or advancing a religion or belief, or teaching the practices of a religion or belief, it is able to restrict membership on the basis of religion or belief, or sexual orientation.[80] There are also exceptions for employers with an ethos based on religion or belief who wish to impose an occupational requirement on employees to be of a particular religion or belief, if this is proportionate having regard to the ethos and nature or context of the work.[81] However, these substantial exemptions were not sufficient to protect Roman Catholic adoption agencies who did not wish to place children with same-sex couples.[82]

There is a general provision allowing for positive discrimination where that is a proportionate way of meeting specific needs. For example, this allows a housing association to confine the services it provides to Orthodox Jewish residents.[83] Political parties are given a specific concession allowing them to operate positive discrimination policies in relation to selection criteria.[84] Associations may also offer age-related concessions, such as lower membership fees or discounts, as an exception to the rules concerning age discrimination.[85] They are allowed to limit the terms of a woman's membership of an association if the existing terms would 'create a risk to her health and safety'.[86] Charities are permitted to restrict the provision of benefits to persons who share a protected characteristic if they do so in pursuance of a charitable instrument and doing so is either generally proportionate or compensates for a disadvantage linked to the protected characteristic.[87] These are just some examples of the ways in which 'equality' is legally tailored to specific groups and activities.

The Equality Act 2000 takes the form of detailed primary legislation which directly regulates the relationships between private individuals and groups – as employers, providers of goods, services and facilities, and in other respects. Practically speaking, it is therefore a far more important source of law in relation to associational life than the Human Rights Act 1998, which only protects abstract rights primarily against public authorities. Courts have sought to develop integrated interpretations of equality obligations in the light of human rights commitments, but it is still arguable that there is an emerging legal

[79] Sch 16, para 1(4).

[80] Equality Act 2010, Sch 23, para 2. See *R (Amicus) v Secretary of State for Trade and Industry* [2004] EWHC 860 (Admin).

[81] Sch 9, para 3.

[82] *Catholic Care (Diocese of Leeds) v Charity Commission for England and Wales* [2012] UKUT 395 (TCC).

[83] *R (Z) v Hackney LBC* [2020] UKSC 40.

[84] ss 104–106.

[85] Sch 16, para 1A.

[86] Sch 16, para 2.

[87] s 193.

privileging of 'equality' over 'liberty'. The outworking of this prioritisation is, however, highly dependent on the particular context of litigation.

VI. CONCLUSION

In reflecting on the law of associations in the United Kingdom, it would be easy to be complacent. In general terms, there is a high degree of liberty under law. Moreover, this liberty is understood not merely as freedom beyond the law, but as the legal empowerment of individuals to generate and contribute to a highly varied and legally secure plurality of social groups. International human rights obligations have contributed relatively little to this legal heritage. At the same time, the law is characterised by increasing public regulation, as sporadic legislative intervention has tended to evolve into more comprehensive legal regimes. Regulation has brought in its wake diversification, as distinct types of social groups are subjected to norms considered suitable for their specific social contribution. The Equality Act 2010 displays these features of the modern law of associations to an unprecedented degree, being both comprehensive in aspiration and reach, yet also containing highly detailed rules, distinctive to particular types of group and activity. The significance of this lies not so much in new (and, it must be said, fairly peripheral) restrictions on associational liberty, as in the fact that it has replaced flexible norms of social acceptability with more rigid legal obligations. This has been supplemented by growing 'soft law' expectations around the proper management and conduct of groups, which means that the impact of public regulation is perhaps felt most in terms of the increased burdens of regulatory compliance on the day-to-day life of groups. In these ways, associative freedom in the United Kingdom may be at risk, not so much of legal limitation as of gradual suffocation.

2

Freedom of Association in Chile

SEBASTIAN SOTO*

I. INTRODUCTION

THE ASSOCIATIVE PRACTICE in Chile has been historically intense. During the nineteenth century, there was active participation of various associations in different areas, including education, social assistance, housing, infant mortality, malnutrition, etc. In the last century, associativism was expressed in trade unions, students' associations, local and rural organisations and religious groups.[1] Many services that are currently in the realm of the state were initially the responsibility of private associations, such as education and childcare. Today, in all of them, the participation of people through civil society organisations continues to be active.

In recent decades, the expansion of civil society organisations has remained high. It was reported that the growth rate of civil society organisations between 2005 and 2023 is 2.25 times higher than that of companies and 6.75 times higher than the population. The same report states that civil society organisations are particularly concentrated in the following areas: community, economic and housing development (eg, neighbourhood councils, housing committees, indigenous communities), culture and recreation (eg, sports clubs) and civic, advocacy and political activities (eg, senior citizens' clubs, social and women's or youth groups). In addition to these formally registered associations, there are a number of other non-formalised associations that are also protected by the right of association.[2]

* I want to thank Luiz Arcaro Conci, Andrés Calderon, Miriam Mora, Magdalena Ortega, Alejandra Ovalle, José Ignacio Ramos and Macarena Sochting. I would also like to thank María Cahill for her suggestions and comments.

[1] LM Díaz de Valdés, 'Trayectorias En Cambio: Un Recorrido Por La Historia de Las Organizaciones de La Sociedad Civil' (Centro de Políticas Públicas UC, 2016) politicaspublicas.uc.cl/publicacion/trayectorias-en-cambio-historia-de-las-organizaciones-de-la-sociedad-civil/ accessed 14 March 2025.

[2] Sociedad en Acción. 'Mapa de las Organizaciones de la Sociedad Civil 2023' (Centro de Políticas Públicas UC, 2024) politicaspublicas.uc.cl/publicacion/mapa-de-las-organizaciones-de-la-sociedad-civil-2023/ accessed 14 March 2025.

This chapter examines the right of association in Chilean constitutionalism. It argues that associativism has grown substantially in the 150 years since the entrenchment of the right of association in the Constitution. The constitutional protection of associations and their autonomy has also been reinforced. From being understood only as the freedom to create associations, it has come to be interpreted as a right as well. In the last half century, protection has also extended to the association itself, seen as a new space of self-determination and autonomy. Section II examines the historical evolution of the right of association in three fundamental debates during Chile's constitutional history. The first was the incorporation of the right into the Constitution in 1874. The second was a few years before the 1973 coup d'état and then in the drafting of the current Constitution of 1980. The last debate is the recent discussion during the two failed constitution-making processes. Section III examines the structure of the right in the Chilean Constitution in its three main elements: the right to form an association, the right not to be forced to belong to an association, and the autonomy of associations. Section IV studies some recent discussions on the right of association in the Chilean context. Among others, I will develop the active debate in Chile based both on the principle of subsidiarity and the role of associations, along with case law regarding the scope of the autonomy of associations. Also, I will analyse one of the most controversial debates regarding the right of association, the idea of institutional beliefs as the basis for an 'institutional conscientious objection' regarding abortion.

II. THREE CENTURIES, THREE DEBATES: EVOLUTION OF THE CONSTITUTIONAL TEXT

A. Constitutional Context: Historical and Regional Considerations

The history of Latin American constitutions has always been interlinked. As Gargarella et al. state, 'institutional outlooks, rights' declarations, ideological underpinnings and canons of constitutional thought display striking similarities that are far from coincidental'.[3] For this reason, an analysis of the regional context contributes to an understanding of the national context.

Latin American constitutions began to entrench the right of association in the mid-nineteenth century. After independence from Spain and Portugal, the new nations wrote their first constitutions without expressly including this freedom. However, several constitutions in the region began incorporating the right of association around the mid-nineteenth century: Argentina in the Constitution

[3] R Gargarella et al., 'Introduction' in *The Oxford Handbook of Constitutional Law in Latin America* (Conrado Hubner and others eds, Oxford, Oxford University Press 2022) xv.

of 1853, Peru in the Constitution of 1856, Chile in an amendment in 1874, Brazil in the Constitution of 1891, and Uruguay in 1934. In some cases, as in Peru, the wording was closer to the right of assembly.[4] In the case of Brazil, the rights to association and assembly were entrenched together.[5] Currently, the constitutions of Latin America entrenched the right of association in provisions of varying length. Among the shortest are the constitutional clauses of Argentina (5 words), Bolivia (recognised together with the right of assembly in 12 words) and Colombia (18 words). Similarly, Jamaica (7 words) and the Dominican Republic (15 words) in Central America.

Most commonly, constitutions recognise the right of association either as a freedom or as a fundamental right. Several constitutions include an explicit prohibition against being compelled to belong to an association. Constitutions with lengthier clauses develop other topics. Brazil, with one of the longest articles, establishes that the compulsory dissolution of a society may only be by 'judicial decision' and that associations have standing to represent their members. Guatemala states that professional associations are an exception to the compulsory association prohibition. Haiti expressly recognises the right of civil service to form associations, Nicaragua refers to the 'social function' of associations, and Paraguay prohibits 'secret associations'. Due to the region's own history of violence, Brazil, El Salvador and Paraguay also explicitly outlaw paramilitary associations.[6]

B. Constitutional Entrenchment in Chile: Nineteenth Century

The Constitution of 1833 was the first to be consolidated in Chile after two decades of constitutional instability, and its original text did not contain the right of association. This should not be surprising since the first Latin American constitutionalism, like the European constitutions, looked at the exercise of this freedom with suspicion.[7] In 1874, the Constitution was amended to incorporate the right of association, together with the right of assembly and freedom of education. This reform was accompanied by other political reforms that marked a shift towards a more open constitutional text, in accordance with the principles of political liberalism.[8]

[4] 'All citizens have the right to associate peacefully, whether in public or in private, without compromising public order' (Art 28).

[5] 'It is lawful for everyone to associate and meet freely and without weapons; The police cannot intervene except to maintain public order' (Art 72.8).

[6] constituteproject.org/ accessed 14 March 2025.

[7] U Preub, 'Associative Rights (the Rights to Freedoms of Petition, Assembly and Association)' in M Rosenfeld and A Sajo (eds), *The Oxford Handbook of Comparative Constitutional Law* (Oxford, Oxford University Press, 2013) 953.

[8] S Collier and W Sater, *A History of Chile. 1808–1994* (Cambridge, Cambridge Latin American Studies, 1996) 121.

The discussion regarding the right of association was intense. Some historians point out that 'it promoted one of the most interesting debates that have taken place in the National Congress, both for its perfection in form and its erudition in substance'.[9] Contrary to what might be expected, conservatives led by Abdón Cifuentes, one of the most important conservative politicians in the nineteenth century in Chile, promoted a broad and unregulated freedom of association. Under this view, the right of association must not only contain the freedom to associate but should also provide a space of autonomy to the new associations. Cifuentes himself argued that 'no authority has the power to confiscate (the right of association) or even to interfere in the internal regime of associations, because it would be to interfere in the internal regime of families'.[10] On the other hand, liberals who were led by Miguel Luis Amunátegui, one of the most famous liberal minds in those decades, promoted greater control over associations and demanded that all associations should have legal personality. This would entail government involvement, as per the rules of the Civil Code, which organises virtually all spheres of private law; government authorisation is a requirement for associations to have a legal personality.

Underlying the whole debate hid a fundamental difference: the degree of freedom that the Catholic Church should have to develop its activities. During the nineteenth century and until 1925, there was no separation between the Church and the state in Chile, so Catholicism was the official religion of the country. In this context, the liberals wanted more civil control over religious authorities, and the conservatives wanted maximum autonomy. The right of association and the autonomy of associations became another area to develop in this discussion. The amendment was finally approved, and since 1874 the Constitution has included the right of assembly and the right of association in two separate articles. In the following decades, the right of association was not the subject of reflection or further discussion in Chile. For example, most of the scholarly work that analyses the constitution of 1833 does not develop this freedom or show substantive debates on the scope of the right.[11]

C. Twentieth Century: Two Moments

The 1925 Constitution, the second most relevant constitution in Chilean history, included the right of association with almost no debate. Its text recognises the

[9] FC Harriet, *Historia Constitutional de Chile*, 4th edn (Casilla, Editorial Jurídica 1969) 342. Also J Heise, *Historia de Chile. El período parlamentario* (Santiago, Editorial Andrés Bello, 1974) 39.

[10] JF García, *La Tradición Constitucional de la P. Universidad Católica de Chile. Vol I* (Santiago, Ediciones UC, 2017) 122.

[11] A Ovalle and S Soto, 'Sociedad Civil y Constitución. Ideas para el debate' (Santiago, Centro de Políticas Públicas UC, 2021) politicaspublicas.uc.cl/publicacion/sociedad-civil-y-constitucion-ideas-para-el-debate/ accessed 14 March 2025.

right to associate without prior authorisation and then adds that this must be 'in accordance with the law'. The constitutional debates that preceded offered no insight into the intended meaning of this latter provision. In any case, what is certain is that it does not seem to have made a difference, as legislation had broad space to regulate rights at that time. It is important to consider that in Chile, judicial review was introduced in the 1925 Constitution, and its exercise was quite limited for decades.[12]

The commentators of the 1925 Constitution gave increasing importance to this right, devoting more efforts to determining its content. While José Guillermo Guerra, a law professor and one of the constitution makers in 1925, dedicated only a few lines to studying this right in 1929,[13] in the 1960s Silva Bascuñán, who was the most prominent scholar of the 1925 Constitution, devoted several pages to it. He was the first author to engage deeper with its content and make explicit that the right of association includes the freedom to form and join any type of organisation, as well as the right not to be forced to join a particular association. Although not explicitly, he was also the first constitutional law scholar to outline the spaces of autonomy of the associations themselves, although he mostly focused on trade unions and political parties.[14]

i. The Statute of Constitutional Guarantees: 1971

In Chile, the debate had its first constitutional expression in 1970 when the Statute of Constitutional Guarantees was approved. This was a set of constitutional amendments negotiated by the Christian Democratic Party and President-elect Salvador Allende in the context of the Cold War. Under the Chilean presidential system of the 1925 Constitution, if no presidential candidate secured an absolute majority of the popular votes in the election, the president was then to be elected from between the two leading candidates by both houses of Congress in a plenary session. Allende, the Socialist Party candidate who represented the leftist forces, including the Communist Party, obtained 36 per cent of the popular vote. Therefore, he needed the support of the majority of the house representatives and senators. With this objective, he reached an agreement with the Christian Democratic Party, a centre-left party, to amend some provisions of the Constitution. The amendments had the objective of providing reassurance that a left-leaning government would not purport to emulate other Latin American leftists' governments that were seen as a threat to democracy.

[12] D Figueroa, 'Constitutional Review in Chile Revisited: A Revolution in the Making' (2013) 51 *Duquesne Law Review*, 394.

[13] JG Guerra, *La Constitución de 1925* (Santiago, Establecimientos Gráficos Balcells y Co., 1929) 114.

[14] A Silva Bascuñán, *Tratado de Derecho Constitucional, Tomo II* (Santiago, Editorial Jurídica, 1963) 249. For a longer review of the right of association in the 20th century, see A Ovalle and S Soto, 'Sociedad Civil y Constitución. Ideas para el debate' (Santiago, Centro de Políticas Públicas UC, 2021).

In this context, the protection of associations was deemed fundamental. The autonomy of unions, educational institutions, the media, political parties and other associations had to be constitutionally reinforced. The justification for this reform was provided by the Christian Democrat Senator (and later President of Chile after the return to democracy) Patricio Aylwin:

> Wherever the Marxist sectors triumph, they immediately begin to apply their methods: they suppress party pluralism (...), they monopolize all the media (...) they completely nationalize education and impose an official ideology on it (...) constitutional guarantees are, as it were, to set the ring for the democratic combat (...) we will have a suitable field to successfully wage the fight that is necessary to give in Chile in this moment.[15]

These amendments incorporated into the constitutional text important rules for the protection of associations.[16] First, it established the freedom to join political parties and the freedom of political parties to organise themselves internally as they deem convenient. Second, private schools were granted autonomy to determine their administrative organisation and the appointment of personnel. Third, the academic, administrative and economic autonomy of universities was established. Fourth, the right to join trade unions was established, as well as the right of unions to legal personality and to federate. Fifth, the right to participate in social, cultural, civic, political and economic life was recognised as necessary to allow for the full development of people. Sixth, the independence and freedom of social organisations[17] that seek 'the solution of their problems' was recognised as well as their freedom to collaborate with the state. The changes made by the reform in 1971 did not last, as the 1925 Constitution was suspended by the 1973 coup d'état. Nevertheless, it was the first time a Chilean constitution contained provisions that strengthened and specified the right of association, and to some extent its effects are found to be present in the third Chilean constitution.

ii. The Current Constitution: 1980

The 1980 Constitution was drafted between 1973 and 1980 during the dictatorship of Augusto Pinochet,[18] and replaced the 1925 Constitution. Since then, it has been profoundly amended. The most important amendments were in 1989, at the end of the Pinochet government and after a political agreement between the outgoing military regime and the democratic opposition, in a reform that

[15] J Fermandois, *La revolución inconclusa. La izquierda chilena y el gobierno de la Unidad Popular* (Santiago, Centro de Estudios Públicos, 2013) 345.

[16] Statute of Democratic Guarantees (ley 17.398).

[17] The amendment mentioned several 'social organisations' such as unions, neighbourhood councils, cooperatives and mothers' centres.

[18] R Barros, *Constitutionalism and Dictatorship. Pinochet, the Junta and the 1980 Constitution* (Cambridge, Cambridge University Press, 2002).

was ratified in a referendum; and then in 2005, in a broad reform that symbolically eliminated Pinochet's name and replaced it with Socialist President Ricardo Lagos' signature. In addition to these two broad reforms, more than 50 constitutional amendment bills have been approved since 1990. Overall, this means that almost all articles of the original constitution have been amended.[19]

The current constitutional text reiterates old constitutional provisions and incorporates new ones. The debates during the 1925 Constitution reinforced the importance of making explicit the two facets of the right: the right to form associations and the right not to be forced to belong to an association. It also established voluntary union affiliation and prohibited compulsory membership in professional associations. Following this lead, it increased the regulation of political parties and established several provisions to strengthen the autonomy of associations and the prohibition of political parties from influencing them. In this vein, it entrenched as a constitutional principle the 'autonomy of intermediate groups' in Article 1 of the Constitution. As we shall see, this last provision has been highly debated in Chile. Finally, it enshrined freedom of association by establishing the right to join unions, recognising the legal personality and autonomy of unions, and prohibiting intervention in political party activities (Article 19.19).

D. Twenty-First Century: The Failed New Constitution Processes

In October 2019, after intense days of mobilisation and high levels of violence, it was agreed in Chile to initiate a process to replace the 1980 Constitution. The first process lasted 12 months, starting in July 2021. In September 2022, 61 per cent of citizens rejected the proposal. This led to the initiation of a second, shorter and more contained process, which took place between March and November 2023. In December 2023, the citizens again rejected the new proposal (55 per cent).[20] Throughout these processes, three constitutional texts were drafted. The first was that of the Convention, composed mainly of left-wing forces. The second was that of the Expert Commission, which achieved a political agreement between the left and the right. The third, also during the second process, was drafted by the Constitutional Council, composed mainly of right-wing forces, which reviewed and rewrote the text of the Expert Commission. The two referenda were over the Convention and the Constitutional Council texts.

[19] For a global review of the current constitution see D Lovera, 'Chile' in *The Oxford Handbook of Constitutional Law in Latin America* (Conrado Hubner and others eds, Oxford, Oxford University Press, 2022).

[20] For an analysis of both failure processes, see S Soto, 'Two Drafts, Three Referendums, and Four Lessons for Constitution-making from Chile' (*ConstitutionNet*, International IDEA, 22 December 2023) constitutionnet.org/news/voices/two-drafts-three-referendums-and-four-lessons-constitution-making-chile accessed 14 March 2025.

The topics discussed during these years were numerous: political system, judiciary, indigenous peoples, right to life, property, etc. No topic was off-limits, although some stirred up more controversy than others. The right of association was not among the most controversial. Even so, it is worthwhile to briefly review the proposals that were made. Although they were rejected, they show consensus and points of differences between both texts. The consensus included the entrenchment of the right, the recognition of the autonomy of associations,[21] a limited right of association for members of the Armed Forces, and the delegation to legislation of the rules for granting legal personality to associations. Among the points of differences, we can highlight that the text of the Convention eliminated the existing restriction on associations that conflict with morality, public order and national security. It also eliminated the right not to be forced to join an association. It also suppressed any references to the autonomy of intermediate groups. The Expert Commission and the Council maintained the mentioned limitations and included the autonomy of 'social groups that freely arise among the people'. In addition, the Expert Commission and the Council extensively regulated political parties. The Convention did not mention them and referred only tangentially to 'political organisations'.[22] Finally, the text of the Convention established a broad right to strike in both the public and private sectors and a strengthening of trade union organisations. The text of the Expert Commission prohibited compulsory membership and delegated various topics to legislation. The Council's text reinstated certain provisions of the current Constitution on union matters.

III. RIGHT OF ASSOCIATION IN THE CONSTITUTION OF CHILE: CONTENTS

The three facets that are in general attributed to this right are entrenched in the constitutional text: the right to form associations, the right not to be forced to belong to them and the right of the association itself to a certain degree of autonomy.[23]

[21] The text of the Convention established that the right of association 'includes the protection of the autonomy of associations for the fulfillment of their specific purposes and the establishment of their internal regulation, organization and other defining elements' Art 72.2. The text of the Expert Commission and of the Council establish that 'the right to associate includes the right to form, organize and maintain associations, to determine their purpose, their officers, members and internal statutes in order to pursue their objectives' Art 16.17.

[22] See S Issacharoff and S Verdugo, 'The Uncertain Future of Constitutional Democracy in the Era of Populism: Chile and Beyond' (2023) 78 *University of Miami Law Review*. They note that 'the Convention reflected the anti-institutionalism of the times'.

[23] For a constitutional approach of the right of association in Chile see JL Cea, *Derecho Constitucional Chileno. Tomo II* (Santiago, Ediciones UC, 2012) and H Nogueira, *Derechos Fundamentales y Garantías Constitucionales. Tomo III* (Santiago, Librotecnia, 2019). For a more theoretical approach see D Loewe, *Multiculturalismo, identidad, plurinacionalidad y todas esas cosas* (Santiago, Fondo de Cultura Económica, 2023).

A. The Right to Form an Association

Article 19.15 of the Constitution assures to all persons 'the right to associate without prior permission'. The provision also forbids associations with objectives 'that are contrary to morality, public order and the security of the State'. Regarding these limits, the ambiguity of these categories has not been disputed, at least at a constitutional level. Both in comparative constitutional law and in international law, the right of association has limits. Article 16 of the American Convention on Human Rights, for example, sets limits on 'national security', 'public order', 'public health or morals' and 'the rights and freedoms of others'. The Chilean Constitutional Court has recognised the centrality of the right and its essential content when it notes that 'the right enshrined in Article 19.15 is not reduced to guaranteeing the freedom to join or leave an association, but, first and foremost, the freedom to create or form any type of group'.[24]

Article 19.15 also refers to the legal personality that associations may obtain. It establishes that 'in order to enjoy legal personality, associations must be constituted in accordance with the law'. Thus, although the power to associate is not subordinated to the law, if an association wants to obtain legal personality and, therefore, to become a legal person that has separate rights and obligations, it is necessary for it to comply with the requirements and forms established by law. Furthermore, it is relevant to consider that legal personhood is an additional benefit but not a requirement to enjoy constitutional protection. In this manner, the Constitutional Court has held that it is not necessary to be formed as legal persons to exercise the right and consequent freedom to create associations. The difference established by the Constitution between the right of association and the right of association with legal personality, is that of genus – species: 'the first, the genus, does not require law for its exercise; the second, the species, must comply with the prescriptions established by the legislature for that purpose'.[25] Decades later, the Court has ratified this approach, protecting to the same degree both types of associations: 'it is true that an association that has legal personality will normally reflect a greater will of permanence in time than one that is not organized in this way. But this type of legal formality is not a requirement of the Constitution'.[26]

The various ways of obtaining legal personality are regulated by common law and offer ample alternatives. This was not the case in the past. The Civil Code, drafted by the jurist Andrés Bello, had a much greater impact than the constitutional enshrinement of the right of association in the Constitution. Cifuentes himself, to whom we referred above, was critical of this and in his memoirs published in 1936 stated that, 'the absurd provisions of the Civil Code on legal personality have continued to govern, in open contradiction with the

[24] *Groups of Senators v Labor Bill* [2016] TC 3016-16, c. 30.
[25] *Constitutional Review of Political Parties Organic Constitutional Law* [1987] TC 43-87, c. 14.
[26] *Groups of Senators v Labor Bill* [2016] TC 3016-16, c. 29.

constitutional precept'.[27] Along the same lines, the 1925 Constitution gave the President the power to grant legal personality to 'private corporations and to cancel them; to approve the statutes by which they must be governed, reject them and accept modifications' (Article 72.11). In 1980 this provision was excluded from among presidential constitutional powers, and at present, the procedures for obtaining legal personality are generally simple and expeditious.

Legislation regulates various types of associations. The text of the 1925 Constitution, as mentioned before, explicitly recognised the right of association 'in accordance with the law'. In the current text there is no explicit mention of the law. This has not prevented legislation from establishing certain proportional and reasonable requirements for the exercise of the right in the multiplicity of associations that recognise civil, commercial and many other legal areas (neighbourhood councils, public interest organisations, trade associations, etc). Associations of civil servants, for instance, were regulated by law in the 1990s and excluded associations of military and police personnel. The last relevant modification was made in 2005, when the authorisation for the formation of non-profit legal entities was moved from the government to local counties.

B. The Right not to be Forced to Belong to an Association

The Constitution also guarantees the negative expression of the right, which, in other words, is the prohibition of being forced to join an association. Article 19.15 states that '[n]o one may be compelled to belong to an association'. This provision is complemented by two other relevant provisions. Article 19.19 states that 'trade union membership shall always be voluntary', while Article 19.16 provides that 'no law or provision of public authority may require membership of any organization or entity as a condition for carrying out a particular activity or work, or disaffiliation to keep it'. These provisions generally prohibit the use of coercion to join an association and specifically prohibit any obligation to join a union or a professional association. These latter provisions were included due to legislation from the 1920s establishing certain mandatory membership mechanisms to work as a lawyer, architect, physician, teacher, journalist, or so on.[28]

The Constitutional Court has stated that 'this freedom consists precisely in the power of self-determination as to whether or not to belong to, create or not, a society, association or specific corporate group, that is, not to be coerced to join a particular corporate body, to freely accept or not, as a member, a particular subject who wishes to join it, and finally to freely withdraw or not from that group or associative body'.[29] In a case involving conflict between a university

[27] A Cifuentes, *Memorias T. II* (Santiago, Nascimiento, 1936) 103.

[28] A Silva Bascuñán, *Tratado de Derecho Constitucional. Tomo XIII* (Santiago, Editorial Jurídica, 2003) 267.

[29] *Constitutional Review of the Bill that Amend Capital Market Laws* [1994] TC 184-1994, c. 7.

student and the student federation of his university, the Supreme Court stated that in a regime of 'automatic affiliation' for those who meet the requirements indicated in the statutes, the right of the students of the university arises 'not only legal but also constitutional, to leave the association'. For that reason, it was deemed unconstitutional for the Student Federation to not accept the student's claim for disaffiliation.[30]

In recent years, some professional associations have promoted the reinstatement of compulsory licensure as a way to reinforce the ethical control of professions. The proposal has generated disagreement, and it is unlikely that such a provision will be approved in the future. There have also been discussions on how to strengthen unions. A few years ago, a bill amending the Labor Code sought to grant trade unions the exclusive right to represent their company in collective bargaining.[31] This reform was declared unconstitutional because it was against, among other things, the right of association of workers outside unions (in Chile known as 'negotiating groups'), as well as the freedom to unionise. Regarding the latter, the Court held that under said regulation, 'if the worker wants to exercise his right to not join a union, their right to bargain collectively will be radically limited'. It added that this established a 'disproportionate difference in treatment in terms of the privileges' that the trade union received and the workers associated in other modalities did not.[32]

C. The Autonomy of the Association

After the right to form an association and the right not to be forced to belong to an association, the third dimension of the right is the autonomy of associations. This third element of the right is recognised in other constitutional norms, and its incorporation in the 1980 Constitution has generated various debates which we will examine in section IV. The first chapter of the Constitution is called 'Bases of Institutionality', and its norms bring together a set of fundamental principles. Article 1 of the Constitution establishes in its third paragraph:

> The State recognizes and protects the intermediate groups through which society is organized and structured and guarantees them adequate autonomy to fulfill their own specific purposes.

The location of this clause is not random. The first paragraph of Article 1 refers to the person; the second, to the family; the third, to intermediate groups; and the fourth, to the state. Thus, the first article of the Constitution is based

[30] *Toro v Student Federation of UCN* [2019] SC 23.233-2018, c. 5.

[31] For a review on labour regulation in Chile from a comparative perspective: OECD 'Negotiating Our Way Up: Collective Bargaining in a Changing World of Work' (Paris, OECD Publishing, 2019) doi.org/10.1787/1fd2da34-en accessed 14 March 2025.

[32] *Groups of Senators v Labor Bill* [2016] TC 3016-16, c. 35 & 36.

on the dignity and freedom of persons, and the following develop the various forms of social relations. As noted previously, the Constitution was drafted in the 1970s during the Cold War, and it was a deliberate political decision to base the Constitution on the person and not on the state.

It is thus assumed that the community is not only made up of individuals and state entities but also of families and a varied set of private organisations that aim to fulfil the most diverse objectives. Arguably, civil society is a core element in the constitutional identity of Chile. The Constitutional Court has pointed out that intermediate groups originate from the exercise of the right of association, unlike public bodies and services that are constituted and configured by virtue of the principle of legality. It has defined them as 'all associations other than the public apparatus, all those that are not organs of the State in all its manifestations, i.e., organs of the State administration, courts, autonomous organs, public law corporations'.[33] However, the autonomy recognised by the Constitution is not unlimited. As various constitutional law professors have pointed out, when 'adequate' autonomy is protected, it is that which is 'appropriate, proportionate or convenient for the specific purposes of the group'.[34] That is why 'the specific purpose of the intermediate society determines the scope and limit within which it can legitimately govern itself with autonomy'.[35]

IV. DISCUSSIONS

In recent years, disputes over the exercise of the right of association in Chile have focused on various issues, which we will examine below.

A. Autonomy of the Associations and the Debate on the Principle of Subsidiarity

Since the 1980s, a highly contested issue in Chile has been the influence of the principle of subsidiarity in constitutional law. Unlike in Europe, where territorial subsidiarity concerns the proper allocation of powers between higher and lower bodies, such as central and local governments,[36] the principle of subsidiarity in Chile emerged as a response to defining the role of the state.

Until the 1970s, the Chilean state apparatus had acquired enormous power. Arturo Valenzuela, author of one of the most renowned books on the Chilean

[33] *Insurance Companies v SVS* [2009] TC 1295-08, c. 55.

[34] JL Cea, *Derecho Constitucional Chileno. Tomo I* (Santiago, Ediciones UC, 2015) 217.

[35] A Fermandois, *Derecho Constitucional Económico. Tomo I* (Santiago, Ediciones UC, 2001) 87.

[36] For a critical analysis of the European interpretation of subsidiarity, see M Cahill, 'Theorizing Subsidiarity. Towards an Ontology-Sensitive Approach' (2017) 15(1) *International Journal of Constitutional Law*, 201–224.

breakdown, wrote that in those years 'the state played a greater role in the nation's economy than it did in the economy of any other Latin American country with the exception of Cuba'.[37] In this context, the new Constitution proposed by the Pinochet regime sought to limit the role of the state and used the principle of subsidiarity as a key justification. Under this principle, the state itself should only assume one specific activity when the private sector could not do so within a reasonable margin of quality. This narrative coincided with the process of economic modernisation that began in the 1980s and was consolidated in the following decades. Both the Pinochet government and the centre-left governments that democratically came to power in the 1990s initiated a series of pro-market reforms that expanded private participation in different areas: health, education, housing, infrastructure, transportation, and so on.[38]

Why is this discussion related to associations and their autonomy? Many argue that the principle of subsidiarity is enshrined in the Constitution. An originalist interpretation of the Constitution often argues that one of the provisions that 'implicitly' uphold the principle of subsidiarity is the autonomy of intermediate groups (in addition to other clauses in the Constitution that limit the entrepreneurial state and favours freedom of choice in health and education). This has allowed many to link the Chilean economic modernisation of the last four decades with the constitutional framework and the principle of subsidiarity.

From the constitutional perspective, the principle of subsidiarity was very present in constitutional adjudication in the 1990s, although it has lost force in judicial argumentation in the following decades. However, from a political perspective, the principle of subsidiarity has maintained its presence as a justification for changing the 1980 Constitution. A decade ago, Ricardo Lagos, a social democrat who served as President of Chile between 2000 and 2006 stated: 'I do not like a constitution that starts by saying that the State is subsidiary.'[39] Although the text does not explicitly consider subsidiarity, criticisms against the Constitution have often become criticisms against that principle.

The failed constitution-making processes opened a new discussion when all three drafts included a clause establishing the social state. The question was whether it is possible that, constitutionally speaking, a social state can coexist with the autonomy of intermediate bodies and the active participation of private associations in all areas. Both the National Congress and the Expert Commission of the second constituent process – which, as noted before, reached a constitutional agreement between left and right – included several clauses in its draft that enshrine the social state clause, the autonomy of associations, and

[37] A Valenzuela, *Chile. The Breakdown of Democratic Regimes* (Baltimore, Johns Hopkins University Press, 1978) 13.

[38] S Edwards, *The Chile Project. The Story of the Chicago Boys and the Downfall of Neoliberalism* (Princeton, Princeton University Press, 2023).

[39] R Lagos, 'La cuestión constitucional: reflexiones de un actor' (2015) 139 *Estudios Públicos*.

public-private provision.[40] Whether this represents a lasting compromise for the future remains uncertain. However, it can be argued that the decades-long constitutional debate between a subsidiary state that relied on the autonomies of associations and the social state clause may find paths of convergence.

B. Politics and Autonomy of Associations

The autonomy of the intermediate bodies was conceived by the drafters of the Constitution as one among several provisions within a constitutional framework that aimed to separate civil society from politics. For many, in the middle of the 1970s, one of the causes of the breakdown of Chilean democracy had been the intervention of political parties in civil society associations. This interference generated ideological instrumentalisation and polarisation of civil society's groups. That is why the 1980 Constitution sought to separate the 'social order' from the 'political order' to protect the autonomy of the 'intermediate associations' from the intervention of politics and parties.

This approach is also expressed in other regulations. Article 23 delegates to legislation the establishment of sanctions for intermediate groups that misuse their autonomy, unduly intervening in activities unrelated to their specific purposes. It then adds that legislation will establish sanctions for union leaders who intervene in partisan political activities, and for political leaders who interfere in the functioning of intermediate groups. Article 19.19 declares that trade union organisations may not intervene in partisan political activities. Another provision states that political parties may not intervene in activities 'unrelated to their own' (Article 19.15). In the same sense, union or neighbourhood leaders must resign from their positions if they register as candidates for the National Congress (Article 57). At present, these constitutional norms are dormant. Some of them call for sanctions without any legislation specifying them, and those that establish the prohibition of non-interference in political activity have not been enforceable.

C. The Autonomy of Associations in Some Decisions of the Constitutional Court and the Supreme Court

Based on the autonomy of intermediate groups, the jurisprudence of the Constitutional Court has built a robust body of case-law that protects these

[40] Most notably, in the second constitution-making process (2023), Congress required that the new constitutional project entrenched the following provision: Chile is a social and democratic state under the rule of law 'that recognizes the fundamental rights and freedoms and promotes the progressive development of social rights, subject to the principle of fiscal responsibility and through state and private institutions' (Art 154).

spaces of autonomy from legislative intrusions that are deemed excessive or disproportionate. It is worth noting that constitutional case-law and doctrine have relied much more on this clause to construct areas of non-intervention than on the right of association. Early on, the Constitutional Court specified that the autonomy of the associative bodies is configured 'by the fact of being governed by themselves; that is, by the necessary and indispensable freedom to organize themselves in the most convenient way according to their statutes, to decide their own acts, the form of administration and to set the objectives or goals they wish to achieve, by themselves and without interference from persons or authorities outside the association, entity or group in question'.[41] In this way, it constructs autonomy as self-determination.

Subsequently, in later rulings, it has gradually established areas of autonomy in different sectors. In the 1995 *Media Law* case, a regulation that required television stations to broadcast certain content was declared unconstitutional. The decision was based on the autonomy of the media and freedom of expression.[42] The result of this ruling was repeated years later in the *People Meter Online* cases (2013), which banned or excessively conditioned the use of online audience measurement systems by television broadcastings. The Court states that it has made clear 'the inconvenience of any form of state interference in the media, in the face of the infringement of the autonomy of intermediate groups'.[43]

In the following decade, new rulings deepened other areas of autonomy. The *Manuel de Salas School* case[44] and *School Day* case established a substantial space of autonomy for educational institutions, connecting the autonomy of intermediate groups with freedom of education. In the latter, the Court held that the autonomy of the association is 'broadly applicable' and also includes schools 'with such capacity to govern themselves in teaching, in the educational, administrative and economic spheres, the aforementioned institutions are empowered by the Constitution to fully exercise their freedom of education, without undue intervention or interference by the State or third parties'.[45]

However, it is uncertain as to whether these decisions are still good law. The Constitutional Court does not adhere strictly to precedent, and changes in case law can occur within just a few years with potentially significant consequences. For instance, the Court has not considered that legislation prohibiting student selection processes in publicly funded elementary or secondary schools violates the Constitution or the autonomy of an intermediate group.[46] It has

[41] *Constitutional Review of the Bill that Amend Capital Market Laws* [1994] TC 184-94, c. 7.

[42] *Group of Deputies v Media Law Bill* [1995] TC 226-95.

[43] *Group of Deputies v Digital Television Bill* [2012] TC 2358-12, c. 18. See also [2013] TC 2509-13, c. 6.

[44] *Group of Deputies v Liceo Manuel de Salas Bill* [2002] TC 352-02.

[45] *Group of Deputies v School Day Bill* [2004] TC 410-04, c. 26. See also A Fermandois, 'Autonomia de los cuerpos intermedios: ¿objeción institucional o protección constitucional? [2018] *Sentencias Destacadas* 2017.

[46] *Group of Senators v School Regulation Bill* [2015] TC 2787-15.

also rejected constitutional challenges against several laws limiting autonomy in universities.[47]

The Chilean Supreme Court also has case law related to fundamental rights. Among its responsibilities, the Court decides actions for the protection of fundamental rights. In this role, it has developed a series of rulings regarding the disciplinary powers of private associations, extending the horizontal effect of the right. In 2023 the Disciplinary Committee of a local organisation in Valparaiso expelled one of its members for 'having unjustifiably caused damage or harm to the assets of the organization and its members'. After following the sanctioning process established in the internal rules, the organisation's assembly expelled one of its members. The Supreme Court affirmed the power of a private association to apply disciplinary measures on its members following the disciplinary procedures by its internal control bodies. This authority derives both from the law that regulates that association and from the Constitution itself, which recognises the autonomy of intermediate groups and the freedom of association. However, it then adds 'that even in the case of a conflict between individuals, which must be resolved within the rules of that association, in the exercise of its autonomy, it is essential that the parties in dispute are on an equal ground so that the dispute can be resolved through proportionate and rational means'.[48] That is why it requires some guarantees of due process to exclude, for example, unreasonable decisions. In this case, the Supreme Court accepted the claim, as various procedural provisions had not been followed to apply the sanction. Many other rulings of the Supreme Court examine sanctions imposed by private associations on their members, such as sports clubs, firefighters, associations of public officials, professional associations, and student organisations, among others.

D. Abortion and Institutional Beliefs

In 2017, the Chilean Congress approved a Bill legalising abortion for three regulated causes: risk of life for the mother, foetal non-viability, and in case of rape of the mother. As is common in this type of debate, the constitutionality of the Bill was challenged before the Constitutional Court, which finally declared its overall constitutionality. The Court's ruling addresses the issue of conscientious objection. The Bill stated that 'conscientious objection is personal and may in no case be claimed by an institution' (Article 1.3 of the Bill). The Court upheld the constitutionality of conscientious objection by medical personnel

[47] *Group of Deputies v Bill on Provisional Administration of Higher Education Institutions* [2014] TC 2731-14.

[48] *NN v Comité de Vivienda Los Estandartes* [2023] CS 68610-23. See also *Corvacho v Asociación Gremial* [2020] CS 143-20; *Pereira v Cuerpo de Bomberos* [2021] CS 30428-21; *Sarzosa Constanzo v Corporación Educacional Newentun* [2022] CS 152329-22.

involved in abortion and extended it not only to physicians, but also to every health professional involved in the procedure. It then declared unconstitutional the prohibition contained in the last part of the provision noted above, in what is colloquially known in Chile as 'institutional conscientious objection'.

In its reasoning, the judgment draws parallels between individual conscientious objection to institutional conscientious objection. It states that both are protected 'by the dignity of persons who – individually or projected in association with others – refuse to perform certain types of actions for ethical, moral, religious, professional or other relevant reasons'.[49] As a second argument, the Court states that the autonomy of institutional ideologies is protected not only by freedom of association, but also by freedom of religion and freedom of education. Regarding the right of association, the decision states:

> conscientious objection can be legitimately raised by legal entities or private associations, in this case, in accordance with the constitutional autonomy that the Fundamental Charter itself recognizes for intermediate groups of society (…). The interposition of this legitimate objection is not exhausted in the individual order, since it also extends and spreads to associations intended to embody the same free thought, in accordance with the right that ensures to all persons the (right of association).

Further in the judgment, the argument relates to religious freedom and freedom of education:

> religious institutions, legal persons or entities with confessional ideals that project themselves into the field of health, under the protection of (religious freedom), can also assert it. As it is also possible for them to oppose the objection in question to educational establishments with a function and ideology in the sense indicated, in accordance with (freedom of education).[50]

The judgment holds that associations may also have beliefs that must be protected. These beliefs are more evident when it comes to educational establishments or religious institutions that exercise not only their right of association but also the freedom of teaching and religious freedom. The same holds true for any association that builds a space of autonomy which unites individuals around a shared position rooted in their freedom of thought. The ruling has generated multiple debates. The possibility that institutional belief can be invoked as a basis for exemption from legal obligations has been extensively discussed. The discussion not only exists in Chile, but also in the rest of Latin America. In recent years, while Argentina and Uruguay have recognised this kind of objection, the Colombia Constitutional Court has declared it unconstitutional.[51]

Years later, the Constitutional Court in Chile had to resolve another related dispute. A regulation issued by the Ministry of Health prohibited private

[49] *Group of Senators and Deputies v Abortion Bill* [2017] TC 3729 (3751)-17, c. 141.
[50] ibid c. 136.
[51] C Asiaín Pereira, 'Los principales desafíos para el ejercicio del derecho de objeción de conciencia en Latinoamérica' (2019) 35 *Anuario de Derecho Eclesiástico del Estado*.

institutions that received public funding from being 'institutional objectors'. The regulation stated that private health facilities that had signed agreements with the Ministry of Health for obstetrics and gynaecology services could not refuse abortions. The rule severely affected hospitals belonging to Catholic universities. The Constitutional Court declared this prohibition unconstitutional for violating the autonomy of the institutions. The ruling states that the constitutional autonomy of intermediate groups

> implies the necessary and indispensable freedom of these groups to set their objectives, to organize themselves in the way their members deem most convenient, to decide their own acts and also the form of administration, as well as the rules by which they are to be governed, without outside interference, whether public or private, unless they violate the legal system or their own statute.

It then adds, in an approach that resembles the American unconstitutional conditions doctrine,[52] that conscientious objection cannot result in punishment against the objecting entity, and that the receipt of public funding does not imply that they gave up their core beliefs.[53]

V. CONCLUSION

In this chapter, I have analysed the evolution of the right of association within Chilean constitutionalism. The constitutional evolution of the right of association can be seen in several important debates over the last three centuries. The first was when the right was entrenched in 1874, which mainly protected freedom of association without previous authorisation. Almost a century later, in 1971, a new constitutional amendment – this time to the 1925 Constitution – introduced important provisions for the protection of various associations, such as political parties, schools, universities, unions and local organisations. Then, the 1980 Constitution transformed the 'autonomy of intermediate groups' into a core constitutional issue. Finally, the last debate on freedom of association took place during the two constitution-making processes that began in 2019, where the limits to freedom of association and the autonomy of associations, among other issues, were discussed.

The current Constitution of 1980 regulates the three facets of the right of association: the right to form an association, the right not to be forced to belong to an association and the autonomy of the associations. Several decisions of the Constitutional Court have recognised the centrality of this right in all its facets. This includes the freedom to create or form any type of group, the protection of both formal associations and associations without legal personality, the

[52] K Sullivan, 'Unconstitutional Conditions' (1989) 102 *Harvard Law Review*. Also, P Hamburger, 'Unconstitutional Conditions: The Irrelevance of Consent' [2012] *Virginia Law Review*.

[53] *Group of Senators v Health Department* [2018] TC 5572-18, c. 10, 21–22.

prohibition of any obligation to join a trade union or a professional association, and a general clause that protects the 'adequate autonomy' of associations 'to fulfil its own specific purposes'.

Finally, we examined some debates concerning this right. Some are local debates, such as the one linking the autonomy of associations and the principle of subsidiarity. There have also been discussions about a series of constitutional provisions that, since the 1970s, have tried to separate civil society from politics. Other debates have focused on relevant case law from other jurisdictions, providing a comparative perspective on how the right has been interpreted in different legal systems. The focus has been on the scope of the autonomy of associations, even in controversial areas such as institutional beliefs and the regulation of abortion, which represent the most recent major judicial debates. This constitutional and jurisprudential trajectory shows that the right of association is strong in Chile, and constitutional provisions have been progressively strengthening this right over the last half-century.

3

Unfolding Pluralism: Freedom of Association in Slovenia's Constitutional Democracy

KATARINA VATOVEC*

I. INTRODUCTION

MANY CENTURIES AGO, Aristotle described human beings as 'political animals'.[1] By nature, people are not inclined toward solitude; rather, they are inherently drawn to form connections with others. Social interaction is indeed intrinsic to human existence. Through relationships, individuals realise their potential, fulfil emotional, intellectual, social, and material needs, and pursue their aspirations. However, not all such relationships fall within the scope of constitutionally protected freedom of association.

In Slovenia, the right of association – closely linked to the right of assembly – is enshrined in Article 42 of the Constitution.[2] Despite the inclusion of the rights of assembly and association within a single constitutional provision, both the wording of the article and prevailing constitutional interpretation indicate that these are two distinct and autonomous rights.[3] Nevertheless, the two rights are substantively interconnected. As noted in jurisprudence and scholarly commentary, the exercise of the right of assembly frequently facilitates the simultaneous

* The views expressed in this work are solely my own and do not represent those of the Constitutional Court. I wish to thank my colleague Tina Mežnar for her valuable comments and the discussions on the legal standing of NGOs before the Constitutional Court in the context of environmental and spatial planning. All remaining errors are my own.

[1] Aristotle, *The Politics*, trans. into English with introduction, marginal analysis, essays, notes and indices by B Jowett (Oxford, Clarendon Press, 1885) Vol 1, 1253a.

[2] The Constitution of the Republic of Slovenia (Official Gazette of the Republic of Slovenia Nos 33/91-I, 42/97, 66/00, 24/03, 69/04, 69/04, 68/06, 47/13, 75/16, and 92/21).

[3] In contrast, many democratic states choose to regulate the two rights separately, recognising their differing legal content and functions. For example, the Spanish Constitution addresses the rights to assembly and association in Arts 21 and 22, respectively, while the Croatian Constitution includes them in Arts 42 and 43.

or subsequent formation of associations.[4] In the Slovenian context, their constitutional recognition reflects the broader commitment to democratic principles and pluralism, situating both rights as essential components of participatory democracy.[5]

Focusing solely on the right of association, the Slovenian Constitution does not explicitly list the various forms of association it protects, except, for example, 'religious communities' (Articles 7(2) and 41(1)), 'commercial organisations' (Article 74), 'trade unions' (Article 76), and 'national communities' (Article 64). Also, the right to strike (Article 77), while not itself a form of association, presupposes collective structures like strike committees, which fall within the broader scope of associational life. These provisions are *lex specialis* in relation to Article 42 of the Constitution.[6] The Slovenian Constitutional Court has repeatedly held that the constitutionally guaranteed freedom of association 'is a fundamental human right that enables the free expression of opinions, the formation of citizens' political will, and self-organisation'.[7]

Beyond the provisions set forth in the Constitution, the right of association within the Slovenian legal framework encompasses a wide range of expressive forms and varying degrees of collective engagement. These include non-profit organisations, political parties and formally constituted for-profit business associations. The right enables individuals to unite around common interests, beliefs, values, and goals, thereby fostering pluralism and encouraging active participation in a democratic society.

This chapter therefore examines the constitutional right of association in Slovenia, situating it within a broader constitutional framework and emphasising the interpretive role of the Slovenian Constitutional Court. Relying on key decisions of the Constitutional Court, the chapter explores how jurisprudence has shaped the content, boundaries, and limitations of the freedom of association, particularly with respect to specific types of associations, often extending its interpretation beyond the Constitution's sparse or narrowly worded text. In doing so, the chapter highlights both the protective scope of Article 42 of the Constitution and the broader legal and political context in which associational life unfolds. It emphasises the importance of constitutional adjudication in shaping its development in Slovenia's democratic society and underscores the right's essential role in enabling civic engagement, collective action, and pluralistic governance.

[4] B Rainey, P McCormick and C Ovey, *Jacobs, White and Ovey, The European Convention on Human Rights* (Oxford, Oxford University Press, 2021) 527.

[5] K Vatovec, '42. člen (pravica do zbiranja in združevanja)' in M Avbelj (ed), *Komentar Ustave Republike Slovenije, Del 1: Človekove pravice in temeljne svoboščine* (Nova Gorica, Nova univerza, Evropska pravna fakulteta, 2019) 403, 405.

[6] ibid.

[7] USRS Decision Up-301/96 of 15.1.1998, ECLI:SI:USRS:1998:Up.301.96, para 11; USRS Order Ps-1/22 of 10.3.2022, ECLI:SI:USRS:2022:Ps.1.22, para 18.

Section II of this chapter contextually analyses the essential characteristics of the right of association through the case law of the Slovenian Constitutional Court. Section III focuses on the influence that freedom of association has had in relation to issues of pluralism and the multi-party system. Section IV draws attention to two significant issues: the absence of references to the freedom of association in constitutional adjudication, and the procedural barriers that associations face in accessing the Constitutional Court. It highlights two contexts where these dynamics are particularly evident: first, during the Covid-19 pandemic, when a wave of constitutional reviews and complaints submitted en masse to the Constitutional Court focused on other rights and largely overlooked the freedom of association; and second, in cases involving non-governmental organisations acting in the public interest – particularly in environmental matters – where legal standing requirements often restricted their ability to challenge regulations before the Constitutional Court. This occurred despite the crucial societal role such associations play and the international recognition of their importance in promoting environmental protection.[8] In conclusion, section V offers some general findings that are also significant from a comparative law perspective.

II. THE RIGHT OF ASSOCIATION: DIVERSITY OF FORMS AND FEATURES

In Slovenia, the constitutional provision that determined the right of association – together with the right of assembly – reads:

> Article 42
>
> (Right of Assembly and Association)
>
> The right of peaceful assembly and public meeting shall be guaranteed.
>
> Everyone has the right to freedom of association with others.
>
> Legal restrictions of these rights shall be permissible where so required for national security or public safety and for protection against the spread of infectious diseases.
>
> Professional members of the defence forces and the police may not be members of political parties.

The Constitution does not define the term 'association' as protected under constitutional law. What distinguishes association from assembly are 'the intensity of connection, the degree of (internal) organisation, and the temporal dimension'.[9] Unlike assembly, association implies a more organised and permanent community of individuals who are more closely connected in the pursuit of

[8] ECtHR Judgment *Verein KlimaSeniorinnen Schweiz and Others v Switzerland [GC]* Application No 53600/20 of 9.4.2024, ECLI:CE:ECHR:2024:0409JUD005360020.

[9] Vatovec (n 5) 409.

common interests.[10] Members of an association voluntarily agree on its purpose and internal rules.[11] The purposive element of the right of association reveals that the coming together of individuals is 'permissible for any common interests or goals (political, religious, economic, social, cultural, scientific, artistic, sporting, social, etc.)'.[12] Indeed, it takes place across various areas of human life, including religious, political, labour-related, cultural, and civil spheres.

The Constitutional Court has elaborated more substantively on the content of this right. As it explained, the freedom of association 'guarantees everyone the ability to connect with like-minded individuals in an association that represents this connected group of people for the purpose of expressing and pursuing common interests'.[13] The Court has also addressed whether mandatory membership in a specific form of association prescribed by law constitutes an interference with the freedom of association. It adopted the position that chambers or other forms of association established by law for the exercise of public authority and primarily for the performance of certain tasks in the public interest do not fall within the scope of associations protected by Article 42(2) of the Constitution.[14] Therefore, prescribing mandatory membership in such forms of association does not constitute an interference with this constitutional right. However, the Court distinguishes these from associations of a private-law nature, which may be based only on the voluntary and free activities of their members and serve to realise their private interests. Only the latter are protected by Article 42(2) of the Slovenian Constitution.[15]

[10] L Šturm, '42. člen (pravica do zbiranja in združevanja)' in L Šturm (ed), *Komentar Ustave Republike Slovenije* (Fakulteta za podiplomske državne in evropske študije, Ljubljana, 2002) 461. The Constitutional Court, for example, held that gathering or socialising in hospitality establishments, due to the specific characteristics of association, cannot, by its very nature, be considered association within the meaning of Art 42(2) of the Constitution (USRS Decision U-I-218/07 of 26.3.2009, ECLI:SI:USRS:2009:U.I.218.07, para 19). See also USRS Decision U-I-155/07 of 9.4.2009, ECLI:SI:USRS:2009:U.I.155.07, para 11.

[11] USRS Decision U-I-290/96 of 11.6.1998, ECLI:SI:USRS:1998:U.I.290.96, para 14.

[12] USRS Decision U-I-155/07 (n 10) para 11.

[13] See, eg, USRS Decision U-I-290/96 (n 11) para 14.

[14] eg, the Constitutional Court has addressed this issue in several cases: regarding the Medical Chamber of Slovenia (USRS Order U-I-48/92 of 11.2.1993, ECLI:SI:USRS:1993:U.I.48.92); the Chamber of Commerce and Industry of Slovenia (USRS Decision U-I-290/96 (n 11) para 16); the Social Chamber (USRS Decision U-I-137/93 of 2.6.1994, ECLI:SI:USRS:1994:U.I.137.93); the Chamber for Private Security (USRS Decision U-I-305/94 of 3.4.1997, ECLI:SI:USRS:1997:U.I.305.94, para 6); the Chamber of Agriculture and Forestry of Slovenia (USRS Decision U-I-283/99 of 20.3.2003, ECLI:SI:USRS:2003:U.I.283.99, para 6); and regarding local public commercial institutions for tourism (USRS Decision U-I-93/00 of 24.10.2002, ECLI:SI:USRS:2002:U.I.93.00, para 11), and hunting organisations (USRS Decision U-I-98/04 of 9.11.2006, ECLI:SI:USRS:2006:U.I.98.04, para 53). Similarly, this view is supported by the case law of the European Court of Human Rights (see, eg, C Grabenwarter, *European Convention on Human Rights: Commentary* (Oxford, Hart Publishing, 2014) 301). The Constitutional Court assesses the obligation of mandatory membership in chambers primarily from the perspective of the so-called general freedom of action under Art 35 of the Slovenian Constitution (see USRS Decision U-I-155/07 (n 10) para 12).

[15] USRS Decision U-I-155/07 (n 10) para 13.

Article 42(2) of the Constitution refrains from identifying any specific types of associations, whether exhaustively or illustratively. The Constitutional Court explains that it is the obligation of the state to provide 'one or more types of associations that will enable individuals to effectively pursue their interests',[16] while leaving the choice of forms to the discretion of the legislature.[17] The freedom of association therefore 'encompasses a very broad spectrum of various types of associations, intended to enable individuals to pursue a wide range of interests'.[18]

Just as a complex, pluralistic society gives rise to a multitude of purposes for association, so too does it foster a diversity of organisational forms. In Slovenia, societies ('*društvo*') are the most general form of association.[19] A society is defined as an independent and non-profit association established for the purpose of pursuing common interests of its members.[20] Its activities are public, and its purpose and operations are not aimed at generating profit, as any surplus of income over expenses is permanently dedicated to achieving the society's purpose and objectives.[21] The Slovenian legal system also recognises institutes ('*zavodi*') as one of the organised forms of association.[22] They are established to carry out socially beneficial activities (such as education, science, culture, sports, and healthcare), provided that the purpose of these activities is not to generate profit.[23] Foundations ('*ustanove*'), on the other hand, are private-law legal entities that have assets tied to a specific purpose, and whose purpose is generally beneficial to the public or charitable in nature, and is typically permanent.[24] Constitutional review in the context of the right of association has also addressed various chambers ('*zbornice*').[25] A cooperative ('*zadruga*') is

[16] ibid para 21.

[17] ibid.

[18] USRS Decision Up-308/00 of 19.12.2000, ECLI:SI:USRS:2000:Up.308.00, para 10.

[19] See USRS Decision U-I-92/07 of 15.4.2010, ECLI:SI:USRS:2010:U.I.92.07, para 117. According to official data in the central register of the competent ministry, as of July 2025, there are over 23,000 registered (but not necessarily active) societies in Slovenia (mrrsp.gov.si/rdruobjave/dr/index.faces).

[20] Art 1 of the Societies Act [Zakon o društvih] (Official Gazette of the Republic of Slovenia No 64/11 – official consolidated text).

[21] ibid.

[22] USRS Decision Up-308/00 (n 18) para 10.

[23] Art 1 of the Institutes Act [Zakon o zavodih] (Official Gazette of the Republic of Slovenia Nos 12/91 et seq). Institutes do not have members but have a founder. They may engage in profit-making activities if these support their non-profit purposes. In addition to private institutes, there are also public institutes, which are not non-governmental organisations, as they are primarily established by the state or municipalities.

[24] Arts 1 and 2 of the Foundations Act [Zakon o ustanovah] (Official Gazette of the Republic of Slovenia Nos 70/05 – official consolidated text et seq).

[25] In particular, the chambers examined by the Constitutional Court were typically a specific form of professional or economic association with obligatory membership, established by law and regulated as public-law entities serving the public interest. These are distinct from voluntary associations protected under Art 42 of the Constitution. See (n 14). However, it is also possible to establish a chamber as a private-law legal entity, which falls within the scope of the constitutional protection of the freedom of association. An example of this is the Slovenian Advertising Chamber, a professional organisation in the field of marketing communications. It is a voluntary, independent, professional,

yet another type of association with an open-ended number of members, based on voluntary membership, established to promote the economic interests and develop the economic or social activities of its members.[26] These various types of organised associations each possess their own distinct legal and functional characteristics. They differ in the purposes they serve, ranging from pursuing the private interests of their members, providing professional or economic services, and engaging in non-profit or charitable activities, to fulfilling public-interest objectives. They also vary in terms of legal form, legal foundation, required number of founders, registration procedures, governance structures, and the costs associated with their establishment.

The freedom of association has an individual dimension.[27] This aspect refers to the individual's right to freely and voluntarily establish, join, or withdraw from an association without coercion or interference. It protects personal autonomy in the pursuit of personal interests, shared goals, or common causes through membership. Importantly, it also encompasses the right not to associate.[28] However, the freedom of association also has a collective dimension.[29] This refers to the rights of the association itself, once established as a legal entity. It includes the right to self-organisation, internal governance, representation of its members, participation in public affairs, and the exercise of collective rights. It ensures the association's ability to function democratically, make collective decisions, and advocate on behalf of its members. As the Constitutional Court has emphasised, 'without this, the freedom of association would often be meaningless'.[30]

These two dimensions – individual and collective – together ensure that both individuals and associations can exercise their constitutionally guaranteed freedom of association in a meaningful and effective manner. The Constitutional Court has clarified that a formally organised association exists

> when it is carried out in a legally predetermined organisational form. [...] The most important legal consequence of formal association is that the law recognises such organised forms of association as holders of rights and obligations [...]. However, this also means that individuals who wish to associate within one of these legally

and non-profit association of legal and natural persons active in advertising and communication. Similarly, as the Constitutional Court has already held, a hunting association ('*lovska družina*') is based on the voluntary decision of its members and is established through registration in the register of associations. It therefore follows that a hunting association is not constituted by a public law act. While such an association may operate in the public interest, exercise public authorisations, or perform public service functions, it is not established by statute, but rather through the autonomous will of its members. Accordingly, its formation must be assessed under Art 42 of the Constitution (USRS Decision U-I-98/04 (n 14) para 53).

[26] eg USRS Decision U-I-155/07 (n 10). Art 1 of the Cooperatives Act [Zakon o zadrugah] (Official Gazette of the Republic of Slovenia Nos 97/09 – official consolidated text et seq).

[27] Vatovec (n 5) 410.

[28] See Grabenwarter (n 14) 299.

[29] ibid.

[30] USRS Decision U-I-155/07 (n 10) para 19.

defined organisational forms must comply with the rules set by law for their establishment and operation.[31]

In its review of the constitutionality of the Religious Freedom Act, the Constitutional Court further held that 'from the perspective of the right to freely establish religious communities, it is not necessary for a religious community to be officially recognised or registered'.[32] It follows, therefore, that associations do not need to be formally recognised or registered to enjoy constitutional protection. Even entirely private or informal associations fall within the scope of the freedom of association guaranteed by the Constitution.[33]

In Slovenia, despite the fundamental importance of the right of association for the development of an individual's personality and for democratic society as a whole, this right is not absolute. Statutory limitations are permissible, but only for exhaustively enumerated reasons: in the interest of national security or public safety, and for the prevention of the spread of infectious diseases;[34] as well as under the general limitation clause, namely, for the protection of the rights of others.[35] When determining such limitations, the legislature – in setting the statutory framework – and the executive and judicial branches – in applying the law – must take into account the particular significance of this right in a free and democratic society. For example, in 1998, the Constitutional Court reviewed the constitutionality of the then-applicable Societies Act, which required that a child's membership in an association be conditional upon the submission of a signed declaration of enrolment by the child's legal representative. The case concerned a scouts association, and the Court held that the prescribed method of enrolment – where only the legal representative signed the enrolment declaration on behalf of the child – failed to sufficiently respect the child's personal autonomy and right to express the will to join.[36] The legal representative's role, the Constitutional Court emphasised, should be to give consent to a decision that the child had already expressed.[37] The Court thus held that the challenged provision constituted a disproportionate interference with the child's constitutionally guaranteed freedom of association. Similarly, the statutory requirement that an association could only be established by at least ten adult citizens of Slovenia was found to be incompatible with the Constitution. In the Court's view, such a requirement interfered with a right of individuals to freely associate; an interference that would only be constitutionally permissible if justified by one of the constitutionally legitimate reasons mentioned above. However, the Court

[31] ibid para 17.
[32] USRS Decision U-I-92/07 (n 19) para 90.
[33] ibid; USRS Decision U-I-155/07 (n 10) para 16.
[34] Art 42(3) of the Slovenian Constitution.
[35] Art 15(3) of the Slovenian Constitution.
[36] USRS Decision U-I-391/96 of 11.6.1998, ECLI:SI:USRS:1998:U.I.391.96.
[37] ibid para 13.

found no constitutionally acceptable justification for such a restriction.[38] As it explained, by its very nature, one cannot associate with oneself, but two or three persons certainly can associate.[39]

Although the Slovenian Constitution does not explicitly state that the freedom of association must be exercised in a peaceful manner, this requirement is implicit in the very nature and scope of constitutional protection.[40] The peaceful exercise of rights is a *conditio sine qua non* – a fundamental prerequisite – for any democratic right to merit constitutional safeguarding. Accordingly, associations that promote or engage in violent, unlawful, or anti-democratic activities fall outside the protective scope of constitutional guarantees.[41]

The right of association possesses certain inherent characteristics. First, there is the *human dimension of the right*, which reveals both its individual and collective facets. Although the right is held by the individual, its very nature dictates that it can only be meaningfully exercised collectively.[42] It is precisely this collective realisation that distinguishes the right of association from many other constitutional rights. Unlike rights that may be exercised individually or jointly, the freedom of association protects the formation of structured, enduring, and autonomous entities – such as political parties and non-governmental organisations – which are capable of internal governance, long-term operation, and independent pursuit of common goals. This right presupposes the existence of a collective legal entity that can act and be recognised independently of its individual members.

Under the Slovenian Constitution, the right of association is guaranteed to everyone, regardless of citizenship, and may be invoked both by individuals who participate in associations and by those who establish them. Private-law associations, where individuals voluntarily unite to pursue private interests and freely carry out activities (eg, a hunting association), are likewise protected under Article 42(2) of the Constitution.[43]

Freedom of association guarantees the ability to come together and form connections within a community, ie, its positive aspect.[44] The Constitutional Court has emphasised (notably in the context of religious associations) that this includes the individual's entitlement to associate with others, jointly establish communities, become a member, and participate in their activities.[45] Equally important is the right not to associate, ie, the negative aspect of this freedom.

[38] ibid para 18.

[39] ibid.

[40] Vatovec (n 5) 409.

[41] A relevant analogy can be drawn with an example of a political party that acts unconstitutionally. (See section III of this chapter.)

[42] Vatovec (n 5) 405.

[43] USRS Decision U-I-98/04 (n 14) para 53. Similarly, the case law of the European Court of Human Rights reflects this understanding (see, eg, Grabenwarter (n 14) 302).

[44] Vatovec (n 5) 407.

[45] USRS Decision U-I-92/07 (n 19) para 89.

This includes the right to refuse membership, abstain from participation, or withdraw from an association.[46] For example, '[e]very Roma association freely decides whether it will join the Roma Community of Slovenia (and thereby gain the possibility to participate in nominating members to its Council).'[47] Although not explicitly enshrined in the constitutional text, the negative aspect 'derives from the very essence of this right and is a necessary component thereof',[48] forming an inseparable counterpart to the positive one. At the core of both aspects lies the principle of voluntariness. Everyone is free to decide whether to exercise their right to associate.

Second, the right of association possesses *an instrumental dimension*, as its value extends beyond its intrinsic significance. This right fulfils an important functional role within society, serving as a means for the realisation of other human rights and fundamental freedoms.[49] For example, it facilitates the effective expression of individual opinions, as affirmed by the US Supreme Court in *NAACP v Alabama ex rel. Patterson*.[50] It also enables individuals, acting collectively, to pursue various legitimate interests – such as those of a sporting, scientific, or cultural nature – and to exercise other constitutionally protected rights and freedoms (eg, freedom of conscience or freedom of expression).[51]

Importantly, the significance of this right is not confined to its constitutional or statutory formulation. What is essential is the effective exercise of this right in practice, which requires an environment characterised by tolerance, open-mindedness, and a pluralism of opinions and beliefs, including the freedom to associate in diverse forms within a democratic society.[52]

Moreover, the right of association holds particular importance for individuals belonging to national, ethnic, and other minority groups.[53] As noted by the European Court of Human Rights, 'forming an association in order to express and promote its identity may be instrumental in helping a minority to preserve and uphold its rights'.[54] In this regard, the Slovenian Constitutional Court has interpreted the right of association for the Italian and Hungarian national communities and their members 'more broadly than for other individuals, namely, as a right that also ensures the preservation of national identity'.[55] In the case at issue, the Constitutional Court held that the contested provision of the Societies Act, which regulated the use of languages in the names of

[46] ibid; USRS Decision U-I-155/07 (n 10) para 15; Vatovec (n 5) 407.

[47] USRS Decision U-I-15/10 of 16.6.2010, ECLI:SI:USRS:2010:U.I.15.10, para 17.

[48] eg, Up-308/00 (n 18) para 10; USRS Decision U-I-155/07 (n 10) para 14.

[49] Vatovec (n 5) 406.

[50] *NAACP v Alabama ex rel. Patterson* of 30.6.1958, 357 U.S. 1958, 459.

[51] USRS Decision U-I-155/07 (n 10) para 14.

[52] Vatovec (n 5) 406.

[53] WA Schabas, *The European Convention on Human Rights: A Commentary* (Oxford, Oxford University Press, 2015) 491; Grabenwarter (n 14) 311.

[54] ECtHR *Gorzelik and Others v Poland* Application No 44158/98, ECLI:CE:ECHR:2004:0217JUD004415898, para 93.

[55] USRS Decision U-I-380/06 of 11.9.2008, ECLI:SI:USRS:2008:U.I.380.06, para 10.

associations, was inconsistent with the Constitution.[56] This was because Italian and Hungarian, as the languages of autochthonous national communities in the regions where they reside, may not be treated by the legislator as foreign languages.[57] In such contexts, it is therefore impermissible to use Italian and Hungarian merely as translations alongside Slovene; rather, the legislator is required to regulate the manner of their direct use, that is, to ensure the use of the Italian and Hungarian languages themselves.

Third, the right of association also encompasses *a political dimension*, which derives from the principle of democracy, as enshrined in Article 1 of the Slovenian Constitution. The understanding that this right is rooted in democratic foundations is both a well-established doctrinal position[58] and a consistent element in the constitutional jurisprudence.[59] While public discourse and the contestation of opinions typically take place through various democratic processes, the right of association plays a crucial role in enabling individuals to organise collectively in order to express shared beliefs, participate in political life, and pursue common interests. As such, it possesses a distinctly political character and functions as an instrument of both participatory and representative democracy.[60] Through free association, individuals are empowered to form political parties, interest groups, and other collective bodies that contribute to democratic pluralism. As the Constitutional Court has emphasised – and as will be thoroughly pointed out later – the 'foundation of a multi-party political system is essential, without which a free democratic society cannot exist'.[61]

III. THE PROMINENCE OF FREEDOM OF ASSOCIATION: ENABLING COLLECTIVE ACTION AND POLITICAL PARTICIPATION

During the initial phase of constitutional jurisprudence, matters relating to political parties featured prominently. Slovenia declared independence from the former Socialist Federal Republic of Yugoslavia (SFRY) in 1991, becoming an independent and sovereign state. The SFRY was not governed by the rule of law; rather, it was marked by serious violations of human rights, national rights, and the rights of its constituent republics and autonomous provinces. This reality is acknowledged in the preamble to the Basic Constitutional Charter on the Sovereignty and Independence of the Republic of Slovenia, which was

[56] ibid para 13.

[57] ibid.

[58] Šturm (n 10) 460–461; Vatovec (n 5) 405.

[59] eg, USRS Decision Up-301/96 (n 7) para 11; USRS Decision U-I-155/07 (n 10) para 14.

[60] Vatovec (n 5) 405.

[61] USRS Decision Up-301/96 (n 7) para 11; USRS Decision Up-239/96 of 5.3.1998, ECLI:SI:USRS:1998:Up.239.96, para 4.

adopted by the then Assembly of the Republic of Slovenia on 25 June 1991.[62] In legal doctrine, the Basic Constitutional Charter has been characterised as constituting 'the foundational act of statehood and constitutionalism to which the Constitution explicitly refers in its preamble'.[63] From a constitutional perspective, it is important to emphasise that the Basic Constitutional Charter established a clear break between the constitutional order of the sovereign Slovenian state and that of the SFRY, of which Slovenia had previously been a federal unit. The Slovenian Constitutional Court has acknowledged this legal discontinuity, particularly in the transition from the former one-party system to the multi-party system characteristic of a constitutional democracy.

The Slovenian Constitution does not contain special provisions on political parties.[64] However, the freedom of association also encompasses the right to establish political parties and to ensure their functioning. The Constitutional Court has linked this freedom to 'the foundation of a multi-party political system, without which no free democratic society can exist'.[65] In this initial phase of the Slovenian Constitutional Court's activity, roughly between the years 1991 and 2000, the freedom of association is mostly understood – given the historical context – as the freedom to associate in political parties and the importance of political parties within a constitutional democracy due to their essential role in ensuring the pluralism of political opinions and the functioning of democracy.

To fully grasp the significance attributed to the existence and operation of political parties and the multi-party system – particularly in light of the historical experience of Slovenian society under the former communist regime – it is important to consider the Constitutional Court's own observation:

> The right to freedom of association constitutes one of the fundamental constitutional values that must be afforded particular respect and whose genuine implementation must be consistently ensured. This is especially significant given that, after assuming power in 1945, the communist regime only nominally guaranteed freedom of association – including the establishment of political parties and their freedom to operate – both constitutionally and through statutory regulation. In practice, however, the communist authorities entirely suppressed the activities of opposition

[62] Basic Constitutional Charter on the Sovereignty and Independence of the Republic of Slovenia (Official Gazette of the Republic of Slovenia Nos 1/91-I and 19/91 – corr.).

[63] P Jambrek, 'Preambula' in M Avbelj (ed), *Komentar Ustave Republike Slovenije, Del 1: Človekove pravice in temeljne svoboščine* (Nova Gorica, Nova univerza, Evropska pravna fakulteta, 2019) 11, 15.

[64] The Constitution refers to political parties only in a few specific contexts: in the prohibition against professional members of the defence forces and the police being members of political parties (Art 42(4)); in provisions on the incompatibility of political party membership with judicial office (Art 133), the office of state prosecutor (Art 136), and the office of Constitutional Court judge (Art 166); and in defining the competences of the Constitutional Court, which include deciding, inter alia, on the unconstitutionality of the acts and activities of political parties (Art 160(1)). USRS Order Ps-1/22 (n 7) para 19.

[65] See USRS Decision Up-301/96 (n 7) para 11; USRS Order Ps-1/22 (n 7) para 18.

political parties through repressive measures, thereby excluding them from the political process.[66]

The constitutional review also stemmed from the fact that the Political Parties Act, adopted in 1994, provided the legal basis for the exercise of the right to freedom of association. It defined a political party as 'an association of citizens who pursue their political objectives, as set out in the party's program, through the democratic formation of the political will of the citizens and by nominating candidates in [various] elections'.[67]

The Political Parties Act stipulates that a political party may be founded by at least 200 adult citizens of the Republic of Slovenia who sign a declaration of establishment.[68] In 1994, a petitioner challenged this provision, arguing that the Act was inconsistent with the right to freely associate, on the grounds that it denied citizens fewer than 200 in number the right to form a political party.[69] The Constitutional Court dismissed the petition, reasoning that the requirement of a minimum number of members to establish a political party does not constitute a restriction of the right of association. On the one hand, every citizen is still permitted to engage in non-organised types of association; on the other hand, when supported by a sufficient number of fellow citizens, one can exercise this right through a properly organised form.[70]

Political parties occupy a distinct position within the Constitutional Court's case law, setting them apart from other types of associations. First, because their functioning is closely linked to the exercise of the principle of popular sovereignty, political parties must be guaranteed freedom in their establishment, their programmes, activities, and in their influence on the formation of citizens' political will. The state must ensure the effective implementation of these guarantees and otherwise refrain from interfering or exerting influence over political parties.[71] Second, any prohibition of their activities can only be a measure of last resort (*ultima ratio*).[72] Third, only the Constitutional Court has the authority to determine whether a political party's acts or activities are unconstitutional.[73] However, a finding of unconstitutionality does not automatically result in the party's removal from the register. The Court must decide separately on this issue, requiring a two-thirds majority vote of all judges, provided it determines that the unconstitutional acts or activities are so severe that merely abrogating

[66] USRS Decision Up-301/96 (n 7) para 7.

[67] Art 1 of the Political Parties Act (Official Gazette of the Republic of Slovenia No 62/94). The definition has been largely retained in the Political Parties Act currently in force (Official Gazette of the Republic of Slovenia Nos 100/05 – official consolidated text et seq).

[68] Art 4(1) of the Political Parties Act.

[69] USRS Order U-I-312/94 of 16.2.1996, ECLI:SI:USRS:1996:U.I.312.94.

[70] ibid para 3.

[71] USRS Decision Up-301/96 (n 7) para 17. USRS Order Ps-1/22 (n 7) para 20.

[72] USRS Order Ps-1/22 (n 7) para 20.

[73] Art 160(1) of the Constitution. See also USRS Decision Up-301/96 (n 7) para 18; USRS Decision Up-239/96 (n 61) para 5.

the unconstitutional acts or prohibiting the unconstitutional activities would be insufficient, and that the elimination of the party from political life is indeed necessary.[74]

In one of its early decisions, the Constitutional Court established the foundational importance of political parties in a constitutional democracy. The case concerned a constitutional complaint in which the complainant alleged a violation of the right to freedom of association, following the rejection of its application for registration as a political party by the competent ministry (ie, the registration authority).[75] The authority justified its decision on the grounds that the complainant's political programme was contrary to the Constitution. Specifically, the complainant advocated for addressing injustices committed during the post-World War II period against individuals from the region of Slovenian Istria by giving them priority in housing allocation. This provision was allegedly contrary to the Constitution, as it placed these individuals in an unequal (and thus privileged) position compared to those who had emigrated from other parts of Slovenia for political or economic reasons.[76] The Constitutional Court found that the registration authority considered a single sentence in the complainant's programme to be unconstitutional.[77] It held that prohibiting the party based solely on the unconstitutionality of that one sentence was, from the outset, unacceptable.[78] Even if such a programmatic provision were found to be unconstitutional, the Constitutional Court could have simply abrogated it without simultaneously ordering the removal of the party from the register.[79]

The Constitutional Court thus held that it was not constitutionally permissible for the registration authority to assess substantive constitutional conditions for the establishment of a political party, as this could result in the party's existence and activities being unacceptably dependent on prior authorisation by an administrative body. The Court stated:

> A registered party cannot be impeded in its political activities until the Constitutional Court, which is the only authority empowered to prohibit a party's activities, reaches a decision on such. As a result, administrative interference with the existence of a political party is excluded, regardless of how hostile its actions may be towards a free democratic constitutional order. This allows each party's activities to continue until their unconstitutionality is established, thereby guaranteeing the highest possible degree of political freedom. A party still operates within constitutionally admissible tolerance, even if it propagates aims that are hostile (contrary) to the Constitution, provided it does so in a constitutionally admissible manner.[80]

[74] USRS Decision Up-301/96 (n 7) paras 18–19; USRS Order Ps-1/22 (n 7) para 22.
[75] USRS Decision Up-301/96 (n 7).
[76] ibid para 28.
[77] ibid para 29.
[78] ibid.
[79] ibid.
[80] ibid para 22.

The role of the registration authority is limited to verifying whether a political party has met the formal requirements prescribed by law; only the Constitutional Court may decide on the substantive conditions, ie, whether the acts and activities of a political party conform to the Constitution.[81] Consequently, the registration authority must reconsider the complainant's application for registration, reviewing only the fulfilment of formal statutory requirements. If these are met, the party must be registered.[82]

To illustrate the preservation of the Constitutional Court's long-standing positions on the importance of political association in a pluralistic society and constitutional democracy, the 2022 order Ps-1/22 is also noteworthy. The case concerned the alleged unconstitutionality of the acts and activities of the political parties that currently form part of the parliamentary coalition: The Left and The Social Democrats.[83] The Constitutional Court was tasked with determining whether the petitioner's allegations about the unconstitutionality of certain provisions of The Left's programme and the activities of both parties were well-founded, and whether such alleged unconstitutionalities would require the abrogation of acts, prohibition of concrete activities, or even removal of these parties from the register of political parties.[84]

Basing its decision on its constitutional powers, the Constitutional Court held that '[i] is not sufficient for a political party to reject, contradict, or not recognise the constitutional order'.[85] According to the Court's position, 'active operation with the intention of destroying (eliminating) the existing constitutional order is required'.[86] Mere criticism, even if well-founded, does not suffice; 'a serious threat to the underlying principles of a free democratic society has to be proven'.[87] Given the special significance of political parties for the existence of a free democratic state, exclusion from political life is not justified as long as parties use lawful means to oppose specific regulations or even constitutional institutions. As the Constitutional Court emphasised, '[s]uch exclusion is only permitted if these parties intend to undermine the fundamental values of a free democratic constitutional state'.[88]

Further, the Constitutional Court set out four criteria for assessing whether the activities and acts of a political party are unconstitutional: (1) threat to fundamental constitutional values, namely respect for human dignity and the core principles of a free democratic order (threats include any incitement to national, racial, religious, or other discrimination; the inflaming of national, racial, religious, or other hatred and intolerance; and any incitement to violence

[81] ibid para 24.
[82] ibid para 26.
[83] USRS Order Ps-1/22 (n 7).
[84] ibid para 21.
[85] ibid para 23.
[86] ibid.
[87] ibid. See also USRS Decision Up-301/96 (n 7) para 15.
[88] USRS Decision Up-301/96 (n 7) para 16. USRS Order Ps-1/22 (n 7) para 23.

and war); (2) severity of the threat (ie, assessed by whether the political party acts systematically and in a planned manner to achieve objectives that are contrary to the constitutional values; there must also be a realistic possibility that such objectives could be realised); (3) means of operation (referring to whether the political party acts in a constitutionally inadmissible manner or uses constitutionally inadmissible means, eg, violence, threats, or other forms of intimidation); (4) source of unconstitutional conduct (whether the unconstitutional nature of the party's activity stems from its own actions, or from those of its members or even sympathisers, provided such actions reflect the party's identifiable objectives or have been explicitly endorsed by the party).[89] The Court subsequently limited its own constitutional intervention regarding the admissibility of the activities of a political party, arguing that such intervention must not be used as a tool to suppress political diversity. It held:

> Namely, the prohibition of the activities of a political party must not be a means to prohibit the expression of a certain worldview, political positions and beliefs, or even political ideologies. The prohibition of the activities of a party merely due to its objection to the legal order in force would entail an inadmissible interference with the foundations of a pluralistic political system and the sanctioning of the party and its members due to conduct that exclusively pertains to the exercise of the right to freedom of expression within the framework of political discourse. Finally, such an understanding of the alleged unconstitutionality of the activities of a party would entail that the Constitution would never be allowed to change because any endeavour in favour of amending the Constitution would be inadmissible. In such context, one must also be aware of the danger of the abuse of law with the intention of eliminating opposition candidates from the election competition and from political life in general.[90]

The petitioner alleged that, through their actions, and in the case of The Left, also through its programme, The Social Democrats and The Left have not distanced themselves from the totalitarian communist regime following the Second World War. This claim was based on statements made by some party members, the use of symbols from the former totalitarian regime at events, expressions of respect for certain figures from that regime, and the parties' advocacy for abolishing private ownership of the means of production in favour of social ownership and workers' management of companies.[91] The Constitutional Court held that, even assuming that the petitioner's allegations were true, it could not be concluded that the political parties in question failed to distance themselves from the ideology of the former totalitarian regime in a manner that would pose a threat to constitutional values. Furthermore, the petitioner did not point to any concrete actions or programme provisions by either party that would threaten the fundamental constitutional values of a free democratic

[89] USRS Order Ps-1/22 (n 7) para 36.
[90] ibid para 32.
[91] ibid paras 33–35.

order. The alleged actions also clearly did not constitute inadmissible activities involving the use of force or threats. In light of these findings, the Constitutional Court deemed the petitioner's allegations – that these actions amount to unconstitutional activities by both political parties, and that the challenged provisions of the Left's programme were unconstitutional – to be manifestly unfounded.[92]

The order was adopted with six judges in favour and three opposed. In the dissenting opinions, it was emphasised that the case was not manifestly unfounded. and it was argued that, rather than dismissing it outright, the Court should have undertaken a substantive review to assess its merits. However, the significance of the case rests in the criteria established by the Constitutional Court for assessing the constitutionality of political parties' acts and activities.

From the Constitutional Court's case law, it is clear that the essence of the freedom of association within political parties resides in its political dimension, as a foundational element of a multi-party system, 'without which a free democratic society cannot exist'.[93] The pivotal role of political parties in a constitutional democracy is deeply influenced by Slovenia's own historical experience. In its early years as the guardian of constitutional order in an independent and sovereign state, the Court emphasised the necessity of departing from a system that suppressed human rights, and embracing one that places those rights, alongside political participation, on a pedestal, as the cornerstone of democratic governance and human dignity. Within this context, the Court's jurisprudence affirms the special status of political parties, distinct from other types of association – a distinction underscored by the exclusive authority of the Constitutional Court to review the constitutionality of their acts and activities. While the Court primarily framed freedom of association in terms of its significance for constitutional democracy and democratic society, it remains essential to recognise that this freedom is, at its core, a human right – protecting both the individual's right to associate based on shared political beliefs and the collective right to organise politically in pursuit of common goals.

IV. ASSOCIATIONS AND CONSTITUTIONAL REVIEW: BETWEEN RECOGNITION AND RESTRICTION

Compared to many other constitutional rights and freedoms, the freedom of association is relatively rarely directly and argumentatively invoked by petitioners or complainants before the Constitutional Court. This was particularly evident in cases arising in the context of the Covid-19 pandemic. During that period, Slovenia – like many other countries worldwide – faced significant

[92] ibid para 40.
[93] USRS Decision Up-301/96 (n 7) para 11; USRS Decision Up-239/96 (n 61) para 4.

challenges and responded by introducing a wide range of measures aimed at containing the virus, managing the pandemic and preventing new outbreaks.[94] These measures (such as restrictions on public protests and gatherings, limitations on movement between municipalities, and social distancing requirements) affected numerous aspects of public life, healthcare, and governance, and were frequently revised in response to the evolving epidemiological situation.

At the time, the Constitutional Court was confronted with a considerable number of cases in which petitioners or complainants argued that their human rights had been excessively restricted. Many also claimed that the government was imposing these limitations through executive ordinances rather than through legislation, despite the constitutional requirement that such restrictions be enacted only by the legislature.[95] Among the human rights alleged to have been infringed were the right to freedom of movement,[96] the right of children with special needs to education and training,[97] and the right of peaceful assembly and public meetings.[98] Notably, despite extensive case law of the Constitutional Court addressing alleged breaches of various constitutional rights during the Covid-19 period, petitioners did not explicitly raise claims concerning the right of association. This absence is noteworthy, as it could be argued that this right was also subject to limitations due to pandemic-related measures, which effectively prevented individuals from exercising it collectively. It appears that rights whose restrictions were felt most directly and immediately – such as access to education through remote schooling, limitations on freedom of movement, or prohibitions and restrictions on public protests – were those most prominently challenged.

The second area relating to associations that introduces an interesting dynamic before the Constitutional Court concerns the *locus standi* of associations. Specifically, it involves the procedural requirement of demonstrating a legal interest in order to initiate constitutional review.[99] While this issue may not seem to directly affect the freedom of association at first glance, it carries a considerable impact on associations – particularly non-governmental organisations (NGOs) – that act to protect public or collective interests.

[94] Unlike some other countries, Slovenia did not declare a state of emergency during this period. Under the Constitution (Art 16), a state of emergency allows, in exceptional circumstances and under specific conditions, the temporary suspension or restriction of most constitutionally guaranteed human rights and fundamental freedoms.

[95] See, eg, USRS Decision U-I-79/20 of 13.5.2021, ECLI:SI:USRS:2021:U.I.79.20; USRS Decision U-I-210/21 of 29.11.2021, ECLI:SI:USRS:2021:U.I.210.21.

[96] USRS Decision U-I-83/20 of 27.8.2000, ECLI:SI:USRS:2020:U.I.83.20; USRS Decision U-I-79/20 (n 95).

[97] USRS Decision U-I-445/20, U-I-473/20 of 16.9.2021, ECLI:SI:USRS:2021:U.I.445.20.

[98] USRS Decision U-I-79/20 (n 95); USRS Decision U-I-50/21 of 17.6.2021, ECLI:SI:USRS:2021:U.I.50.21.

[99] A legal interest is deemed to be demonstrated if the regulation directly interferes with the petitioner's rights, legal interests, or legal position (see Art 24(2) of the Constitutional Court Act, Official Gazette of the Republic of Slovenia, No 64/07 – official consolidated text et seq).

In the past, the Constitutional Court, in line with its established case law, recognised legal interest for political parties or other associations only when they challenged regulations that directly interfered with their own rights, legal interests, or legal position.[100] Petitions submitted on behalf of their members, in their interest, or to advance the general public interest traditionally did not satisfy the legal interest requirement.[101] As a result, a situation emerged in which individuals exercised their constitutional right to freedom of association by forming various types of associations; yet these associations were not necessarily recognised as having the legal interest required to file petitions for the review of regulations. This restrictive interpretation was largely shaped by the Court's need to balance its broad jurisdiction with an increasing caseload, acting as both the guardian of constitutionality and human rights[102] and as a court of last resort – particularly in environmental and spatial planning law, where it often adjudicated matters that might otherwise have been more appropriately addressed, at least initially, by ordinary courts. This approach had a significant impact on environmental NGOs, which often found themselves excluded from constitutional review despite playing a vital role in promoting environmental protection, a field that inherently serves the public interest.

This tension came to the fore in Order U-I-25/17, where the Constitutional Court revisited, and ultimately revised and softened, its strict interpretation of legal interest.[103] The case involved a challenge to a Decree on the Plan for the Reconstruction of a Power Line. The petitioners, mainly private landowners and the Association of Ecological Movements of Slovenia – an environmental NGO with recognised public-interest status under the Environmental Protection Act – argued that the project amounted to new construction, not reconstruction, and should have required an environmental impact assessment.[104] They also claimed that they were excluded from the decision-making process and that the public had been denied participation in the preliminary procedure.[105]

While in previous cases such NGOs would likely have been denied standing for failing to show direct legal effects, the Constitutional Court changed its approach. Drawing on Article 9(3) of the Aarhus Convention, as interpreted by the Court of Justice of the European Union, the Court recognised that imposing

[100] eg, USRS Order U-I-41/94 of 7.4.1994, ECLI:SI:USRS:1994:U.I.41.94.

[101] Thus, in Decision No U-I-386/06 (of 13.3.2008, ECLI:SI:USRS:2008:U.I.386.06), the Constitutional Court held that the mere fact that the petitioner had the status of an association operating in the public interest was not sufficient to establish legal interest for submitting a petition. Furthermore, in Order No U-I-316/12 (of 21.2.2013, ECLI:SI:USRS:2013:U.I.316.12), the Court clarified that the public interest which the petitioners sought to protect through their activities was also not sufficient to demonstrate legal interest.

[102] In Slovenia, the Constitutional Court is 'the highest body of the judicial power for the protection of constitutionality, legality, human rights, and fundamental freedoms' (Art 1(1) of the Constitutional Court Act).

[103] USRS Order U-I-25/17 (n 101).

[104] ibid para 1.

[105] ibid.

overly restrictive requirements (such as the need to demonstrate personal legal interest) could effectively prevent access to legal remedies for all environmental NGOs acting in the public interest.[106] Importantly, it adopted the position that NGOs active in the field of environmental protection and recognised as operating in the public interest meet the requirement of demonstrating their own legal interest when, with the aim of protecting the environment, they challenge implementing regulations governing that field.[107] Therefore, in the view of the Constitutional Court, the assumption that legal interest must be of a personal nature must, in the case of environmental NGOs operating in the public interest, be interpreted in light of their role and the purpose of their activities.

In the case at issue, the petitioner failed to meet the burden of demonstrating that the modification of the draft spatial act made after the public consultation was of such a nature as to require repeated public consultation, and therefore did not establish that the procedure by which the Decree was adopted was inconsistent with the right to public participation. Although the petitioner did not succeed in having the Decree declared unconstitutional, the decision marks an important evolution in the Court's jurisprudence, shifting from a narrowly individualistic understanding of legal interest to one that better reflects the collective nature of environmental rights and the role of NGOs in protecting them. While the right of association was not explicitly invoked, the ruling nonetheless significantly strengthens its practical exercise by ensuring that associations established for public-interest purposes, especially in the environmental field, have meaningful access to constitutional review.

V. CONCLUSION

The freedom of association is undoubtedly one of the fundamental rights in modern constitutional democracies, including Slovenia. Its significance lies in enabling political participation within a representative democracy. In Slovenia, this was particularly vital during the early years of statehood, as the country transitioned from a one-party to a multi-party system. While this shift was made possible by the new Constitution, it also required internalisation through the actual exercise of the freedom of association. Aristotle's notion of the human being as a 'political animal' speaks not only to political life but also to the broader social nature of human beings – our need for cooperation, interaction, and the pursuit of shared interests among like-minded individuals, as well as the tolerance and acceptance of differing views in a constitutional democracy. In this context, and given the essential role that the right of association plays in a modern, pluralistic society, it is all the more important that this right be

[106] ibid para 19.
[107] ibid para 20.

interpreted *in favorem associationis*, that is broadly, both in terms of who may exercise it and the variety of forms it may take.

This chapter examines the scope and practical limitations of the freedom of association within the framework of constitutional adjudication in Slovenia. Despite the freedom of association being a fundamental constitutional right, it has been relatively rarely directly and argumentatively invoked by petitioners or complainants before the Constitutional Court, especially when compared to many other constitutional rights and freedoms. This was particularly evident during the Covid-19 pandemic, when broad public health measures constrained associational freedoms, yet the right was largely absent from the wave of constitutional complaints and reviews submitted at the time.

Furthermore, this analysis underscores the procedural challenges confronting associations – most notably NGOs acting in the public interest – in establishing legal standing for constitutional review. The jurisprudential shift from a narrowly individualistic conception of legal interest toward a more collective and functional understanding constitutes a significant advancement in the Constitutional Court's approach. This shift was influenced by international instruments and EU law.

By contributing these insights, the chapter enhances scholarly understanding of the interplay between constitutional rights, judicial procedure, and civil society, offering implications for both theory and practice in the constitutional protection of collective rights within contemporary democratic governance. Slovenia serves as a revealing case study in this regard: its historical background, together with its international and European legal obligations, provides a valuable lens through which to examine the tension between formal constitutional guarantees and their practical enforceability. Ultimately, the Slovenian experience highlights a deeper structural challenge common to many constitutional democracies, namely the need to ensure that collective rights are not diminished by procedural barriers or narrow interpretations. In this light, the freedom of association emerges not merely as a constitutional human right, but as a democratic necessity; one that must be defended not only in principle but also in practice, through a legal culture that embraces its pluralistic and participatory potential.

4

Freedom of Association in Germany

LEANNÁN MARTAN O'GRADY

I. INTRODUCTION

WITHIN THE BASIC Law for the Federal Republic of Germany (*Grundgesetz* GG[1]), the freedom of association (*Vereinigungsfreiheit*) is enshrined as a fundamental right (*Grundrecht*). Fundamental rights are an expression of a community of values and culture and serve both as defensive rights against state interference and, as in the case of freedom of association, as participatory rights (*Mitwirkungsrechte*) in the political and democratic process.[2] They are delineated in Article 1 to Article 19 of the Basic Law[3] and significantly shaped by the opposition between state authority and individual rights. This is also expressed through the Basic Law's commitment to a so-called militant democracy (*wehrhafte* or *streitbare Demokratie*),[4] which refers to the idea that a democratic state has the right and duty to defend itself against those who seek to abolish democracy using democratic means.[5]

Whilst many of the fundamental rights defined in Article 1 to Article 19 have strong historical roots,[6] sometimes dating back to the Middle Ages, contemporary German law is also deeply influenced by the legacy of the Nazi era,

[1] For an English translation of the Articles of the Basic Law see: www.gesetze-im-internet.de/englisch_gg/.

[2] G Robbers, *Einführung in das deutsche Recht*, 8th edn (Baden-Baden, NomosEinführung, Nomos, 2023) 43; see also: K Hesse, *Grundzüge des Verfassungsrechts der Bundesrepublik Deutschland*, 20th edn (Zurich, Müller 1999) 178.

[3] Other legal guarantees scattered throughout the constitution, as Robbers highlights, are considered equal to fundamental rights. Robbers (n 2) 45.

[4] Other terms used to describe this concept include defensive or combative democracy.

[5] Federal Constitutional Court, 'Headnotes to the Order of the First Senate of 13 July 2018', *1 BvR 1474/12, Rn 1-167* (13 July 2018) www.bundesverfassungsgericht.de/SharedDocs/Entscheidungen/EN/2018/07/rs20180713_1bvr147412en.html.

[6] As an example, Art 17 GG, the right to petition, is one of the oldest fundamental rights in Germany, being already prevalent during the Middle Ages. The functionality as an early warning system was relevant for many different state forms, and as such, it was also included in the constitution of the DDR and certainly the Basic Law of Germany. V Epping and others, *Grundrechte*, 10th edn (Cham, Springer-Lehrbuch, Springer Publishing, 2024) 552; for a further insight into the historical development of relevant ideas in Germany, see Robbers (n 2) 39–41.

with both legislation and legal practice shaped by a lasting determination to prevent the recurrence of totalitarianism.[7] In this context, freedom of association assumes particular significance, as it safeguards (political) pluralism and reinforces other fundamental rights that inherently challenge the authority of a dictatorship – as demonstrated by the Nazi regime's determined efforts to abolish it entirely. While freedom of association existed in the 1919 Weimar Constitution (*Weimarer Verfassung* WRV), it was abolished by the Reichstag Fire Decree of 1933 and further undermined by dissolving existing trade unions into the German Labour Front, banning all other political parties and forcibly coordinating civil society organisations, youth groups and religious associations.[8]

Only after the capitulation and occupation of Germany was the right to freedom of association restored by the Western Allies.[9] Initially, a number of state constitutions were adopted in West Germany that guaranteed freedom of association, whereby the Parliamentary Council (*Parlamentarischer Rat*), which developed the Basic Law between 1948 and 1949, also decided in favour of including freedom of association in the new federal constitution.[10] It was enshrined as Article 9 GG as a specialised extension of the general freedom outlined in Article 2 paragraph 1; while both articles provide overlapping protections, Article 9 paragraph 1 takes precedence in matters related to associations.[11] When it does not fully address a situation, Article 2 paragraph 1 acts as a fallback, ensuring, as will be later discussed, protection against forced membership in public-law associations and safeguarding the rights of foreign individuals and associations.[12] Additionally, even though rooted in Article 9 GG, the freedom to form political parties or religious associations is not covered by the general freedom of association. Those are, as will be further elaborated upon in section IV, covered by Article 21 GG (political parties), Article 4 paragraph 1 GG (freedom of faith and conscience) and Article 140 GG (law of religious denominations).[13]

Generally, fundamental rights, and therefore freedom of association, hold superior status, requiring legislative alignment according to Article 142 GG at a federal and state level; conflicting laws are invalidated. Therefore, fundamental rights are not just legally protected – they are higher law. This hierarchy is further exacerbated by Article 31 GG, which establishes that federal law takes precedence over conflicting state law – and the homogeneity clause in

[7] Robbers (n 2) 23.

[8] For more insights see RJ Evans, *The Third Reich in Power, 1933–1939* (London, Penguin Press, 2005).

[9] Generally speaking, German contemporary law is heavily shaped by the catastrophic crimes of the National Socialist rule. Robbers (n 2) 23.

[10] Epping and others (n 6) 1–10.

[11] BVerfGE 1, 264 (274); BVerwGE 54, 211 (220).

[12] D Merten, 'Vereinsfreiheit' in J Isensee and P Kirchhof (eds), *Handbuch des Staatsrechts der Bundesrepublik Deutschland*, 3rd edn (Heidelberg, CF Müller Juristischer Verlag, 2003) 1064.

[13] D Schroeder, *Grundrechte*, 5th edn (JURIQ Erfolgstraining Öffentliches Recht, Heidelberg, CF Müller. 2019) 152; see also: Hesse (n 2) 177–78.

Article 28 para 1 GG requires that the constitutional order in the federate states aligns with the principles of a republican, democratic, and social state governed by the rule of law in accordance with the Basic Law. Consequently, whilst the federated states have their own constitutions, their scope is limited by the Basic Law,[14] though they retain some autonomy in specific areas – as an example, where the Basic Law does not explicitly grant fundamental rights, those provided by state constitutions are valid.[15]

As fundamental rights serve both as a legal function and as an expression of societal values, they establish a profound interconnection with political discourse. This interrelation frequently gives rise to debates concerning their interpretation. Understanding them necessitates studying their exact content as well as landmark decisions, especially those of the Federal Constitutional Court (*Bundesverfassungsgericht* BVerfG) and the German Federal Court of Justice (*Bundesgerichtshof* BGH). The Federal Constitutional Court, established by the Basic Law, plays a crucial role in upholding constitutional rights. Its rulings, according to Section 31(1) of the Federal Constitutional Court Act (*Bundesverfassungsgerichtsgesetz* BVerfGG), are legally binding upon all constitutional institutions at both the federal and state levels. This includes governmental bodies, judicial authorities, and administrative institutions. Through this, the Federal Constitutional Court ensures compliance with the constitution and can, in some cases, even constitute law.[16]

This chapter looks at these landmark decisions alongside ongoing discourses in literature on their interpretation to delineate the contemporary situation of freedom of association in Germany, especially in the context of a developing legal interpretation and implementation.[17] After providing an overview of the contemporary culture of associations in Germany, it focuses on the legal outline of freedom of association, which includes special cases and different dimensions within the Basic Law. Following this, the still relevant debate revolving around the inclusion of the negative right to freedom of association as well as the actual beneficiaries within the legal framework will be discussed. The

[14] Furthermore, Art 25 of the Basic Law integrates general rules of international law into German federal law, granting them precedence over statutes and direct applicability to individuals when relevant, while ensuring that widely accepted norms, such as diplomatic protections and wartime prohibitions, override conflicting statutory law unless of constitutional rank. However, other aspects of international law, particularly treaty law, require explicit domestic incorporation through parliamentary approval under Art 59(2) to attain legal force within Germany. Hesse (n 2) 43.

[15] Similarly, the material legal status of rights already enshrined in the Basic Law (eg, through Art 142 GG) or incorporated by reference does not create additional guarantees. Despite their constrained legal authority, state constitutions, as Hesse highlights, play a crucial role in political practice. They influence constitutional life within the federate states and shape their legal culture. This is particularly relevant for older state constitutions, which often have historical significance, even if some of their provisions have become obsolete due to federal constitutional developments. ibid 35.

[16] Robbers (n 2) 27.

[17] T Kingreen and others, *Grundrechte Staatsrecht II*, 39th edn (Staatsrecht 2, Heidelberg, CF Müller, 2023).

chapter concludes with the highly relevant possibility of severe interference with freedom of association by the German state, which will provide the basis for final remarks and a brief commentary on the current situation within the German legal system.

II. ASSOCIATIONS IN GERMANY

While it is widely accepted that an association under Article 9 paragraph 1, already forms with two persons,[18] in Germany, associations can be either registered (*eingetragene Vereine*, e.V.) or informal. Registered associations require at least seven members, a written constitution, and entry into the register of associations (*Vereinsregister*) at the local district court (*Amtsgericht*), gaining full legal capacity under the Civil Law Book (*Bürgerliches Gesetzbuch* BGB; explicitly sections 21–79), with public law aspects governed by the Law on Associations (*Vereinsgesetz*). The Law on Associations also allows the state to monitor and, if necessary, ban or dissolve associations that violate constitutional principles or threaten public order.

Protected and organised by this legal framework, the culture of associations plays a central role in German civic life. According to the discussion paper *Vereine in Deutschland im Jahr 2022* – published by the NPO *Stifterverband* – as of April 2022 there were 615,759 registered associations in Germany.[19] This represents a substantial component of organised civil society, further illustrated by the fact that in 2021, between 25 and 28 million individuals engaged in voluntary activities within associations, with the economic contribution of such volunteerism estimated at approximately 40 billion euros per annum.[20]

Although the overall number of associations continues to increase, the rate of growth is decelerating. In 2021, only 9,352 new associations were registered in the association register, compared to more than 15,000 ten years earlier. This slowdown in growth is not due to an increased removal of inactive associations by local courts, as the number of deletions – which can be enacted due to a voluntary dissolution of the association under section 41 BGB, inactivity or, in severe cases, bans – has remained relatively stable over the past ten years. Rather,

[18] G Manssen, *Staatsrecht II: Grundrechte* (Munich, CH Beck, 2020) 171; an association formed by one person is excluded, mainly because of the collective nature of Art 9 para 1. This is also the case for one-person demonstrations, which are not covered by Art 8 para 1 of the Basic Law either. Merten (n 12) 1051.

[19] Regional variations are notable, with the Saarland exhibiting nearly 11 associations per 1,000 inhabitants, whereas Bremen registers approximately 5 per 1,000 inhabitants. Furthermore, the dynamics of new association formation differ markedly across federal States; eg, Berlin has seen 31 per cent of its associations registered after 2012 in contrast to the Saarland's 16 per cent. P Schubert and others, *Vereine in Deutschland Im Jahr 2022. Aktuelle Zahlen Zum Strukturwandel Der Unterschiedlichen Geschwindigkeiten*, vol 3 (Discussion Paper Series, Stifterverband, 2022) 1.

[20] *Bewertung Und Einschätzung Des Dritten Sektors Der Gesellschaft* (Bundesverband der Vereine und des Ehrenamtes eV 2021) 4–5.

there has been a significant decline in new registrations, meaning that due to the decreasing number of new entries and the constant number of deletions, the total number of registered associations is, according to the discussion paper, expected to decline within this decade.[21] Recent trends also suggest that support associations (*Fördervereine*) are becoming increasingly dominant, signalling a shift from traditional sectors such as sport and leisure towards areas including education and civic engagement. This is accompanied by an increasing institutionalisation of civil society through associations, supporting the thesis that civil society organisations are becoming more engaged in interest representation and political decision-making.[22]

In the political sphere, membership in major political parties such as the CDU/CSU and the SPD stands at around 360,000 members each, while the Greens count roughly 150,000 members. This is notwithstanding occasional surges such as the influx of over 20,000 new members for the Greens in November 2024; in the same month, 2,500 new members applied for the SPD and over 1,000 for the CDU.[23] Whilst this sudden growth can be attributed to the collapse of Chancellor Olaf Scholz's coalition government on 6 November 2024, as well as his announcement to call a vote of confidence, it also highlights the engagement and public participation in the political sphere.

Another relevant sector of associations discussed here concerns religious groups. According to the *Research Group on Worldviews in Germany* (fowid), as of 31 December 2023, there were 38.9 million Protestant and Catholic Christians in Germany, making up 45.9 per cent of the population. This marks a profound shift in religious affiliation within Germany, as membership in the Evangelical Church in Germany (EKD) and the Roman Catholic Church has declined significantly. In 2019, these two churches collectively accounted for 52 per cent of the population, which already reflected a downward trend over previous decades. Additionally, in 2023, there were 3.2 million Muslims affiliated with a religious denomination (3.8 per cent), 3.5 million members of other religious communities (4.1 per cent), and more than 39 million people without any religious affiliation (46.2 per cent). Consequently, in 2023, for the first time, the proportion of individuals identifying as non-denominational surpassed that of Christians, highlighting a remarkable transformation in the country's religious landscape.[24] This trend is generally attributed to various factors, including

[21] Schubert and others (n 19) 2–3.

[22] The data does not provide evidence for a growing prevalence of a culturally nationalist orientation among newly founded associations. ibid 10–11.

[23] Other, smaller parties also recorded astonishing surges in memberships; the Left Party (Die Linke) and the FDP registered 4,860 and 2,000 membership applications, respectively. '"Großartiger Rückenwind" – Grüne Jubeln Über Zehntausende Mitgliedsanträge Seit Ampel-Aus', *Welt* (29.11.2024) www.welt.de/politik/deutschland/article254710376/Gruene-jubeln-ueber-Zehntausende-Mitgliedsantraege-seit-Ampel-Aus.html?utm_source=chatgpt.com accessed 22 February 2025.

[24] 'Religionszugehörigkeiten 2023', *Forschungsgruppe Weltanschauungen in Deutschland fowid* (28.08.2024) fowid.de/meldung/religionszugehoerigkeiten-2023.

secularisation, demographic changes, and individual decisions to distance themselves from traditional religious institutions.[25]

Finally, trade unions (*Gewerkschaften*) also constitute a significant element of association culture in Germany, historically playing a key role in shaping labour relations. However, membership figures have generally declined over recent decades. As of 2023, approximately 16 per cent of German employees are members of a trade union, representing a significant decline compared to the approximately double proportion recorded in 1980.[26] The German Confederation of Trade Unions (*Deutscher Gewerkschaftsbund*, DGB) serves as the primary umbrella organisation, representing eight major unions, including IG Metall (covering the metal and electrical industries) and ver.di (United Services Union), which advocates for employees in the service sector.[27] Despite the decline in membership, German trade unions continue to wield considerable influence in wage negotiations and working conditions through collective bargaining agreements. In recent years, tensions between employers and unions have increased, particularly in industries facing restructuring and job cuts, such as the automotive sector.[28] This has resulted in rising strike actions and industrial disputes.[29] Accompanying this, unions are at the forefront of advocating for reduced working hours and enhanced work-life balance, reflecting broader societal trends in Germany.[30]

III. ARTICLE 9 PARAGRAPH 1 OF THE BASIC LAW

Article 9 GG belongs together with Article 8 (freedom of assembly) and Article 5 GG (freedom of expression, arts and sciences) to the fundamental rights of communication. This relevance within the Basic Law is constituted by their function against totalitarianism, enabling the formation of political

[25] As a glimpse on the global development, in the United States, a Gallup survey found that in 2020, only 47 per cent of Americans reported being a member of a church, synagogue, or mosque, compared to 70 per cent in 1999. This decline in religious group memberships suggests a similar trend to that observed in Germany, with more people turning away from organised religions. JM Jones, 'U.S. Church Membership Falls Below Majority for First Time', *Gallup* (29.03.2021) news.gallup.com/poll/341963/church-membership-falls-below-majority-first-time.aspx accessed 22 February 2025.

[26] *Institutional Characteristics of Trade Unions, Wage Setting, State Intervention and Social Pacts.* (OECD/AIAS ICTWSS database no date); L Goerken and Y Huang, *Job Satisfaction and Trade Union Membership in Germany* (Discussion Paper Series, Institute of Labor Economics, 2022) 1.

[27] 'Unions in Germany', *deutschland.de* (23.02.2023) www.deutschland.de/en/topic/business/globalization-world-trade/unions?utm_source=.

[28] For an in-depth insight into contemporary German civil society see also H Krimmer (ed), *Datenreport Zivilgesellschaft* (Bürgergesellschaft und Demokratie, Cham, Springer VS, 2019).

[29] C Steitz and T Käckenhoff, 'Germany Faces Year of Industrial Strife as Companies Go into Battle with Workers', *Reuters* (13 February 2025) www.reuters.com/markets/europe/germany-faces-year-industrial-strife-companies-go-into-battle-with-workers-2025-02-13/ accessed 22 February 2025.

[30] B Benoit, 'A Nation of Workaholics Has a New Fixation: Working Less', *The Wall Street Journal* (20.08.2024) www.wsj.com/lifestyle/workaholics-work-less-germany-aa9c5a09 accessed 22 February 2025.

will in a free, pluralistic and democratic state. Both freedom of association and freedom of assembly are complementary guarantees to the freedom of expression.[31]

Article 9 contains two fundamental rights.[32] Article 9 paragraph 1 GG guarantees the so-called general freedom of association, covering the formation, organisation and ongoing existence and activities of, as well as participation in, an association, containing a broader right to action.[33] As (almost[34]) all fundamental rights in the Basic Law, the right to form and participate in associations is directed at the state, not third parties or the association itself.[35] Furthermore, for the association itself, any obligation for 'democratic' decision-making is excluded; Article 9 paragraph 1 rejects, rather than mandates, the alignment of state and society.[36] It also does not support claims to state support. Accordingly, freedom of association is a permissive right (*Darf-Recht*), not an entitlement right (*Kann-Recht*). While every German citizen may form and join associations, Article 9 paragraph 1 GG does not guarantee the resources to do so.[37] Accordingly, Article 9 paragraph 1 GG neither requires nor forbids state funding for associations,[38] however, if the state provides support, claims to equal access may arise, particularly from Article 3 paragraph 1 GG at the constitutional level,[39] and from statutory regulations at the legislative level.[40]

What is meant by an 'association' (*Verein*) is determined on the basis of section 2 VereinsG (1)[41] as an organisation where a majority of individuals or entities unite for a common purpose voluntarily, adhering to a uniform decision-making process over time. Voluntariness is essential for an association's existence under Article 9 paragraph 1 GG, as compulsory associations of a public or private law nature are not covered by the scope of protection of Article 9.[42] The protection provided by Article 9 paragraph 1 includes all types of associations, whether they are registered or informal, economic – like corporations and joint partnerships[43] – political, or purely ideological in nature; no specific limitations are imposed here, except for the mandatory alignment with constitutional principles.[44] The legal form of the association is also irrelevant.

[31] D Murswiek, 'Grundfälle Zur Vereinigungsfreiheit – Art 9 I, II GG' [1992] *JuS* 116, 117; Hesse (n 2) 177.

[32] Schroeder (n 13) 152.

[33] Merten (n 12) 1057.

[34] See Art 9 para 3, further elaborated on in the following section of the chapter.

[35] As into internal affairs, like access to member information. BVerfGE 84, 372 (377–378); see also Merten (n 12) 1044, 1058.

[36] ibid 1055.

[37] ibid 1041.

[38] BVerfGE 22, 180 (216–218).

[39] BVerfGE 70, 191 (214).

[40] Merten (n 12) 1042.

[41] Gesetz zur Regelung des öffentlichen Vereinsrechts (Vereinsgesetz). s 2 Begriff des Vereins.

[42] Manssen (n 18) 171; Epping and others (n 6) 490.

[43] Schroeder (n 13) 152; Merten (n 12) 1053; see also s 21 BGB and s 22 BGB.

[44] Merten (n 12) 1052.

Thus, a loosely connected citizens' initiative is considered an association, just like a joint-stock company. The primary criterion is whether there is a *certain*[45] degree of organisational stability, which may be reflected in a process of collective decision-making.[46] The key features of 'permanence' and 'organized decision-making' differentiate associations from gatherings under Article 8 paragraph 1 GG, as Article 9 paragraph 1 GG can even encompass temporary groups with structured decision-making.

This, as Konrad Hesse aptly writes, standardises a general principle of the structure of German society: the free formation of social groups. The social system established by the Basic Law and especially Article 9 is designed to avoid both a feudal-corporate structure, characteristic of earlier societies, and state-controlled organisation dictated by the values of the ruling group, as seen in modern totalitarian regimes.[47]

IV. SPECIAL CASES OF FREEDOM OF ASSOCIATION

Detlef Merten aptly highlights that 'in some sections of the Basic Law, there are qualified special cases of general freedom of association, so that these are, according to their specific scope, leges speciales'.[48] As was previously mentioned, Article 9 of the Basic Law contains two fundamental rights,[49] whereby Article 9 paragraph 3 GG specifically protects so-called coalitions (*Koalitionen*), particular cases of associations[50] with the purpose of safeguarding labour and economic conditions.[51] A coalition, to qualify under paragraph 3, is more narrowly defined than associations under paragraph 1 and must have the primary purpose of promoting working conditions, with the improvement of economic conditions potentially serving as a supplementary aspect.[52] The right, therefore, essentially refers to trade unions and employers' organisations, making Article 9 as much a fundamental economic right as it is a right of communication.[53]

[45] The requirements are not rigid; therefore, even loosely organised groups are entitled to protection under Art 9 para 1 of the Basic Law. ibid 1051.

[46] Epping and others (n 6) 490.

[47] Hesse (n 2) 178.

[48] Translation by author. Original version in German: 'An einigen Stellen des Grundgesetzes finden sich qualifizierte Sonderfälle der allgemeinen Vereinigungsfreiheit, so daß diese entsprechend ihrer tatbestandlichen Reichweite leges speciales sind' Merten (n 12) 1064.

[49] Schroeder (n 13) 152.

[50] Manssen (n 18) 177.

[51] The emphasised relevance not just of freedom of association, but also that of coalitions, is among others highlighted in its implementation in Art 11 of the European Convention on Human Rights (ECHR) and Arts 12 and 28 of the Charter of Fundamental Rights of the European Union (CFR).

[52] Manssen (n 18) 177.

[53] Epping and others (n 6) 486; Schroeder (n 13) 152.

Furthermore, a coalition must be freely formed on a private law basis, and it is required that its members do not include their social counterparts, ensuring legal and factual independence.[54] The Federal Constitutional Court views coalition freedom as essential for the orderly regulation of working life, with the state retracting its regulatory role to allow parties to manage their affairs independently.[55] It also establishes a foundation for the so-called tariff autonomy (*Tarifautonomie*), the cornerstone principle that trade unions and employers' associations have the independent right to negotiate and establish collective agreements on wages and working conditions without state interference.

The origins of this specific paragraph can be traced back to the nineteenth century as a direct reaction to industrialisation. Volker Epping et al. note that paragraph 3 is almost identical to Article 159 of the WRV;[56] and this historical position is still influential for decisions by the Federal Constitutional Court to this day.[57] Interestingly, the only change in Article 9 was made to paragraph 3 over the course of the emergency legislation of 1968, which expressly excluded certain crisis instruments from being used against industrial action.[58] This is a rare occurrence, as amendments of the Basic Law require a two-thirds majority in both the Bundestag and Bundesrat.

Within paragraph 3, coalitions are granted special constitutional protection with potential third-party effects.[59] This is relevant, because, as mentioned in the previous section, private individuals and entities are usually not directly bound by fundamental rights, as these rights are conceived as entitlements of individuals rather than obligations imposed upon them;[60] hence, Article 9 paragraph 3 GG is the sole exception.[61] Consequently, under this provision, it is impermissible for an employer to make an individual's employment contingent upon membership in, or non-membership of, a particular trade union.

According to the Federal Constitutional Court, Article 9 does not extend to political parties,[62] parliamentary groups, churches, or religious organisations, as they are not considered associations within the meaning of this provision.[63] Firstly, Article 21 of the Basic Law supersedes Article 9 in regulating the formation and activities of political parties.[64] Only those political

[54] Manssen (n 18) 177.
[55] BVerfGE 44, 322 (340); BVerfGE 50, 290 (367); BVerfGE 58, 233 (246).
[56] Epping and others (n 6) 489.
[57] See, eg, BVerfGE 19, 303; 38, 386.
[58] S Schmid, 'Deutscher Bundestag – Vor 55 Jahren: Bundestag beschließt Notstandsgesetze' (*Deutscher Bundestag*, no date) www.bundestag.de/dokumente/textarchiv/2023/kw21-kalenderblatt-notstandsgesetze-556672 accessed 25 June 2024.
[59] BVerfGE 84, 212 (224).
[60] Robbers (n 2) 48.
[61] ibid.
[62] Murswiek (n 31) 876.
[63] BVerfGE 83, 341 (354–356); Federal Constitutional Court (n 5).
[64] BVerfGE 2, 1 (13); 12, 296 (304).

associations that do not meet the criteria of a 'party' under Article 21 fall under the scope of Article 9 paragraph 1;[65] yet, despite this legal separation, the freedom granted to political parties has historical roots in the broader right of association.[66] Within Germany's organised landscape, political associations remain relatively insignificant, both in number and structural development, when compared to the multitude of organisations dedicated to various other objectives.[67]

Furthermore, the protection of religious freedom of association is also enshrined as a distinct fundamental right and specific form of the freedom of association,[68] explicitly guaranteed by Article 4 of the Basic Law and Article 137 paragraph 2 sentence 1 of the Weimar Constitution, in conjunction with Article 140 of the Basic Law.[69] Unlike general freedom of association, it does not depend on the broader provisions of Article 9 paragraph 1 or utilise the restrictions imposed by Article 9 paragraph 2.[70]

The German Basic Law thus grants specific protections to certain forms of associations that take precedence over the general freedom of association enshrined in Article 9 paragraph 1 GG. This can be attributed to historical influences, as already outlined in the WRV,[71] and the prominent role these types of associations hold within German society. While the subsequent sections of this chapter will focus on Article 9, as it constitutes the fundamental right to freedom of association, the examples of political parties and religious organisations illustrate that this freedom extends beyond its core formulation within the fundamental rights framework of the Basic Law.

V. THE COLLECTIVE AND INDIVIDUAL DIMENSION OF ARTICLE 9

Both the general freedom of association and the freedom of coalition are considered individual fundamental rights as well as collective fundamental rights.[72] The individual general freedom of association guarantees the activities of current or future members, encompassing, as was previously elaborated upon, both the freedom to establish associations and the freedom to participate in their actions. Individual freedom of coalition especially protects collective bargaining autonomy, participation in company co-determination,

[65] This mainly includes local or smaller political groups. BVerfGE 17, 155 (166); 69, 92 (104–105).
[66] Merten (n 12) 1039.
[67] ibid 1041.
[68] ibid 1058.
[69] BVerfGE 42, 312 (322–323); 53, 366 (387); 83, 341 (354–356).
[70] Art 9 para 1 GG continues to protect religious associations that were explicitly mentioned under Art 124 para 1 sentence 3 WRV as part of the general freedom of association. Merten (n 12) 1067.
[71] ibid 1066–67.
[72] Murswiek (n 31) 873; Schroeder (n 13) 154; Epping and others (n 6) 501 BVerfGE 146, 71 (114).

advertisement, industrial action (strikes and lockouts)[73] and prevents sanctions for membership.[74]

As fundamental collective rights, they apply to the association and coalition themselves,[75] as the association's right to exist and function is also explicitly protected; within the German Basic Law, associations can claim their own fundamental rights, not just those of their members,[76] even if the extent to which the activities of the association, specifically its external impact, are protected is a matter of controversy.[77] According to the Federal Constitutional Court, at least a core area of the association's continuity and activity is included, guaranteeing the right to the establishment and existence of an organisation. This contains the formation and functioning of an association, the self-determination over its own organisation, as well as the process of decision-making and management. In this context, the Federal Constitutional Court has explicitly ruled that the usage of the name[78] and effective self-promotion[79] are protected, since they can be essential for the existence of the association. Furthermore, as clarified by the Federal Constitutional Court, the right of the association to determine the admission and exclusion of members is included,[80] because the association and participation of opposing members can be detrimental to the function of the association.[81] Since Article 9 paragraph 1 GG does not, unlike paragraph 3, have a direct third-party effect of fundamental rights, an individual cannot claim the right to freedom of association when seeking admission to, or facing exclusion from, an association,[82] and associations can exclude individuals based on gender, ethnicity, or (political) views. The state can only intervene in associations that put discrimination at the forefront of their purpose.[83]

The most relevant exception to this autonomy is in the case of monopolistic associations or those with significant economic or social power,[84] which may be required to accept members if they have a substantial or

[73] This has been clarified during the aforementioned emergency legislation in 1968, where the following sentence has been added to Art 9 para 3 GG: 'Measures taken pursuant to Article 12a, to paragraphs (2) and (3) of Article 35, to paragraph (4) of Article 87a or to Article 91 may not be directed against industrial disputes engaged in by associations within the meaning of the first sentence of this paragraph in order to safeguard and improve working and economic conditions.' Schmid (n 57).

[74] Epping and others (n 6) 503; BVerfGE 50, 290 (367).

[75] Manssen (n 18) 178.

[76] BVerfGE 16, 147 (158), Merten (n 12) 1047.

[77] Epping and others (n 6) 492.

[78] BVerfGE 30, 227 (241).

[79] BVerfGE 84, 372 (378).

[80] BVerfG, Decision of the 2nd Chamber of the First Senate of 2 February 2023, 1 BvR 187/21, Rn. 1-12, www.bverfg.de/e/rk20230202_1bvr018721.html.

[81] Murswiek (n 31) 873.

[82] Epping and others (n 6) 492.

[83] Merten (n 12) 1052.

[84] BGHZ 63, 282 (284); 77, 32; 93, 151 (152).

fundamental interest in joining.[85] This was, among others, further clarified on 2 December 1974, when a cycling association sought membership in the German Sports Confederation (*Deutscher Sportbund*).[86] The confederation rejected the application based on its statute permitting only one peak association per sport – which, in this case, was already occupied by the German Cycling Federation (*Bund Deutscher Radfahrer*). The plaintiff argued that the DSB's monopoly rendered this restriction invalid, as the rejection led to disadvantages such as reduced funding, exclusion from key events, and membership loss. In this context, the Federal Court of Justice in civil matters clarified the following:

> If a monopoly association rejects the admission of an applicant for membership by invoking a restriction on admission under its articles of association, the purpose of which is in itself objectively justified, the restriction on admission may nevertheless be ineffective if the purpose pursued by the monopoly association can also be achieved by another, 'milder' formulation of the articles of association that would allow the applicant to become a member.
>
> The alternative may apply if the applicant is able to fulfil the admission requirements set by the monopoly association without disproportionate sacrifice.[87]

The Federal Court of Justice therefore confirmed the obligation of a monopoly association to admit a membership applicant despite statutory restrictions.[88] The ruling establishes that such restrictions, even if substantively justified, may be invalid if a less restrictive framework could achieve the same objective.

This interpretation is even further exemplified within rulings by the Federal Constitutional Court and Federal Court of Justice regarding unions, as they are more likely to assume a position that constitutes a fundamental interest in joining[89] – as their decisions, in certain cases, can significantly impact access to economic, professional, or social participation.[90] A fitting example for this is a decision by the German Federal Court of Justice in 1984, focusing on the IG Metall.[91] The Court established that IG Metall is generally subject to an obligation to admit applicants within its sphere of influence, even if it is not strictly speaking monopolistic,[92] as the IG Metall has an exceptionally high membership, granting it an overwhelmingly dominant position within the metal industry.

[85] Merten (n 12) 1056; Schroeder (n 13) 154.

[86] The German Sports Confederation (DSB) served as the overarching organisation for state sports federations and sports associations in Germany, operating as a registered association (e. V.). On 20 May 2006, it merged with the National Olympic Committee for Germany to establish the German Olympic Sports Confederation (DOSB).

[87] Translation by the author. For the original version in German, see BGHZ 63, 282.

[88] BGHZ 63, 282 (284).

[89] BGHZ 63, 282; 29, 344 (347); BGH NJW 1973, 35.

[90] P Annerfelt, 'Grenzen Gewerkschaftlicher Autonomie Bei Aufnahme Und Ausschluss von Mitgliedern' (2021) 69 *Arbeit und Recht* 14, 14–15.

[91] BGHZ 93, 151.

[92] Annerfelt (n 90) 16.

No other union within its jurisdiction has ever approached its significance or bargaining power, making membership in IG Metall effectively obligatory for those seeking adequate and effective representation.[93]

Nonetheless, this admission obligation is not absolute. Within the same decision, the Court recognised that unions have a legitimate interest in maintaining their organisational integrity and can reject applicants in specific circumstances. Grounds for rejection may include prior membership in organisations hostile to the union or conduct detrimental to its principles. In such cases, the Court balances the applicant's fundamental interest in joining against the association's right to self-preservation. An especially valuable example for this involved the exclusion of a police officer from the Police Union (*Gewerkschaft der Polizei*) due to his membership in the far-right National Democratic Party of Germany (NPD) and election as a representative in the Bavarian State Parliament in 1966,[94] which was elaborated on by the German Federal Court of Justice in 1972. The union expelled him on the basis that membership in organisations deemed incompatible with its principles was not permitted under its internal rules. The plaintiff argued that his exclusion violated his fundamental rights, particularly political neutrality, freedom of association under Article 9 of the Basic Law, and freedom of opinion. He further contended that the NPD, not being a banned party under Article 21 GG, should be treated as a democratic entity and that his expulsion caused reputational damage, for which he sought compensation. The Court upheld the exclusion, ruling that the union had the right to protect its integrity and prevent members from supporting organisations whose goals conflicted with its fundamental principles. The reason for the plaintiff's affiliation with the NPD being incompatible with the union's democratic values is a direct consequence of the NPD's conviction that, for the maintenance of industrial peace, it is prudent to establish unified organisations of both employees and employers – effectively calling into question the continued existence of free trade unions.[95]

This is in accordance with the collective and individual dimension of Article 9 GG; while monopolistic or dominant associations generally have autonomy in deciding membership, their influence can impose legal constraints to prevent unjust exclusion, especially if their decisions unjustly infringe upon fundamental rights.

[93] '[...] wenn der Verein oder Verband im wirtschaftlichen oder sozialen Bereich eine überragende Machtstellung innehat und ein wesentliches oder grundlegendes Interesse am Erwerb der Mitgliedschaft besteht.' BGHZ 93, 151.

[94] BGH NJW 1973, 35 (36).

[95] P Annerfelt highlights in this context the historical dimension of the relationship between National Socialists and Unions, whereby the suffering experienced by thousands of trade unionists under National Socialist rule resulted in the conviction of irreconcilability of the idea of free trade unions and fascism. Annerfelt (n 90) 18.

VI. NEGATIVE RIGHT TO FREEDOM OF ASSOCIATION

Although not explicitly mentioned in the text of the article, the right to form associations under Article 9 paragraph 1 GG is often interpreted to include the mirrored right to a so-called negative right to freedom of associations, ie, the freedom to leave associations under private law or to keep away from them from the outset.[96] Yet, there is some – if limited – debate on this, which does not question the existence of a negative right to freedom of association, but rather its protection under Article 9 GG; even if not included, it would be covered by the general freedom of action guaranteed by Article 2 paragraph 1 GG.[97] Regardless of the association's legal nature, within the Basic Law, compulsory membership constitutes an intrusion into general freedom of action.[98]

From a critical perspective, it must be noted that other fundamental rights in the GG explicitly include a negative component, such as the prohibition of forced labour in Article 12 paragraphs 2 and 3, and the right not to disclose religious beliefs in Article 136 paragraph 3 WRV (incorporated into the GG by Article 140 GG).[99] Furthermore, the freedom to act implies the freedom to abstain, which exists even without explicit constitutional protection. A state does not need to permit someone not to do something, and since Article 9 paragraph 1 expresses no general duty to found or participate in associations, there is strictly speaking no need for a specific permission not to associate.[100] It is, however, generally agreed that it exists. Some of the reasons include that the decision to join one association can exclude membership in another, and mandatory membership can therefore eliminate genuine choice,[101] therefore necessitating an implication of the negative right within Article 9 paragraph 1 GG. Building on this, proponents of the existence within Article 9 paragraph 1 further argue that true freedom of association requires the freedom not to associate,[102] and there is a certain consensus on this position. In the context of this work, it is assumed that it exists within Article 9 paragraph 1 and is also deeply embedded in the general conception of the Basic Law.

The debate regarding the negative right to freedom of coalition entailed in Article 9 paragraph 3 GG is inclined to reach a consensus that it exists,[103] but it remains uncertain whether the negative right to freedom of association

[96] BVerfGE 50, 290 (354).

[97] Johannes Hellermann, *Die Sogenannte Negative Seite Der Freiheitsrechte* (Schriften zum öffentlichen Recht, Duncker & Humblot 1993) 250.

[98] BVerwG NJW 2021, 406; Epping and others (n 6) 493–95.

[99] BVerfGE 52, 223 (239) (Schulgebet).

[100] Epping and others (n 6) 494.

[101] Merten (n 12) 1060.

[102] Manssen (n 18) 171; Epping and others (n 6) 493.

[103] BVerfGE 50, 290 (367); P Leydecker, *Der Tarifvertrag als exklusives Gut: Die rechtliche Zulässigkeit und Erstreikbarkeit von Differenzierungsklauseln* (Schriften zum Sozial- und Arbeitsrecht 243, Berlin, Duncker & Humblot, 2005) 110; Epping and others (n 6) 493.

is limited to the right to refrain from joining or extends to protection against the effects of coalitions.[104] The Federal Constitutional Court consistently holds that the negative right to freedom of coalition is only affected if significant pressure to join is exerted; therefore, the protection under Article 9 paragraph 3 GG is not infringed if an employer is required to apply collective agreements, regardless of his membership in the employers' association, to obtain public contracts, as seen in the Berlin regulation on compliance with collective agreements.[105]

Last but not least, it is important to mention that the protection under Article 9 GG against compulsory membership in public law associations is debatable, as the negative right to freedom of association within paragraph 1 protects the right to leave, or refrain from joining, *private law* associations.[106] Public law associations, on the other hand, aim to involve citizens in state administration, such as the Federal Bar Association (*Bundesrechtsanwaltskammer* BRAK), the Chamber of Industry and Commerce (*Industrie- und Handelskammer* IHK), student bodies and the Chamber of Craft (*Handwerkskammer* HWK).[107] As Epping et al. highlight, the negative right to freedom of association protects the right to leave, or not join, private associations but does not extend to public law associations since citizens cannot form such associations.[108] Still, counterclaims exist, stating that the negative right to freedom of association within Article 9 paragraph 1 GG should protect against public law associations, as there is no difference to the individual whether the association they are compelled to join is of a private or public nature;[109] especially since historically, freedom of association was meant to protect against compulsory guilds.[110] Also, any state-enforced affiliation with specific organisations would limit the freedom to create or join private associations.[111] However, as Epping et al. further elaborate, this would make it difficult to justify existing public law compulsory associations under constitutional law.[112] It must therefore be agreed that public law associations are not covered by Article 9 paragraph 1, but by Article 2 paragraph 1 GG; an interference with the general freedom of action – which it would be, regardless of whether the association was established under private or public law – would have to be justified.

[104] BVerfGE 64, 208 (213); Leydecker (n 103) 84–86.
[105] BVerfGE 116, 202 (218).
[106] BVerfG, NJW 2001, 2617 (2617).
[107] Epping and others (n 6) 495.
[108] ibid.
[109] KH Friauf, in K Pleyer and R Reinhardt (eds), *Festschrift für Rudolf Reinhardt zum 70 Geburtstag, 7 Juni 1972* (Goldbach, Keip, 1995) 395.
[110] Murswiek (n 31) 118–19; H Bethge, 'Grundrechtsprobleme Einer Zwangsmitgliedschaft in Verbänden Des Öffentlichen Rechts' [1979] *Juristische Arbeitsblätter* 281, 284–85; for an overview see also Epping and others (n 6) 495.
[111] Merten (n 12) 1060–61.
[112] Epping and others (n 6) 495.

VII. BENEFICIARIES OF ARTICLE 9 OF THE BASIC LAW

Article 9 paragraph 1 GG constitutes a fundamental right of Germans, including all Germans within the meaning of Article 116 GG as natural persons.[113] Pursuant to Article 19 paragraph 3 GG, domestic legal persons who wish to form an association within the meaning of Article 9 paragraph 1 GG may also be entitled to fundamental rights. Non-Germans are also allowed to form associations, but they cannot invoke a specific fundamental right and must rely on Article 2 paragraph 1 GG.[114] This does not apply to EU citizens, for whom the Federal Republic of Germany is obliged to guarantee the same protection of fundamental rights within the scope of application of the EC Treaties via Article 2 paragraph 1 GG as Germans via Article 9 paragraph 1 GG. The Federal Constitutional Court has not yet decided if freedom of association under Article 9 applies to economic entities, including large corporations or mutual insurance associations with extensive memberships, where individual participation becomes increasingly marginal. However, precisely defining the threshold at which an organisation no longer qualifies as an association in this sense remains a complex challenge.[115]

Foreign associations, which are led by, or mostly composed of, foreigners[116] or which have no registered office in Germany, are not protected under Article 9, paragraph 1 GG[117] and can be banned for reasons beyond Article 9 paragraph 2 GG under section 14 of the Associations Act. In such instances, as in the case of individual freedom of association, fundamental rights are protected solely in accordance with Article 2 paragraph 1 GG.[118]

Unlike paragraph 1, the freedom of coalition under paragraph 3, is a fundamental right for everyone. This right is defined by its connection to dependent employment and protects all individuals in their professional roles, whether as employees or employers, without excluding any occupational groups.[119]

VIII. SEVERE INTERFERENCE

The limitations of Article 9 paragraph 1 GG are contained within Article 9 paragraph 2 GG, which defines a narrow qualified legal reservation

[113] Within the German Basic Law, there is a distinction between the above-mentioned fundamental rights that protect all Germans and those that are general human rights of all individuals, independent of nationality. As an example, these include the freedom of religious belief or freedom of expression. Robbers (n 2) 47.

[114] Epping and others (n 6) 488.

[115] BVerfGE 124, 25/34; Manssen (n 18) 172–73.

[116] Whereby, according to s 14 para 1 of the Associations Act, associations are explicitly not considered foreign associations if their members or leaders are all or predominantly foreign nationals of a Member State of the European Union.

[117] Manssen (n 18) 172.

[118] Merten (n 12) 1046, 1048.

[119] Murswiek (n 31) 873; Epping and others (n 6) 501.

to the freedom of association and allows for preventive protection of the constitution. The necessity for this has been clarified by the Federal Constitutional Court, stating that

> freedom of association is dependent to a greater or lesser extent on regulations that integrate the free associations and their life into the general legal system, guarantee the security of legal transactions, secure the rights of members and take into account the interests of third parties or public interests that require protection.[120]

This is reflective of the aforementioned commitment of the Basic Law to a militant democracy[121] and allows the state to target criminal organisations specifically by focusing on the collective actions of their members rather than individual behaviour. The reasoning for this is aptly summarised in a 1956 ruling by the Federal Constitutional Court concerning the ban of the Communist Party of Germany (KPD): 'No unconditional freedom for the enemies of freedom'.[122]

As further delineated by the Federal Constitutional Court in its 2018 decision, addressing constitutional complaints against three association bans, an association is prohibited under Article 9 paragraph 2 GG if it incites or supports criminal actions, adopts an aggressive stance against constitutional principles, or actively promotes violence or terrorism, including through third-party support[123] – whereby it is acknowledged that humanitarian aid in crisis regions can have an indirect effect on terrorism that is not necessarily grounds for prohibition.[124] Interestingly, even if individual acts are not criminal, if they are part of a group's activities or tacitly accepted by the group, the state can intervene[125] as organised collectives pose greater risk compared to individuals.[126] This is also relevant in the context of international understanding, which is a key value under protection; actions directed against specific nations or groups and breaches of sections 102 to 104 of the German Criminal Code (*Strafgesetzbuch* StGB) are only significant if they challenge international cooperation itself. As

[120] Translation by author. Complete passage in original language: 'Art. 9 Abs. 1 GG schützt die Vereinigungsfreiheit allerdings nicht schrankenlos, und die Gewährung der Vereinigungsfreiheit kann nicht bedeuten, dass jede staatliche Regelung der Organisation und Willensbildung von Vereinigungen ausgeschlossen ist. Vereinigungsfreiheit ist in mehr oder minder großem Umfang auf Regelungen angewiesen, welche die freien Zusammenschlüsse und ihr Leben in die allgemeine Rechtsordnung einfügen, die Sicherheit des Rechtsverkehrs gewährleisten, Rechte der Mitglieder sichern und den schutzbedürftigen Belangen Dritter oder auch öffentlichen Interessen Rechnung tragen. Demgemäß ist mit der verfassungsrechtlichen Garantie der Vereinigungsfreiheit seit jeher die Notwendigkeit einer gesetzlichen Ausgestaltung dieser Freiheit verbunden, ohne die sie praktische Wirksamkeit nicht entfalten könnte.' BVerfG, NJW 2001, 2617 (2617).

[121] Federal Constitutional Court (n 5).

[122] Translation by author. Complete passage in original language: 'keine unbedingte Freiheit für die Feinde der Freiheit'. BVerfGE 5, 85.

[123] Federal Constitutional Court (n 5).

[124] BVerfGE 149, 160; Kingreen and others (n 17) 864–66.

[125] BVerwGE 80, 299 (307).

[126] Merten (n 12) 1070.

Merten highlights, Article 9 paragraph 2 of the Basic Law does not safeguard foreign interests or sensitivities.[127]

The Federal Ministry of the Interior (*Bundesinnenministerium für Innen und für Heimat*) oversees bans on associations operating across state borders, while state interior ministries handle bans within their respective territories.[128] They are obligated to maintain a high threshold for prohibition and adhere to the principle that there can be no limitation of otherwise applicable liberty rights. Restrictions on fundamental rights are only justified to safeguard the fundamental rights of others or other constitutional legal interests.[129] This is especially prominent in cases where the association's opinions are covered by the freedom of expression enshrined in Article 5 paragraph 1 GG, as these stances cannot be grounds for a prohibition of an association.[130] A total of 55 associations and 109 partial and substitute organisations have been banned in Germany under Article 9 paragraph 2 of the Basic Law since the foundation of the Federal Republic of Germany in 1949,[131] whereby these associations actively and aggressively opposed the constitutional order to lose their protection. Merely having a critical stance is generally insufficient, as Article 9 paragraph 2 GG does not prohibit ideologies or beliefs. However, it is not necessary for the association to immediately threaten fundamental constitutional principles, nor must there be an imminent danger or potential for achieving unconstitutional goals[132] – other than the prohibitions of political parties under Article 21 paragraph 2 GG, whereas there must be a concrete danger for the basic democratic order to justify a prohibition.[133]

The wording of the provision suggests that associations directed against the legal interests mentioned therein are constitutionally prohibited. However, as Gerrit Manssen notes, such an interpretation would be hostile to fundamental rights. Associations would have no certainty regarding whether they are prohibited or not.[134] Therefore, as declared in section 3 VereinsG, any prohibition does not occur automatically but must first be decreed by the competent state authority.[135] Until the prohibition order takes effect, the association must not be treated as prohibited.[136] This prohibition order has a constitutive effect, but the association is, in the context of judicial protection, still capable of litigation and

[127] Murswiek (n 31) 116; Merten (n 12) 1071.

[128] Robbers (n 2) 43.

[129] BVerfGE 28, 243 (261); 81, 278 (292–293); 94, 268 (284); Merten (n 12) 1072.

[130] BVerfGE 149, 160; Manssen (n 18) 175.

[131] There were a total of 20 bans in the area of right-wing extremism, 1 in left-wing extremism, 19 in Islamism, 7 in foreigner extremism, 79 of an illegal nature (rock clubs; organised crime) and 2 bans for other reasons. Bundesministerium des Innern und für Heimat, 'Öffentliches Vereinsrecht' [no date].

[132] BVerfGE 149, 160 (197–199).

[133] BVerfGE 144, 20 (199, 223). See also Robbers (n 2) 67.

[134] Manssen (n 18) 175.

[135] Hesse (n 2) 180.

[136] Manssen (n 18) 2020; Epping and others (n 6) 490; *cf* BVerwGE 4, 188.

fundamental rights.[137] This is a relevant difference to the freedom of assembly enshrined in Article 8 GG, which only provides protection to peaceful assemblies without weapons.[138]

The topic of prohibition of associations is one of the most intricate debates surrounding Article 9 today, as it comes up in a variety of contexts; and the recurring topic of far-right parties or organisations generates particular publicity. The annual Report on the Protection of the Constitution (*Verfassungsschutzbericht*)[139] highlights the ban of several associations for activities that violated constitutional principles, fostered extremism, or opposed democratic values. As an example, right-wing extremist groups, particularly the 'Reichsbürger' and 'Selbstverwalter'[140] movements, were targeted for rejecting the legitimacy of the German state and promoting xenophobic and antisemitic ideologies. The 2023 report highlights the 'suspicion of continuing a prohibited organisation'[141] in regard to the association *Geeinte deutsche Völker und Stämme* (GdVuSt; roughly translated to mean United German peoples and tribes). The group and its sub-organisations were initially banned on 19 March 2020 by the Federal Minister of the Interior, Horst Seehofer, which marked the first time that a group from the Reichsbürger milieu had been prohibited. The ban was executed through coordinated searches and seizures across ten German states, involving approximately 400 law enforcement officers, resulting in the confiscation of the group's assets.[142]

Since then, different cases have underscored the actuality of this problem. On 6 March 2025, members of the *Vereinte Patrioten* were sentenced to prison terms of up to eight years for plotting the violent overthrow of the German government, including plans to abduct then Health Minister Karl Lauterbach and reinstate the 1871 imperial Constitution.[143] On 13 May 2025, Federal Minister of the Interior Alexander Dobrindt banned the biggest group within the milieu, the *Königreich Deutschland* (Kingdom of Germany), citing its

[137] Federal Constitutional Court (n 5).

[138] Epping and others (n 6) 20, 490.

[139] Bundesministerium des Innern und für Heimat, *Verfassungsschutzbericht 2023* (2024); for a summarised version in english translation see: Federal Ministry of the Interior and Community, *Brief Summary. 2023 Report on the Protection of the Constitution* (2024).

[140] Bundesministerium des Innern und für Heimat, *Verfassungsschutzbericht 2023* (n 139) 62–63, 132–42.

[141] Translation by author. Section in original language: 'Wegen des Verdachts der Fortführung einer verbotenen Vereinigung […]' ibid 138.

[142] For more information see the press release of the Federal Ministry of the Interior at the time of the ban: Bundesministerium des Innern und für Heimat, 'Bundesinnenminister Seehofer Verbietet Mit "Geeinte Deutsche Völker Und Stämme" Erstmals Reichsbürgervereinigung' (19 March 2020) www.bmi.bund.de/SharedDocs/pressemitteilungen/DE/2020/03/verbot-reichbuergervereinigung.html accessed 3 March 2025.

[143] 'Geplante Lauterbach-Entführung – Gericht Verurteilt "Reichsbürger" Zu Mehrjährigen Haftstrafen', *Welt* (7 March 2025) www.welt.de/politik/deutschland/article255621884/Geplante-Entfuehrung-von-Karl-Lauterbach-Gericht-verurteilt-Reichsbuerger-zu-mehrjaehrigen-Haftstrafen.html accessed 13 March 2025.

anti-constitutional activities and criminal operations. Also in this case, authorities conducted nationwide raids, seizing assets and arresting key figures, including leader Peter Fitzek, for operating an illicit financial network.[144]

It is controversial whether Article 9 paragraph 2 GG can also be applied to Article 9 paragraph 3 GG, as it defines a very specific kind of freedom of association that has an equally specific position within the system.[145] Still, outside the scope of Article 9 paragraph 2 GG, both the freedom of association and freedom of coalition can be restricted by conflicting constitutional law, ie, fundamental rights of third parties and other constitutional rights.[146] In the case of freedom of coalition under Article 9 paragraph 3 GG, the topic of interference can become relevant in the context of multiple strikes by different unions against the same employer, in which instance the legislature has considerable discretion.[147] The Federal Constitutional Court has also approved laws mandating fixed-term employment for academic staff at universities and state research institutions, excluding alternative collective agreements.[148] This measure, interfering with freedom of coalition, is justified by the need to periodically create new positions for junior researchers to protect academic freedom.[149] Still, as with every interference, all restrictions must adhere to the principle of proportionality (*Verhältnismäßigkeitsprinzip*).[150]

IX. CONCLUSION

It was demonstrated that freedom of association in Germany is enshrined as a fundamental right and therefore higher law in the Basic Law, shaped by historical experiences and constitutional principles. Positioned at the beginning of the constitution, it underscores the importance of individual rights in response to past authoritarianism, aligning Germany with European and North American human rights traditions by emphasising both individual and collective liberties. In particular, the Federal Constitutional Court has, on many occasions, reinforced these protections, ensuring that associations can function freely within the legal framework.

The diverse aspects of freedom of association, such as the definition of specific cases outside of Article 9 GG, the duality of an individual and a

[144] For more information see the press release of the Federal Ministry of the Interior at the time of the ban: Bundesministerium des Innern und für Heimat, 'Bundesinnenminister Dobrindt Verbietet Den Verein "Königreich Deutschland"' (Berlin, 13 May 2025) www.bmi.bund.de/SharedDocs/pressemitteilungen/DE/2025/05/verbot-koenigreich-deutschland.html accessed 5 June 2025.

[145] Murswiek (n 31) 875; Epping and others (n 6) 509; Manssen (n 18) 179.

[146] Schroeder (n 13) 158.

[147] This is especially relevant as strikes themselves must adhere to the principle of proportionality. See BAGE 23, 292 and BVerfGE 84, 212.

[148] BVerfGE 94, 268 (270).

[149] Art 5 para 3 GG.

[150] Manssen (n 18) 179.

collective dimension and the highly relevant option for severe interference within the German Basic Law, combine with a particular jurisdiction that emphasises proportionality-based jurisprudence, a combative democracy, a federal structure – including legal diversity – and social state (*Sozialstaat*) principles. Especially the latter views associational rights also as tools for social justice and economic fairness, as evident in labour law (*Arbeitsrecht*) and the freedom of coalition enshrined under Article 9 paragraph 3, where collective bargaining rights are strongly protected.[151] This constitutes a flourishing environment of a multitude of associations in Germany today, enabling individuals to unite for manifold purposes.

In this context, ongoing debates, particularly concerning the negative freedom of association and instances of severe state interference, illustrate the dynamic nature of freedom of association and its application over time. They have to be perceived as healthy disputes concerning some of the most fundamental aspects of a democratic system. In this way, Germany's approach has influenced European human rights law, particularly through engagement with the European Court of Human Rights (ECtHR) and the European Court of Justice (ECJ). As an example, the ECtHR is drawing from the proportionality approach, which originated in Germany,[152] into broader European legal standards and also those concerning freedom of association enshrined in Article 11 of the European Convention on Human Rights.[153]

While Germany's legal framework therefore offers an influential and functional model for freedom of association, certain issues arise or persist that highlight potential threats to its current stability. The handling of Palestinian solidarity movements – which mainly fall under Article 8 but are, as previously highlighted, heavily linked with Article 9 – has drawn criticism, with the UN Special Rapporteur on the Promotion and Protection of the Right to Freedom of Opinion and Expression, Irene Khan, considering 'the response [from Germany] among the toughest, imposing a blanket ban on all demonstrations in support of Palestinian people from 7th to 21st October 2023, and pre-emptively banning several such gatherings'.[154] Amnesty International argues that restrictive measures on Palestinian organisations and pro-Palestinian demonstrations conflate legitimate political dissent with hate speech, limiting public discourse on foreign policy and disproportionately targeting these movements – and 'calls on the Berlin authorities to refrain from blanket bans of assemblies, so that the

[151] As an exemplary and insightful ruling in this context, see especially BVerfG 92, 365, whereby the Federal Constitutional Court reinforces the principle that collective bargaining must remain free from undue state interference while ensuring a fair balance between negotiating parties.

[152] L Hirschberg, *Der Grundsatz Der Verhältnismässigkeit* (Göttinger rechtswissenschaftliche Studien Bd. 106, Cham, Schwartz, 1981) 6.

[153] eg, Case 34503/97 *Demir and Baykara v Turkey* ECLI:CE:ECHR:2008:1112JUD003450397, [2008] ECHR 1345.

[154] United Nations, 'Global Threats to Freedom of Expression Arising from the Conflict in Gaza. Report of the Special Rapporteur on the Promotion and Protection of the Right to Freedom of Opinion and Expression, Irene Khan' (23 August 2024) www.un.org/unispal/document/report-special-rapporteur-23aug24/ accessed 14 March 2025.

rights to freedom of expression and freedom of peaceful assembly in Berlin are preserved for everyone'.[155] Such constraints not only raise concerns regarding all fundamental rights of communication but also set a precedent that may be used to curtail other forms of political advocacy.

Additionally, the aforementioned groups linked to the Reichsbürger movement showcase the immediate threat certain associations pose to the Federal Republic of Germany, and the necessity of balancing freedom of association against severe interferences by the state. This is potentially exacerbated by further, fundamental issues; as former Federal Constitutional Court President Andreas Voßkuhle warns, Germany risks a decline in its state capacity, potentially weakening its ability to uphold fundamental rights. He has called for significant state reforms to prevent the country from falling behind globally, highlighting a crucial concern: if governance structures become ineffective, the enforcement and protection of constitutional rights, including freedom of association, may be jeopardised.[156] These considerations are further reinforced through discussions on state reform, with calls for a more 'action-capable state' gaining prominence. Initiatives seeking structural changes to increase governmental efficiency aim to address current political and administrative challenges,[157] highlighting a contemporary necessity and also potential weaknesses. This is exacerbated by new challenges, particularly the preservation and development of European integration and the inclusion of new population groups. With Russia's war of aggression against Ukraine, there is also a renewed focus on the restoration and securing of peace in Europe,[158] whereas actors with various intentions apply pressure from the outside.[159]

Whilst these developments should not be considered to be the cause of an inevitable decline in fundamental rights in Germany, they clearly indicate that challenges persist, and, in some cases, are becoming even more urgent. The broader implications extend beyond individual cases, raising essential questions about the resilience of democratic freedoms in times of political and societal transformation. Ultimately, ongoing legal and political debates will shape the interpretation and application of these rights, emphasising the paradox that a stable democracy requires a functioning right to freedom of association, and such a freedom also necessitates the existence of a stable democratic system.

[155] Amnesty International, 'Protect the Protest: Against Blanket Bans of Demonstrations for the Rights of Palestinians' (12 September 2023) 4 www.amnesty.org/en/documents/eur23/7180/2023/en/ accessed 14 March 2025.

[156] ER Lautsch, 'Diese Vorschläge Sollen Deutschland Aus Der Lähmung Befreien', *Zeit* (12 March 2025) www.zeit.de/politik/deutschland/2025-03/initiative-fuer-einen-handlungsfaehigen-staat-staatsreform-bundespressekonferenz-peer-steinbrueck.

[157] 'Ex-Verfassungsrichter Fürchtet Deutschlands Abstieg Zum "Zweite-Welt-Land"', *Welt* (12 March 2025) www.welt.de/politik/deutschland/article255678502/Deutschland-in-der-Krise-Ex-Verfassungsrichter-fuerchtet-Abstieg-zum-Zweite-Welt-Land.html accessed 13 March 2025.

[158] Robbers (n 2) 42.

[159] T Paternoster and L Stroud, 'The Musk Effect: Could the X Owner Actually Impact Germany's Election?', *Euronews* (10 January 2025) www.euronews.com/my-europe/2025/01/10/the-musk-effect-could-the-x-owner-actually-impact-germanys-election accessed 13 March 2025.

5

*Freedom of Association in Türkiye**

FATIH ÖZTÜRK**

I. INTRODUCTION

FREEDOM OF ASSOCIATION in Türkiye, including the right to form associations and join them, is protected by the Turkish Constitution. Article 33 of the Constitution explicitly guarantees this right. Article 33 of the Turkish Constitution states that everyone has the right to form associations, or to become a member of an association, without prior permission. This is a fundamental right aimed at supporting democratic participation and civil society activities. The Law on Associations (Law No 5253) and other relevant regulations provide the legal basis for the establishment, operation, and supervision of associations in Türkiye. This law outlines the requirements for forming an association, including the minimum number of founders and the necessary documentation.

In this chapter, I will first examine Article 33 of the Constitution of Türkiye, the Law on Associations (Law No 5253), and relevant regulations. Second, I will explore cases from first instance courts. Third, I will examine cases from the Turkish Constitutional Court to analyse how the country's highest judicial body has interpreted the right to freedom of association. Finally, I will conclude with my reflections on the protection of freedom of association in Türkiye.

* Since 1 June of 2022, 'The United Nations changed the country's name from "Turkey" to "Türkiye" in foreign languages following Türkiye's request. UN Secretary-General's Spokesperson, Stephane Dujarric, stated that they received a letter from Foreign Minister Mevlüt Çavuşoğlu on June 1, in which he requested the country's name to be changed to "Türkiye" in foreign languages. Dujarric noted that the name change became effective as soon as the letter was received.' See turkiye.un.org/tr/184798-t%C3%BCrkiyenin-ad%C4%B1-bmde-yabanc%C4%B1-dillerde-de-art%C4%B1k-t%C3%BCrkiye.

** I would like to express my sincere thanks to Professor Maria Cahill for giving me the opportunity to be part of this book project.

II. THE TURKISH LEGAL SYSTEM

Modern Türkiye has a civil law system similar to that of most other European countries. Legislation is the main source for law and is binding on courts.[1] According to the classifications of European law, Turkish law belongs to the family of Continental European law.[2] This form of law contains separate classes such as Common law, Continental European law, Islamic law, Socialist law, and American law.[3] After the disintegration of the Ottoman Empire and the creation of the Republic of Türkiye, the Turkish state aimed to establish its legal and social order according to western norms.[4] To this end, the framers of the Republic took very radical actions. In 1924, the Turkish Grand National Assembly (TBMM) passed a law to abolish the Sharia (religious) courts (Ser'iye Mahkemeleri). In 1926, the TBMM abolished Islamic law and forced the Swiss Federal Code Civil law system (with adaptations for Turkish society) into the new state's legal system. The German Commercial Code was added into Turkish Commercial law. In addition, the Italian Criminal Code of 1889 was adapted and put into effect in July 1926.[5] However, a new Turkish Criminal law became effective in June 2005 in order to come in line with the law of the European Union (EU). Turkish law was made to resemble the Continental European Civil law. The Turkish Parliament now enacts new laws and regulations on a daily basis to conform to EU standards.[6]

There is currently great conflict in the legal arena of modern Türkiye. In the First Constitution of the Republic (The Constitution of 1924), Article 2 stated that the state religion was Islam. However, the fathers of the Republic believed that secularism was to be one of the most important tools of modern Turkish society. Thus in 1928, although the religion of the state was Islam, this was removed from the Constitution.[7] In 1937, secularism was added into the Turkish constitutional system,[8] and today, the modern Turkish state struggles with its

[1] See T Ansay and EC Schneider (eds), *Introduction to Turkish Business Law* (Ankara, TK, 2002) 3.

[2] MK Oğuzman, *Medeni Hukuka Giris* [*Introduction to Civil Law*] (Istanbul, Filiz, 1990) 17–25.

[3] ibid 18–19.

[4] See Atatürk's strategy to establish a western style state, P Dumont, 'Hojas For Revolution: The Religious Strategy of Mustafa Kemal Ataturk' (1980) 1 *Journal of the American Institute for the Study of Middle Eastern Civilization* 17–32.

[5] See Oğuzman (n 2) 20–22.

[6] See about Türkiye's efforts to become the EU member, PR Hugg, 'The Republic of Türkiye in Europe: Reconsidering the Luxembourg Exclusion' (2000) 23 *Fordham International Law Journal* 606–706. Moreover; ES Hurd, 'Negotiating Europe: The Politics of Religion and the Prospects for Turkish Accession' (2006) 32 *Review of International Studies* 401–418. DD Banani, 'Reforming History: Turkey's Legal Regime and Its Potential Accession to the European Union' (2003) 26 *Boston College International and Comparative Law Journal* 113–127.

[7] See K Boyle and J Sheen (eds), *Freedom of Religion and Belief* (London and New York, Routledge, 1997) 389.

[8] See AS Gözübüyük, *Hukuka Giriş* [*Introduction to Law*] (Ankara, TK, 2006) 61.

secularist traditions in light of an Islamic citizenry.[9] Traditional Turkish state officials prefer to follow the French and German version of secularism, instead of that of the UK, Canada and America. The Turkish state still continues to seek influence over individual thought and religious belief.[10] Some foreign observers of Türkiye believe that the orientation of secularism will be one of the keystones to the future of Turkish society and policy practices.[11] Rigid adherence to secularism may compromise democracy if religious freedom is curtailed in the name of protecting secularism.

Lastly, I would like to give some basic information about the Turkish court system. The Turkish judicial system sets out the civil law court system as composed of:

a) General First Instance courts, including: i) criminal courts: magistrate, general criminal, and heavy penalty courts; and ii) civil courts: civil courts of peace, general civil courts, and commercial courts;
b) Specialised First Instance courts, including juvenile courts, land registration courts, labour courts, intellectual property courts, and family law courts;
c) The Supreme Court of Appeals (in Turkish '*Yargıtay*') as the court of last instance for reviewing decisions and judgments given by criminal and civil courts;
d) The administrative court system is composed of administrative courts, tax courts and regional administrative courts;
e) The Council of State (in Turkish '*Danıştay*') as the court of law instance for administrative and tax court decisions; and
f) The Constitutional Court (in Turkish '*Anayasa Mahkemesi*'), which examines the constitutionality of laws in respect of both their form and substance, and judicial review decrees having the force of law and the rules of procedure of the Turkish Parliament.[12]

The Turkish Constitutional Court may reach one of two different outcomes when reviewing the constitutionality of laws (judicial review): either rejecting the annulment request or annulling the law. Annulment decisions ensure that unconstitutional laws are repealed. According to Article 153 of the 1982

[9] See about secularism and secular practices, Y Sezen, *Turk Toplumunun Laiklik Anlayışı* [*Turkish Society's Understanding of Secularism*] (Istanbul, MUIFVY, 1993).

See also Edip Yuksel, who is a Kurdish Human Rights Activist, and fled from Türkiye to the US claiming that the Republic secular ideology, controls, manipulates and exploits religious beliefs and attacks those who are not converted to the official version. See E Yuksel, 'Cannibal Democracy, Theocratic Secularism: The Turkish Version' (1999) 7 *Cardozo Journal of International & Comparative Law* at 467.

[10] See more with examples, C Morris, *The New Turkey: The Quiet Revolution on the Edge of Europe* (London, Granta Books, 2005) 60–86.

[11] FS Larrabee and IO Lesser, *Turkish Foreign Policy in an Age of Uncertainty* (Santa Monica, Rand, 2003) xiv. See more, JS Szyliowicz, 'Religion, Politics and Democracy in Turkey' in W Safran (ed), *The Secular and The Sacred: Nation, Religion and Politics* (London, Frank Cass, 2003) 188–216.

[12] See Ansay and Schneider (n 1) 14-6.

Constitution, a law is repealed after the annulment ruling is published in the Official Gazette. Established in 1961, the Constitutional Court has sometimes overstepped its primary purpose by acting as a legislative body. However, constitutional courts are primarily designed to review and protect legal changes related to fundamental political issues, such as fundamental rights, freedoms, and minority rights. Their main duty is to oversee whether the decisions of political authorities and the legislature comply with the constitution. Consequently, their work unavoidably involves political decisions, and complete neutrality in such matters contradicts the very nature of their function. In Turkish constitutional jurisprudence, the doctrine of judicial activism leads the Constitutional Court to interpret its authority as broadly as possible. While the US Supreme Court tends to limit its own powers, the Turkish Constitutional Court has shown a tendency to expand its jurisdiction. The ambiguous, subjective, and ideological provisions in the 1961 and 1982 Constitutions have made judicial activism highly feasible.

In fact, the Constitutional Court has gone so far that, in a 1993 ruling, it asserted the authority to suspend the enforcement of laws, despite the fact that neither the 1961 nor the 1982 Constitution granted such authority. In general, the Turkish Constitutional Court has engaged in judicial activism, particularly in areas such as privatisation, government savings in the social sector, suspension of executive decisions, and constitutional amendment reviews. Like other state elites, the Turkish Constitutional Court has perceived itself as the guardian of the state and a supreme tutelary body, consistently viewing elected political elites with suspicion, considering them opportunistic representatives of temporary and partial interests.

Lastly, the so-called 'Turkish-Sstyle presidential system', which has been in place since the 2017 Constitutional Amendment, appears to be a hybrid of the parliamentary and presidential systems. However, in reality, it resembles neither a true parliamentary system nor a presidential system, presenting a unique and unprecedented model of governance.

III. ARTICLE 33 OF THE CONSTITUTION OF 1982 AND THE LAW ON ASSOCIATIONS (LAW NO. 5253)

Article 33 of the Turkish Constitution is titled under the heading 'Freedom of Association' and reads as follows:

> Everyone has the right to form associations, or become a member of an association, or withdraw from membership without prior permission. No one shall be compelled to become or remain a member of an association. Freedom of association may be restricted only by law on the grounds of national security, public order, prevention of commission of crime, public morals, public health and protecting the freedoms of other individuals. The formalities, conditions, and procedures to be applied in the exercise of freedom of association shall be prescribed by law. Associations may be

> dissolved or suspended from activity by the decision of a judge in cases prescribed by law. However, where it is required for, and a delay constitutes a prejudice to, national security, public order, prevention of commission or continuation of a crime, or an arrest, an authority may be vested with power by law to suspend the association from activity. The decision of this authority shall be submitted for the approval of the judge having jurisdiction within twenty-four hours. The judge shall announce his/her decision within forty-eight hours; otherwise, this administrative decision shall be annulled automatically. Provisions of the first paragraph shall not prevent imposition of restrictions on the rights of armed forces and security forces officials and civil servants to the extent that the duties of civil servants so require. The provisions of this article shall also apply to foundations.

In Turkish Civil Code No 4721 and the Associations Law No. 5253, the definition of an association is almost identical. Associations are defined as legal entities formed by at least seven real or legal persons who pool their knowledge and efforts continuously to achieve a specific and common purpose, excluding profit-sharing (Turkish Civil Law Code, Article 56/1 and Associations Law, Article 2-a). The individuals who form associations are called members, and two key elements in the definition of associations are members and purpose. The reason for the existence of associations is their objectives; if it is no longer possible to achieve their objectives, the associations are considered to have ceased to exist on their own (Turkish Civil Law Code, Article 87/1-1). The most significant distinction between associations, trade unions, and political parties lies in the differences in their objectives. According to the accepted view in Turkish law, the broad definition of the concept of associations includes both political parties and trade unions. Therefore, in the absence of specific regulations, these two institutions are subject to the legal provisions applicable to associations. Turkish Civil Code, Article 56-1, in parallel with the Associations Law, Article 30, states that associations cannot be established for purposes that are contrary to law and morality. In other words, in Turkish law freedom of association provides protection for various forms of organisations, such as political parties, trade unions, associations, or foundations.

The Constitution of Türkiye, Article 34, regarding the 'right to organize meetings and demonstrations', states that '[e]veryone has the right to organize meetings and demonstrations, unarmed and non-violent, without prior permission.' Article 51, concerning the 'right to form trade unions', reads, '[w]orkers and employers have the right to establish unions and confederations to protect and improve the economic and social rights and interests of their members, as well as the right to freely join and withdraw from them, without prior permission.'

These provisions affirm that these rights can be exercised by everyone without the need for prior authorisation. However, the articles also specify situations where these rights can be restricted. Such restrictions may apply in cases of national security, public order, prevention of crime, public health, public morality, and the protection of the freedoms of others.

In recent years, the amendments to association legislation in our country clearly reflect an intent by the ruling power to intervene in the liberal structure of the 'civil' sphere. It is evident that these changes impose restrictions on the citizens' most fundamental constitutional right – the right to association. As an author rightly stated,

> [i]t is a legitimate expectation within the scope of the right to legal security that every legal regulation should comply with the Constitution, which is the fundamental text, and be consistent with other legislation governing the field. The amendment made to Article 23 of the Law on Associations, requiring membership admissions and resignations to be reported in writing to the local authority, is a clear example of the state's attempt to bring associations under public control through an additional reporting obligation, despite the information already being available to public authorities. This provision of the law evidently violates the freedom of association.[13]

The author emphasises two fundamental principles of constitutional law: the principle of legal certainty and freedom of association.

It is stated that every legal regulation must comply with the fundamental provisions of the constitution and not contradict other relevant legislation. This is essential for ensuring individuals' trust in the legal system and enhancing predictability. The requirement to notify local authorities of membership admissions and resignations, despite the existing information infrastructure, mandates an additional reporting obligation. This has been criticised as imposing unnecessary administrative burdens and indirectly restricting individuals' right to association. Gümüş rightly argues that the regulation violates freedom of association. Freedom of association is one of the cornerstones of democratic societies, encompassing the right of individuals to form groups, establish associations, and carry out their activities. Excessive oversight or bureaucratic barriers can hinder the effective exercise of this right. In conclusion, the critique underlines the importance of safeguarding constitutional principles and avoiding unnecessary restrictions on individual rights and freedoms. Such regulations should undergo a constitutional review process to ensure that freedoms are not unnecessarily curtailed.

Although the Turkish Constitutional Court stands at the top of the judicial system in Türkiye, most Turkish lawyers avoid taking their cases to the Constitutional Court after finalising them in the Court of Cassation (*Yargıtay*) to prevent an additional two to four years of legal delay. For this reason, we will examine two interesting cases ruled by the Court of Cassation, which are directly related to our topic of the right to form associations.

[13] M Gümüş, 'Dernekler Mevzuatında Son Dönemde Yapılan Değişikliklerin Örgütlenme Özgürlüğüne Etkileri' [The Impact of Recent Amendments to Association Legislation on Freedom of Association], (2022) 3 *Ankara Barosu Dergisi* 497.

A. The Supreme Court of Appeals, 9th Criminal Chamber, Decision Dated May 22, 2003, Case No. 2003/627 – Decision No. 2003/870

In this case, the defendants were accused of establishing an association that violated the principles stated in Article 5 of the Associations Law No 2908, Article 174 of the Turkish Constitution, and Law No 677, which mandates the closure of all dervish lodges, tekkes, and tombs. The defendants allegedly continued their activities in violation of these 'laws' and faced prosecution under Article 76/1 of the Associations Law for their association's activities. The Court sentenced the defendants to punishment and ordered the closure of the association. The specific case concerned an association named 'Hatay Tombs and Shrines' Protection and Beautification Association.' The association's founding statute included goals and activities that violated the prohibitions in Article 5/9 of the Associations Law and Article 174 of the Constitution, such as attempting to repeal or revive revolutionary laws and forbidden matters. The association was also accused of violating Law No 677, which prohibits the reopening or re-establishing of closed tekkes, dervish lodges, or tombs, and engaging in activities related to prohibited titles or services associated with them. However, after examining the case, it was found that the association's statute did not involve any prohibited activities, and no evidence was found to show that the defendants engaged in activities contrary to the law. Furthermore, the defendants were previously acquitted in another case concerning the same issue, where the Court found that the purpose of the association was merely to ensure the proper maintenance of the tombs in Antakya and provide a clean environment for visitors. Given this, there was no intent to commit a crime. The Court, after reviewing the evidence, found that there was insufficient evidence to convict the defendants, and the decision to convict them was overturned. The case emphasised that the association's activities did not violate the law and the defendants' actions were not criminal. This decision was made under the previous Associations Law No 2908, which was later repealed and replaced with more restrictive regulations. This decision reflects a more liberal interpretation of the association's activities at the time and highlights the importance of distinguishing between lawful association activities and those that violate legal or constitutional principles.

B. The Supreme Court of Appeals, 9th Criminal Chamber, Decision Dated November 18, 2003, Case No. 2003/1993 – Decision No. 2003/2113

The defendants were members of the board of directors of the *Anadolu Tutuklu ve Hükümlü Aileleri Yardımlaşma Derneği* (TAYAD). They had decided to stage a hunger strike to prevent the establishment of F-type prisons and had also distributed a declaration supporting a death fast. The decision recorded in the association's Minutes of Meetings dated 29 November 2000, stated:

> The state intends to place our detained and convicted children in F-type prisons. Our children are determined not to enter these F-type prisons, and as a result, they are on an indefinite hunger strike and death fast. To support their rightful demands and to prevent their deaths, the association members unanimously decided to begin an indefinite hunger strike on December 1, 2000.

The police report dated 4 December 2000, confirmed that some of the defendants began their hunger strike in accordance with the board's decision. The association's stated purpose in its bylaws was to 'assist among families of detainees and convicts, help meet all their material, social, and other needs in a manner worthy of human dignity, and strive for the full realization of human rights and freedoms'. The defendants were convicted of violating Article 37/1 of the Associations Law No 2908, which states that members of an association can only engage in activities related to the purpose and activities as specified in the bylaws. They were sentenced to six months in prison under Article 77/3 for participating in activities beyond the scope of the association's purpose. The prison sentences were later converted into fines. The Court of Appeals upheld the conviction of the defendants who signed the board's decision for the hunger strike. However, for the defendants who did not sign the 29 November 2000 board decision and whose names were not listed in the 4 December 2000 report, the Court ruled that there was an insufficient amount of definitive and convincing evidence needed to prove that they had participated in unlawful activities or committed the alleged crime. Therefore, the convictions were overturned. Although a similar penal provision exists in Article 30/a of the Law No 5253 on Associations, a subsequent amendment by Law No 5728 changed the penalty for such offenses to a judicial fine instead of imprisonment. This decision highlights the legal limits placed on associations, especially regarding activities that fall outside their stated purposes. The case also demonstrates how legal penalties for associations that engage in prohibited activities can be adjusted through legal amendments, particularly when changing the scope of penalties from imprisonment to fines.

IV. TURKISH CONSTITUTIONAL COURT CASES REGARDING FREEDOM OF ASSOCIATION

According to the Turkish Constitutional Court's ruling in the Emin Aydın Case (Application No 2013/2602, Decision Date: 23/01/2014): 'Freedom of expression not only includes the freedom to 'hold opinions and beliefs' but also the freedom to 'express and disseminate' these thoughts and beliefs'. Additionally, it encompasses the right to 'receive and impart information and opinions'. In this context, the Constitutional Court ruled in the same decision that freedom of expression or speech means that 'individuals should be able to freely access news, information, and the opinions of others, should not be condemned for the thoughts and beliefs they hold, and should be able to express, explain, defend, convey, and disseminate these ideas alone or together with others through various means'. Since the right to freedom of expression is inherently closely linked to the right to freedom of association, it would not be an exaggeration to say that they are like two sides of the same coin – one cannot truly exist without the other.

The Turkish Constitutional Court has addressed various cases concerning the freedom of association. For instance, in the case of *Kristal-İş Sendikası* (Application No 2014/12166, 2/7/2015), the Court examined issues related to trade union rights. Similarly, in *Birleşik Metal İşçileri Sendikası* (Application No 2015/14862, 9/5/2018), the Court dealt with matters pertaining to union activities. Another notable case is *Muharrem Çimen* (Application No 2016/5002, 23/3/2023), which also delved into aspects of the freedom of association.

The *Kristal-İş Sendikası* case before the Turkish Constitutional Court dealt with the right to freedom of association, specifically in the context of trade union activities. The case was brought by Kristal-İş, a labour union representing workers in the glass industry. The union argued that certain actions and decisions by the authorities interfered with their rights under the Constitution and international law, including the right to freely organise and engage in collective bargaining. The union claimed that administrative or judicial decisions limited their ability to organise and represent workers effectively. They alleged that these restrictions undermined the rights of workers to collectively negotiate working conditions. The case addressed whether the actions taken against the union violated the constitutional guarantee of freedom of association. The Constitutional Court assessed the case within the framework of Article 51 of the Turkish Constitution, which guarantees the right to form and join trade unions. It also considered international treaties, such as the European Convention on Human Rights (Article 11) and International Labour Organization (ILO) conventions, which Türkiye has ratified. The Court held that any restrictions on the activities of a union must be proportional, necessary in a democratic society, and pursue a legitimate aim. Unreasonable interference with union activities constitutes a violation of the right to freedom of association. The case is significant, as it reaffirms the principles protecting trade unions and highlights the importance of ensuring workers' rights to organise without undue state interference.

The *Muharrem Çimen* case before the Turkish Constitutional Court addressed the alleged violation of trade union freedom due to disciplinary action taken against an employee for participating in a slowdown strike. Muharrem Çimen, the applicant, was an employee who participated in a slowdown strike organised by his trade union. In response, his employer imposed disciplinary measures against him. Çimen contended that these actions infringed upon his constitutional right to trade union freedom. The applicant argued that participating in union-organised actions, such as slow-down strikes, is a fundamental aspect of trade union freedom. The case examined whether the disciplinary actions taken were proportionate and justified, considering the nature of the union activity involved. The Court evaluated the case in light of Article 51 of the Turkish Constitution, which safeguards the right to form and join trade unions. It also referenced international conventions, including the European Convention on Human Rights (Article 11), which protects freedom of assembly and association. The Court arrived at the conclusion that participation in a slowdown strike, as a form of industrial action, falls within the scope of legitimate trade union activities. Imposing disciplinary penalties on an employee solely for engaging in such union activities constitutes a violation of the right to trade union freedom. This judgment underscores the importance of protecting employees' rights to participate in union activities without fear of retaliation, reinforcing the constitutional guarantee of trade union freedom.

In another interesting case, the Court concluded in the *Tayfun Cengiz* decision that

> freedom of association not only includes the right of individuals or legal entities to establish an organization and become a member of one, but also encompasses the ability to request human, material, and financial resources from local, foreign, and international sources, as well as the right to receive and utilize these resources.[14]

The Constitutional Court of Türkiye has adjudicated several significant cases concerning the freedom of association, particularly focusing on the dissolution of political parties and the rights of trade unions. For example, the *Welfare Party* (*Refah Partisi*) case; in 1998 the Constitutional Court dissolved the Welfare Party on the grounds that its activities violated the principle of secularism enshrined in the Turkish Constitution. The party appealed to the European Court of Human Rights (ECHR), arguing that the dissolution infringed upon their rights to freedom of association and expression. However, the ECHR upheld the decision, stating that the party's policies were incompatible with democratic principles. Another one was the *Democratic Society Party* (*DTP*) case, in 2009 the Constitutional Court ordered the closure of the pro-Kurdish DTP, citing its alleged connections with the Kurdistan Workers' Party (PKK), which is designated as a terrorist organisation by Türkiye. The Court also imposed political bans on several party members. This decision was met with criticism from the European Union, which viewed it as a setback for democratic reforms in Türkiye. In the very recent *Şerafettin*

[14] AYM (Turkish Constitutional Court), Tayfun Cengiz Decision, App No 2013/8463, Verdict dated 18/9/2014, § 36. See more about freedom of association in Türkiye, U Karan, *Örgütlenme ve Toplanma Özgürlüğü: Anayasa Mahkemesine Bireysel Başvuru El Kitapları Serisi 3* [*Freedom of Association and Assembly: Individual Application to the Constitutional Court, Handbook Series 3*], (Ankara, Avrupa Konseyi, MRK Baskı, 2018).

Can Atalay case, in 2023 the Constitutional Court ruled that the continued detention of Şerafettin Can Atalay, a member of Parliament (Workers' Party of Türkiye), violated his rights to be elected and to engage in political activity. Atalay had been convicted of attempting to overthrow the government and was elected as an MP while his appeal was pending. The Court's decision underscored the importance of legislative immunity and the protection of political rights. The Constitutional Court ruled twice in favour of Atalay, but the Court of Cassation did not implement these rulings, and the first-instance court followed the Court of Cassation's decision. As a result, the elected member of Parliament, Atalay, is still in prison.

These cases reflect the Constitutional Court's pivotal role in interpreting and enforcing the principles of freedom of association in Türkiye, balancing state interests with individual and collective rights. However, it should not be forgotten that the main issue in Türkiye is the freedom of expression, as in a place where there is no real freedom of expression, it is impossible for other freedoms to exist and develop. Therefore, just like in other countries, the key to freedoms in Türkiye is through freedom of expression. Without building a system based on the rule of law, a constitutional republic cannot be established. In my view, the construction of a constitutional republic is only possible in a system where freedom of expression is absolute. To understand why freedom of expression is the most crucial issue in Türkiye, one must consider the events of 19 March 2025, when Istanbul's elected mayor, Ekrem İmamoğlu, was detained and arrested. In response, millions of people participated in protests under the framework of freedom of expression. However, the blocking of social media platforms and the disruption of public transportation in Istanbul served as further proof of the restrictions on this fundamental right.[15]

Between 1959 and 2016, the European Court of Human Rights (ECHR) issued a total of 656 violation rulings related to freedom of expression – 265 of these decisions (40 per cent) were against Türkiye.[16] This statistic clearly demonstrates that freedom of expression is the most significant legal issue in Türkiye. As a legal scholar and academic with 20 years of experience, I argue that the root cause of this problem lies in the positivist legal education taught in law schools. This approach has produced legal professionals who, instead of prioritising justice, have developed a culture of submission to those in power. Therefore, unfortunately, it does not seem possible to speak of judicial independence in Türkiye, especially in the last 200 years since the 1800s. On the contrary, it would be more accurate to call it the judiciary of the executive.

[15] See more, E Wither (BBC) 'Turkish President Etrdogan's main rival jailed' www.bbc.com/news/articles/c0egjvj8vdro, last accessed 24 March 2025.

[16] See violation by Article and by states (1959–2016), www.echr.coe.int/documents/d/echr/Stats_violation_1959_2016_ENG, last accessed 24 March 2024.

V. CONCLUDING REMARKS

The constitutional republic of a society or country is determined by looking at the functioning of the legal system built in that society or country. In fact, one can easily understand whether rights and freedoms are respected in that society simply by observing the functioning of traffic. You can even gauge the level of law and justice in a country by noticing whether people smoke without considering those walking behind them. In Türkiye, the system which has been in place since the 1800s was built upon elitist pillars and causes the innocent and honest people of this country to be the ones made to lose in the struggles that take place above. They have no race or religion. Sometimes they are Muslim, sometimes Jewish, sometimes Christian, and sometimes atheist. But their common point is being honourable in the face of the dishonourable. We believe that the disease of elitism is most evident in the fields of law and medicine. In a constitutional republic, people, citizens, will fear the power of the laws, not of individuals. Individuals will derive their power from the laws, not from their positions or the wealth they have accumulated.

Constitutionalism refers to the limitation of state or political power and the protection of individual freedoms. The goal of constitutionalism is to ensure as much freedom as possible for individuals, while also restraining the power of political authorities. Contrary to popular belief, constitutionalism existed in these lands long before the 1808 *Sened-i İttifak* (Deed of Agreement). In fact, constitutional judicial review, meaning the subjection of first-instance court decisions to the highest norm, the constitution, existed centuries ago in Turkish-Islamic states (the Great Seljuk State 1037–1194) through the *Divan-ı Mezalim* (the court of atrocity) institution, where the decisions of judges were corrected by a higher judicial body.

In conclusion, constitutional rights in Türkiye should begin with first-instance courts, and it is essential to move away from the Napoleonic model where agents of the administration are protected by legal loopholes. Instead, a system should be adopted where lawsuits can be directly filed and administrators are held accountable. In Türkiye, freedom of association is a constitutional right protected under Article 33 of the 1982 Constitution, which guarantees everyone the right to form associations without prior permission. This right is also subject to Türkiye's international obligations under instruments such as the ECHR, particularly Article 11. While the legal framework permits a wide range of associational activity, restrictions can be imposed on grounds such as national security, public order, or the prevention of crime. In practice, the Constitutional Court has played an active role in upholding associational rights, particularly in cases involving the closure of associations or political parties, emphasising proportionality and democratic pluralism. However, concerns persist regarding limitations on certain civil society organisations, especially those critical of the government.

6

Freedom of Association and its Restrictions in Indonesia

INNA JUNAENAH*

I. INTRODUCTION

THIS CHAPTER EXAMINES freedom of association in Indonesia, which encompasses the legal recognition of the rights held by civil society organisations. The author follows Salamon, Sokolowski and List by defining civil society organisations in a broad sense, ie, those organisations that exist outside the institutional structures of the government.[1] Within this definition, the term 'civil society organisations' signifies self-governing associations, allowing people to join, participate and/or channel their solidarity voluntarily, including both informal and formal registered organisations, as well as those of a religious and secular nature. Salamon et al. provide some instances that exist as a broad grouping of entities, such as the following:

> hospitals, universities, social clubs, professional organisations, day care centers, grassroots development organisations, health clinics, environmental groups, family counseling agencies, self-help groups, religious congregations, sports clubs, job training centers, human rights organisations, community associations, soup kitchens, homeless shelters, and many more.[2]

The broad sense of association may include the interpretation that an established association manifests sector-based characteristics, such as those in economics and politics.[3] This is why, under Elfudllatsani et al.'s notes, several laws[4]

* I thank Ghaniya, a Maldivian PhD graduated from Universiti Teknologi MARA, Malaysia, for language editing of my manuscript. Gratitude also goes to Center for State Policy Studies of Unpad for supporting the author to get connected with this collaboration.

[1] Preface, LM Salamon, SW Sokolowski and R List, *Global Civil Society: An Overview* (Center for Civil Society Studies Institute for Policy Studies The Johns Hopkins University, 2003).

[2] ibid 1.

[3] The economics sector allows the establishment of an association of trade unions and the politics sector is indicated in joining political parties. NS Hafid, T Arifin and I Fauzia, 'Hak Berserikat Dan Berkumpul Menurut UUD Pasal 28E Ayat 3 Dan Pasal 21 Ayat 1 DUHAM; Tinjauan Aktivitas Ekonomi Islam' (2025) 10 *Al-Muamalat: Jurnal Ilmu Hukum & Ekonomi Syariah* 49, 56.

[4] Such as the act regulating political parties, inherited from Dutch colonial law in *Staatsblad* No 64 of 1870, the Environmental Act 1982, and the Civil Society Organisation Act No 2 of 2017.

recognise a type of alliance, including associations involving political parties, incorporated organisations, non-governmental organisations and civil society organisations.[5] Following Elfudllatsani et al.'s work, this chapter considers 'associations' through the lens of non-governmental organisations and civil society organisations.

The broad sense of such a meaning allows us to depict Indonesia as home to about 568,884 registered organisations and societal groups, as released by the Ministry of Home Affairs in January 2024.[6] Of the 509 surveyed, 302 entities are classified as incorporated organisations.[7] A similar survey also suggests that 21 entities are affiliated with unincorporated organisations.[8] It indicates that Indonesia also respects unregistered associations as they exist, and no prohibition is explicitly articulated on establishing an organisation. In addition, the main concerns asserted by the 509 organisations vary. The utmost concern is with people empowerment, including among women, children, persons with disabilities, and other marginalised groups (190 organisations). Other prominent concerns articulated in the survey include health (69), human rights and democracy (63), environment and climate change (55), broadening protection for marginalised groups (30), public services (28), SDGs (24), diversity, tolerance, and peace (12), legal aid (6), and labour (3).[9]

Drawing from Rukmana Amanwinata's doctoral thesis, Raja Adil Siregar highlights the crucial value of freedom of association, as it allows individuals to channel their aspirations, assert their collective interests, and participate in decision-making processes.[10] This chapter emphasises the concept of civil society organisations in relation to the freedom of association within the legal framework centred on the 1945 Constitution, the Human Rights Act No 39 of 1999, and the Civil Society Organisations Act of 2013, with its amendment in 2017. As for a brief introduction to Indonesia, the Constitution also grants the President the authority to participate in international agreements, one of which may include ratifying a covenant under United Nations initiatives.[11] The legal framework underpinning freedom of association, therefore, includes Act No 12 of 2006, which ratifies the International Covenant on Civil and Political

[5] B Elfudllatsani, I and A Riwanto, 'Kajian Mengenai Kebebasan Berkumpul Dan Berserikat Pasal 28E Ayat (3) Undang-Undang Dasar 1945 Melalui Organisasi Kemasyarakatan Kaitannya Dengan Teori Kedaulatan Rakyat Dan Hak Asasi Manusia' (2019) 7 *Jurnal Hukum dan Pembangunan Ekonomi* 52, 56.

[6] INFID, 'Laporan Survei Kondisi Eksisting Dan Kapasitas Kelembagaan OMS Di Indonesia' (2024) 1.

[7] ibid.

[8] ibid.

[9] ibid 34–35.

[10] RA Siregar, 'Tinjauan Yuridis Terhadap Kebebasan Berserikat, Berkumpul Dan Mengeluarkan Pendapat Berdasarkan Undang-Undang Nomor 17 Tahun 2013 Tentang Organisasi Kemasyarakatan' (2015) 2 *Jurnal Online Mahasiswa Fakultas Hukum Universitas Riau* 1, 6 www.neliti.com/publications/34427/tinjauan-yuridis-terhadap-kebebasan-berserikat-berkumpul-dan-mengeluarkan-pendap.

[11] Art 11 of the 1945 Constitution of Republic of Indonesia.

Rights.[12] The Convention binds Indonesia as a State Party to the United Nations, and it was ratified in 2006.[13]

The Civil Society Organisations Act 2013, as amended in 2017, encourages associations to be aligned with the primary purposes of the nation-state of Indonesia. Any violation of this alignment may result in a restriction. Since the 2017 amendment, there have been few discussions or criticisms regarding the provisions that removed the role of the court in the process of banning an association. Instead, recent regulations have been enacted with provisions deemed to address criticism of organisations over the government's policies. In addressing this, this chapter highlights the queries on the extent of legal positions underpinning the freedom of association. It seeks to establish whether the Constitution recognises the right to freedom of association, by the extent of the rights translated into legislation and any indications to restrict particular behaviour of associations.

This chapter proceeds as follows: section II considers the nature of freedom of association as a constitutional right and in light of background controversies between those involved in drafting the 1945 Constitution. Section III outlines the scope of the right to freedom of association as protected under the terms of the Civil Society Organisations Act 2013 as amended in 2017. Section IV, meanwhile, draws attention to various ways in which the autonomy of civil society organisations is compromised and the right to freedom of association is restricted. A conclusion reflects on the contours of the right within Indonesia's legal and political culture.

II. FREEDOM OF ASSOCIATION AS A CONSTITUTIONAL RIGHT

Fundamentally, freedom of association is recognised by the 1945 Constitution.[14] Article 28 and 28(3) of the 1945 Constitution consider freedom of association as one package with the freedom of assembly and freedom of thought, both in oral and written form, and further to be governed by law. As sourced from minutes of the constitutional amendment, some concerns highlighted several matters about recognising human rights in the constitutional provision in the initial independence and constitutional rights, which secure freedom of association in the amendment of the 1945 Constitution.[15]

[12] International Covenant on Civil and Political Rights (16 December 1966).

[13] 'Status of Ratification Interactive Dashboard' indicators.ohchr.org/.

[14] The origin of the 1945 Constitution was prepared in upholding the independence of Indonesia inherited by the civil law legal tradition brought about the Netherlands post colonialism. The then additional provisions providing human rights were enacted through the second phase of constitutional amendments in 2000.

[15] Editors, *Naskah Komprehensif Perubahan Undang-Undang Dasar Negara Republik Indonesia Tahun 1945, Latar Belakang, Proses, Dan Hasil Pembahasan 1999-2002, Buku VIII Warga Negara Dan Penduduk, Hak Asasi Manusia, Dan Agama* (Revisi, Sekretariat Jenderal dan Kepaniteraan M ahkamah Konstitusi, 2010).

A debate behind such a constitutional right occurred where the framers of the Constitution were of two main distinct contentions concerning the narratives of 'human rights,'[16] ie, they were in opposition as to whether human rights should be materialised into the Constitution. Soekarno and Supomo disagreed, whereas Mohammad Hatta and Mohammad Yamin agreed with materialising human rights in the constitutional provisions. For Soekarno, the freedom of association, alongside freedom of speech and assembly, was perceived as prejudiced in reflecting individualistic and liberal values, which might contrast with the collective realm of the Indonesian nation-state.[17]

Contrariwise, Mohammad Hatta and Mohammad Yamin raised the counterargument that ignoring human rights in the Constitution might lead to an autocratic government, which risked undermining protection for the country's people. Yamin argues that the absence of a stipulation recognising people's right to protect their rights would contradict the notion of the 'republican' principle. A compromise was agreed upon to include several rights, including freedom of association; however, those entitlements were to be further regulated in legislation.

It was decided that fundamental ideas about human rights were best accommodated in the then-inaugurated Constitution, ultimately taking the central issue of freedom as its core. Such consensus reflects that the framers of the 1945 Constitution did not neglect the important and historical role of pioneering civil society organisations prior to Indonesian independence in 1945. For instance, the *Sarekat Dagang Islam* (Islamic Trade Union, 1868–1956) was among the organisations acting in the collective movement during the National Revival period. In a similar era, *Jong Java* (Young Java, 1918), the *Jong Sumatranen Bond* (Young Sumatrans Union, 1917), the *Studerenden Vereeniging Minahasa* (Minahasan Study Union, 1918), *Jong Ambon* (Young Ambon, 1918), the *Sarekat Ambon* (Ambonese Union, 1920), and the Pasundan (Land of the Sundanese, 1914) represented youth movement organisations. Others were also found to be faith-based organisations, such as Muhammadiyah (1912), the first women's organisation – Aisyiyah (1917), Nadhlatul Ulama (NU, 1926), and *Persatuan Islam* (Islamic Union, 1923).[18]

Recently, Nadhlatul Ulama and Muhammadiyah have been progressively developing several sub-autonomous divisions and foundations, serving communities by preparing and implementing programmes to address social problems. For instance, Nadhlatul Ulama and Muhammadiyah work to establish numerous educational institutions, from kindergarten to university, and operate numerous hospitals and medical clinics.[19] In 2018, USAID also acknowledged Nahdlatul

[16] ibid 26–29.

[17] In Indonesia's culture, this spirit is well-known as '*gotong-royong*' (hand-in-hand teamwork) and '*kekeluargaan*' ('kinship', or sometimes, it can also imply a sense of familial closeness).

[18] MC Ricklefs, *A History of Modern Indonesia since c. 1200*, 4th edn (London, Macmillan International Higher Education 2008) 204–218.

[19] USAID, 'Civil Society Organizations In Indonesia' (2018).

Ulama and Muhammadiyah as among the active faith-based organisations providing services in education, health, and other developmental sectors.[20] Discussed later, the important strategic position of these organisations creates concern that the government may restrain their criticisms, but not by directly banning mechanisms.

During the discussion of the second phase of amendment of the 1945 Constitution, the Ad Hoc Commission for the 1945 Constitutional Amendment agreed more with the sense of 'regulation', rather than a provided 'guarantee', for the freedom of association, in addition to freedom of assembly. To emphasise the sense of 'regulation', Gregorius Seto Harianto, Khaliq, and Nursyahbani perceive that those freedoms shall be regulated in legislation, so their actualisation avoids enjoyment without an order.[21] Hence, as Dewa Gede Atmadja agreed during the amendment debate, there should be no restriction on fundamental freedoms except for reasons of public order and morality and to protect the broader public interest.[22] The Constitution anticipates the restriction over the enjoyment of human rights when falling under the criteria of: i) established by law, ii) to guarantee the recognition and respect of the rights and freedoms of others, and iii) due to morality, religious values, security, and public order in a democratic society.[23] Henceforth, the discussion involves: a) the interpretation of the extent of the freedom of association provisions, and b) the anticipation of employing restrictions over the association.

III. THE SCOPE OF FREEDOM OF ASSOCIATION PROVISIONS

Among studies on freedom of association in the context of Indonesia, there are limited works that elaborate on interpreting the extent of the respected rights.[24] Therefore, this part of the discussion primarily examines the subject matter of the Civil Society Organisations Act 2013, with the 2017 amendment as a reference to outline the scope of rights provided therein. The relevant explanation is also found within other laws, such as the Human Rights Act 1999. The respected Act divides this matter into several salient features, including: 1) the nature and types of associations, 2) the extent of entitlements, 3) registered and incorporated associations: the conditions and procedures, 4) the internal rules of organisations,

[20] ibid.

[21] Editors (n 15) 204–205.

[22] ibid 236, 280.

[23] Art 28J(2) of the 1945 Constitution of Republic of Indonesia.

[24] Such as the work from Siregar (n 10); F Mursid, 'Indeks Demokrasi Indonesia Naik, Perludem: Masih Diklasifikasikan Cacat' *Republika* (Jakarta, 16 March 2022) www.republika.co.id/berita/r8uflx487/indeks-demokrasi-indonesia-naik-perludem-masih-diklasifikasikan-cacat; Elfudllatsani, Isharyanto and Riwanto (n 5); R Herlambang Perdana Wiratraman, 'Hak-Hak Konstitusional Warga Negara Setelah Amandemen UUD 1945: Konsep, Pengaturan Dan Dinamika Implementasi' (2007) 1 *Hukum Panta Rei* 1.

5) empowerment of associations, 6) internal disputes within associations, and 7) prohibition and penalties. Each of these will be dealt with in turn.

First, we consider the nature of civil society organisations. Prior to narrowing down the extent of rights, the Civil Society Organisations Act 2013 defines a civil society organisation as an organisation established by society voluntarily, based on shared aspirations, willingness, needs, interests, activities, and goals, to participate in development for the sole purpose of the nation-state.[25] As Putra Setiawan and Riwanto agreed, an established association represents a vehicle for society to actualise its freedom of peaceful assembly. Additionally, it is a realisation of public participation in enhancing democracy to uphold freedom, equality, brotherhood, and honesty.[26] Setiawan and Riwanto point out that there were 349,203 registered organisations in 2017.[27] The earlier-mentioned 568,884 registered ones are developing in 2024,[28] demonstrating that people exercise and implement this freedom as part of democracy and human rights.[29]

Second, we turn to the extent of entitlements afforded. The Civil Society Organisations Act recognises the right to freedom of association, which includes the right to form associations; thus, the organisation deserves legal protection due to its existence and activities.[30] In parallel, the Human Rights Act entitles everyone to the right to establish political parties and civil society organisations.[31] The author subscribes to Joseph Raz in advocating the importance of freedom of association, among other fundamental rights, as a liberty for everyone, whether they choose to exercise it or not.[32] Their individual right to join an association signifies a decision to surrender certain personal rights in order to preserve others' fundamental rights.[33]

Under the Human Rights Act, the right to establish an organisation is a path to the right to participate in state governance, inalienable from the right to freedom of peaceful assembly.[34] Accordingly, the significance of freedom of association is interdependent with the right to take part in public affairs, as pointed out by Article 28C(2) of the 1945 Constitution, justifying everyone to promote and assert his or her rights collectively in developing society and country. Moreover, under the Human Rights Act, the right to take part in public affairs includes participation in: a) proposing a law or policymaking, b) being engaged in the protection, enforcement, and promotion

[25] Art 1.1 of the Civil Society Organisations Act No 17 of 2013.

[26] AP Setiawan and A Riwanto, 'Pembubaran Organisasi Kemasyarakatan Dalam Perspektif Hak Asasi Manusia' (2020) 4 *Res Publica* 273 digilib.uin-suka.ac.id/id/eprint/31708/.

[27] ibid.

[28] INFID (n 6) 1.

[29] Setiawan and Riwanto (n 26).

[30] Art 20(e) of the Civil Organisations Act No 17 of 2013.

[31] Art 24(1) of Human Rights Act No 39 of 1999.

[32] J Raz, 'Rights and Individual Well-Being' (1992) 5 *Ratio Juris* 127, 132.

[33] I Salevao, *Rule of Law, Legitimate Governance & Development in the Pacific* (B Maidment and M May eds, Kambri, ANU E Press 2005) 26.

[34] Art 24(1) and (2) of the Human Rights Act No 39 of 1999.

of human rights, and c) submitting a petition as an indication of a human rights violation.[35] In proposing a law or policymaking, Article 102 provides civil society organisations with their entitlement to channel aspirations about policymaking on human rights matters by submitting to human rights institutions. Engagement in human rights promotion is permitted for civil society organisations, as well as for other stakeholders, such as groups and political organisations.[36] Moreover, Article 90 of the Human Rights Act allows a group or organisation – and not only an individual – to represent itself in submitting a petition indicating a human rights infringement of its members' rights or based on shared legal interests.

Freedom of association is considered a parallel framework covering individual rights, which is important for reflecting a collective interest in achieving shared goals.[37] Under the Civil Society Organisations Act 2013, Article 20 entitles civil society organisations to:[38]

i. to regulate and manage the internal organisation independently and openly;
ii. to obtain the intellectual property rights due to the name and symbol of the organisation under the legal framework;
iii. to assert the organisation's goals;
iv. to organise activities to achieve the respective goals;
v. to collaborate with the government, local government, the private sector, and other parties to develop and sustain the organisations.

These entitlements suit accommodating collective action on behalf of the organisation. It is worth noting that freedom of association is commonly intended to assert collective bargaining.[39] Mutual rights under freedom of association, as enshrined in the Human Rights Act, are considered aimed at protecting, enforcing, and promoting human rights within the national legal framework.[40] However, the collective purpose under the Civil Society Organisations Act tends to be designed as a part of achieving national purposes, which leads to the consequence that a civil society organisation is allowed to be sponsored by the government. The respective terms and conditions are closely interlinked with the following provisions that underpin an organisation.

Thirdly, we consider the types of civil society organisations that are protected. Marking the types of civil society organisations is deemed identical to identifying the status of an organisation. The Civil Society Organisations Act regulates institutional matters such as classifying the status of incorporated

[35] Art 44 of the Human Rights Act No 39 of 1999.
[36] Art 100 of the Human Rights Act No 39 of 1999.
[37] Hafid, Arifin and Fauzia (n 3) 56.
[38] Art 20 of the Civil Organisations Act No 17 of 2013.
[39] BH Weston, 'Human Rights' (1984) 6(3) *Human Rights Quarterly* 257 www.jstor.org/stable/762002; M Haas, *International Human Rights: A Comprehensive Introduction*, 2nd edn (Abingdon, Routledge, 2014).
[40] Art 24(1) and (2) of Human Rights Act No 39 of 1999.

and unincorporated associations.[41] Since only incorporated organisations are allowed by the Act to become registered, the classification is also meticulous with regard to the type, ie, incorporated but unregistered organisations. Considering the survey found that 21 of the 509 institutional respondents are unregistered,[42] the other organisations are both unincorporated and unregistered. The Act attempted to accommodate unincorporated organisations on an equal footing with registered ones. Under the former Articles 16, 17, and 18, the local government was authorised to generate a type of letter of certification acknowledging that an unincorporated organisation was equally registered *(Surat Keterangan Terdaftar)*.[43] Those provisions are no longer in force, as the Constitutional Court[44] invalidated this authority. In Verdict No 82/PUU-XI/2013 and No 3/PUU-XII/2014, the Court clarifies that even though unregistered, a social organisation has the right to exist, provided it does not compromise public safety and order and/or infringe upon the rights and freedoms of others.[45] Thus, no judgment expressed by the government should be justifiable for marking the unregistered organisation as prohibited and prohibiting their activities, as long as they do not violate the law.[46]

After all, a registered status is beneficial, as the law allows an association to receive social funds and government facilitation.[47] Conversely, it is understandable that unregistered organisations may be unlikely to be the beneficiaries of government charity and aid initiatives. Nevertheless, it is risky to disregard the eligibility of those unregistered associations to participate in legislation-making. This is because Act No 13 of 2022 concerning the legislation-making process includes the registered civil society organisation among eligible parties to participate in legislation making.[48] To be considered registered, a civil society organisation shall be verified as an incorporated association.[49] Regrettably, this provision may narrow the extent of freedom of association, as mentioned in the previous section, the opportunity to take part in public affairs.

Fourthly, we turn to the internal rule of organisations. It appears that no force is imposed to join an association, as the Civil Society Organisation Act 2013 recognises the principle of a voluntary basis, along with social, independent,

[41] Art 10(1) of the Civil Society Organisations Act No 17 of 2013.

[42] INFID (n 6) 1.

[43] Arts 16, 17, and 18 of the Civil Society Organisations Act No 17 of 2013.

[44] The Indonesian legal system recognises separated judiciary bodies (the Constitutional Court and the Supreme Court) to review the written law. The Constitutional Court has power to review the constitutionality of a primary Act, while the Supreme Court is authorised to review whether the subsidiary legislations contravene the primary Act or the higher legislation. Art 24 of the 1945 Constitution of Republic of Indonesia.

[45] E Nugroho, 'Sengkarut Hukum Pembubaran Ormas' (PSHK, 2022).

[46] Siregar (n 10) 14–15.

[47] ibid.

[48] Interpretation of Art 96(3) of the Legislation-Making Act No 13 of 2022.

[49] Art 15(1) of the Civil Society Organisations Act No 17 of 2013.

non-profit, and democratic elements.[50] Thus, Article 4 is consistent with the definition of a 'civil society organisation' under Article 1.1 as an organisation established and founded by the society voluntarily, which shares aspirations, willingness, needs, interests, activities, and goals in a way to participate in national development for the sake of the state goals. Nevertheless, an anomaly appears in Article 5, where the law frames the purpose of the organisations, among others, as assisting public services and preserving natural resources and the environment.[51] Such an incoherent provision may undermine the autonomy of the internal organisation, as entitled under Article 20(a), specifically in governing and administering internal affairs independently. In Verdict Nos 82/PUU-XI/2013 and 3/PUU-XII/2014, the Constitutional Court of the Republic of Indonesia reviewed several provisions in the Civil Society Organisations Act 2013 to determine whether they contravened the 1945 Constitution. The petitioner argues that the state should barely be justifiable in controlling anybody's manifestation of a school of thought. Therefore, in respect of the enjoyment of freedom of association and peaceful assembly, Article 5 should not be necessary to determine any goal of the organisation.[52]

Article 29 is a protective provision against laws that impede the organisational autonomy to determine how to structure the organisation by deliberation and consensus. In the Constitutional Court Verdict No 3/PUU-XII/2014, it is argued that the state should not limit or interfere with the internal association mechanism.[53] In responding so, the Court concluded the above assertions concerning those clauses as unconstitutional. On the one hand, the judges appreciated the importance of the law that directs the association's goals. However, on the other hand, such a treatment may undermine the notion of independence and autonomous association. This is because the sustainability of social organisations should be a primary concern of internal affairs.[54] Holding this contention, the Court invalidated Article 34(1), which had imposed equal rights and duties on members of the associations as determined in each organisational Constitution.

Fifthly, in relation to the empowerment of civil society organisations, Chapter XII of the Civil Society Organisations Act 2013 authorises the government programme to enhance the capacity of social organisations. It aims to enhance both its performance and sustainability.[55] Under the

[50] Art 4 of the Civil Society Organisations Act No 17 of 2013.

[51] Art 20 of the Civil Organisations Act No 17 of 2013.

[52] Minutes of Verdict of Constitutional Court of Republic of Indonesia Numbers 82/PUU-XI/2013 and 3/PUU-XII/2014. MKRI, 'Risalah Sidang Perkara Nomor 82/PUU-XI/2013 Perkara Nomor 3/PUU-XII/2014 Perihal Pengujian Undang-Undang Nomor 17 Tahun 2013 Tentang Organisasi Kemasyarakatan Terhadap Undang-Undang Dasar Negara Republik Indonesia Tahun 1945 Acara Mendengarkan Keterangan' (2014) 9.

[53] MKRI (n 52); *Verdict 3/PUU-XII/2014* 1.

[54] *Verdict 3/PUU-XII/2014* (n 53) 127.

[55] Arts 40 and 41 of the Civil Society Organisations Act No 17 of 2013.

coordination of the Ministry of Home Affairs, the government provides an information system to improve public services and administrative order.[56] This provision is impressive in implementation, especially in terms of pursuing the obedience of civil society organisations and in fostering bonds with the government.[57] Not to mention that facilitation in the form of financial aid is expected to enable civil society organisations to grow independently and be accountable and professional.[58] The author disagrees with the opinion that the respected empowerment is intended to steer the dependency of civil society organisations clear of the interference of any parties (including foreign institutions), which potentially jeopardises their existence and breaks the law.[59] Such prejudice is inappropriate due to its tendency to undermine the autonomy of organisations and label them arbitrarily in general. In practice, it is noticeable that the empowerment initiative is uneven across civil society organisations.[60] The factors include uneven socialisation, the selection process, and the lack of a government budget.[61] All in all, the independence of civil society organisations should be the priority, and above all, for them to maintain their criticisms and freedoms, and keep them aware of meaningful participation in the decision-making process of government policies.

Sixthly, we consider internal disputes within civil society organisations. To some extent, civil society organisations suffer from internal disputes due to several factors, such as a lack of empowerment and capacity building, as well as being labelled as illegal organisations because they are unregistered.[62] In situations where the internal mechanisms of an organisation fail to resolve internal conflicts, Article 57 provides a mediation instrument offered by the government. Even if mediation fails, a dispute before the Court is allowed.[63]

Seventhly and finally, we turn to prohibition and penalties. Through the amendment under the Act 2017, Article 59 is revised to warn the civil society organisations of any prohibitions. Considering that the penalty is classified as administrative and criminal punishment, the current clauses (1) and (2) of Article 59 characterise administrative issues,[64] while clauses (3) and (4) indicate

[56] Art 42 of the Civil Society Organisations Act No 17 of 2013.

[57] AI Nurhadi, E Eviany and U Madjid, 'Implementasi Kebijakan Program Pemberdayaan Organisasi Kemasyarakatan Di Provinsi DKI Jakarta' (2024) 10 *Jurnal Kajian Pemerintah* 127, 128 journal.uir.ac.id/index.php/JKP/article/view/17011/6410.

[58] ibid.

[59] ibid.

[60] ibid.

[61] RA Medellu, S Sambiran and DK Monintja, 'Kinerja Badan Kesatuan Bangsa Dan Politik Dalam Pembinaan Dan Pemberdayaan Organisasi Kemasyarakatan Di Kabupaten Minahasa Selatan' (2023) 3 *Eksekutif* 1; Nurhadi, Eviany and Madjid (n 57).

[62] Medellu, Sambiran and Monintja (n 61) 2.

[63] Art 58 of the Civil Society Organisations Act No 17 of 2013.

[64] Such as the misuse of the name or symbol of organisations and managing donations and some funds against the law.

specific criminal conduct.[65] It leads to a discussion on the reasons for banning an organisation as an expression of restrictions.

IV. RESTRICTIONS ON FREEDOM OF ASSOCIATION

Prohibition or breaking the law may cause a restriction on the associations. As mentioned earlier, the 1945 Constitution favours the restriction over the enjoyment of human rights under the criteria of: i) established by law, ii) to guarantee the recognition and respect of the rights and freedoms of others, iii) due to morality, religious values, security and public order in a democratic society.[66]

To some extent, civil society organisations may express their views on the law and policymaking, which can enrich and challenge draft legislation and government policies. This freedom should be guaranteed, as civil society organisations play a crucial role in a democratic society. As illustrated by Amnesty International for Indonesia, the existence of civil society organisations is valuable in opposing the majority tyrant, who is often described as the enemy of democracy.[67]

Hans Thoolen marks the 1970s and 1980s as the age of government policies being made to reduce the number of political parties, a prohibition of civil servants from joining independent political parties, a conversion of peasant associations and trade unions into government-sponsored organisations, and an effort by the government to restrain the influence of student associations.[68] Also, legislation regarding the dissolution of civil society organisations has evolved since 1985 (replaced in 2013 with the latest amendment in 2017).[69]

[65] Such as arbitrarily overriding the responsibilities of law enforcement institutions and violating the principles of *Pancasila*. Articulated in the Preamble of the 1945 Constitution, *Pancasila* contains five principles as follows:

1. a belief in the One and Only God;
2. just and civilised humanity;
3. the unity of Indonesia,
4. democratic life led by wisdom of thoughts in deliberation amongst representatives of the people,
5. social justice for all the people of Indonesia.

[66] Art 28J(2) of the 1945 Constitution of Republic of Indonesia.

[67] T DA, 'Amnesty International Indonesia Beberkan 4 Syarat Pembubaran Ormas' *Hukumonline.com* (31 March 2022) www.hukumonline.com/berita/a/amnesty-international-indonesia-beberkan-4-syarat-pembubaran-ormas-lt6245ccd6c78d7/.

[68] H Thoolen, 'Indonesia and the Rule of Law: Twenty Years of "New Order" Government: A Study' (International Commission of Jurists, 1987) 116.

[69] The Civil Society Organisations Act 2013 is amended by the Government Regulation in Lieu of Law No UU No 2 of 2017. In the Indonesia legal system, the Act of Parliament, namely *Undang-Undang*, is under a hierarchy of law below the 1945 Constitution. The Government Regulation in Lieu of Law (so-called *Perppu*) is equal to the main legislation and justifiable to be

There is an indication of concern about the unfair treatment of freedom of association linked to reports submitted to the National Human Rights Commission (*Komnas HAM*). They were supposed to be in effect from 2013 (the year of the original enactment) until 2017, the year the latest amendment to the Civil Society Organisations Act was enacted. Due to the data not being available during the initial period, the petition was only submitted in 2015. The records in 2015, 2016, and 2017 emphasised petitions concerning the issue of infringement of freedom of association. The total number of reports in 2015 hit 18 records, decreased in 2016 (16 records), and re-increased in 2017 (19 records).[70]

This situation seems to have persisted until recently, as indicated by the Universal Periodic Review submitted by the Indonesian Government. Indonesia received a recommendation to repeal the undue restrictions on freedom of association and peaceful assembly, including Law No 17 of 2013 on Civil Society Organisations (United States of America) and Law No 19 of 2016 on electronic information and transactions (Switzerland). Costa Rica also recommends that Indonesia harmonise the regulations that govern freedom of expression and association in accordance with its respective international obligations (Costa Rica).[71]

Those reviews sound fair in criticising the experience of banning organisations in Indonesia. The author subscribes to the standard proposed by Usman Hamid, Executive Director of Amnesty International for Indonesia, who advocates that there should be four conditions to justify banning an association. It includes legal aspects, necessities, proportionality, and accountability. First, legal aspects of dismissing an association necessitate the existence of prohibited characteristics.[72] Second, there should be adequate arguments and measurements to establish the urgency of the need for an organisation to be banned. Third, when it is justifiable, proportionality shall be reflected to limit the right to freedom of association without excessive treatment. Thus, Hamid urges the provision of a procedure to dismiss an organisation, in addition to the crucial due process of law in a fair trial. To avoid arbitrary dismissal, a judicial proceeding allows the parties to present proof to persuade the judges whether the disputed organisation shall be concluded or dismissed. Fourth, the dismissal of an organisation must be justified through accountable means, by which the reason behind its decision is explainable without absolutist reasoning.[73]

issued by the President in the event of an administrative emergency. A *Perppu* shall be passed by the Parliament (the People Representative Body) to be validated as a main legislation. This chapter emphasises that the *Perppu* No 2 of 2017 is validated by the enactment of the Act No 16 of 2017; *(Undang-Undang Nomor 16 Tahun 2017 tentang Penetapan Perppu No. 2 Tahun 2017 tentang Perubahan Atas UU No.17 Tahun 2013 tentang Organisasi Kemasyarakatan).*

[70] 'Periodic Data Report' dataaduan.komnasham.go.id/#/periodic-data/actual-data.

[71] UN_HRC, 'Thematic List of Recommendations-UPR of Indonesia' (2022) www.ohchr.org/en/hr-bodies/upr/id-index.

[72] DA (n 67).

[73] ibid.

The legal position in Indonesia suggests that an administrative penalty is treated as a temporary ban for an association. In the event of disobedience following this sanction, it is justifiable for the government to permanently revoke the official status of the organisation as a registered entity after a final judicial decision.[74]

Acknowledging that historical context shows the experience of many civil society organisations being banned, the current law no longer requires a court decision. Instead, it requires an executive decree to justify the banning of a civil society organisation. This recent mechanism was applied within the last decade to ban Hizbut Tahrir Indonesia and the Front Pembela Islam (the Islam Defenders Front). As introduced earlier, the Civil Society Organisations Act has been designed to safeguard the uniformity of a single, interpreted state philosophy, known as the 'Pancasila'.[75] This matter was used as the ultimate reason for the dissolution of Hizbut Tahrir Indonesia. Hizbut Tahrir Indonesia was banned by revocation of its incorporation status through the Decree of the Ministry of Law and Human Rights No AHU-30.AH.01.08 of 2017.[76] By applying the principle of *contrarius actus*, the reason for dismissing Hizbut Tahrir Indonesia was that the internal constitution of this association was allegedly set to an ideology that contravened Pancasila.[77] The other banned organisation is Front Pembela Islam, which has been banned since 2020 by a joint government decree involving the Minister of Home Affairs, the Minister of Law and Human Rights, the Minister of Informatics, the Attorney General, the Chief of the Indonesian National Police, and the Head of the National Agency for Counter-Terrorism.[78] The two main reasons for banning this organisation were that the Front Pembela Islam, as a matter of law, had not renewed its registration status since 21 June 2019, due to failure to fulfil the updated requirements.[79] The government considers such disobedience sufficient grounds for dissolution.

Moreover, as a civil society organisation, the Front Pembela Islam has been recorded committing activities that frequently disrupt public order and security,

[74] Art 68(1) and (2) of the Civil Organisations Act No 17 of 2013.

[75] Articulated in the Preamble of the 1945 Constitution, *Pancasila* (n 65).

[76] *Surat Keputusan Menteri Hukum dan HAM Nomor AHU-30.AH.01.08 tahun 2017 tentang Pencabutan Keputusan Menteri Hukum dan HAM Nomor AHU-0028.60.10.2014 tentang Pengesahan Pendirian Badan Hukum Perkumpulan HTI.*

[77] 'Ahli Hukum Administrasi: Badan Hukum HTI Dicabut Sesuai Asas Contrarius Actus' (*Direktorat Jenderal Administrasi Hukum Umum 2014, Kementerian Hukum Republik Indonesia*, 2018) portal.ahu.go.id/id/detail/75-berita-lainnya/1840-ahli-hukum-administrasi-badan-hukum-hti-dicabut-sesuai-asas-contrarius-actus accessed 26 December 2024.

[78] *Surat Keputusan Bersama Nomor 220/4780 Tahun 2020, Nomor M.HH/14.HH05.05 Tahun 2020, Nomor 690 Tahun 2020, Nomor 264 Tahun 2020, Nomor KB/3/XII Tahun 2020, dan Nomor 320 Tahun 2020 tentang Larangan Kegiatan Penggunaan Simbol dan Atribut Serta Penghentian Kegiatan FPI.*

[79] S Mubarak and A Arsyad, 'Pembubaran Ormas Islam Oleh Pemerintah; Studi Komparatif Undang- Undang Ormas Dan Hukum Islam' (2021) 2 *Shautuna* 780.

breaking the laws, and exhibiting violence, such as anarchism and provocation.[80] The acts were found to contravene Article 59 of the Civil Society Organisations Act 2023.[81] Other societies admit that the Front Pembela Islam committed acts of violence and damaged property during several actions. Although this is the case, they disagree with responding to these actions by simply banning the organisation's status instead of prosecuting under criminal law.[82]

Those examples of the dissolution of society organisations entail a change in provisions from proceeding through judicial mechanisms under the Civil Society Organisations Act 2013 to one-sided decisions by the executive government (through its amendment in 2017).[83] Asfinawati opines that ignoring a fair trial in a judicial process to determine the dismissal of an organisation may create a precedent and reveal an arbitrary process afterwards.[84] Therefore, the author coincides with the contention that reviewing the mechanism regarding the absence of the court's power in the process of banning an organisation is critical.[85]

In advocating for the doctrine to encompass the role of the court in a proceeding for the dissolution of an organisation, an expert (Atip Latifulhayat), who presented in the judicial review of the Civil Society Organisations Act amendment 2017, outlined his two primary standing positions.[86] Firstly, the position of Pancasila[87] as the source of principle for any civil society organisation movement is, indeed, a settled preposition in the ideological realm in Indonesia. Regardless of that, as he asserted, whether an organisation has proven guilty of violating Pancasila should be clear.

Secondly, it is undeniable that one of the limitations of human rights is the prohibition to violate the human rights of others. The matter is how to characterise the respected limitation. The expert argues that a defined limitation should be based on the due process of law framework, as a universally well-received legal concept. Additionally, Latifulhayat agrees with the three

[80] 'Gov't Officially Bans Activities of Islam Defenders Front' (*Office of Assistant to Deputy Cabinet Secretary for State Documents & Translation*, 2020).

[81] H Hafansyah and T Syahuri, 'Pembubaran Organisasi Kemasyarakatan Front Pembela Islam (FPI) Dalam Perspektif Hukum Tata Negara' (2023) 10 *Jurnal Yuridis* 74.

[82] D Nurita, 'FPI Dibubarkan, Pakar: Idealnya Melalui Pengadilan, Bukan Oleh Pemerintah' *Tempo.co* (Jakarta, 30 December 2020).

[83] Under the amendment in 2017, Art 68 authorising the court to perform due process of law in banning process of an organisation is revoked.

[84] Asfinawati represents a CSO, namely Yayasan Lembaga Bantuan Hukum Indonesia (YLBHI), in an interview by a TV channel (Kompas TV). R Andidi, 'Pembubaran FPI Tanpa Peradilan Membahayakan Demokrasi, Pemerintah Bisa Seenaknya' (2021) rmol.id/politik/read/2021/01/08/469545/pembubaran-fpi-tanpa-peradilan-membahayakan-demokrasi-pemerintah-bisa-seenaknya accessed 24 December 2024.

[85] FR Rabbina and A Irfani, 'Membincang Pembubaran Front Pembela Islam Dalam Framing Pemberitaan Republika.Co.Id' (2022) 4 *Jurnal Studi Jurnalistik* 53.

[86] *Verdict of Constitutional Court of Republic of Indonesia No 38/PUU-XV/2017, 38/PUU-XV/2017, 39/PUU-XV/2017, 41/PUU-XV/2017, 48/PUU-XV/2017, 49/PUU-XV/2017, 52/PUU-XV/2017, and 58/PUU-XV/2017.*

[87] (n 47).

requirements to uphold the due process of law, ie, reasonable, just, and proper. In a banning mechanism, Latifulhayat asserts that a prosecuted organisation shall be entitled to defend its rights during a fair trial. Otherwise, it is risky to be arbitrarily labelled as guilty.[88] Aligning with this argument, the Court notes the government's explanation that the executive branch's subjective power should not be applied arbitrarily, as the judiciary should confirm its decision.[89] Unfortunately, the Constitutional Court is uncertain about whether to reinstate the role of the judiciary in deciding the dissolution of a civil society organisation. It suggests that denying a guarantee of a fair trial in decreeing the dismissal of an organisation due to allegations of violating the law and Pancasila principles prompts an infringement of comprehensive freedom of association.

The author believes that promoting further legal improvement would be achieved by reinstating the judiciary's role in determining whether an association is justified in being banned. This is due to an indication that the national government's guarantees of freedom of association depend on access to a fair trial if an organisation is alleged to have committed a violation. In support of this argument, the author agrees that ignoring due process of law in this matter could potentially contravene the right under the Human Rights Act 1999, which recognises the protection of a fair and impartial trial for the sake of human dignity.[90] Additional entitlement is strengthened by Article 17, which states that the protection of a fair trial plays a crucial role in safeguarding procedural law. This entails an objective examination before the Court by an honest and impartial judge to obtain a fair and truthful verdict.

Accordingly, the virtue of a fair trial to determine whether banning an organisation is necessary should be promoted, as it enables an opportunity for a hearing. In this context, Agus Riwanto cited Suparman Marzuki, advocating that a fair trial hearing is crucial. The reason is that it allows a defendant to defend and present the evidence. Moreover, a fair trial signifies that the state respects human rights and freedom and performs equality before the law.[91] Unfortunately, the law continues to undermine, or in other words, delete the power of the judiciary in the process of banning an organisation.

It can be argued that the above-mentioned model of state restriction over freedom of association reveals a repressive style. Such a manner might reflect the government's explicit and direct control over certain groups in society, given its pivotal role in overseeing government policies and decisions. The Indonesian Government may use the Civil Society Organisations Act as amended in 2017 to

[88] *Verdict of Constitutional Court of Republic of Indonesia No. 38/PUU-XV/2017, 38/PUU-XV/2017, 39/PUU-XV/2017, 41/PUU-XV/2017, 48/PUU-XV/2017, 49/PUU-XV/2017, 52/PUU-XV/2017, and 58/ PUU-XV/2017* (n 86).

[89] ibid 108.

[90] Art 5(1) and (2) of the Human Rights Act (HRA) No 39 of 1999.

[91] Setiawan and Riwanto (n 26).

justify its administrative conduct and restrict organisations with counterviews to the ruling government by directly labelling them as anti-Pancasila and paralysing their official existence.[92]

In practice, banning an organisation is not the only restriction used in anticipation of the potential criticisms from societal organisations. The law exhibits excessive regulation of the behaviour of civil society organisations. Although it is unclear and not articulated in any provisions, another manner used with a similar intention of restricting civil society organisations' activities can be seen as a soft, persuasive, or hidden means of controlling an organisation's autonomy. Suspicious of soft intentions to undermine the association, recent law is seen as attempting to facilitate, particularly under a mining concession offered to faith-based organisations.

Indonesia is home to the world's largest Muslim population. Muslim faith-based organisations are one category of well-known social organisations that play important roles in society and politics.[93] It demonstrates specific sociological realms in Indonesia, where several faith-based organisations, such as Nahdlatul Ulama and Muhammadiyah, play important roles in disseminating religious teachings. NU is estimated to have around 95 million members, while Muhammadiyah is estimated to have 60 million members.[94]

On 30 May 2024, former President Joko Widodo (known as Jokowi) signed a policy through Government Regulation No 25 of 2024,[95] which regulated the employment of mineral and coal mining business activities.[96] With less than one year until the end of his second term as President, Jokowi had planned to grant mining permits for faith-based organisations in Indonesia, ie, Nahdlatul Ulama, Muhammadiyah, the Indonesian Catholic Bishop's Conference, Protestant Indonesian Communion of Churches, Buddhism, and Hinduism organisations.[97] The concession granted to Special Mining Business Permit Areas underwent an amendment with Government Regulation No 96 of 2021, which added a provision under Article 83A(1) with the expressed purpose of

[92] Andidi (n 84).

[93] G da Costa, 'Government Offers Coal Mining Concessions to Six Religious Organizations' *Indonesia Business Post* (10 June 2024) indonesiabusinesspost.com/insider/government-offers-coal-mining-concessions-to-six-religious-organizations/; Elfudllatsani, Isharyanto and Riwanto (n 5).

[94] Van Der Schaar Investments B.V., 'Indonesia Investments Report: "Coal Mining Update Indonesia: Religious Organizations to Become Coal Miners?"' (2024) www.indonesia-investments.com/id/budaya/penduduk/item67?.

[95] In the Indonesian legal system, a government regulation is considered a type of subsidiary legislation supposed to implement the primary Act of Parliament (legislation, or interchangeably Act, namely *Undang-Undang*). The supreme law in the hierarchy is the 1945 Constitution, followed by the Act. It implies that the President is merely authorised to enact a government regulation without being compelled to involve meaningful public participation in its making procedure. Unlike the making of the Constitution, and the primary Act shall involve representative bodies.

[96] *Peraturan Pemerintah (PP) Nomor 25 tahun 2024 tentang Perubahan atas Peraturan Pemerintah (PP) Nomor 96 Tahun 2021 tentang Pelaksanaan Kegiatan Usaha Pertambangan Mineral dan Batu Bara.*

[97] Costa (n 93).

enhancing public welfare. This provision authorises the government to offer the designated concession to a corporation under the management structure of a faith-based organisation.

Likewise, the offer is tempting for the targeted groups, most prominently Nahdlatul Ulama and Muhammadiyah, who have openly expressed their support for the mining permit. In June, Nahdlatul Ulama was the first to declare that it had accepted the offer, claiming that the concessions would be used to finance religious and charitable initiatives.[98] Muhammadiyah later accepted the offer in July at a 'national consolidation' gathering, under the guise that it would provide improved mining methods for the purposes of social welfare and environmental protection.[99] Predictably, the acceptance of mining permits by the two most prominent Muslim organisations in Indonesia drew criticisms from both internal and external members and groups. For instance, Busyro Muqoddas, a prominent legal expert within Muhammadiyah, disagreed with such a decision, as did Aisyiyah, an internal women's organisation. Both expressed dissent from such a leader's decision, considering the risk of exacerbating agrarian conflicts, environmental damage, and human rights violations.[100] Among external voices are also those who disapprove of the Muslim leaders' decisions. It reveals concerns, such as Ahmad Rizky M. Umar's label of 'religious clientelism'[101] and Nina A Loasana and Radhiyya Indra's indication of 'pork barrel politics' for Nahdlatul Ulama.[102] They interpreted this as a signal of legislation favouring religion, and a tendency to jeopardise the essential role of political institutions and pressure groups in monitoring the ruling government.[103]

By promising a concession for mining projects to civil society organisations based on religion, the author argues that Government Regulation No 25 of 2024 offers bribes to 'lure the kindness' of society in return for withholding potential criticisms of the government. This type of manipulation between the government and the critical civil society organisation may reduce the potential head-to-head opposition. However, it may paralyse society's control over the executive government. The editor of *Tempo Magazine* also warns of the risk that a gift from the government to the most prominent Muslim organisations

[98] ARM Umar, 'Religious Coal Rush: Why Do Indonesian Muslim Leaders Accept Coal Mining Concessions?' (*Indonesia at Melburne*, 2024) indonesiaatmelbourne.unimelb.edu.au/religious-coal-rush-why-do-indonesian-muslim-leaders-accept-coal-mining-concessions/ accessed 7 January 2025.

[99] AntaraNews, 'Mining Concession -Muhammadiyah to Meet President Jokowi' *AntaraNews* (Yogyakarta, 29 July 2024) en.antaranews.com/news/320275/mining-concession-muhammadiyah-to-meet-president-jokowi.

[100] Umar (n 98).

[101] ibid.

[102] 'NU Mining Permits Slammed as Pork Barrel Politics' *Jakarta Post* (Jakarta, 4 June 2024) www.thejakartapost.com/indonesia/2024/06/04/nu-mining-permits-slammed-as-pork-barrel-politics.html.

[103] I Junaenah, 'Izin Tambang: Modus Melawan Oposisi' *Pikiran Rakyat* (Bandung, 7 August 2024).

could trigger horizontal conflict.[104] Inevitably, such a prediction proves to be accurate. The provision in government Regulation No 25 of 2024 underpinning the mining concession was challenged by several religious, legal, and environmental organisations on Tuesday, 1 October 2024, through judicial review in the Supreme Court.[105] Wahyu Agung Perdana, one of the petitioners, explained that he filed for judicial review because mining concessions for religious organisations violated state ethics. Similar to the author's earlier remark, Wahyu argues that the concession may serve more as a template for political bribery than simply being a legal flaw.[106]

To emphasise, the role of a civil society organisation is ideally to function as a means of public oversight and a tool to contribute to public policy that may impact public interests through some of their alternative, dialectical ideas. Ferdian Andi, also a member of Muhammadiyah, wondered whether this organisation would change its relationship with the government, that is, from maintaining its criticism to becoming a rubber stamp.[107] This question was highlighted recently, as Nahdlatul Ulama took a stand alongside Jokowi, after the release of an international organisation's report ranking corrupt leaders worldwide.

Towards the end of 2024, the Organised Crime and Corruption Reporting Project, an international journalism organisation based in Amsterdam, Netherlands, released the 'Person of the Year' in Organised Crime and Corruption.[108] Surprisingly, the report nominated Indonesia's former President Joko Widodo among the finalists for the most corrupt leaders in the world. Although the final decision concluded that Bashar al-Assad was the top finalist, the Organised Crime and Corruption Reporting Project received many votes in favour of the former President, among five others.[109] The respective annual list characterises the finalists as having 'done the most to advance crime and corruption globally, thus damaging democracy and human rights'.[110]

[104] Editor, 'From Religious Mass Organizations to Mining Mass Organizations' *Tempo Magazine* (5 August 2024).

[105] The respected group referred to itself as Tim Advokasi Tolak Tambang (Anti-Mining Advocacy Team). N Nur Fauziyah, 'Anti-Mining Group to Challenge Mining Concessions for Religious Groups at Indonesia's Supreme Court' *Tempo.co English version* (Jakarta, 1 October 2024) en.tempo.co/read/1923158/anti-mining-group-to-challenge-mining-concessions-for-religious-groups-at-indonesias-supreme-court.

[106] ibid.

[107] F Andi, 'Izin Tambang Dan Mandat Ormas Keagamaan' (reposted from koran.tempo.co/read/opini/490130/risiko-izin-tambang-ormas-keagamaan, Jumat, 4 October 2024.) graduate.uinjkt.ac.id/id/izin-tambang-dan-mandat-ormas-keagamaan accessed 8 January 2025.

[108] A Sood, 'Indonesia's Widodo Slams "Baseless" Report Listing Him as Leading Corruption Enabler' *South China Morning Post* (4 January 2025) www.scmp.com/week-asia/politics/article/3293374/indonesias-widodo-slams-baseless-report-listing-him-leading-corruption-enabler?module=perpetual_scroll_0&pgtype=article.

[109] MR Fadillah, 'Jokowi: The Most Corrupt Leader in the World' *6:30 am in English Edition* (8 January 2025) kbanews.com/english-edition/jokowi-the-most-corrupt-leader-in-the-world/.

[110] Sood (n 108).

The author considers Ferdian's speculation as validated by how the leader of Nahdlatul Ulama, Yahya Cholil Staquf, who reacted to the release, argued that the Organised Crime and Corruption Reporting Project announcement nominating Jokowi had no strong basis and may distract from national stability.[111]

Back to the model of state restriction over the freedom of association, instead of evaluating Article 8A(1) and (2) of the GR of 25/2024, the current President Prabowo Subianto even proposes that the mining concession be strengthened in the proposed Act. The *Dewan Perwakilan Rakyat-DPR* (House of Representatives) passed the proposed provision, which allows businesses owned by social and religious organisations to manage mining concessions by granting Mining Business Permit Areas.[112] The author notes that the provisions position the civil society organisations as prospective permit beneficiaries, compromising their objectivity due to vested interests and weakening their role in overseeing the ruling government. The big civil society organisations, both as allies and opponents to the government in Indonesia, face more challenges and temptations as President Prabowo Subianto incorporates nearly all of the political actors (political parties and faith-based organisations) to be engaged in the current overextended ministries.[113] Thus, it is recommended that faith-based organisations restrain themselves from being influenced by the ruling government's incentives in return for softening their criticisms.

V. CONCLUSION

To summarise, this chapter presents the legal framework for freedom of association in Indonesia and discusses the legal position. It outlines that freedom of association in Indonesia resulted from constitutional debate among the country's founding leaders. It is marked by a debate on whether the subject matter of human rights deserves to be materialised as constitutional rights. Eventually, the 1945 Constitution established fundamental recognition, which was strengthened by the Human Rights Act 1999 and a commitment to international human rights law, specifically the International Covenant on Civil and Political Rights.

However, the interpretation of the right is actualised by the Civil Society Organisations Act 2013, with its amendment in 2017. It is observed that freedom of association remains limited, but it can be enjoyed under certain conditions. This Act aims to instil obedience within organisations through their registered

[111] Editor, 'Bela Jokowi Atas Tuduhan OCCRP, PBNU-PSI-Noel Diolok-Olok Netizen' *orines.id* (5 January 2025) orinews.id/2025/01/05/bela-jokowi-atas-tuduhan-occrp-pbnu-psi-noel-diolok-olok-netizen/.

[112] Y Paat, 'DPR Passes Revised Mineral and Coal Mining Law' (February, 18 February 2025) jakartaglobe.id/news/dpr-passes-revised-mineral-and-coal-mining-law.

[113] Y Lai, 'Indonesian President Prabowo Presents Largest Cabinet in Decades' *Jakarta Post* (22 October 2024) asianews.network/indonesian-president-prabowo-presents-largest-cabinet-in-decades/.

status, which qualifies them to receive certain funds. Moreover, this status ensures their eligibility to participate in law-making.

A legal mechanism to ban an association is also justifiable as a form of restriction. Nevertheless, the procedure now excludes the power of the judiciary to ensure a fair trial in proving allegations that an organisation is violating the law. Moreover, the recent situation has shown a decline in discourse on this issue. The reality also demonstrates the attempt to restrain the criticism of organisations, especially faith-based ones, by facilitating them with special licenses for a mining project. Suspiciously, this policy serves as a lure to undermine their potential criticisms of government policy. It is acknowledged that for the purpose of ongoing academic questions concerning the role of society in its relation to public affairs, this chapter takes note of the trends in the persistently flawed democracy status in Indonesia, marked by the change in the current President from Joko Widodo to Prabowo Subianto. Hence, this work remains open to further study on how particular civil society organisations may decide to assert or restrain genuine participation in policymaking through the freedom of association.

7

Freedom of Association in Kenya: Constitutional Foundations, Judicial Reasoning, and Democratic Tensions

NJOKI MBOCE

THIS CHAPTER EXAMINES the right to freedom of association in Kenya. It seeks to provide a comprehensive, descriptive understanding of how the right is codified, interpreted, and applied in the Kenyan legal system and by her courts. The right to freedom of association in Kenya emerges as both a constitutional guarantee and a site of contestation, where the regulatory role of the state must balance democratic pluralism with the internal accountability of associations, physical associational life and emerging trends, including digital platforms and online mobilisation.

The legal system in Kenya is primarily influenced by English common law traditions from British colonial rule, doctrines of equity, and statutes of general application which were transplanted into the Kenyan context through the reception clause of the East Africa Order in Council, 1897 – repealed by the 1902 Order and later consolidated in the Judicature Act.[1] Alongside this, elements of African customary law were selectively recognised, particularly in matters of personal law, provided they were not 'repugnant to justice and morality' or inconsistent with written law.[2] After independence in 1963, Kenya retained

[1] 'Judicature Act, Chapter 8 Laws of Kenya'. The full texts of the East Africa Order in Council, 1897 and the subsequent East Africa Order in Council, 1902 are not readily available in open-access online repositories. This is because colonial constitutional instruments were primarily published in the *London Gazette* and archived within the *Kenya Gazette* and the British Colonial Office records, which remain dispersed across physical archives such as the UK National Archives (CO series) and the Kenya National Archives. The 1902 Order expressly repealed and replaced the 1897 Order, and thus is the more commonly reproduced instrument in accessible legal sources. Additionally, most contemporary references – including judicial history materials and secondary scholarship – summarise their positions rather than reproduce the entire text. See kenyalaw.org:8181/exist/kenyalex/actview.xql?actid=CAP.%208 accessed 11 July 2020.

[2] Atuguba, 'Customary Law Revivalism: Seven Phases in the Evolution of Customary Law in Sub-Saharan Africa' [2022] Inter Gentes intergentes.com/seven-phases-in-the-evolution-of-customary-law-in-sub-saharan-africa/ accessed 27 August 2025.

this mixed heritage but gradually indigenised its legal framework, consolidating it through successive constitutions and statutory reforms.[3] The current 2010 Constitution of Kenya, marks a transformative departure by entrenching constitutional supremacy, judicial independence, and a robust Bill of Rights, while still reflecting the enduring interaction between English common law, African customary law, and international law.[4]

This chapter is divided into six sections. Section I begins by tracing the legal system in Kenya and highlights the pre-colonial, colonial, and post-colonial context of the regulation of the right to freedom of association in Kenya. Section II discusses constitutional foundations of the right to freedom of association in Kenya, situating the right within both domestic law and international legal frameworks. This lays the basis for section III, which discusses the statutory pillars of the rights. Section IV then examines key judicial decisions that have shaped the scope of freedom of association. It mainly focuses on cases on the registration and regulation of political parties and civil society organisations, and the intersection of associational freedom with speech and religion. It also highlights the persistent tension between judicial protection of autonomy and the regulatory role of the state, including instances of legislative overreach where statutory provisions have threatened to undermine constitutional guarantees. Section V turns the discussion to reflections on the legal protection of the right to freedom of association, including highlighting the tension between legitimate public interests in the implementation of the role of the state in regulating associations and the constitutional imperative of autonomy. Political parties and civil society organisations are considered as the prevailing primary vehicles of collective action, before engaging with contemporary and emerging trends – including digital associations and online movements – that expand the terrain of associational life. Section VI concludes the chapter by drawing together these strands to acknowledge Kenya's progress and gaps in realising the right to freedom of association under the 2010 Constitution. It also highlights the need for reform and vigilance to optimally secure the right as the anchor of democratic practice and pluralist society.

I. THE PATH TO FREEDOM OF ASSOCIATION IN KENYA

While statutory regulation of the right to freedom of association emerged during colonial and post-colonial periods, collective organisation in Kenya through

[3] HWO Okoth-Ogendo, *Constitutions without Constitutionalism: Reflections on an African Political Paradox* (New York, American Council of Learned Societies, 1988).

[4] YP Ghai and JPWB McAuslan, *Public Law and Political Change in Kenya: A Study of the Legal Framework of Government from Colonial Times to the Present* (Oxford, Oxford University Press, 1970) Arts 2, [160], and ch 4, respectively.

customary norms predates statutes.[5] During the colonial era, the right was mainly regulated through ordinances that significantly limited union activity.[6] The Trade Unions Ordinance of 1935 permitted African workers to form labour organisations but imposed strict registration controls and government oversight.[7] Subsequently, political associations such as the Kenya African Union (1944) and the Kenya African National Union (1951) emerged as vehicles for anti-colonial mobilisation.[8]

Upon independence in 1963, the new Constitution nominally guaranteed fundamental freedoms, including the right to freedom of association.[9] These rights were eroded as the Kenya African National Union consolidated power into a de facto one-party state between 1969 and 1991.[10] Constitutional amendments and legislation banned multi-party politics, imposed arduous licensing requirements on civil society groups, and absorbed trade unions into government-aligned structures, effectively stifling independent collective organisation.[11] The then President Daniel Moi initially argued that a single-party system was essential to preserving social order and preventing tribalism.[12] This claim illustrates the enduring tension between state-centred stability and the right to freedom of association. In 1991 – driven by domestic and international pressure – the one-party laws were repealed, reintroducing multi-party democracy.[13]

[5] JS Mbiti, *African Religions & Philosophy* (Heinemann 1990) books.google.com/books?hl=en&lr=lang_en&id=eTUpo9lH-fYC&oi=fnd&pg=PR10&dq=John+S.+Mbiti,+African+Religions+and+Philosophy+&ots=Min3Ulypn4&sig=lojdP4RXU__EVtvUwW-1HadHMgE accessed 28 August 2025; BA Ogot and WR Ochieng, *Decolonization & Independence in Kenya, 1940–93* (Columbus, Ohio State University Press, 1995) books.google.co.uk/books/about/Decolonization_Independence_in_Kenya_194.html?id=jBxkzgEACAAJ&redir_esc=y accessed 28 August 2025; J Lonsdale, 'Moral Ethnicity and Political Tribalism' [1994] Occasional Paper 131.

[6] Ghai and McAuslan (n 4).

[7] 'History of COTU(K)' *(Central Organization of Trade Unions (COTU-K)*, 8 November 2015) cotu-kenya.org/history-of-cotuk/ accessed 27 May 2025; M O Makoloo, and YP Ghai, *Kenya: Minorities, Indigenous Peoples and Ethnic Diversity* (Minority Rights Group International London, 2005) minorityrights.org/app/uploads/2023/12/download-147-kenya-minorities-indigenous-peoples-and-ethnic-diversity.pdf accessed 17 May 2025.

[8] D Anderson, *Histories of the Hanged: The Dirty War in Kenya and the End of Empire* (New York, WW Norton & Company, 2005).

[9] '1963_Constitution.Pdf' kenyalaw.org/kl/fileadmin/pdfdownloads/1963_Constitution.pdf accessed 17 May 2025, art 14 (b).

[10] 'On the History of the Restoration of a Multi-Party-Political System in Kenya' ResearchGate www.researchgate.net/publication/363512299_On_the_History_of_the_Restoration_of_a_Multi-Party_Political_System_in_Kenya accessed 27 May 2025.

[11] 'Democratisation and the Rule of Law in Kenya: ICJ Mission Report | ICJ' (*International Commission of Jurists*) www.icj.org/resource/democratisation-and-the-rule-of-law-in-kenya-icj-mission-report/ accessed 27 May 2025; 'U.S. Department of State Country Report on Human Rights Practices 1994 – Kenya' (*Refworld*) www.refworld.org/reference/annualreport/usdos/1995/en/25793 accessed 27 May 2025.

[12] Kenya Human Rights Commission, 'Ethnicity-and-Politicization-in-Kenya.Pdf' khrc.or.ke/wp-content/uploads/2024/02/Ethnicity-and-Politicization-in-Kenya.pdf accessed 27 August 2025.

[13] DW Throup and C Hornsby, *Multi-Party Politics in Kenya* boydellandbrewer.com/book/multi-party-politics-in-kenya-pb/ accessed 27 August 2025; KB Richburg, 'Kenyan Leader Opts for

The 2010 Constitution marked a transformative moment by explicitly guaranteeing the right to freedom of association, covering political parties, trade organisations, and any group formed to protect interests.[14] It also incorporates international treaties which Kenya has ratified and general rules of international law directly into domestic law.[15] As the supreme law, it binds all persons and state organs, and renders any inconsistent law or action void to the extent of the inconsistency.[16] Consequently, courts in Kenya have actively referenced international obligations, especially in areas lacking detailed local legislation. In *Mitu-Bell Welfare Society v Kenya Airports Authority & 2 others*; the Supreme Court articulated a nuanced position that domestic courts must take cognisance of international law when resolving disputes, if it does not clash with the Constitution, statutes, or final court decisions.[17] In *Barasa v Cabinet Secretary, Ministry of Interior and National Co-Ordination & 3 others; Nderitu & 2 others (Interested Parties)*, the Court recognised the Rome Statute under the International Crimes Act as domestically operative after Kenya's ratification.[18] In *Josephine v Attorney General*, the Court of Appeal emphasised that courts only interpret international instruments insofar as needed to resolve domestic rights and obligations,[19] and stressed that treaties are tools for interpretation, not sources of standalone legal obligations.[20]

Before the 2010 Constitution, Kenyan courts mainly applied dualism, requiring treaties to be domesticated before enforcement.[21] However, the 2010 Constitution, through Article 2(6), grants treaties which Kenya has ratified direct effect.[22] In *Karen Njeri Kandie v Alassane Ba & Another*, the Supreme Court of Kenya confirmed that the direct application affects both the treaties ratified before and after the 2010 Constitution, which remain binding unless revoked.[23]

Multi-Party Rule – Ruling Party Shift Stirs Cautious Reaction' *The Washington Post* (3 December 1991) www.washingtonpost.com/archive/politics/1991/12/03/kenyan-leader-opts-for-multi-party-rule/4e0fb998-a0d7-434c-bc75-efa43c626c0c/ accessed 27 August 2025; 'Constitution of Kenya (Amendment) (No. 2) Act, 1991' www.kenyalaw.org/kl/fileadmin/pdfdownloads/Constitution/HistoryoftheConstitutionofKenya/Acts/1991/ActNo.12of1991.pdf accessed 27 May 2025.

[14] 'Constitution of Kenya' (n 2) Arts 36 and 41.

[15] ibid Art 2(6) and (5), respectively.

[16] 'Constitution of Kenya' (n 14) Art 2(1), (2), and (4), respectively.

[17] *Mitu-Bell Welfare Society v Kenya Airports Authority & 2 others; Initiative for Strategic Litigation in Africa (Amicus Curiae) (Petition 3 of 2018)* [2021] KESC 34 (KLR) (11 January 2021) (Judgment).

[18] *Barasa v Cabinet Secretary, Ministry of Interior and National Co-Ordination & 3 others; Nderitu & 2 others (Interested Parties) (Constitutional Petition 488 of 2013)* [2014] KEHC 7542 (KLR) (Constitutional and Human Rights) (31 January 2014) (Judgment).

[19] *Josephine v Attorney General (Criminal Appeal 128 of 2009)* [2015] KECA 407 (KLR) (25 September 2015) (Judgment).

[20] ibid.

[21] Orago, 'The 2010 Kenyan Constitution and the Hierarchical Place of International Law in the Kenyan Domestic Legal System: A Comparative Perspective – African Human Rights Law Journal (AHRLJ)' www.ahrlj.up.ac.za/orago-n-w accessed 25 August 2025.

[22] 'Constitution of Kenya' (n 14) Art 2(6).

[23] *Kandie v Alassane BA & another (Petition 2 of 2015)* [2017] KESC 13 (KLR) (28 July 2017) (Judgment).

Article 94(5) reserves law-making for Parliament.[24] To align treaty ratification with legislative control, Parliament enacted the Treaty Making and Ratification Act 2012, prescribing that while the Executive negotiates and ratifies treaties, parliamentary approval is mandatory before those treaties can be ratified.[25]

II. CONSTITUTIONAL PROTECTIONS FOR FREEDOM OF ASSOCIATION IN KENYA

The right to freedom of association includes the ability to join or form groups, decline membership, or withdraw, and maintain organisational autonomy free from undue interference. It also includes the right to exclude.[26] It imposes both positive and negative obligations on the state – to avoid unjustified intrusion and to facilitate its exercise – with judicial review available for registration, deregistration, and internal disputes. The right to freedom of association is therefore a qualified right.[27]

Article 36 of the 2010 Constitution of Kenya guarantees the right to freedom of association.[28] It affirms that every person is entitled to freely associate – whether by forming, joining, or participating in groups – without undue pressure, and that any legal requirement for registration of an association must not allow arbitrary refusal or cancellation.[29]

Article 38 builds on this by securing the political rights that depend on the right to freedom of association – allowing individuals to form or join political parties, participate in political activities, and seek public office.[30] Together, the two provisions reinforce participatory democracy by protecting both the organisational and political dimensions of civic engagement. Article 24 permits limitations; they must be reasonable, justifiable, and not undermine the essence of the right. In this regard, where deregistration is sought, it must follow due process, including the right to a fair hearing.[31]

As discussed in section I, the 2010 Constitution recognises international law as part of Kenyan law, thereby giving effect to international human rights treaties such as the International Covenant on Civil and Political Rights (ICCPR)

[24] 'Constitution of Kenya' (n 14) Art 94(5).

[25] Treaty-Making and Ratification Act 2022, ss 8 and 12.

[26] A Gutmann, *Freedom of Association*, vol 17 (Princeton, Princeton University Press, 1998) books.google.com/books?hl=en&lr=lang_en&id=oUxgcs6cJx4C&oi=fnd&pg=PP9&dq=emy+guttmann:+Freedom+of+Association&ots=yMJu34vGNU&sig=iBFn9NBOZB4iQxxzemAt6Rtk09c accessed 27 August 2025.

[27] 'Democracy, Freedom of Expression and Freedom of Association: Threats to MPs' publications.parliament.uk/pa/jt201919/jtselect/jtrights/37/37.pdf accessed 27 August 2025.

[28] 'Constitution of Kenya' (n 14) Art 36.

[29] ibid Art 36.

[30] ibid Art 38 (1).

[31] ibid Art 36(3)(b).

and the African Charter on Human and Peoples' Rights, both of which safeguard the right to freedom of association.[32]

The 2010 Constitution expressly regulates the limitation of rights under Article 24(1), which provides that a right or fundamental freedom may be limited only by law, and only to the extent that the limitation is reasonable and justifiable in an open and democratic society based on human dignity, equality and freedom, taking into account factors such as the nature of the right, the purpose and importance of the limitation, the extent of the limitation, and whether there are less restrictive means to achieve the intended purpose.[33] This framework reflects the globally recognised compelling state interest/least restrictive means test, which requires that state regulation of rights be both substantively necessary and narrowly tailored.[34]

III. LEGISLATIVE REGULATION OF THE RIGHT TO FREEDOM OF ASSOCIATION

Kenya's statutory framework for the right to freedom of association reflects a layered legal evolution fashioned by its shifting political climate.[35] This framework is outlined below, before the chapter goes on in section IV to consider how judicial interpretation of the right to freedom of association has also played a significant role in affirming and expanding the contours of freedom of association.

The Public Benefit Organisations Act, operationalised in May 2024, replaced the Non-Governmental Organizations Co-Ordination Act of 1990 (the NGO Coordination Act), significantly aligning Kenya's civil society regulation with the 2010 Constitution, especially the right to freedom of association under Article 36.[36] Unlike the NGO Coordination Act – criticised for discretionary registration, fragmented regulation, weak self-regulation, lack of dispute resolution, and enforcement practices found unconstitutional – the Public Benefit Organisations Act introduces clearer registration timelines, a consolidated framework, stronger self-regulation through the National Federation of Public

[32] ibid Art 2(5) and 2(6). 'International Covenant on Civil and Political Rights' (*OHCHR*) www.ohchr.org/en/instruments-mechanisms/instruments/international-covenant-civil-and-political-rights accessed 17 May 2025; 'African Charter on Human and Peoples' Rights' (*African Commission on Human and Peoples' Rights*, 21 October 1986) achpr.au.int/en/charter/african-charter-human-and-peoples-rights accessed 17 May 2025.

[33] 'Constitution of Kenya' (n 14) Art 24(1)[(a)–(e)].

[34] A Barak, *Proportionality: Constitutional Rights and Their Limitations* (Cambridge, Cambridge University Press, 2012) www.cambridge.org/core/books/proportionality/6E9C523D5653FEE453068DEFECF4C4F5 accessed 27 August 2025.

[35] 'Constitution of Kenya' (n 14) Art 2. The discussion in the 'Introduction' (Sec I) establishes this in great detail, including the relationship between the 2010 Constitution, Kenyan Statute, international law principles, and treaties which Kenya has ratified.

[36] Public Benefits Organizations Act (2025) new.kenyalaw.org/akn/ke/act/2013/18/eng@2025-06-20 accessed 21 August 2025; Non-Governmental Organizations Co-Ordination Act (2022) new.kenyalaw.org/akn/ke/act/1990/19/eng@2022-12-31 accessed 16 June 2025.

Benefit Organisations, a dedicated Disputes Tribunal, and enhanced transparency and accountability.[37]

Under the Public Benefit Organisations Act, an organisation seeking registration must first apply to the Public Benefit Organisations Regulatory Authority in the prescribed form, signed by its authorised officials.[38] The application must be accompanied by the organisation's constitution, details of its founders, officials, and physical address, as well as the required registration fee.[39] The Authority then reviews the application to ensure compliance with statutory requirements, including that the objectives fall within the definition of a public benefit organisation.[40] Where satisfied, the Authority issues a certificate of registration, conferring legal personality and the rights and obligations of a PBO.[41] If refused, the Authority must provide written reasons, and the applicant has a right of appeal to the Public Benefit Organisations Disputes Tribunal.[42]

Despite recent legislative reforms, Kenya continues to face challenges in fully realising the constitutional right to freedom of association. On 30 April 2025, the High Court of Kenya in *Otieno & 2 others v Attorney General & another; Katiba Institute & 9 others* invalidated multiple provisions of the Public Benefit Organizations Act as unconstitutional – for infringing the constitutional rights to privacy, fair trial, institutional independence, and freedom from compelled association.[43] Among the key outcomes, the Court ordered the automatic

[37] Public Benefits Organizations Act (n 36); W Arthur and Rödl & Partner, 'Kenya: The Dawn of a New Era: The Operationalisation of the Public Benefits Organization Act' www.roedl.com/insights/kenya-public-benefits-organization accessed 21 August 2025. It also has transition provisions requiring NGOs to re-register (deadline extended to May 2026), thereby creating a more predictable, transparent, and constitutionally compliant environment that better supports the right of civil society to organise and operate freely.

[38] Public Benefits Organizations Act (n 36) ss 6, 7.

[39] ibid s 7(3).

[40] ibid ss 5, 8.

[41] ibid ss 9, 10.

[42] ibid ss 19, 20.

[43] *Otieno & 2 others v Attorney General & another; Katiba Institute & 9 others (Interested Parties) (Petition E519 of 2024)* [2025] KEHC 8557 (KLR) (Constitutional and Human Rights) (30 April 2025) (Judgment). The court declared paragraphs 5(1) & 5(2) of the Fifth Schedule (which required organisations previously registered under the repealed NGO Co-ordination Act to re-apply) null and ordered the automatic transition and registration of such organisations as Public Benefit Organizations. It held that section 32 (on compelled disclosure of members and donors) violated the right to privacy (Art 31[c]), and found the composition and appointment framework for the Public Benefit Organizations Authority Board and Public Benefit Organizations Disputes Tribunal (section 35, the Third Schedule, and parts of the Fifth Schedule, and sections 50[1], 50[5] and 50[6][c]) incompatible with constitutional requirements for institutional independence and judicial/security-of-tenure safeguards. The Court also ruled that mandatory membership of Public Benefit Organizations in the National Federation (sections 21[1] & 21[9]) and the prescription that only 'significant' self-regulatory forums (section 23[2]) be recognised were unconstitutional – reading those provisions as voluntary rather than compulsory – because they infringed freedom from compelled association (Art 36[2]) and related guarantees. Finally, the Court held that suspension/cancellation procedures in sections 18(1)–(3) and section 19(1)(b) breached the right to a fair hearing and fair administrative action (Art 50), and therefore were invalid. The relief included declaratory orders, a mandamus directing the Public Benefit Organizations Authority to effect the automatic transition.

transition of non-governmental organisations registered under the repealed NGO Coordination Act to Public Benefit Organizations status, eliminating their need to reapply.[44]

The decision in the *Otieno* case further clarified that membership in the National Federation of PBOs must be voluntary, reinforcing the principle of freedom of association.[45] Provisions allowing deregistration without a fair hearing were invalidated for breaching the right to fair administrative action.[46] Lastly, the Court found that the structure and appointment processes of the PBO Regulatory Authority and Disputes Tribunal compromised institutional independence and were therefore unconstitutional.[47] Overall, the decision marks a significant step forward in protecting civil society organisations and ensuring that regulatory frameworks align with Kenya's constitutional values. As at the date of this chapter, the state still has room to challenge the decision.[48]

The Political Parties Act of 2011, enacted in the wake of the 2010 Constitution, regulates the formation and functioning of political parties – an essential vehicle for exercising the right to freedom of association in a democracy.[49] The Act reinforced democratic principles by obliging political parties to incorporate democratic principles in their constitutions, including internal political party structures and transparency through regular, free, and fair internal elections, participatory governance, and transparent financial management through annual audited accounts submitted to the Registrar of Political Parties.[50]

The Act, however, also imposes a high threshold for full registration that may constrain political pluralism, such as the requirement that a party have at least 1,000 registered members in at least half of Kenya's 47 counties and ensure its membership and governing body reflect regional and ethnic diversity, gender balance (no more than two-thirds of its governing body are of the same gender), and representation of minorities and marginalised groups.[51] Additionally, only parties that secure at least 5 per cent of the national vote qualify for public funding.[52] While intended to ensure national representation and prevent fragmentation, such rules can disproportionately disadvantage smaller or emerging political parties, thereby limiting the diversity of political competition.

Meanwhile, the Labour Relations Act 2007, adopted in a period of expanding civil liberties, modernised union structures by outlining clear procedures for trade union registration, and strengthening the framework for collective

[44] ibid.
[45] ibid.
[46] ibid.
[47] ibid.
[48] Appellate Jurisdiction Act 2022.
[49] Political Parties Act 2022.
[50] ibid s 6(2), s 9(2)(c), s 21(1)(f). To ensure compliance with the Political Parties Act, the Register's mandate includes registration, regulation, monitoring, investigation, and supervision of political parties.
[51] ibid s 7(1) and 7(2)a–d.
[52] ibid s 25(2).

bargaining.[53] However, certain procedural controls – particularly the requirement for notice and balloting before strikes, and the Registrar's discretionary powers in registration – predate the 2010 constitutional reforms and can still constrain workers' associational rights.[54]

The right to freedom of association in Kenya is not absolute. It may be limited where such restriction is 'reasonable and justifiable in an open and democratic society'.[55] Therefore, certain associations are often banned, particularly those considered as threats to national security or public order. The criteria for determining 'reasonable' and 'justifiable' remain relatively subjective – an unruly horse.[56] Under Kenya's Prevention of Organised Crimes Act, the government has proscribed numerous groups and intensified security operations targeting them, on grounds of involvement in violence, extremism, and criminal activities.[57]

Another example of when freedom of association was limited under Article 24 of the Constitution concerns civil society groups: following a terrorist attack at the Garissa University, in the northeast of Kenya in 2015, the government froze bank accounts and began deregistering NGOs allegedly linked to funding terrorism.[58] These included Muslims for Human Rights (MUHURI), Haki Africa, and the Agency for Peace and Development (APD).[59] The board invoked powers under the POCA.[60] However, courts later ruled that the process violated due process and ordered restoration of their registrations and bank accounts.[61]

Finally, while informal associations are not prohibited, formal legal registration becomes necessary once an association seeks to operate publicly – such as opening bank accounts, owning property, hiring employees, or entering legal

[53] Labour Relations Act 2022, ss 12–18, and ss 54–59, respectively.

[54] ibid ss 76–78, and ss 19–21, respectively.

[55] 'Constitution of Kenya' (n 14) Art 24.

[56] 'Enderby Town Football Club Ltd v. Football Association Ltd' (*vLex*) vlex.co.uk/vid/enderby-town-football-club-793216057 accessed 28 August 2025. The reference 'Unruly horse' is to borrow the words of Lord Denning.

[57] Prevention of Organised Crimes Act, Chapter 59 Laws of Kenya 2022. These designations, made under section 22(1) of POCA, allow the government to criminalise group membership, seize assets, and restrict operations. Affected groups may appeal the decision in the High Court within 21 days, ensuring legal oversight while enhancing public safety. Some of the groups that have been proscribed include: Al Shabaab, Amachuma, Angola Msumbiji, Banyamulenge, Baghdad Boys, Charo Shutu, Chinkororo, Coast Housing Land Network, Congo By Force, Dallas Muslim Youth, Forty Brothers, Forty Two Brothers, Jeshi La Embakasi, Jeshi La Mzee, Jeshi La King'ole, Japo Group, Kamjesh, Kamukunji Youth Group, Kaya Bombo Youth, Kenya Youth Alliance, Kosovo Boys, Kuzacha, Makande Army, Mombasa Republican Council, Mungiki Movement, Mungiki Organization, Mungiki Sect, Republican Revolutionary Council, Sabout Land Defence Force (SLDF), Sakina Youth, Siafu, Sungu Sungu and Taliban.

[58] 'Country Reports on Terrorism 2015 – Kenya' (*Refworld*) www.refworld.org/reference/annual-report/usdos/2016/en/110410 accessed 16 June 2025.

[59] ibid.

[60] ibid.

[61] ibid.

agreements.[62] The Societies Act, which regulates the registration and control of societies in Kenya, requires that any group of ten or more persons formed for a common purpose must register if it falls within the Act's definition of a 'society'.[63] Unregistered associations that operate in such a formal manner risk being declared unlawful and may face legal sanctions.[64]

IV. JUDICIAL INTERPRETATION OF THE RIGHT TO FREEDOM OF ASSOCIATION

Section IV examines select landmark judicial decisions on the right to freedom of association in Kenya, as they provide interpretive guidance and a measure of how constitutional guarantees are balanced against state regulation and illuminate the practical scope and limitations of the right.

In *Council of County Governors v Attorney General & another*, the High Court of Kenya upheld the constitutionality of section 10 of the Election Laws (Amendment) Act 2017, which required political parties to submit membership lists 120 days before a general election.[65] The petitioners argued that the provision violated the right to freedom of association under Article 36 of the Constitution by limiting political mobility and party affiliation.[66] However, the Court found that the law pursued a legitimate public interest – ensuring credible, timely, and orderly elections – and imposed a reasonable and proportionate limitation on the right.[67] It emphasised that constitutional rights, including freedom of association, are not absolute and may be justifiably limited under Article 24.[68] The Court dismissed the petition, affirming that electoral integrity can necessitate lawful constraints on individual political freedoms.[69]

In *Attorney General & another v Randu Nzai Ruwa & others*, the state appealed a High Court decision that had invalidated the proscription of the Mombasa Republican Council (MRC) under the Prevention of Organized Crime Act.[70] The government argued that the MRC was unlawful and a threat to national security.[71] The Court of Appeal, however, upheld the position of the High Court, holding that a blanket ban was unconstitutional.[72] It stressed that Articles 36 (freedom of association), 37 (assembly), and 38 (political rights)

[62] 'Societies Act, CAP. 108' www.kenyalaw.org/lex//actview.xql?actid=CAP.%20108 accessed 11 August 2025.

[63] ibid.

[64] ibid.

[65] *Council of County Governors v Attorney General & another* [2017] KEHC 6395 (KLR).

[66] ibid.

[67] ibid.

[68] ibid.

[69] ibid.

[70] *Attorney General & another v Randu Nzai Ruwa & 2 others* [2016] KECA 418 (KLR).

[71] ibid.

[72] ibid.

protect even unpopular or controversial groups, unless clear and proportionate justification is provided under Article 24.[73] The Court emphasised that the state must use less restrictive measures – such as monitoring or regulating the group's activities – rather than outright prohibition, and that due process, including the opportunity to register as a political party, could not be circumvented.[74]

In February 2023, the Supreme Court of Kenya upheld the right to freedom of association by affirming that the National Gay and Lesbian Human Rights Commission (NGLHRC) must be allowed to register as an NGO.[75] The Court held that denying registration based on sexual orientation was unconstitutional, stressing that freedom of association is a fundamental right inherent to all, regardless of whether the views advanced are popular.[76] This judgment which concluded a ten-year legal battle initiated by Eric Gitari in 2013, reaffirmed earlier decisions by the High Court (2015) and the Court of Appeal (2019) that the refusal to register NGLHRC violated constitutional guarantees of association.[77] In addition to underscoring the right to freedom of association, the decisions also expose the state's recurrent attempt to limit recognition of associations perceived as politically sensitive.

In *Thuranira & 4 others v Attorney General & Others*, the High Court scrutinised amendments introduced by the Political Parties (Amendment) Act 2022, which sought to restructure the regulation of political parties. While most provisions were upheld, two were struck down: section 31(3) for removing the Auditor-General's constitutionally mandated role in auditing party finances under Article 229, and section 34(fd) for attempting to transfer the regulation of political party nominations from the IEBC to the Registrar of Political Parties, contrary to Article 88(4). The Court anchored its reasoning primarily in Article 38 (political rights) rather than in Article 36 (freedom of association), underscoring the centrality of party autonomy to democratic participation.

This decision captures the enduring tension between state regulation and associational autonomy. On one hand, the state has a legitimate role in ensuring accountability, transparency, and fairness in the management of political parties as public actors. On the other, excessive state control – such as reallocating core constitutional functions or undermining independent oversight – threatens the autonomy of parties and the broader right of citizens to organise freely for political purposes. Although the Court did not extend its analysis to associations beyond political parties, the underlying principle – that state regulation must not extinguish autonomy – resonates with the broader freedom of

[73] ibid.

[74] ibid.

[75] 'Supreme Court Petition No.16 of 2019, NGOS Co-Ordination Board vs. Eric Gitari & 5 Others. Judgement – The Judiciary' judiciary.go.ke/download/supreme-court-petition-no-16-of-2019-ngos-co-ordination-board-vs-eric-gitari-5-others-judgement/ accessed 27 May 2025.

[76] ibid.

[77] Petition 440 of 2013 – Kenya Law; *Non-Governmental Organizations Co-ordination Board v EG & 5 others (Civil Appeal 145 of 2015)* [2019] KECA 902 (KLR) (22 March 2019) (Judgment).

association framework. It illustrates how Kenya's constitutional order attempts to balance oversight with independence in the governance of associations.

Freedom of association underpins collective action, political participation, and organisational autonomy, complementing individual rights. It is closely tied to the right to freedom of expression, as political speech often occurs within associative contexts; to freedom of religion and belief, which depends on the ability to form religious organisations; and to equality and non-discrimination, a lens courts have applied to challenge exclusionary practices, as seen in the *Eric Gitari* case.

Moreover, the *Fugicha* litigation illustrates the unresolved tension in Kenya between freedom of association, speech, and religion.[78] The High Court upheld a school's uniform policy, holding that institutional discipline outweighed claims to religious expression.[79] The Court of Appeal reversed, stressing that pluralism is a constitutional value and that associations such as schools must accommodate diversity rather than enforce uniformity that erases identity.[80] On further appeal, however, the Supreme Court set aside the judgment on procedural grounds, declining to address the substantive constitutional issues.[81] The case thus highlights the fragile balance between institutional autonomy and individual liberty, and the judiciary's ambivalence in fully reconciling associational order with freedoms of expression and religion.[82]

Overall, Kenyan courts emphasise three rationales: individual liberty (citizens' freedom to pursue shared goals); democratic pluralism (enabling diverse voices in governance); and autonomy of associations (self-regulation in line with democratic norms). This approach is evident in how courts assess both state and intra-association actions.

The courts recognise freedom of association as an aspect of individual liberty, protecting the ability of citizens to pursue common goals without unjustified interference. In *Eric Gitari v Non-Governmental Organisations Co-ordination Board & 4 others*, the High Court, Court of Appeal and Supreme Court all upheld that denying registration of an association solely because it represented sexual minorities was unconstitutional, affirming that individuals have the right to come together in pursuit of lawful objectives.[83] This principle underscores that the state cannot curtail personal liberty through restrictions on collective identity.[84]

[78] *Fugicha v Methodist Church in Kenya (Suing Through its Registered Trustees) & 3 others (Civil Appeal 22 of 2015)* [2016] KECA 273 (KLR) (7 September 2016) (Judgment); Supreme Court, *Methodist Church in Kenya v Fugicha & 3 Others (Petition 16 of 2016)* [2019] KESC 59 (KLR) (23 January 2019) (Judgment) (with Dissent – JB Ojwang, SCJ) (2019) new.kenyalaw.org/akn/ke/judgment/kesc/2019/59/eng@2019-01-23 accessed 26 August 2025.

[79] *Fugicha v Methodist Church* (n 78).

[80] ibid.

[81] Supreme Court (n 78).

[82] ibid.

[83] 'Supreme Court Petition No.16 of 2019' (n 75).

[84] YP Ghai and J C Ghai, *Kenyas-Constitution-Instrument-for-Change.Pdf* katibainstitute.org/wp-content/uploads/2021/08/Kenyas-Constitution-Instrument-for-Change.pdf accessed 26 August 2025; W Mutunga, 'The 2010 Constitution of Kenya and Its Interpretation: Reflections from the Supreme Court's Decisions' (2015) 6 *Speculum Juris* 1.

Additionally, the courts view association as essential for democratic pluralism, ensuring that diverse social, political, and cultural voices are represented in governance. In *Party of Independent Candidates of Kenya v Attorney General & 2 others*, the High Court addressed the tension between freedom of association and the regulation of political parties under the Political Parties Act.[85] While the petitioners argued that strict registration requirements violated Articles 36 and 38 by stifling political organisation, the Court upheld them as reasonable limitations designed to foster national integration and discourage ethnically or regionally based parties.[86] From the perspective of democratic pluralism, the case illustrates how Kenyan courts balance the need for diverse political voices with safeguards to ensure that such diversity does not fragment governance or undermine multiparty democracy.[87] In this sense, pluralism is recognised not as an absolute proliferation of associations but as regulated diversity that strengthens democratic stability.[88]

Kenyan jurisprudence strongly supports the autonomy of political parties in managing internal affairs, while ensuring accountability through judicial oversight. This is evident in *Thuranira & others v Attorney General*, where the High Court underscored that state interference in internal decision-making is justified only in cases of constitutional or democratic violations.[89] Complementing this, multiple decisions of the Political Parties Disputes Tribunal demonstrate how the tribunal and courts emphasise the exhaustion of internal dispute resolution mechanisms before parties can escalate conflicts to the Tribunal and courts.[90] This reinforces internal governance. Together, these decisions affirm that associations are protected from arbitrary state and judicial intervention, while preserving pathways for redress when internal mechanisms fail.[91] Further, PPDT jurisprudence on internal party disputes reflects the struggle between the autonomy of associations and judicial oversight to enforce democratic norms.[92]

[85] *Party of Independent Candidates of Kenya v Attorney General & 2 others* [2012] KEHC 5853 (KLR).

[86] ibid.

[87] ibid.

[88] ibid.

[89] *Thuranira & 4 others v Attorney General & 2 others; Registrar of Political Parties & 3 others (Interested Parties) (Petition E043, E057 & E109 of 2022)* [2022] KEHC 482 (KLR) (Constitutional and Human Rights) (20 April 2022) (Judgment).

[90] 'Commission Validates Report and Case Digest of 2022 Pre-Election Dispute Resolution' www.iebc.or.ke/news/?Commission_Validates_Report_and_Case_Digest_of_2022_Pre-election_Dispute_Resolution accessed 26 August 2025 The author is in possession of a copy of the Political Parties Disputes Tribunal Case Digest: Emerging Jurisprudence of the PPDT 2022 Electoral Cycle (published with the support of the Judiciary Committee on Elections, ELGIA and USAID), which can be availed upon request.

[91] *Thuranira & 4 others v Attorney General & 2 others* (n 89); 'Commission Validates Report and Case Digest of 2022 Pre-Election Dispute Resolution' (n 90).

[92] *Lilian Gogo v Joseph Mboya Nyamuthe & 4 others* [2017] KECA 454 (KLR).

V. REFLECTIONS ON THE LEGAL PROTECTION OF THE RIGHT TO FREEDOM OF ASSOCIATION

Kenyan non-state observer groups emphasise the right to freedom of association as foundational to democratic governance.[93] Theories emphasise civic engagement, checks on power, and minority protection. Specifically, political theory underscores the importance of association.[94] Liberal and pluralist traditions stress rights and institutional checks.[95] Participatory democracy highlights that participation in civic associations and institutions is necessary for democratic legitimacy, political efficacy, and citizen inclusion.[96] Deliberative democracy views freedom of association as crucial for inclusive public debate and collective decision-making.[97] Civic republicanism highlights active vigilance against domination.[98] Together, these frameworks underscore why freedom of association is not merely an individual liberty but a collective right that underpins democratic resilience.

Observer groups stress that the right to freedom of association in Kenya is underutilised and should be better understood in terms of its enabling function in civil society, especially for youth, women, and marginalised communities.[99] For instance, the International Center for Not-for-Profit Law (ICNL) notes that while Kenya's legal framework formally supports public participation and civil society, implementation gaps – including limited civic education, poor engagement mechanisms, and lack of access for women, youth, and persons with disabilities – impede the full realisation of association rights.[100]

Ongoing reform discussions focus on simplifying registration processes, enhancing oversight under the Political Parties Act and expanding civic education

[93] S Gaballa, 'A Crucial Case on Freedom of Association in Kenya' katibainstitute.org/a-crucial-case-on-freedom-of-association-in-kenya/ accessed 26 August 2025.

[94] T Adeate, 'Mbiti on Community in African Political Thought: Reconciling the "I" and the"We"' (2023) 24 *Phronimon* 1.

[95] 'Democracy in America by Alexis de Tocqueville (1840)' www.marxists.org/reference/archive/de-tocqueville/democracy-america/index.htm accessed 26 August 2025; R Dahl, *Who Governs?* yalebooks.yale.edu/book/9780300103922/who-governs/ accessed 26 August 2025.

[96] C Pateman, '71. Participation and Democratic Theory' in R Blaug and J Schwarzmantel (eds), *Democracy* (New York, Columbia University Press, 2016) www.degruyter.com/document/doi/10.7312/blau17412-086/html accessed 26 August 2025.

[97] J Habermas, 'Postscript to Between Facts' (1996) 135 Habermas, Modernity and Law books.google.co.uk/books/about/Between_Facts_and_Norms.html?id=4SK1CgAAQBAJ&redir_esc=y accessed 26 August 2025; J Habermas and W Rehg, *Contributions to a Discourse Theory of Law and Democracy* (Cambridge, Polity Press, 1996) teddykw2.wordpress.com/wp-content/uploads/2012/07/jc3bcrgen-habermas-between-facts-and-norms.pdf accessed 26 August 2025; JS Dryzek, *Deliberative Democracy and beyond: Liberals, Critics, Contestations* (Oxford, OUP, 2002) books.google.com/books?hl=en&lr=lang_en&id=9iTqPrZAYX8C&oi=fnd&pg=PA1&dq=Dryzek,+John+S.+(2000).+Deliberative+Democracy+and+Beyond:+Liberals,+Critics,+Contestations.+Oxford:+Oxford+University+Press.&ots=Wx6ORYYfJh&sig=ZTS6fwjdPqK90kVjwYm5d7LHZoc accessed 26 August 2025.

[98] A Bose, 'Vigilance as a Practice of Postcolonial Freedom' (2024) 118 *American Political Science Review* 1614.

[99] 'PROTECT: Building a Free, Open, and Inclusive Kenya – Together' (*ARTICLE 19*) www.article19.org/protect/ accessed 22 August 2025.

[100] 'Kenya' (*ICNL*) www.icnl.org/resources/civic-freedom-monitor/kenya accessed 22 August 2025.

on associational rights, amid consensus that Kenya's political associational potential remains under-realised; unlocking it will require easing bureaucratic barriers, safeguarding the rights of dissenting and minority groups, and aligning statutory frameworks more closely with constitutional guarantees.

The wave of Gen Z-led protests in Kenya in June 2024 and June 2025, that were ignited by widespread opposition to the Finance Bill 2024 and characterised by digital mobilisation like TikTok, Telegram, and X (formerly Twitter), has redefined freedom of association in a digital context, particularly during the mobilisation phase of recent protests. The use of fluid, non-hierarchical networks, and leaderless organisation but highly organised collective action, challenges traditional legal frameworks governing freedom of association.[101] Social justice actors, especially those with strong influence on social media, were instrumental in rallying public support. They created online communities and informal associations to advocate for specific reforms.

These digital spaces became powerful platforms for collective action, demonstrating that the right to freedom of association can thrive even outside formal registration frameworks. Many participants chose not to formally register or be publicly identified as members of any existing organisation, yet still exercised their constitutional right to organise and advocate. This evolution reflects a more flexible, inclusive, and contemporary interpretation of freedom of association in Kenya's civic landscape.

As discussed in the preceding sections of this chapter, existing statutes such as the PBO Act, Political Parties Act, Labour Relations Act, and Societies Act presuppose structured, registered, hierarchical organisations, thereby failing to accommodate loosely coordinated, issue-based, or digitally convened groups exercising their Article 36 rights. This gap risks marginalising vibrant, decentralised civic movements and undermines the modern ethos of freedom of association, calling for a more inclusive legal framework that recognises and protects non-traditional forms of public assembly and collaboration. Additionally, the state's response to these protests – including brutal dispersal of assemblies, attempts to attribute responsibility to informal leaders, and the use of registration-based compliance measures – highlights the tension between current law and the constitutional commitment to political participation and association.[102]

In *Law Office of Ghazi Suleiman v Sudan*, the African Commission held that Sudan's punitive actions against a human rights advocate constituted a

[101] O Madung, 'Tortured over a Tweet: How the War between Kenya's Gen Z and Their President Has Moved Online' *The Guardian* (1 May 2025) www.theguardian.com/global-development/2025/may/01/kenyans-tortured-for-a-tweet-president-ruto-satire-x-youth-gen-z accessed 22 August 2025.

[102] 'Kenya: Concerns over Deaths in Protests' (*OHCHR*) www.ohchr.org/en/press-briefing-notes/2025/07/kenya-concerns-over-deaths-protests accessed 22 August 2025; 'Freedom of Expression: Treatment of Kenyan Protestors during Summer Unrest Draws Concern' www.ibanet.org/kenyan-protestors accessed 22 August 2025; O Madung, '"This Is Lawfare": Kenya "Weaponising the Law" to Silence Critics and Protesters' *The Guardian* (8 August 2025) www.theguardian.com/global-development/2025/aug/08/kenya-weaponises-law-mass-arrests-crackdown-critics-protesters accessed 22 August 2025.

disproportionate violation of freedoms of expression, association, and assembly under the African Charter.[103] Complementing this, General Comment No 37 (2020) clarifies that informal, spontaneous gatherings – like those observed in the Gen Z protests – are protected under Article 21 of the ICCPR even when the participants are not part of any registered entity.[104] Together, the decision and provisions illustrate the interdependence of assembly and association: communities can leverage rights to freedom of assembly to express collective dissent, and rights to freedom of association to sustain organised discourse, without necessarily entering into formal registration.

A reconsideration of the legal framework may be necessary to recognise and protect decentralised, issue-based movements while ensuring public order. Such reforms could include clarifying the application of registration laws to informal civic movements, strengthening protections against arbitrary restrictions, and embracing digital spaces as legitimate forums for association and political expression.

VI. CONCLUSION

While Kenya has made significant strides in implementing the right to freedom of association since the enactment of the 2010 Constitution, the persistence of state overreach and control shows that Kenya is not immune to 'façade constitutionalism'.[105] Despite significant jurisprudence and legislative developments fortifying this right, implementation gaps and bureaucratic obstacles persist. With thoughtful reform and sustained judicial vigilance, Kenya can advance the full promise of associational freedom as a cornerstone of democratic governance and pluralism.

[103] 'Law Offices of Ghazi Suleiman / Sudan – 228/99' (*African Commission on Human and Peoples' Rights*, 22 August 2025) achpr.au.int/index.php/en/decisions-communications/law-offices-ghazi-suleiman-sudan-22899 accessed 26 August 2025.

[104] 'General Comment No. 37 on Article 21 (Right of Peaceful Assembly)' (*OHCHR*) www.ohchr.org/en/documents/general-comments-and-recommendations/general-comment-no-37-article-21-right-peaceful accessed 26 August 2025; 'International Covenant on Civil and Political Rights' (n 32).

[105] CM Fombad, 'The Swaziland Constitution of 2005: Can Absolutism Be Reconciled with Modern Constitutionalism?' (2007) 23 *South African Journal on Human Rights* 93.

8

Judicial Review of Associative Agreements: Insights from a Civil Law Perspective

JOSÉ JUAN ANZURES GURRÍA*

I. INTRODUCTION

ONE OF THE protected areas under freedom of association concerns the ability of associations to organise themselves and make their own decisions without interference from third parties, mainly the state. This does not mean, however, that the associations' decisions are outside the law or that they cannot be appealed to the courts. But how far should the intervention or control of the courts over the actions of associations go? Freedom of association includes the autonomy of associations to self-organise, meaning state authorities must be kept away from any intervention in their internal activities. However, this does not mean that their actions are free from any intervention by state courts.[1] There is no private dispute that can escape the control of the judiciary. Internal association agreements are no exception. Any decision taken by the association according to its organisational autonomy may be reviewable by ordinary courts.[2] This does not mean that, once the association's internal instances have been exhausted without reaching the desired result, a member must go to court and request the rectification of the association's agreement. If

* I would like to thank Professor Maria Cahill for inviting me to contribute to this book and for her suggestions and comments on this chapter.

[1] In Germany, legal precedents are cited by abbreviating the name of the court and the case law journal, followed by the year and page number of the resolution. The precedent cited corresponds to *RG* JW 1925, 224, (Reichsgericht, Juristischen Wochenschrift, year 1925, page 224). Also, it mentions the book and page number where the resolution is found. See, in this regard, resolution RGZ 153, 267; 165, 140, which means *Entscheidungen des Reichsgerichts* in Zivilsachen (book 153, page 267 and book 165 page 140). From 1879 to 1945, the *Reichsgericht* was the Supreme Court of the German Reich responsible for ordinary jurisdiction.

[2] Ruling of the Spanish Constitutional Court 218/1988, 22 November 1988. From now on, the rulings of the Spanish Constitutional Court will be abbreviated with the initials STC.

a member contests a decision made by the association, it is because he does not agree with it. However, this does not mean it should be corrected by the courts.

Therefore, the problem is not whether the agreements of associations should be under judicial control, nor if members of associations have the right to effective judicial protection and can appeal to the courts, or even if the courts can and should hear disputes arising within associations. Rather, the problem lies in determining how far this control by state courts can go. As Vidal Marín says, 'in determining the limits to this judicial control'.[3]

This dilemma has been resolved in various ways in different jurisdictions. In common law countries, there may be greater respect for associative autonomy, limiting judicial interference.[4] In contrast, in Roman-Germanic countries such as Spain and Germany, respect for the autonomy of the association is maintained, but members are also protected against possible abuses or violations by the association. There are three perspectives: one suggesting that the court's intervention should be merely formal, another advocating for a substantive intervention, and the third based on a *reasonable basis* criterion. Based on the study and systematisation of decisions from the constitutional courts of Spain and Germany, this paper offers some insights in respect of judicial review of associative agreements, intended to guide judges across different jurisdictions. The first consideration is the type of association; if it is an association with public relevance, such as political parties or trade unions, the judge's intervention should be greater. Another criterion is the type of associative agreement, whether it refers to a strict application of the statutes or an interpretive agreement of them. In the latter case, it must also be considered whether it is an agreement on the organisational structure of the association or whether it affects the members' rights. The chapter proceeds as follows: section II analyses the normative framework relevant to judges resolving associative conflicts. Section III considers the case of formal judicial review while section IV considers material or substantive judicial control. Section V explores the reasonable ground criterion. Section VI presents guidelines to orient judicial judgment in the case of judicial review of associative agreements.

II. APPLICABLE LAW

To respect the freedom of associations to self-organise, when hearing an associative dispute, the judge must first ensure that the statutes of the association are being respected.[5] The judge's task is to verify that the association's

[3] TV Marín, 'El Derecho fundamental de asociación y el control judicial de la actividad interna de las asociaciones', in JD Revorio and EE Templado (eds), *La justicia constitucional en el estado democrático* (2000) 270.

[4] Also in common law countries, *Foss v Harbottle* (1843) 67 ER 189; *Wedderburn*, 'Shareholders' Rights and the Rule in Foss v Harbottle' [1957] *CLJ* 194196–198; *Hopkins v Marquis of Exeter (1867)* L.R. 5 Equity 63; *Fisher v Keane, (1878)* 11 Ch. D. 353, *Dawkins v Antrobus*, (1881) 17 Ch. D. 615, *Labouchere v Earl of Wharncliffe (1879)* 13 Ch D 346; *Young v.s. Ladies Imperial Club* (1920) 2 KB 523.

[5] STC 218/1988.

agreements comply with its statutes. This can be very clear in the case of regulated agreements, where the statutes assign a specific, detailed, and clearly defined authority to the association's bodies, which they are obliged to comply with. Therefore, if an agreement adopted by the association's bodies contravenes the provisions of the statutes, it is clearly evident the agreement will be null and void.

Furthermore, the judge must also check that the association's agreements are in conformity with both the law and the Constitution. In this regard, the Spanish Constitutional Court pointed out in its decision ATC 213/1991 that the judge can nullify an association agreement not only when the association does not comply with its own statutes, but also when its agreements are contrary to the national system of law.

At the outset of this book, an interesting case is presented that bears relevance to the situation under consideration. The 'Soup Kitchen' scenario concerns *Cairde ar son Cairde*, a soup kitchen founded by Gráinne and friends, which operates using leftover food from local groceries and receives assistance from neighbours. *Cairde ar son Cairde* is not formally constituted, lacks a formal structure, and is not registered as a charity.[6] It also has no bank account or bookkeeper. However, if *Cairde ar son Cairde* is a charity, and there is a law (such as the Charity Act) governing the operation of such associations, then it should be constituted and organised accordingly.

The Spanish Constitutional Court on 5 March 1995, in its decision 56/1995, pointed out that the courts may not only annul the agreements of association bodies for contravening their statutes, but also for infringement of the legal system, as well as for violating constitutional rights.[7] The Spanish Supreme Court has also stated that judicial review of association agreements must take place when the management of the legal entity deviates from its own statutes or when it contravenes mandatory rules of the legal system or violates constitutional principles.[8]

Thus, the associative freedom of self-organisation is firstly limited by the association's own statutes, but also by the legal system, the laws, the Constitution and its principles and values. Judicial control is therefore nothing more than verifying the association's conduct is carried out within the framework of legality and constitutionality. According to R Ernst, if the association conduct is not bound by these restrictions, it could be considered an abuse of power by the association.[9]

[6] M Cahill, 'Introduction: Comparative and Interdisciplinary Interfaces of Associational Life and Freedom' in M Cahill and G Lasagni (eds), *Associational Life and Freedom: Insights from Philosophy and Law* (Oxford, Hart Publishing, 2026), 15–16.

[7] On trade union matters, this position is defended by Antonio Ojeda Avilés in AO Avilés, *Derecho Sindical*, 3rd edn (Madrid, Tecnos, 1986) 122. See also STS 7 May 1988.

[8] STS 5 July 2004, (FD 2°.); also STS 1153/2007, 6 November (FD 2°.). From now on, the rulings of the Spanish Supreme Court will be abbreviated with the initials STS.

[9] R Ernst, *Die Ausübung der Vereinsgewalt* (Diss., Köln, 1969) 48.

While freedom of association includes the establishment and functioning of any association, such associations must be constituted and registered in accordance with the associative models stipulated by law. The laws governing the different types of associations do not infringe on the autonomy of associations; on the contrary, these regulations are designed to protect the diverse types of associations and their members.

If Gráinne and her partners have a conflict that goes to court, they will have the legal certainty that the conflict will be resolved based on established law. The legislation the judge must apply is known – for example, the Charity Act. Then, there is no reason to argue that a judge should not apply the laws of the state when resolving an associative conflict.

III. FORMAL JUDICIAL CONTROL

Once it has been clarified that courts must ensure that the association's conduct complies with its own statutes, the problem is to determine the scope of judicial control within associations. Insofar as the freedom of self-organisation of an association is the manifestation of a *negativus* status right, its exercise consists of a non-intervention of the state in the internal functioning of the association. In this sense, one of the first positions of scholars and case law in Germany was that the interference of the courts in conflicts over association agreements should be kept to a minimum.[10]

In this sense, a decision rendered by the *Reichsgericht* in 1922 held that a judicial review of the facts that led to an expulsion agreement constituted an undue interference in the autonomy of the association.[11] Similarly, another decision held by the German Supreme Court stated that the courts only have to check whether the decision of the association body was based on a provision of the statutes. This is because the assumption of facts in accordance with the statutes falls within the scope of the association's autonomous powers.[12]

From this perspective, the courts' task focuses on examining the facts that have occurred within the association and determining whether they are based on the statutes of the association. It is a matter of proving that the factual circumstances contained in the statutes have occurred. According to this position, it must be the association bodies, no one else, which must assess the facts that have occurred and adopt the decision they deem appropriate.[13] The courts cannot assess the correctness of the decision adopted by the association's bodies, nor

[10] JA Águila-Real, 'La expulsión de asociados y la confianza en el derecho privado', *Anuario de Derecho Civil*, 1997, 167.

[11] *RGZ* 49, 150, 155. *RGZ* means 'Entscheidungen des Reichsgerichts in Zivilsachen', (Decisions of the Supreme Court of Justice in civil matters, (book, page).

[12] *NJW* 66, 1951. NJW refers to 'Neue Juristische Wochenschrift' (New Legal Weekly Newspaper), where the first number corresponds to the year and the second to the page.

[13] TV Marín (n 3) 274.

can they substitute their assessments or reasoning, because this would imply a violation of the association's autonomy.[14]

In this respect, Stöber points out that the assessment and evaluation of the facts is not the task of the courts. Such an intervention would be an interference of the essential domain protected by the association's autonomy.[15] The will of the association would be replaced by that of the state, thus encroaching on the spontaneous vitality of associations and paralysing their internal functioning.

IV. MATERIAL JUDICIAL CONTROL

After the First World War, several court decisions became more influential in deciding certain association disputes. In 1922, the *Reichsgericht* heard a case on the expulsion of a doctor from the social security doctor's association (*Kassenarzt Entscheidung*) and ruled not only on the procedure followed by the association, but also on its decision. The Court stated that the expulsion constituted a 'manifest injustice'. Since expulsion from the association also prevented the doctor from practicing his profession, membership of the association was a matter of vital importance for him.[16] The Court understood that when questions of survival or the livelihood of a partner are at stake, judicial control must be substantive. From this court decision rendered on the 20th of April 1976, the German Supreme Court radically changed its judicial criterion.[17] Instead of recognising a minimal judicial intervention, it recognised a more intensive intervention. Moreover, with this decision, the tension between the individual interests of the members and the autonomy of the association became more evident.[18] As a result of this judgment, the autonomy of the association and the principle of state non-intervention have ceased to be treated as dogma.[19] The German Supreme Court gradually extended its interpretation to various aspects of members' lives, such as their economic, social and cultural development.[20]

Although it is true that the state is, and remains, a potential threat to the organisational and operational freedom of associations, it is also true that the social and democratic state governed by the rule of law is the guarantor of individual freedoms. This results in the constitutional obligation of the courts to observe and enforce these rights both in public relations, of the citizen vis-à-vis

[14] The Spanish Supreme Court also holds that in no case can the court substitute the will of the associative body. STS, 5th of July 2004 FD 2°. Also STS 1153/2007, 6th of November, Legal Ground (FD) 2.

[15] *cf* K Stöber, *Handbuch zum Vereinsrecht* (Köln, Auflage, 2004) 9, 390.

[16] *RGZ* 106, 120; 107, 386.

[17] *BGHZ* 47, 381. BGHZ means 'Entscheidungen des Bundesgerichtshofes in Zivilsachen', (Decisions of the Federal Court of Justice in civil matters, book, number page).

[18] U Meyer-Cording, *Die Vereinsstrafe* (Tübingen, J. C. B. Mohr, 1957) 112.

[19] J Schmitz, *Innere Vereinsfreiheit*, Inaugural-Disertation (zur Erlangung der Doktorwürde einer Hohen Rechtswissenschaftlichen Fakultät der Universität zu Köln, 1976) 71.

[20] *RGZ* 140, 24; 147, 15.

the state, and in private relations, which include endo-associative ones, and this perspective justifies a more intensive judicial intervention. In this sense, a more intensive judicial review consists not only of assessing whether the facts fit the statutes' requirements, but also of assessing the validity of the association agreement. In other words, it concerns the assessment made by the association's organ of the facts that led to the decision.

From this perspective, judicial review consists of making a value judgement on the facts or reasons that gave rise to the association agreement, irrespective of its decisions. The courts must review not only the facts that gave rise to the association agreement, but also the association organ's subsumption of those facts under the relevant statutes.[21] This is undoubtedly a substantial interference with the association's autonomy and is therefore only justified when it is intended to protect a member from possible abuses by the association or when the decision was notoriously arbitrary.

To defend the autonomy of associations, it is often argued that the fact that the courts decide on the substance of the dispute does not automatically mean excessive and arbitrary intervention. It is argued that this is not an infringement of the associations' autonomy, since the judicial decision will be taken in a well-founded and reasoned manner, based on the legislation that regulates each type of association, and on the principles and values of the legal system, including fundamental rights.

There should be no doubt that the courts must resolve the associative conflict in accordance with the law. The doubts of this position derive from the fact that when the courts hear an associative conflict and interpret the association's statutes, they overlook the interpretation made by the association's body of its own rules and regulations. An association's interpretation of its statutes is also part of the association's autonomy, so replacing its interpretation could indeed constitute an infringement of the association's freedom of self-organisation.

V. THE REASONABLE GROUND CRITERION

In Spain, the dilemma of judicial control over associations' internal decisions was solved to some degree by decision number 218/1988, rendered by the Constitutional Court on the 22nd of November 1988, which adopted the concept of 'reasonable ground'. An association appealed an ordinary court decision which assessed the consistency of the association's decision with its own statutes, as well as the reasoning of the association's body, and ultimately substituted the court's own judgment for that of the association. The Constitutional Court found that the ordinary court's decision had infringed the association's freedom of self-organisation. The Court ruled that the judge's role is not to

[21] STS of the 24th of March 1992, 13th of June 1996 and 26th of October 1995.

assess the member's conduct, independently of the judgement already made by the association's organs; rather, he must confine himself to checking whether there was a reasonable ground for the association's organs to adopt the expulsion decision.

This concept of reasonable ground has been well accepted and regularly used by the Constitutional Court, the Supreme Court, and other ordinary courts as a sufficient reason to resolve intra-association conflicts concerning the freedom of self-organisation of associations.[22]

Thus, in decision ATC 2/1993, the Constitutional Court reiterated the precedent it had maintained in decision STC 218/1988 and set it out in a more refined and complete manner. The Court stated that once the legality of the statutes has been verified by the judge, his task is strictly formal and must focus on two specific aspects: the competence of the associative body and the legality of the procedure. In addition to this review, the judge can verify the circumstances and reasonable grounds of the decision taken by the associative body, but must leave the discretion of the decisions to the association's body on how it will function.

In its decision STC 42/2011 from the 11th of April, the Constitutional Court stated that according to precedent, judicial review is less intense in substantive aspects than in procedural ones, and that judicial review should be limited to determining whether the decision lacks all reasonableness in accordance with the applicable legal and regulatory provisions.

The Spanish Supreme Court has also held in its decision STS, dated 6th of July 2000, that the right to self-organisation of a trade union prevents the judge from reviewing the reasoning of the association's body when it is sanctioning a member. But it does allow the judge to 'verify the fulfilment of the procedural guarantees established in the statutes to impose a sanction, and also to verify whether the adopted decision lacks a reasonable ground and is, therefore, arbitrary'.[23]

Although the concept of reasonable ground has been very useful, it is an indeterminate legal concept and therefore does not solve all problems. According to Marín López, we must ask what should be understood as reasonable, what the criterion of reasonableness is, what it consists of and how the judge should assess this reasonableness.[24] According to this author, a judge cannot decide whether the decision of an associative body is reasonable or not without assessing the facts; and if this is so, it must be accepted that this assessment must be made independently from the one made by the associative body, in which case it is possible to reach different conclusions. If this approach is not accepted,

[22] In its decision STS 846/2007 of the 13th of July 2007, the Supreme Court used the concept of reasonable grounds not to justify the expulsion of a member, but to deny membership to an applicant.

[23] STS of 23 December 1997, 7 April 1989 and 7 May 1988.

[24] JJ Marín López, 'La intervención judicial en los conflictos endoasociativos: el caso de la expulsión de asociados' (1989) 14 *Poder Judicial* 156.

judicial review would have no practical operational effect. In short, according to this author, the reasonable ground is a justification for the judge to carry out a thorough judicial review of the association agreements.

On the other hand, this concept has been overused, including to justify the validity of all association agreements when perhaps it was not necessary. In this regard, the decision STS 654/2006 from the 23rd of June 2006 (Civil Chamber, 1st Section) of the Spanish Supreme Court is very illustrative. In this sentence, the Supreme Court ruled that the agreement adopted by the association to expel one of its members was based on reasonable grounds. The conduct carried out by the member were evident acts constituting reason for expulsion: the member engaged in self-contracting, which was prohibited by Article 48.3 of the association's statutes; he spoke out against the association in the media; he did not approve the 1995–1996 budgets; he made reverse charge calls; and he engaged in other sanctionable conduct. Therefore, what happened in this case was not that there was a reasonable cause to expel the member from the association, but rather that there was a clear and flagrant violation of the association's statutes, and the member's conduct was in accordance with those acts.

The concept of reasonable ground is not to be understood as the conformity of the association agreement with the statutes of the association. It is not a question of whether the facts were correctly subsumed under the factual conditions set out in the statutes. In that case we would be dealing with a purely formal review, and this concept would be meaningless. Rather, the concept of reasonable ground is to be applied when an association agreement is in accordance with the statutes, but the interpretation of the statutes by the decision-making body is apparently erroneous. This was precisely the case in the decision STC 218/1988 rendered by the Supreme Court, in which the expelled members claimed that the sanctioning body's interpretation of the statutes was incorrect.

Rather, the concept of reasonable grounds should be understood as a way for the judge to hear the association agreements without replacing the value judgement made by the association, ie, without infringing the discretionary capacity and the faculty of appreciation that every association has in the exercise of its organisational autonomy. Then, the reasonable ground concept is applicable when the association agreement is discretionary or appreciative, to determine that it has not been arbitrary, irrational or out of proportion.

The golf case scenario presented at the commencement of this book pertains to the Kilmartin Golf Club, which was established 40 years ago.[25] Although there is no explicit rule prohibiting female membership, women are not admitted. This is attributed to an internal nomination procedure wherein a current member must nominate a prospective member, and to date, no woman has been nominated. A local businesswoman and amateur golfer seeks membership at the Kilmartin Golf

[25] Cahill (n 6) 16–17.

Club. Should the case go to court, the judge would need to assess whether the club's decision to deny the woman's entry was based on reasonable grounds.

In short, according to constitutional case law precedents, it can be affirmed that judicial control over associative conduct should be minimal, and should focus on merely formal or procedural aspects, but not on the substance of the matter. In any case, the judge will determine whether this decision has been taken on a reasonable ground, whether it appears logical and not manifestly unfair or arbitrary. However, the judge's decision should not replace the reasoning made by the associative bodies.

VI. GUIDELINES TO DETERMINE THE SCOPE OF JUDICIAL CONTROL

Trying to determine whether judicial intervention in association agreements should be of a formal or substantive nature, or on reasonable grounds, is a question that cannot be solved in *abstracto*. The scope of judicial intervention in associative agreements will depend on the circumstances of each case. These circumstances can be grouped mainly into two categories: the type of association and the type of agreement adopted by the association.

A. The Type of Association

One of the most important issues to take into consideration to determine the scope of judicial control over association agreements is the type of the association. As Bilbao Ubillos points out, 'if the associative reality is heterogeneous, the legal treatment cannot be uniform'.[26] Indeed, the type of each association or its special condition affects its freedom of self-organisation and, consequently, the scope of the judicial control.

Salvador Coderch and Ferrer Riba have distinguished between associations with 'ideological aims' and those of an 'economic nature'.[27] Regarding the first, judicial control must remain separate from any debates or controversies surrounding ideological aspects. In this type of association, judicial control should be limited to verifying the conformity of the association agreement with the statutes, without being able to make an ideological judgement.

The agreements of religious associations or associations with a certain ideology or world view are basically not subject to judicial control. Any conflict or debate between different beliefs or ideologies within the association must remain outside the scope of judicial control. The courts are not the forum for

[26] JM Bilbao Ubillos, *Libertad de asociación y derechos de los socios* (Universidad de Valladolid, 1997) 12.

[27] STC 56/1995, 6 March 1995.

deciding ideological questions, and ideological associations could not survive if judges and courts imposed their ideology.

As outlined in the Soup Kitchen scenario at the beginning of this book, the Charity Act pertains to the financial aspects of charity associations, not their ideological goals. Thus, if a judge encounters a conflict related to *Cairde ar son Cairde*, the judge's inquiry should focus on their financial stability, not their ideological principles.

For example, according to the facts of the decision rendered by the Supreme Court on 26 July 1993, Mr Antonio Mª Peña Esturo, a member of the Popular Political Party of Spain, appealed against a resolution made by the party's National Executive Committee which proposed setting up a Management Committee on the grounds that there were serious circumstances which justified it. The action was dismissed at all levels. When hearing the case, the Supreme Court underlined the discretion of the party's governing bodies in assessing the causes justifying such an agreement, as well as the fact that, in these disputes, 'political and opportune (circumstances) tend to predominate in relation to the management and activity of the party'.

On the other hand, the Court underlined that voluntary adhesion to a political party implies the acceptance and fulfilment of the statutes, especially in matters with a strong political dimension. The Supreme Court also determined that ordinary courts can only review the associative decisions that contradict the statutes of the association. Thus, with respect to political parties, associations with a specific ideology, and any other association, judicial control will be kept minimal when the internal agreement concerns matters related to their own ideology. We understand that, although not all associations have ideological aims, they are all governed by certain principles and values. In such cases, judicial control cannot reach the correctness or incorrectness of a particular agreement. As far as political parties are concerned, it must be said that they are associations which play an important role in the social and democratic state under the rule of law.[28] Consequently, judicial control of their internal decisions must be far more extensive when it comes to examining their democratic structure and organisation.

The same applies to trade unions. Trade unions have a privileged place in the social and democratic state under the rule of law. Trade unions are associations of constitutional relevance, and their internal decisions are therefore submitted to thorough judicial control. However, it is true that there must always be room for their organisational autonomy.[29] In this sense, the decision of the Supreme Court from the 6th of July 2000 amends the precedent of the Constitutional Court in its decision 218/1988 from the 22nd of November. The Supreme Court

[28] STC 185/1993.

[29] JT Poveda 'Sobre el control judicial de la actividad sindical, Comentario a la sentencia del Tribunal Supremo de 6 de julio de 2000' (2000) 12 *Revista de Derecho social* 162.

stated that 'maintaining trade union freedom in its auto-organizational scope could violate the constitutional right of every worker to remain in the trade union of his choice'.[30]

If judicial control is far more extensive for associations with constitutional relevance (political parties and trade unions), a more thorough judicial review can also be justified for associations with public relevance, not in the political sense, but in the social, economic or cultural field. This perspective can be supported by the Soup Kitchen scenario described at the beginning of this book. Due to the social importance of charities, judicial oversight of their internal agreements could be more extensive.

In the case of associations with economic relevance, judicial control should be greater because of the 'financial damage that may result' for the association's members.[31] In Germany, for example, given the financial implications of membership in a co-operative association, judicial control of its internal decisions is not only formal but also substantive.[32] The aim is to protect the economic interests of the members.[33] This also seems to be the understanding of the Spanish Constitutional Court in its decision 96/1994 from the 21st of March 1994. The Court understood that in the case of significant economic damage to a member – as in the case of the expulsion of a co-operative member – 'the courts have full awareness' of the internal activity of the association.[34]

On the other hand, the extent of judicial control will also depend on the internal regime of the association, ie, whether it has a democratic structure and organisation. In associations with a non-democratic structure and functioning, there is an increased risk of inadequate protection for members. In such associations, the infringement of members' constitutional rights seems more likely than in the case of associations with an internal democratic regime. However, case law seems to show the opposite, that violations of members' rights occur mainly

[30] ibid 169.

[31] Bernard Reichert, Franz J. Dannecker and Christian Kühr proposed a substantive judicial review of the association's decisions if the amount of the matter was equal to or greater than 5,000. Handbuch Vereins- und Verbandsrecht, Luchterhand, Köln, 2010. Pablo Salvador Coderch and Josep Ferrer I. Riba point out that this proposal is based on the idea that judicial intervention is only justified if there is substantial and quantifiable damage to the member. PS Coderch and JoF I Riba, 'Asociaciones, democracia y Drittwirkung' in PS Coderch, (coord.), *Asociaciones, derechos fundamentales y autonomía privada* (Madrid, P Lang, 1997) 157 y ss.

[32] RGZ 57, 154; 88, 193 y ss., 196; 129, 48; JW 08, 250; 27, 691; 30 2697; 32, 1010.

[33] It has been pointed out that in common law countries also judicial intervention will be more intense to defend the rights of the partner when property rights are at stake. *Rigby v Connol (1880)*, 14 Ch. D. 482; *Osborne v Amalgamated Society of Railway Servants, 1911*, 1 Ch. 540; in Canada *Abbott v Sullivan*, [1952] 1 KB 189; in the United States *Otto v Journeyman Tailors* P. & B. TJ *(1888)* 75 Cal. 308.

[34] In similar terms, the Supreme Court ruled in its decision STS 846/2007 of the 13th of July 2007 that the ordinary court may substitute the association body decision for its own if the expulsion causes relevant harm to the expellee, yet the court must reason why the expulsion causes relevant harm to the expellee.

in democratic associations, sometimes due to a simple violation of the statutes, and sometimes due to arbitrary decisions of the associative bodies.[35]

It could therefore be argued that judicial control will be far more extensive for associations with a democratic regime than for those without. When an association has a democratic internal regime, stipulated by law, the state must ensure that this structure is followed and that members' rights are respected. If, on the other hand, an association is not obliged to have a democratic regime and follows another type of organisational model, such as a hierarchical one where members have freely accepted the restriction of some of their rights, the intervention of the courts should be limited.

In conclusion, if the association has constitutional relevance, ie, it guarantees a constitutional and democratic state under the rule of law, like political parties and trade unions, it is evident that its internal autonomy will be limited. Therefore, judicial control over its internal decisions must be greater, not regarding its ideology, but its structure and functioning.

If the association has no constitutional relevance but holds a dominant or monopolistic position in a certain economic, cultural or social sphere, so that denial of membership implies a significant detriment for the member, the scope of judicial control can also be thorough. This could be exemplified by the Kilmartin Golf Club case, as described in scenario number 2 at the beginning of this book. This suggests that even for a private association, its social and economic relevance in a specific town, and the value of membership for building social networks and businesses, could be significant factors for a judge to consider when intervening in the association's internal organisation. Indeed, the value of Kilmartin Golf Club membership extends beyond the membership itself to the associated rights and benefits.

On the contrary, if an association is strictly private, receives no public funding, is supported by its own income, carries out purely private activities and pursues private needs, and doesn't have any social or economic relevance, it will enjoy a very wide autonomy in adopting its own association agreements, and consequently, the judicial control would be minimal.[36]

B. The Type of the Associative Agreement

The scope of judicial review in an associative conflict depends on the type of agreement. The validity of an association agreement primarily depends on its concordance with the association's statutes. Based on this link between an association's agreements and its statutes, a significant portion of German legal

[35] AE Perales, 'Asociaciones y democracia interna' in AA VV, *La democracia constitucional: estudios en homenaje al Profesor Francisco Rubio Llorente* vol. I (Madrid, 2002) 628.

[36] JJ Marín López, 'El derecho de ingreso en las asociaciones' in *Los Alardes: Una Perspectiva Jurídica: Libertad e Igualdad en Las Relaciones entre Particulares* (Irún, Casino de Irún, 2000) 13, 22.

scholarship has identified a similarity between association agreements and acts of public administration. Thus, association agreements can be classified into regulated agreements, discretionary agreements, and value-based agreements. This classification is merely a proposal that may be useful for understanding the operation of any association and for determining the scope of judicial intervention.

To define these, we can say that: 1) Regulated agreements are the acts of the association's bodies that execute the powers conferred upon them by the statutes, according to their design and structure.[37] The adoption of these agreements consists solely of applying the statutes to the specific case by the competent body. 2) Discretionary agreements are those that require an association body to interpret gaps or silences in the statutes. Discretionary associative agreements may concern, for example, the time or occasion of member elections, the election of members to associative bodies, the economic amount of a pecuniary sanction, or the number of days a member will remain suspended from the association.[38] 3) Value-based agreements refer to the power that the association's bodies have to interpret or apply an indeterminate legal concept contained in the association's statutes, such as the social interest, the common good, the associative order, a serious fault, or a just cause for the expulsion of members, among many others.[39]

Value-based agreements differ from discretionary agreements in that value-based agreements interpret and give meaning to a vague concept, whereas discretionary agreements consist of a subjective appraisal by the association body of several options. For clarity, let us consider moot Scenario 2 described at the beginning of this book. The statutes of Kilmartin Golf Club are silent on the admission of women to the club, but traditionally the members, who nominate new members, have never nominated a woman. Given the silence of the statutes, an association's interpretation of its own statutes is a discretionary agreement. On the other hand, if an association decides to expel a member for committing serious misconduct, which is an indeterminate concept, the interpretation of that concept is a value-based agreement.

i. Judicial Review of the Association's Agreements in Relation to its Statutes

If judges are clear about the type of association agreement, they will also be clear about the scope of their decision. Referring to regulated agreements, the judicial control is not a major problem: it is sufficient to check that the body's decision is in conformity with the statutes of the association; if the agreement adopted by the body contravenes the statutes, the agreement is manifestly null

[37] *Cf* Ernst (n 9) 24.
[38] Id.
[39] P Schlosser, *Vereins- und Verbandsgerichtsbarkeit* (München, Goldmann, 1972) 106.

and void. Consequently, the judicial control should be minimal, as it is limited to verifying that the agreement complies with the statutes.

If an association's organs adopt discretionary or value-based decisions, the courts must restrict their review to verifying whether the interpretation made by the association body has been adopted on reasonable grounds and remained within the limits of its discretion, and whether it has not acted maliciously, or in a notoriously arbitrary or disproportionate manner. However, under no circumstances can the courts replace the will of the association.

We have already said that an association has the faculty to interpret their own status, but this does not mean that association bodies have the right to take arbitrary or disproportionate decisions, agreements contrary to the aims of the association, its own values, or even the legal system.

ii. Judicial Review of the Association's Agreements Based on their Content

The scope of judicial control will also depend on the content of the association agreement. They can be organic, ie, relating to the organisation of the association, or dogmatic, ie, relating to its ideological content.

In Germany, the Supreme Court pointed out in the *Traberzucht* case that the correction by the ordinary court regarding the adopted agreement of the association should only occur in the case of punitive agreements.[40] Therefore, if the association agreement is merely organic, ie, it concerns itself with structure and functioning, there is no room for substantive judicial intervention, nor for the substitution of the association agreement.

In the case of agreements with dogmatic content, the constitutional rights of the members come into play as against the organisational autonomy of the association. It is precisely in relation to these agreements that the choice between formal or substantive judicial control has significant implications for both the association and its members.

Formal judicial intervention would benefit the autonomy of the association, but could violate the constitutional rights of the members, and, consequently, the state would fail in its duty to protect these rights.[41] If, on the other hand, a substantive judicial intervention is sought to protect members vis-à-vis the association, there is a risk of infringing the association's autonomy.[42] Among the dogmatic association agreements, case law has mainly dealt with association agreements for the admission of new members and association agreements for expulsion.

[40] *BGH* LM Nr. 2 zu § 35 BGB = DB 56, 473.

[41] JA Águila-Real, 'Autonomía privada y derechos fundamentales', *Anuario de Derecho Civil*, 1993, 93.

[42] JJ Marín López, 'La intervención judicial en los conflictos endoasociativos: el caso de la expulsión de asociados' (1989) 14 *Poder Judicial* 155. Also Ubillos (n 26) 71. See also SSTC 218/1988, 96/1994 and ATC 213/1991.

As narrated in the Golf Club scenario at the beginning of this book, the central issue is a dogmatic agreement of an association. The Kilmartin Golf Club has the power to determine membership, including the exclusion of women, but this directly opposes Rósin's freedom to associate and her right to equality.

In the case of association agreements to admit or not admit new members, a judicial review consists of verifying the reasons for the refusal, but not the facts that gave rise to the agreement.[43] The control cannot be very intensive because, in principle, the refusal of membership by the association does not violate any rights of the applicant, as there is no subjective right to join a certain association. From this point of view, Róisín has no right to join Kilmartin Golf Club, and Kilmartin Golf Club is not obliged to accept Róisín as a member.

If significant damage is caused or the applicant is prevented from carrying out a certain activity due to the specific status of the association, judicial control must be material because of the damage that may be caused to the member. Perhaps in this case, Róisín could argue that Kilmartin Golf Club's denial of admission is causing her harm, as it prevents her from conducting business or engaging in social networking in her own town.

Judicial control has been more intense in relation to associative agreements for the removal of members. The Spanish Constitutional Court has recognised that in the exercise of its autonomy, the association may expel its members, but on the other hand, this may imply the violation of the member's constitutional right to remain in the association. In this sense, Lahera Forteza points out that the scope of judicial control is greater because it can gauge the tension between self-organisation and the member's right.

When a member is expelled from the association, judicial review will consist of verifying: 1) whether the punishable conduct is determined in its statutes (statutory agreement); 2) whether the punishable conduct contained in the statutes has been correctly interpreted by the association's decision-making body; 3) whether the association's body has correctly applied the sanction using its discretion,[44] and finally 4) whether the sanction does not appear unjust or arbitrary, in other words, whether the association's decision is not manifestly unreasonable.[45]

German scholars and case law have established that the expulsion decision must not be manifestly unjust. Therefore, the courts must consider not only

[43] E Sauter, G Schweyer and W Waldner, *Der eingetragene Verein*, 19th edn (Munich, C.H. Beck, 2010) 54. In Italy, Aldo Bardusco rejects substantive judicial review of association agreements on admission or rejection of new members. According to this author, judicial control should be limited to procedural aspects. The judge cannot replace the will of the parties and directly recognise the applicant's right to admission. A Bardusco, *La ammissiones del cittadino ai parti*, Instituo edn (Varese-Milano, Cisalpino, 1967) 97–101.

[44] *Cf* RGZ 72, 191; *cf* Meyer-Cording (n 18) 114.

[45] *Cf* Stöber (n 15) 390.

the loss of membership, but also the possible harm that the member may suffer because of the expulsion.[46]

VII. CONCLUSION

When disagreements between an association and a member come before the courts, the court must consider different aspects and circumstances to rule for or against one or the other. The arguments presented in this chapter can guide judges from different countries, regardless of their legal tradition, when they must resolve internal disputes of associations.

In the first instance, the judge is required to verify that the association agreement adheres to its statutes, the law, the Constitution, and the legal system. In the second instance, the judge must take into consideration the nature of the association. A private association enjoys greater freedom of self-organisation and less interference from public authorities, whereas a public association with greater relevance experiences less freedom of self-organisation and more interference from public authorities. In the third instance, the judge must examine the type of associative agreement. In the case of a regulated agreement, judicial interference is limited to formal review; in the case of a discretionary or value-based agreement, the judge may assess the reasonableness of the agreement but must not alter the value judgment rendered by the associative body. Finally, the content of the agreement is also a relevant consideration: if the agreement pertains to organic matters, the judicial review is limited to formal aspects; if the agreement pertains to dogmatic matters, the judicial review may be substantive if it infringes upon a constitutional right of the member or causes them significant harm.

[46] A.A. OLG Celle NJW-RR 1989, 313; JR 1990, 317, 323.

9

Schisms and Internal Disputes within Religious Associations under the European Convention on Human Rights

NICHOLAS McMURRY

I. INTRODUCTION

THIS CHAPTER WILL explore the approach of the European Court of Human Rights to the question of dissent, division, or contentious schism within associations. There is a tension between the association's right to manage its own affairs and the rights of members of that association to disagree. We will start by looking at philosophical perspectives on this problem, then discuss how the European Court of Human Rights approaches it in light of these perspectives. The caselaw cited relates to religious associations, but the Court frequently refers to freedom of association in establishing the application of the rights concerned. The Court distinguishes between dissent within an association and a deep internal division and has a different approach to each scenario.

Broadly speaking, there are two philosophical approaches to this question, though there are disagreements within as well as between these approaches. For liberal theorists, membership of an association is a voluntary act and places one under the control of the rules of the association in question, with the proviso that one must be permitted to leave the association. Kukathas, who emphasises this principle more than other liberals, holds that the freedoms of association and dissociation are fundamental to a free society and states that if members of an association wish 'not to leave their community but to assert rights recognized by the wider society but not by their particular community or culture, they receive no recognition'.[1] In contrast with other liberals, he states that a society

[1] C Kukathas, *The Liberal Archipelago: A Theory of Diversity and Freedom* (Oxford, Oxford University Press, 2003) 103.

cannot be based on principles of social justice, because there is inevitably disagreement over these, and we must permit persons to associate in order to follow their own vision of the good life without interference.[2] The state, therefore, should not impose its own values onto associations.

There must, however, be limitations to this principle. Toleration may acquiesce to 'much that liberals are often unwilling to countenance'.[3] Kukathas is willing to countenance associations that torture their members through genital mutilation,[4] but surely society cannot tolerate associations that have ordered their members to commit suicide, have engaged in systematic child abuse, or which have murdered their members. He argues that associations should be 'bound by the norms and conventions or the laws of the communities to which they belong',[5] but this seems to apply solely to relations outside the association. A tolerant society should 'give groups … carte blanche to do as they wish in the case of children'.[6] He argues that persuasion is preferable to coercion,[7] and no doubt in many cases he is correct. But not to intervene is an acceptance that, within the association at least, might be right. Leaving an association can have enormous costs, as Kukathas acknowledges.[8] Furthermore, Kukathas does not indicate how the law should rule if there should be internal disagreement as to what decision an association has made. The role of the law cannot be entirely distant: there will be questions of ownership of property, fulfilment of contracts and membership that will need to be decided by some authority.

In contrast to the liberal tradition, which differentiates between a right and the cost of exercising that right, the republican tradition is not content to ignore power disparities between persons within an association.[9] Pettit aspires to achieve freedom from domination and he defines domination as meaning that those in power '(1) … have the capacity to interfere (2) on an arbitrary basis (3) in certain choices that the other is in a position to make.'[10] For him, initial consent is not conclusive: domination may arise in relationships that were originally established voluntarily through consent.[11] Interference is arbitrary if it is 'subject just to the arbitrarium, the decision or judgement, of the agent … without reference to the interests, or the opinions, of those affected.'[12] The role of the state is to regulate associations in order to protect people from domination.

[2] ibid 85.
[3] ibid 120.
[4] ibid 135.
[5] ibid 144.
[6] ibid 147.
[7] ibid 136–37.
[8] ibid 107.
[9] P Pettit, *Republicanism: A Theory of Freedom and Government* (Oxford, Oxford University Press, 1997).
[10] ibid 52.
[11] ibid 61–62.
[12] ibid 55.

Thus, it can be said that the liberal approach, somewhat counterintuitively, considering its basis in individual rights, gives associations strong powers over their members, as long as there is a right to leave the association. The republican approach requires of associations certain standards in their decision-making and their treatment of their members. Cahill outlines three approaches, one where the courts 'give a wide latitude to the association itself to define the terms of its own existence', one where they 'engage in substantive review of the internal rules', and the third where they 'engage in procedural review, examining the matter to see if the association has followed its own rules'.[13] As we will see, the European Court of Human Rights largely follows the first approach in understanding freedom of association.

The chapter will now proceed to explain the role of the European Court of Human Rights and the law that it applies. It will then look at a number of cases and establish that these pertain to freedom of association despite the fact that the findings made relate to freedom of religion. It will describe the limits to the role of the state in the case of a 'deep division' within an association. It will examine the Court's sparse findings on the question of property, particularly in relation to schism within a religion. It will then proceed to explore the question of dissent within an association, before analysing these findings in light of the philosophical approaches outlined above. Exploring the caselaw of the Court provides an overview of how the question of internal disagreements within associations can be addressed when looking at them from a relatively abstract perspective of fundamental human rights.

II. EUROPEAN COURT OF HUMAN RIGHTS

The European Court of Human Rights is an international Court established to implement the European Convention on Human Rights and its protocols. This is an instrument of the Council of Europe, and the core Convention and most of the protocols have been ratified by all 47 Member States of the Council. The Convention imposes obligations on Contracting States and the role of the Court is not to make rulings that directly impact on associations, but to determine whether the actions of the state and its courts have breached Convention rights. This means that when the Court states that there is no right to dissent under the Convention, it does not imply that there can be no right to dissent under national law, merely that the actions of the state are in keeping with the Convention if they support the authority of associations over their members, assuming that this does not impinge on other rights under the Convention. On the other hand, interference in an association on behalf of the members would

[13] M Cahill, 'Considering How and Why Freedom of Association is Protected: Reflections on the State of the Art' in A Amaya, C Michelon and N Walker (eds), *Law and the Ties that Bind* (Proceedings of the British Academy, 2026, forthcoming).

amount to the limitation of freedom of association, though we have not found such a case in the caselaw. Under the Convention, such limitations can be justified as long as they are clearly laid out in domestic law, have a legitimate aim listed in the Convention, and are proportionate.

The current research has not uncovered a relevant case where a violation was found of freedom of association, but there are several cases in which findings have been made in relation to freedom of religion, in many cases interpreting this in light of freedom of association. Freedom of religion and freedom of association constitute Articles 9 and 11 respectively, of the European Convention on Human Rights:

> 9.1: Everyone has the right to freedom of thought, conscience and religion; this right includes freedom to change his religion or belief and freedom, either alone or in community with others and in public or private, to manifest his religion or belief, in worship, teaching, practice and observance.
>
> 11.1: Everyone has the right to freedom of peaceful assembly and to freedom of association with others, including the right to form and to join trade unions for the protection of his interests.[14]

As we can see, Article 9 provides some rights that persons can assert on an individual basis, including freedom of thought, conscience, and religion, and the right to manifest one's religion or belief alone. However, this article also provides rights that can be asserted 'in community', such as through religious associations, including the manifestation of 'belief, teaching, practice and observance'. Freedom of religion does not explicitly provide a right to form religious associations, though the Court has found that it does provide such a right when read in light of freedom of association.[15] It does provide the right to manifest one's religion or belief, whereas non-religious associations have no explicit right under the Convention to carry out specific activities related to their purpose.

The legitimate limitations that may be imposed on the rights, contained within the second paragraphs of each article, are broadly similar, though phrased somewhat differently:

> 9.2: Freedom to manifest one's religion or beliefs shall be subject only to such limitations as are prescribed by law and are necessary in a democratic society in the interests of public safety, for the protection of public order, health or morals, or for the protection of the rights and freedoms of others.
>
> 11.2: No restrictions shall be placed on the exercise of these rights other than such as are prescribed by law and are necessary in a democratic society in the interests of national security or public safety, for the prevention of disorder or crime, for the protection of health or morals or for the protection of the rights and freedoms of

[14] Convention for the Protection of Human Rights and Fundamental Freedoms (Rome, 4 November 1950) (ECHR).

[15] *Church of Scientology Moscow v Russia* (2007) 46 EHRR 304, para 72: 'Since religious communities traditionally exist in the form of organised structures, Article 9 must be interpreted in the light of Article 11 of the Convention, which safeguards associative life against unjustified State interference.'

> others. This article shall not prevent the imposition of lawful restrictions on the exercise of these rights by members of the armed forces, of the police or of the administration of the State.[16]

Freedom of association may be restricted on the additional grounds of national security and prevention of crime, but other grounds appear to be the same between the two articles. Freedom of association may also be restricted for those working within the state, largely in order to enable states to restrict the establishment of trade unions for military and security forces.

Freedom of religion thus does not only provide a right to carry out certain activities together, but, in combination with freedom of association, it provides a right to create organisations. These organisations can own property, enter contracts and employ people. In order to do this, they can create internal decision-making structures that provide certain persons and bodies with authority over others. These persons of authority can regulate the activities that take place on the organisation's properties, and the activities of its members, and can ultimately sanction and expel its members. This gives the leadership within the religion considerable power.

III. CASELAW

Disputes within religious organisations have led to legal problems. In the *Scottish Churches case* in 1904, following a split within the Free Church of Scotland, the House of Lords in the UK caused consternation, by recognising the small minority faction as being the continuing manifestation of that Church, providing it with all of the associated assets and responsibilities, contractual rights and obligations.[17] That situation was ultimately resolved through the intervention of Parliament to create a process for the peaceful transfer of assets from one party to the other.[18]

The caselaw of the European Court of Human Rights, which we will consider now, makes findings in relation to freedom of religion, but in most cases this is interpreted in light of freedom of association. While the Court had previously found that criminal sanctions against a controversial claimant to a religious leadership role were disproportionate,[19] the most comprehensive judgments arose in response to tensions within the Orthodox Church and the Muslim community in Bulgaria during the democratisation process after the fall of the Communist regime. Both of these communities were initially led by persons who had been appointed by the Communist regime,[20] and within both

[16] ECHR (n 14).

[17] *Bannatyne v Overtoun* [1904] AC 515 (HL).

[18] Churches (Scotland) Act 1905.

[19] *Serif v Greece* ECHR 1999-IX (1999) 31 EHRR 20, para 13. See also paras 49–54.

[20] *Holy Synod of the Bulgarian Orthodox Church (Metropolitan Inokentiy) & ors. v Bulgaria* (2009) 50 EHRR 3, para 12; *Hasan & Chaush v Bulgaria* ECHR 2000-XI (2000) EHRR 35, para 11.

there developed alternative structures and alternative leaders that were allied with the democratic movement.[21] Through the 1990s and into the following decade, there were effectively two claimants for leadership of each community. The state recognised alternative leaders depending on which political party was in power and removed those from the other side of the disputes.[22]

Cases were taken to the European Court of Human Rights against Bulgaria by both sides within the Muslim community (the *Hasan* case and the *Supreme Council* case), and by the alternative synod of the Orthodox Church. In each case, the complainants argued that their freedom of religion had been violated, and in each case, the Court found in their favour.[23] In all three cases, the Court found that Article 9 should be 'interpreted in the light of Article 11'[24] in relation to the organisational elements of religion. In the *Hasan* case, the Court found that 'no separate issue arises under Article 11 of the Convention'.[25] The state disputed in that case whether the Muslim community formed an association as understood under Article 11,[26] but the Court established that questions of organisation within the community concerned the 'associative life' of the community,[27] implicitly invoking freedom of association, though the question of whether the community consisted of an association under the Convention was left unanswered. Freedom of religion therefore requires, not merely that persons are enabled to carry out the basic public and private requirements of their religion, but that they be permitted to organise themselves freely. Given that freedom of association is explicitly cited to support the Court's approach, it seems likely that these principles, inasmuch as they relate to the organisational features of religion, will apply also to non-religious associations were they to face a similar situation of division.

IV. INTERNAL DISPUTES

The Court established that there existed within each community a dispute over the leadership of the religion in question. The Court referred to the Muslim community as a 'divided religious community'[28] and the Orthodox Church as containing 'deep division and incompatible claims to legitimacy by two opposing

[21] *Holy Synod v Bulgaria* (n 20) para 23; *Hasan & Chaush v Bulgaria* (n 20) paras 12 & 16.

[22] *Holy Synod v Bulgaria* (n 20) paras 17–18, 24–28, 42–48 & 55–61; *Hasan & Chaush v Bulgaria* (n 20) paras 11 & 21.

[23] *Holy Synod v Bulgaria* (n 20) para 160; *Hasan & Chaush v Bulgaria* (n 20) para 89; *Supreme Holy Council of the Muslim Community v Bulgaria* (2004) 41 EHRR 3, para 99.

[24] *Hasan & Chaush v Bulgaria* (n 20) para 65; *Supreme Holy Council v Bulgaria* (n 23) para 73; *Holy Synod v Bulgaria* (n 20) para 160.

[25] *Hasan & Chaush v Bulgaria* (n 20) para 91.

[26] ibid para 90.

[27] ibid para 62.

[28] ibid para 78, *Supreme Holy Council v Bulgaria* (n 23) para 82.

groups'.[29] The Court distinguished between this situation and a question of dissent within a religious association,[30] a question to which we will return. In the context of an internal dispute, any state support for one side at the expense of the other, will amount to an intervention in the internal affairs of the association in question.[31]

The Court then proceeded to establish whether this interference was justified. The Court's well-established approach to this is to determine firstly whether it is 'prescribed by law', a phrase that it interprets to require a law that provides clear direction and is not applied in an arbitrary manner.[32] Secondly, the interference must aim to meet a legitimate aim, one of those listed in Article 9.2 of the Convention. The Court grants the state a considerable margin of appreciation in this regard in the sense that it assumes that the state's intentions are reasonable.[33] Finally, it determines whether the interference is 'necessary in a democratic society', a phrase it interprets to require both that the interference is necessary, ie, that no less disruptive measures would have achieved the same desired outcome, and that it is proportionate.

In the *Hasan* case, the Court found that the state action in refusing to recognise Hasan's leadership was arbitrary. The legislation concerned did not provide any criteria to guide the decision, and Hasan was not notified of any decision or any reasons for it. Therefore the Court did not consider the interference to be 'prescribed by law'.[34] This would have required not only that the legislation countenance the actions of the state but also that it must also 'afford a measure of legal protection against arbitrary interferences by public authorities'.[35] The Court also separately noted that the state had failed to implement decisions of the Bulgarian Supreme Court, further undermining the rule of law.[36]

In the *Supreme Council case*, in contrast, the Court neglected to make a finding on whether the interference was 'prescribed by law', noting that the complaint concerned its justification rather than its legality and noting that in this case the state had made greater effort to follow an agreement made by the different factions.[37] Furthermore, it found that the interference had a legitimate aim, namely 'protection of public order and of the rights and freedoms of others'.[38] However, it did find that the interference was not 'necessary in a democratic society' as the state had not explained why their

[29] *Holy Synod v Bulgaria* (n 20) para 107.
[30] ibid para 141.
[31] ibid paras 110 & 113; *Hasan & Chaush v Bulgaria* (n 20) paras 82–83; *Supreme Holy Council v Bulgaria* (n 23) para 85.
[32] *Hasan & Chaush v Bulgaria* (n 20) para 84; *Holy Synod v Bulgaria* (n 20) paras 114–15; *Supreme Holy Council v Bulgaria* (n 23) paras 87–89.
[33] *Holy Synod v Bulgaria* (n 20) para 131; *Supreme Holy Council v Bulgaria* (n 23) paras 91–92.
[34] *Hasan & Chaush v Bulgaria* (n 20) paras 85–86.
[35] ibid para 84.
[36] ibid para 87.
[37] *Supreme Holy Council v Bulgaria* (n 23) paras 88–90.
[38] ibid para 92.

aim could not have been achieved by less drastic means than 'compelling the divided community under a single leadership'.[39] Forcing unity on a religious community is therefore seen as inherently disproportionate considering the goal of preserving pluralism.

In the *Orthodox Church* case, while noting that the state's action was taken on the basis of legislation, the Court declined to examine whether the measures taken provided adequate legal protection.[40] While the Court did establish that the aim of the government was, broadly speaking, to 'improve the legal regulation of religious denominations',[41] it failed to identify the specific aim from the Convention that this sought to achieve. When considering the necessity of the measures taken, the Court found that the state's actions of 'suppression of the applicants' activities as an alternative leadership within the Church and their expulsion from temples, monasteries and other Church premises' were disproportionate.[42] The inappropriate use of criminal law to settle a private dispute was a factor in this conclusion.[43] It specifically found that 'religious pluralism as a basic fabric of democracy' prevented the state from imposing unity upon a religious association.[44] Citing freedom of association directly, the Court established that 'the fact that what was at issue touched on national symbols and national identity is not sufficient'.[45] The Court reiterated its requirement that the State remain neutral in an internal dispute within a religion.[46]

The reasoning behind the finding that restrictions were illegitimate therefore varied between the different cases. In the *Hasan* case it was sufficient to find that the complainants were not given adequate legal protection. However, even when the process may have been sufficient, forcibly imposing unity upon a religious community is not 'necessary in a democratic society', at least to achieve the legitimate aims of promoting community cohesion and protecting the rights of the other side of the dispute. The state may not force 'the community to come together under a single leadership against its own wishes'.[47] While the state can act to try to repair disputes, 'matters changed [in the *Supreme Council case*] at the moment when the Directorate continued to insist on 'unification' despite the fact that the leaders of the applicant organisation decided to withdraw'.[48] In a succinct summary, the Court found that 'The role of the authorities in a situation of conflict between or within religious groups is not to remove the cause

[39] ibid para 97.
[40] *Holy Synod v Bulgaria* (n 20) paras 116–17.
[41] ibid para 122.
[42] ibid para 142.
[43] ibid para 140.
[44] ibid para 148.
[45] ibid para 148, citing *Stankov and the United Macedonian Organisation Ilinden v Bulgaria* ECHR 2001-IX (2001) para 107.
[46] *Holy Synod v Bulgaria* (n 20) paras 119–20, 139 & 151.
[47] *Hasan & Chaush v Bulgaria* (n 20) para 78.
[48] *Supreme Holy Council v Bulgaria* (n 23) para 84.

of tension by eliminating pluralism, but to ensure that the competing groups tolerate each other.'[49]

The Court therefore has more nuanced requirements than the House of Lords had in the *Scottish Churches* case. Both sides from a divided community must be recognised. There appears to be a deviation from this principle, however, in the case of *Cha'are Shalom ve Tsedek v France*.[50] The applicants in this case represented a Jewish organisation that, inter alia, produced kosher food that conformed to the stricter Sephardic standards than those applied by the state-recognised Jewish association.[51] The failure of the state to authorise the meat production of the applicant organisation was not considered an interference with freedom of religion because its members could obtain meat that met their standards from other sources: 'there would be interference with the freedom to manifest one's religion only if the illegality of performing ritual slaughter made it impossible for ultra-orthodox Jews to eat meat from animals slaughtered in accordance with the religious prescriptions they considered applicable'.[52] The Court therefore declined to consider the rights of individuals to act in a certain religious capacity on behalf of a religious association, in this case in ritual slaughter. It may have been pertinent that this case centred on one niche aspect of the religious tradition: the Court's conclusions would hardly have been the same if the state was restricting the association from establishing synagogues, even if existing synagogues were considered adequate for its members. The judgment in this case was made by a slender majority, with the seven dissenting judges objecting particularly strongly to the idea that the association could have obtained permission from the larger Jewish association to practice under their authority, as this appears to directly contradict the principle of equal recognition of both sides to a schism.[53]

V. PROPERTY DISPUTES

In all of these cases, the Court has very little to say on the principal bone of contention within the *Scottish Churches* case, namely ownership, control, and access to property. A claim was made in the *Orthodox Church* case that the right to property was infringed, but the Court neglected to consider this on the basis that the complaint did 'not concern State action dispossessing the legal person of the Bulgarian Orthodox Church but State interference in the internal organisation of the Church'.[54] In the *Hasan* case, the European Commission on

[49] ibid para 96.
[50] *Cha'are Shalom ve Tsedek v France* (27 June 2000) (27417/95) 9 BHRC 27.
[51] ibid paras 36–44.
[52] ibid para 80.
[53] ibid Joint Dissenting Opinion of Judges Sir Nicolas Bratza, Fischbach, Thomassen, Tsatsa-Nikolovska, Panţîru, Levits and Traja, para 1.
[54] *Holy Synod v Bulgaria* (n 20) para 173.

Human Rights had found that 'changes in [the Muslim] leadership by no means constitute a deprivation of property',[55] and the claim was not pursued before the Court.[56] A claim in relation to property was not made in the *Supreme Council* case. The Court's understanding of property appears therefore purely contractual: the right to property concerns the legal ownership of property, and persons cannot claim a violation of that right on the basis of lack of access to, or use of, property due to an internal dispute within an association. The question of the right to property will only be raised, therefore, in the case of a schism within an association, which results in more than one legal entity.

It should be noted that the right to property may be legitimately restricted, including with the aim of protecting the rights of others. Freedom of religion can require access to property both for the purposes of public worship and for administrative purposes. In the *Hasan* case, one of the factors used to indicate that there had been interference in freedom of religion was that he 'was apparently not able to retain control over at least part of the property belonging to the community'.[57] In the *Orthodox Church* case, the Court found that the alternative Synod members could not be regarded merely as 'persons occupying churches unlawfully'[58] and that the evictions were disproportionate, though for reasons of the legal process rather than interference with religion.[59] Thus it is possible in a dispute within an association, that the state would need to ensure access to property for both sides of the dispute, where it is necessary for maintaining their administrative and religious functions. If the property rights of others need to be restricted to achieve this, this may nevertheless be required.

However, it should be noted, that in the *Griechische Kirchengemeinde* case, the Court emphasised that the Convention does not give religious communities the right to be provided with a place of worship and that the question of whether removal of access to a place of worship can be an interference with freedom of religion is dependent on the reasons given for the removal.[60] This case concerned a church building which had been provided for use by the Greek community by a historic ruler of Bavaria. The congregation had defected to a schismatic branch of the Greek Orthodox Church known as the True Orthodox Church, and the authorities had removed their access from the church building in question. The Court in this case declined to determine whether this constituted an interference in freedom of religion, and instead determined that even if it was an interference, it was legitimate. The decision was made according to law and was made to protect the rights of others, namely those of the Greek Orthodox community.

[55] *Hasan & Chaush v.Bulgaria* App no 30985/96 (European Commission of Human Rights, 26 October 1999) para 118.

[56] *Hasan & Chaush v Bulgaria* (n 21) para 109.

[57] ibid para 79.

[58] *Holy Synod v Bulgaria* (n 20) para 134.

[59] ibid para 140.

[60] *Griechische Kirchengemeinde München und Bayern e. V. c. l'Allemagne* App no 52336/99 (18 September 2007). The paragraphs are not numbered within this judgment.

In determining whether it was proportionate, they determined merely that the decision was made according to a reasonable interpretation of the existing law and was not discriminatory. The question of which party was schismatic was not considered by the Court: it was assumed that the mainstream Greek Orthodox Church was the true manifestation of the Greek community, while the claims of the True Orthodox Church were not even mentioned. The schism in question occurred many decades before the defection of the congregation in the case.

It was mentioned that the applicant congregation was offered the use of another church building, but the Court found that its refusal to accept on the basis that it was insufficient for their needs was irrelevant: '*il s'agissait de toute façon d'une raison purement intra-ecclésiale que la requérante ne pouvait opposer à la demande des autorités bavaroises*'. This conclusion is weakened by the fact that the Court also sought to demonstrate that the congregation's claims were not substantiated. It appears from this that the offer of an alternative property was a factor in determining whether the eviction of a religious group from the building they used breached their freedom of religion, but that this offer does not have to be overly generous: refusal for 'intra-Ecclesial reasons' is not sufficient to indicate an interference.

It therefore appears that prevention of access to property can be an aspect of a violation of freedom of religion, including both religious and administrative buildings. Where religious groups are being evicted from buildings in order to serve another religious community, the Court encourages the state to offer an alternative but is not too stringent in this regard. The state therefore enjoys some margin of appreciation in this area: it must not intervene if to do so would interpose in an internal religious dispute but may choose to do so with churches that had formally split. It is clear also that the state may, if it wishes, restrict the right to property in order to protect freedom of religion, but no cases have challenged such a restriction on the basis of the right to property.

VI. DIVIDED COMMUNITIES OR INTERNAL DISSENT

The other question that arises from this case-law is how to identify whether a disagreement within an association amounts to a divided community or whether it is merely a question of internal dissent. The Court itself uses both words, 'dissent' and 'division', to describe the state of the Bulgarian Orthodox Church,[61] implying that the distinction may not be straightforward despite the contrasting legal implications of each term. The Court makes a distinction between the two, apparently on the basis of a 'genuinely deep division and incompatible claims to legitimacy by two opposing groups',[62] for which it provided evidence

[61] *Holy Synod v Bulgaria* (n 20) para 134.
[62] ibid para 107.

that 'the Church conventions which supported the two rival leaderships were each attended by hundreds of representatives of local parishes and other clergy and believers' and that there was 'no authoritative decision by the community settling this dispute'.[63] It therefore appears that a genuine dispute within a religious body, and by inference any association, can be discerned by the number of persons involved on either side, especially those in leadership positions, the attempt by both sides to follow the processes of the association in question, and the lack of authoritative internal settlement. There appears to be a considerable grey area here, but a finding of internal division requires the State to recognise both sides, whereas a finding of dissent creates no legal rights for dissenters.

This raises the question of why there is no right to dissent under the European Convention on Human Rights. The Court appears to take a liberal perspective, referring to the principle of dissociation: 'it is sufficient that dissenters should be free to leave the community'.[64] However, it should be stressed that the overall regime of the European Convention on Human Rights does not conform to Kukathas' understanding of freedom of association being central. Within the Convention, restrictions on freedom of association may be legitimate as long as they adhere to certain conditions, and freedom of association is merely one right alongside many others, including some, such as freedom from torture and slavery, that are absolute. Nevertheless, the Court's approach does provide established power structures within associations with considerable power. In one case the Court found that maintaining the integrity of the religion as a whole was a legitimate reason to restrict the right of ministers of that religion to form a trade union.[65]

If one takes a perspective from the republican tradition, this becomes problematic. A right to dissent is critical if vulnerable persons are to be protected by the law when abused by persons in power within associations that they belong to. This is particularly troubling in the area of religion. The costs of leaving a religious association can include loss of participation in activities and rituals, loss of family and friends, loss of connection to one's ancestry, loss of home and loss of benefits and employment. Furthermore, some groups, and particularly, but not solely, religious groups, may display cultish behaviour where one individual or a small group within the religion may have the power to make any decisions on a completely arbitrary basis, and may interject themselves more intrusively into more pervasive aspects of the lives of their members, another factor that Pettit considers important.[66] If the state and the law are not permitted under any circumstances to interject themselves in the decisions of an association, this effectively means that the only protections afforded members will be those established within the association in question.

[63] ibid para 109.
[64] ibid para 141.
[65] *Sindicatul "Păstorul Cel Bun" v Romania* ECHR 2013 (2013) 58 EHRR 10, para 171.
[66] Pettit (n 9) 58.

There are competing priorities here between permitting associations to manage their own affairs without state interference and protecting members of associations from domination by their own structures. This is clearly a difficult balancing act, but insisting on non-interference would appear to be an indiscriminate endorsement of power structures that exist within associations. For Kukathas the theoretical right of dissociation is enough to mitigate this. Pettit, on the other hand, clearly believes that law is necessary to ensure non-domination, and the intervention of national laws may be required for this purpose, but this would appear to be discouraged by the European Court of Human Rights. An approach that might adhere more closely to Pettit's vision would be that followed by the courts in Germany and Spain described in the chapter by Anzures Gurría in this volume.[67]

VII. CONCLUSION

To summarise, the approach of the European Court of Human Rights to disputes within religions, and by implication within other associations, is nuanced, but only where the dispute is characterised as dividing the community. If this is the case, the state must remain neutral in the dispute: it may encourage dialogue, but may not impose unity on a divided association, and should not intervene to support either side. However, where the dispute is characterised merely as dissent, or where it accepts that one party is schismatic, interference on behalf of the official association becomes justifiable, and interference on behalf of the dissidents is restricted. Any removal of access to property for administrative or religious purposes may constitute an interference with freedom of religion, and by implication freedom of association, although the Court declined to make a finding on this issue in a number of cases. It is clear, though, that interference can be justified by existing laws where the affected community is understood to be schismatic. It seems likely that the principles developed by the Court with regard to divisions within religious communities will also apply to disputes within other associations, though the question of dissent has been discussed by the Court solely with reference to freedom of religion.

[67] JJ Anzures Gurría, 'Judicial Review of Associative Agreements: Guidelines from a Civil Law Perspective' in M Cahill and G Lasagni (eds), *Associational Life and Freedom: Insights from Philosophy and Law* (Oxford, Hart Publishing, 2026) 151.

10

Portraits of Associational Participation: Exploring Personal Narratives

ERIN JACKSON*

I. INTRODUCTION

REAL STORIES OR non-fictional narratives can be a meaningful or powerful way to ground human rights in real experience. They have long been used to pinpoint the intersection of human rights and personal testimony, or 'life narrative', often through emotive stories.[1] Keeping with this tradition, and as a foray into the multi-faceted chapters in this volume on freedom of expression, this opening narrative chapter seeks to briefly capture real moments of participation in associations.

The purpose of this chapter's narrative focus is to highlight stories of lived experience in associations as a gateway to thinking more about associational living as a whole in our societies. From the city band to the local book club, portraits of participation illuminate motives and meaning, and give a small snapshot of associational participation from several angles. Why do people join or leave them? What do they experience within them? And what do they take with them when they are no longer involved? This chapter engages with this purpose by drawing on an empirical pilot study conducted under the auspices of the Societās project.[2] The

* With thanks to Professor Maria Cahill and Dr Giulia Lasagni for their valuable feedback in the development of this chapter. This work was produced as part of the author's position as Research Assistant on the Irish Research Council/Research Ireland Laureate Project 'Societās: Exploring the Value of Freedom of Association' IRCLA/2022/3860 led by Professor Maria Cahill and based at the School of Law, University College Cork.

[1] See, eg, K Schaffer and S Smith, *Narrated Lives: The Ethics of Recognition* (New York, Palgrave Macmillan, 2004).

[2] The pilot study comprised 30 in-depth semi-structured interviews with (former) students and staff of an Irish university about their experiences with and perceived value of associational participation over the course of their lives. The project formed part of wider Societās project led by Professor Maria Cahill and based at the School of Law, University College Cork. Ethical approval for this project was sought and granted by the UCC Social Research Ethics Committee (SREC). The data has been anonymised, and the names of participants, places and other identifying references or data have been omitted or changed.

stories captured within these narrative portraits are drawn from broad exploratory interviews on the value of associations in people's everyday lives. They are presented here as portraits in respect to key themes pertaining to associational involvement. This chapter does not purport to be exhaustive but instead offers a glimpse of lived experience. Through these portraits, it illustrates some of the myriad ways associations affect our lives.

The narratives in the chapter are the result of interviews conducted as part of a pilot study in Ireland on the value of associations and how people experience them in different ways across their life course. In the interviews, participants had the opportunity to share experiences of associations throughout their life and what they meant to them. With a qualitative empirical approach as its basis, this chapter draws on the experiences of a sample of university students and staff to capture a range of lived experiences and memories of participation. The portraits of pursuit, fulfilment, frustration and impact are stories used to exemplify motivations, perceived value, challenges, and lasting legacy.

By means of the empirical research conducted in this pilot study, the chapter aims to spotlight some of these facets of associational experiences – good and bad – with real-life examples through storytelling and to set the stage for wider and more legal and philosophical contributions of this book. After an explanation of the dataset from which these portraits are derived (section II), this chapter presents a series of stories under the four main themes: motivations, value, challenges and legacy (section III) and then concludes (section IV). This food-for-thought exploration of narratives brings to life, in a personal way, how associations touch daily life.

II. THE DATASET: AN IRISH PILOT STUDY

The narratives in this chapter stem from a pilot study on experiences of associational involvement carried out within the Societās project,[3] which expands upon background research that gathered a series of testimonials from participants of associations. As part of the study, a total of 30 in-depth semi-structured interviews were carried out with students and staff of a university in Ireland. The university is situated in a city where associational involvement is deeply embedded in the culture of the surrounding area. It is also home to over 200 clubs and societies. A flyer was distributed amongst students and staff outlining the purpose of the research and a call for participation. Participants could be current or former students or staff from any discipline, as long as they were currently participating or had at some point participated in an association

[3] For more on the Societās research project on freedom of association, please see: www.associationalfreedom.org/.

(for easy understanding, 'club or society') in their lifetime. Participants could be of any nationality and any age (adult), and participation could be in any type of association for any length of time. No parameters of specific involvement (such as leadership roles) were placed on participation, though these were discussed where relevant.

The resulting pool of participants ended up as follows: 12 male, 17 female and 1 non-binary participant aged between approximately 18 and 65 years old. Of these, 17 were university staff and 13 were (current or former) students. Of the participants, 26 were Irish and 4 were from outside Ireland. Of these participants, 25 spoke about associations based in Ireland, and 5 spoke about associations based outside of Ireland. A couple of participants (2) spoke about associations that were international (either because the association was based abroad or because it had chapters abroad), one about a national association (1), and the remainder about locally based associations (27).

The interviews, carried out in May 2024 in person (and online in a few instances), lasted between 30 to 60 minutes and were audio recorded (with one exception). This empirical pilot study of the project was approved by the research ethics committee of the research project's host university. In line with the ethical approval of the project, participants were informed at the beginning of the interview of the purpose of the study, their right of withdrawal and confidentiality, and they signed consent forms. The narratives presented here are derived from the interview transcripts.[4] To preserve the anonymity of the data, names of participants and places in the portraits have been changed, and associations are referred to only by subject matter.

The participants' experiences ranged in scope and formality from recreational book clubs, to choirs and music clubs, to more structured student societies, professional associations, and athletic clubs.[5] Given that many participants had been part of multiple associations over the course of their lifetime, also at different stages of life, they were first invited to share their history with associational involvement and then allowed to self-select the experience most meaningful to them or that they wished to talk about. The participants were first asked: what associations have you been a part of in your life? After a full account, they were asked: which experience would you like to speak about?

[4] Meta data for the project, including the information sheet and transcripts, has been published via the Digital Repository of Ireland and is accessible online: doi.org/10.7486/DRI.8c980s15f. In line with the ethical approval by the SREC, the project data is stored with Professor Maria Cahill for a minimum period of ten years.

[5] The activities of participants included: local choirs, book clubs, prayers groups, performance and music bands, athletic associations (eg, badminton, tennis, national sports, Taekwondo, golf, yoga), and a diverse variety of societies including medieval costumers, LGBT, skydiving, board games, and national volunteer organisations.

III. PORTRAITS OF EXPERIENCE: ASSOCIATIONAL PARTICIPATION IN DAILY LIFE

Within their chosen experience, participants were further asked about their motivations for entering and leaving associations, their experiences within them and the lasting impact they felt their involvement has had on their lives. In addition to their practical experiences or tasks, this often led to more philosophical discussions on lessons learnt, stories of personal growth or trials that accompanied decisions in life to join or leave groups. At times, it led to displays of grief, sadness or gratitude related to their participation. While the participants spoke on the subject with ease, it became clear that associations touch upon life milestones in a way that evokes emotion, and for some participants these questions prompted a first reflection on the meaning of their associational involvement throughout their life.

The narratives presented below are selected from the interview transcripts. They comprise different experiences and exemplify a theme or part of a theme found to be expressed in the pilot study. In this way, they make three-dimensional some aspects of the choices of joining, the experiences of being within associations and their impact long after. Naturally, in the cycle of any individual's experience, they may have experiences that fit all themes. After all, each person joins an association, has an experience within and leaves it. The chosen portraits have been placed under the theme where they best illustrate something meaningful.

In what follows, each of the core themes of motivations, value, challenges and legacy are illuminated by two or three stories from participants. As such, each theme presents a set of portraits that bring to life experiences related to that theme. Under each theme there is a brief summary of the characters about to be introduced. Following that, each story is told through a stylised summative narrative of the story told in the interview. Each narrative is followed by a short quote in participants' own words to encapsulate part of their experience or message.

A. Portraits of Pursuit: Motivation for Associational Involvement

Two women, two life transitions, one keeping a connection to home, and the other searching for like-minded individuals in a new home. One man training his kids' teams out of a sense of obligation. One woman joining a band and finding music and friends. The stories of Elaine, Emma, Joe and Gwen are stories of what motivates people to participate in associations.

i. Elaine: Keeping a Connection to Home

When Elaine joined the book club, she did not really need friends; she already had a lot of things to keep her busy. A friend invited her to come along, and she thought it would be a good idea. She knew that she would be expected to read a book a month and thought this would instil the habit of reading. She was nervous at her first meeting and thoroughly prepared for the discussion of Colm Tóibín's 'Brooklyn', but everyone was very nice and welcoming. You had to speak, but it was not an exam, and she quickly became part of the core five of the group. That was 18 years ago now. Now she has moved away, as she had a few times over the years, and lives an hour and a half away. Still, she travels once a month to be there. There are other book clubs where she lives now that she could join, but for her it would not be the same. Everyone has their place in the group, and the familiarity is stabilising. It gives some structure. As she has gotten older, it has been harder to meet people, and the book club has become about friends after all. She is now the second-longest member of the group, and her involvement over time has given her long-lasting friendships and self-confidence, just by being consistently involved. As an added bonus, when she travels back for the book club, she meets other old friends and has a reason to go back home. In Elaine's words:

> We have moved around the country quite a lot, and I just find it quite stabilising to be able to return to something which is familiar. … The structure, the coherence, the predictability, those kind of things, even the regularity, the discipline of having to read the book and all of that. That I think is what it provides. … You know, there are all sorts of promises to stay in touch and whatever and sometimes it's hard to do that unless you have a particular reason to go back somewhere. So, if I say go back to the book club there, I can then attach to that meeting other people whom I've known in the past. And I think it's a very useful hook as well for that because otherwise, you know, you go back aimlessly to somewhere and you don't really keep doing it.

ii. Emma: Looking for Connection in a New Place

When Emma moved to the UK ten years ago, she had already found her passion in historical reenactment. A chance encounter with a student society led her through her student years, punctuated by medieval weapons training and events with a close-knit group of friends. She'd learnt to sew her own costumes and took carefree trips across the country to attend fairs. So, it was only natural her first stop in her new home abroad would be to seek the same. She searched online and tried to find the closest possible thing. It took six months, but she found a medieval dance renaissance group. Some of the group cared more about the dances, while she preferred the costumes, but through it she was able to find what she was looking for – people with similar interests and a new community. For that reason, she would take the train to the lessons and return late in the evening, and she kept going up until it was time to move back to Ireland. Now back in Ireland, she regularly goes back to the UK to see her friends she made in the dancing class. They keep in touch and are some of her closest friends. When she gets the chance, she travels back to attend balls and to hang out with them, just like they did when she was in a new place away from home. In Emma's words:

> I've been doing this for probably 25 years. I don't see it changing at all. And I think the fact that so many of my friendships are founded on it, it's always there in the background. So even if none of us are doing it again at some point in the future, it will always have that grounding. That sounds bad in the sense that we're not friends just because of the thing. They're obviously really important people in my life, you know, [but] I can't change the fact that that's how I met them and that's how we became friends. That's the history. … I feel that if I was to sum it up, it really enriches my life. Not to say that I wouldn't have an enriched life if I had another hobby, but I'm so glad it's this one.

iii. Joe: Coaching His Children's Sports Teams

Joe has three sons. Like most kids their age, they play sport at the local club. The youngest plays soccer, and the oldest plays Gaelic football with his local Gaelic Athletics Association (GAA).[6] Both local clubs run on the work of volunteers. He grew up playing sports himself, and he does not believe in standing on the sidelines and not helping out. He would have to be there pitch-side every week as a parent anyway, and so he takes it upon himself to be a coach for the team. Who else will do it, he thinks. The parents at times seem ungrateful. They often do not express any thanks, and some seem to see it as free daycare, with little interest in the sport. Still, the fathers are expected to pitch in. He is left wondering, why does a swimming coach get paid for their coaching while we receive no compensation? After all, he has to go through training for his coaching badges. It is not about the money per se, but it just does not seem right. In any case, he has been doing it for three years already, and he will probably be doing it for a few more. He appreciates the time bonding with his kids and seeing the children improve their skills, but as soon as his sons leave the teams, so will he. For him, it is primarily a practical way to be involved and spend quality time with his kids, but without them on the team, the coaching itself would not be personally fulfilling enough to maintain. In Joe's words:

> There's no way off this merry-go-round. There can be a bit of politics. People can get emotional about these things, some dads are there to win and to live out their dreams through their children. They can be competitive and that causes tensions. … The upside is you would get to know the other dads well and you'd see them at the schoolyard. You meet kids and other parents that as they get older you will know them as they grow up. You feel like you're contributing something. You're standing there, you might as well be helping. … I do get fulfilment from seeing the children develop and improve [but] I have no attachment to doing it, I see it as a responsibility.

[6] Gaelic football is a team sport played in Ireland. It is governed by the Gaelic Athletics Association (GAA), Ireland's largest sporting organisation, which promotes amateur Gaelic sports, including Gaelic football, hurling and camogie. On Gaelic football, see further: www.gaa.ie/my-gaa/getting-involved/gaelic-football.

iv. Gwen: Venturing into a New Hobby and Feeling Less Alone

Gwen had no musical training, but she had always loved music. She had seen the large, Latin American city band around and always wanted to join. After leaving her job and starting to freelance, she found she had more free time but not much of a social life. She found the band's email address online and contacted them. She was in luck. They were just taking on new members, and she was invited to join a practice. The leader had two simple criteria for membership: participants should have a bit of rhythm and be nice people; the rest was just a matter of practice. That made it easy to join and get started. Like every member, Gwen started on the smaller, simpler instruments and worked her way up to the big ones. After the first practice, someone suggested they all go out for some drinks, a tradition they kept up, and so she got to know everyone. She spent six years in the group, with people from all different backgrounds. They practiced, they travelled, they performed – all for free and because they loved it. It was unstructured and free-flowing in those days, and that suited her. During the Covid-19 pandemic, their practices came to a standstill. A group chat formed, and they joined an online quiz twice a week to stay social during the lockdown. She felt included. One night she did not show up online because she was not feeling up to it. A text popped up – someone from the band checking in – are you okay? She cries as she recalls it. It was a level of care that she had not expected. After all, they did not know much about each other's lives outside of the band. The connection they had formed through their mutual love of music was the basis of making memories together. Yet, those check-ins during the pandemic showed her how much her bandmates truly cared. Despite otherwise not being deeply involved in each other's lives, they took the time to reach out to her, and she felt less alone during what was a difficult and isolating time. In Gwen's words:

> Within those years, it was my social life. And because of [the band leader's] two criteria, he had gathered a group of people who were really similarly minded but had completely different backgrounds. … At the same time, our other lives weren't that relevant to the band. There was a lot of people I still don't know what they do and it doesn't matter. … With the lockdown, it was really intense at the beginning and at the time it was a little bit, maybe too much, but we were frantic when we were all trying to connect. But they always included me, and I remember one night I just wasn't feeling it. And I got a message, one of the guys, he was like, 'everything okay'? … And he made it his business then to check in. So, I mean, that's [a level of care] completely separate to the band"

B. Portraits of Fulfilment: Perceived Value

One man on a mission to make tangible change to society. One woman seeking solace and meaning among people who share her faith, and another lost in her career, searching for a way forward. The stories of Stephen, Mary and Donna are stories of value.

i. Stephen: Fighting for Change within Society

When Stephen joined a national advocacy group, he was annoyed. He disagreed with the religious laws (governing schools and oaths) in Ireland, which he did not think fit within a secular society. He wanted to make a change. After the death of his wife, he had left behind a time-consuming job that he loved and had taken up law as a new career path. He had more time, and he wanted to make a real change. Though he had been a part of other NGOs or associations, this one was different. He felt as though they were all on the same page. They wanted to fix a problem. More than that, he admired and learnt from the way other members advocated for their cause – some with humour, some with great tenacity – and he learnt from them along the way. Together, they made an impact on how the law is written, and their campaign featured prominently during a referendum that passed country wide. For his part, he stayed behind the scenes, letting others talk to the cameras, but wrote letters and volunteered his time to make the campaigns a success. Now he is a retired pensioner, and with his child grown up, he stays involved and funds change for the future. In Stephen's words:

> I was in therapy after my wife died and the therapist said, you can't fix the whole world. I was like, oh yeah, but you can try. … It hasn't really changed me, but I see it, especially having children, that there's like a humanist principle that you're custodians of the world for the next generations. And part of that philosophy is that you improve the world and build a better world. And that's the way I would sum it up.

ii. Mary: Finding a Faith-Based Community

When Mary first joined a large youth prayer group, she was looking to make friends with similar values. Her faith was really important to her, and she wanted to expand her social circle. She was a self-described slow starter and often left straight after the prayers were finished, even though she wanted to meet people. She was not prepared for how enthusiastic everyone would be and found that she would only join in every few weeks. She found that most young people were looking to meet their future girlfriend or boyfriend there, and there was a lack of oversight in the group. It lacked leadership and rules, she felt, and was too casual. She wanted friends, but she did not want the pressure that she experienced when joining group activities. Instead, she found a different group, with mostly older people, where she found she could just attend and pray, where the pressure to socialise was not as intense. She was the youngest member in the group by far, but there she felt completely safe, and she appreciated that there was an authority figure to lead the group. Even though it was an hour away, she went twice a week, and it was worth it. The membership got younger over time, and one day in walked her future husband. They now have five children together. In Mary's words:

> I got the space to find my faith in a more deep way. It was really a space out of the week to just think and pray and then really enjoy the company of people afterwards. I went there for a long time, for three or four years, and as time went on, it wasn't just old

> people. In the beginning, literally, there were like 70s and 80s and me. Then as time went on, it got younger, but for about two years that was it. So those two years really gave a lot of space, gave a lot of peace. It just gave the chance to decompress from the business of the week. … I met people who revealed parts of themselves that were very personal and very deep and who shared their faith and that impacted and strengthened mine.

iii. Donna: Keeping Ties to a Professional Community

Donna had been struggling with her career. After finishing a PhD three years prior in a niche topic, she found herself with no prospects and not knowing how to keep connected to academic circles without a university position. She was about to leave university life – her opportunities were waning, and she was not sure how to make progress in her field. Academically speaking, she had one lifeline remaining, and that came through a society that had asked her to give a talk. The group met a few times each year and discussed their work amongst talks, teas and lunches together. They were not judgmental, and they did not exhibit the usual competitive air of people jockeying for success. She remembers, as a junior scholar, she was invited to sit at the right hand of the chairperson, and she felt treated as an equal. The elder scholars in her field filled the group with knowledge. She received encouragement, she found an academic position. and her career began to flourish. When the secretary stepped down, she took up the role, and she continued it for 10 years, stepping down when she felt it was time for someone else to take over. Over time, things changed. The meetings moved online, and some older inspirational scholars were lost, but she still remembers it fondly. It got her where she is today – a successful scholar. If it were not for them, she is not sure she would be doing what she does now. In Donna's words:

> I feel it was a huge part in saving my career, actually, because it kept me in touch. And they were just such a supportive group and completely non-judgmental, because there are certain academic societies and groups that if you're an independent scholar or you're not involved in a post, they just don't want to know you, but this group was the opposite. … I was really grateful to them and I felt that they'd been good to me.

C. Portraits of Frustration: Challenges of Associational Involvement

One person builds an organisation and loses it to differences of opinion. Another spends years in a temporary role helping a society grow and finds it hard to step away and watch their successors take it in a new direction. The stories of Jennifer and Finn are stories of challenges.

i. Jennifer: Leaving what You Started

When Jennifer got her first car, she joined her first search group. She had always loved animals, and since she had seen search dogs on the back of a van as a child, she had always wanted to be a part of it. She met her husband right away. He was passionate about dogs too. Together, they started their own group, training a breed of dog that until then had not been included in the Irish search force. She invested her own money and time. Sometimes it was difficult, and assisting the police and families with missing persons could be heavy emotionally, but she was proud of her work. Together, they did that for almost 10 years. By then, the group had grown and become more structured. Initially, there was no paperwork, but then people got titles, and the atmosphere of the group changed. There were disagreements about the allocation of funds and the future direction of the group. She felt they were losing track of what it was about. After a disagreement with the management, Jennifer and her husband left the group on bad terms. The chairman had the power, and so she left. Looking back at it, she wishes she had stood her ground and said 'this is our club, you leave', but at the time she did not feel empowered to do so. The club felt like their child in some ways because it was something they had built together. Even now, she feels bitter that it still exists and that other people are running it. She takes part in a music group now, but finds she invests less in the people there and remains more guarded. She does not let herself become friendly with others too fast. In Jennifer's words:

> It seems like a lifetime ago now, I suppose, but it is something that hurts a lot. I think because of the fact that we were so invested in it, when it all went apart, even our relationship was around all that kind of stuff. And then, there was nothing. It was one of the weirdest kind of things. Yeah, it was a big loss to us at the time, I think. … I really am bitter that it still exists and people are there running the club. That was our club that we started for a reason and its purpose is turned into something which it was never supposed to be.

ii. Finn: Watching what You have Made be Reassembled

As a student, Finn was involved in a multitude of societies. Within the LGBT society, which they were a part of for five years, they took on roles in inclusivity, finance and coordination. To be more involved, they took a one-year student sabbatical, staying fully registered but taking no classes and being fully committed to the society. They became a go-to person for guidance, integral to advising other students on taking on committee roles and managing their workload to make sure they did not suffer a burnout. They used their own experience taking on too many activities to help others avoid the same mistakes. It felt good to pass those things on to others. Without that, a lot gets lost. Over time, Finn noticed that a huge amount of institutional knowledge is gained and lost each year. They saw it happen a few times – a society passes from one group to the next, and it inevitably changes. Finn begrudgingly watched his successors make mistakes from information not being passed on or from trying new things, and saw cherished events get cancelled and replaced with new ones. It was always hard to watch it get broken down and rebuilt, even if the society was built back in a better way. It is a cultural evolution, they know, but it can still hurt to see parts of what you have created be taken apart or altogether replaced. In Finn's words:

> I wasn't ready to admit that the version of these groups that I first came into was changing and was gone. Once it happened with three or four of them, I was like, OK, this just happens. Because with the first one, I was like, what's going on? I got so angry. Why are they ruining it? And then when the second one happened, I was like, are these young guys all just idiots? Do they not know how to do things? And then it happened again. I was like, oh, I'm the problem. I get it now."

D. Portraits of Impact: The Legacy in One's Life

Two women grow up in highly active sports-based communities and follow similar paths but with two different outcomes. The stories of Aoife and Olive, here intertwined, are about the lasting impact of associational involvement.

i. Aoife and Olive: Contrasting Legacies from a Similar Path

Aoife grew up immersed in her local GAA sports club,[7] playing traditional Irish sports at all age levels, making friends and sharing a sense of purpose with them. As a college student, now in a competitive medical programme in another county, she still travels home regularly to train and play with the club and takes the communication and leadership skills she learnt with her into her academic pursuits. Olive, who also started playing Irish sports from an early age, was similarly deeply involved in her local club throughout her childhood and recalls with fondness making friends and having fun. Yet, the pressure from coaches, lack of support and rigid training schedules took away from the joy of camaraderie and collective wins and affected her mental health. She abruptly quit. Now a student in the same medical course as Aoife, she stays active through the gym but has never found that exuberance of being part of a team, and wonders whether, if she had stayed, she might still be part of the lasting friend groups she sees on social media.

For both, involvement in a vibrant local sports club throughout their childhood sparked friendships and demanded ongoing time and effort to be part of a team. Both experiences left a lasting impact on their lives, though one was positive and the other not so. One leaves a lasting legacy of ongoing connection to her home, a source of pride and enduring, transferrable life skills. The other leaves a feeling of something lost and lasting doubts about ever joining a club

[7] The GAA is a community-based organisation with over 2,200 clubs across Ireland in all 32 counties, and typically people join the local club in their county or parish. For more on the GAA generally, see: www.gaa.ie/the-gaa/about-the-gaa.

again due to lingering anxiety about the requisite commitment and pressure. In Aoife's and Olive's words, respectively:

> I suppose just kind of having more people stay in sport and even the younger girls on the team coming up, seeing like she's still able to give her time to her sport while doing quite a big course and she's still able to balance her life. She's still able to be organised and she's still getting through the year. I feel like it would be nice to kind of just be a kind of a motivation for other girls, especially in the club.
>
> I felt like I was letting people down when I wouldn't give 100% to it. So, I think I kind of struggled with that to keep it up to the standard that I would have wanted to do it at. … They just expect a really high standard of commitment from you, and for an amateur sport at a young age, I think that was quite difficult. … Let's say if I couldn't go to a training, then my teammates would be annoyed if I was starting a match ahead of them. It was just a lot of pressure and a lot of stress on me. That was kind of the main reason why I gave up in the end was because I just couldn't keep up with it.

IV. CONCLUSION

Personal stories have often been used to give insight into the lived experience of human rights. In the context of freedom of expression, for example, Special Rapporteur on the Promotion and Protection of the Right to Freedom of Opinion and Expression, Irene Khan, has used them to chronicle experience and give voice to communities whose rights are at stake.[8] In the context of this volume, the purpose of these narrative portraits is to offer a first set of reflections, in the context of a set of essays exploring the nature of associational life and freedom from legal and philosophical perspectives, on the meaning that associations have in everyday life. The experiences chronicled may sometimes be mundane, but they hold meaning for the participants involved. The stories of Aoife, Olive and others demonstrate how associations intersect with one's personal life. In the end, associations are made up of individuals who are filled with their own desires, who contribute in their own ways and who have their own experiences.

As stated at the outset, the purpose of this narrative chapter is not to be exhaustive in its survey of the daily lived experience of associations. After all, eight portraits cannot capture the entire breadth of means or ways that involvement in associations can affect people's lives. Instead, the stories presented here give a brief glimpse of experience and open a door to thinking about how associations touch daily life in different ways. For the participants in the present pilot study, the associations in their lives had specific purpose or meaning at different times and left a long-lasting impact.

[8] UNESCO, UN Special Rapporteur Irene Khan launches essay collection '#JournalistsToo' on personal stories of harassment by women journalists, 25 November 2021, available at: www.unesco.org/en/articles/un-special-rapporteur-irene-khan-launches-essay-collection-journaliststoo-personal-stories.

These stories give a 'face' to some of the facets of associational living. They journey through some wider themes of the motivations to join, the value and challenges and the legacy. They are not intended here to be empirically consequential (generalisable) or the basis of a wider estimation on the value of associations, but rather a more visceral and imaginative capturing of lived experience, in this case from an Irish perspective. Still, there are other stories, from other parts of the world, which might include a different narrative, and where involvement in associations might raise concerns not seen in this national context. Other narratives might intersect with abuse of government powers, (fighting) authoritarianism, and experiences of danger, fear, rebellion, protest or backlash. Different contexts would produce different stories and portraits of how we might think about the value or impact of associations across the globe.

With this in mind, these narratives form a modest backdrop to the depth of this collection. We can remember these stories – of real people and their meaningful experiences – as we cross the legal and philosophical terrain of the right to freedom of association globally, be it in Chile, Germany, Indonesia, Kenya, Slovenia, Türkiye or the United Kingdom, and examine more technical aspects of associative agreements and disputes. It can serve as a reminder that at the heart of freedom of association is the lived experience of individuals for whom associational participation can be meaningful, impactful and even crucial to their life experience.

Part II

Philosophical Perspectives on Associational Freedom

11

Social Ontology and Collective Intentionality: A Philosophical Perspective on Human Association

GIULIA LASAGNI*

ASSOCIATIONAL LIFE LIES at the heart of our human experience. It concerns the ways in which individuals forge bonds, build societies, and act in concert towards shared goals. When law seeks to regulate and protect these dimensions of social life, it is confronted with a complex terrain as associational life unfolds within a space where the boundaries between individual and collective, formal and informal, legal and social, are often porous and fluid. Legal systems across jurisdictions are tasked with navigating not only this complex space but also the cultural, political, and social particularities that characterise each context.

Philosophy may not offer a rulebook, but it does provide a rich array of theories and concepts – tools that can illuminate, provoke reflection, and deepen our understanding of human sociality and life together. This is precisely the kind of contribution that this part of the edited volume, *Associational Life and Freedom: Insights from Philosophy and Law*, aims to offer. It brings together perspectives from law and philosophy to engage with the lived experience of associational life and freedom. Part I of the book, 'The Law of Associational Freedom', comprises chapters examining how freedom of association is protected and understood in various jurisdictions, particularly in Chile, Germany, Indonesia, Kenya, Slovenia, Türkiye, and the United Kingdom. It also features chapters addressing specific cross-cutting

* This publication is a contribution to the *Societās: Exploring the Value of Freedom of Association* project, led by Professor Maria Cahill at the School of Law, University College Cork, and funded by the Irish Research Council (now Research Ireland) under grant IRCLA/2022/3860. The chapter introduces the philosophical part of the book, featuring contributions from scholars who participated in the interdisciplinary workshop *Exploring Associational Life: From Social Ontology to Law and Back Again*, held at University College Cork on 25–26 April 2024.

issues, such as judicial review and schism, before concluding with an empirical exploration of human associational experience. Meanwhile, Part II, 'Philosophical Perspectives on Associational Freedom', includes five chapters in addition to this introduction. It picks up where the legal section leaves off, beginning with a chapter that explores the familiar and habitual grounds of associational life. The next chapter builds upon this, layer by layer, moving through shared practices and formal articulations to reach the level of established associations. The subsequent chapter offers a reflection on the nature of such entities. Spanning from informal collective experience to the realm of incorporated associations, the final two chapters engage with the complexity of the domain encompassed by freedom of association, exposing apparent tensions and working towards theoretical reconciliations.

The philosophical reflections presented in this volume are from the field of social ontology, which investigates the social world, how we make it, and how we live in it together. In recent years, there has been a growing wave of interest in the intersection between social ontology and law.[1] This volume sits in a unique position within this developing area, offering a pioneering perspective framed through the theme of freedom of association.

The very idea of 'association' gives rise to cross-disciplinary and philosophically intriguing questions about the nature of groups and our life together. What does it mean to say that associations exist, or that they can hold certain rights? What is involved in forming an association and being part of it? What is an association in the first place? And what is the relationship between spontaneous collective experience and regulated group life? Social ontology offers tools for addressing such questions by examining the fundamental components of social reality, particularly the collective intentions, actions, emotions, norms, and other facets of experience that are central to associational life. These aspects are particularly important to understand in relation to a human right that protects associational freedom specifically.

In this chapter, I introduce the philosophical part of the book by providing a theoretical framework, drawing on the literature, to guide the reader through the subsequent chapters. Section I presents the field of social ontology and its relevance to the interdisciplinary debate on freedom of association. In section II, I introduce the notion of collective intentionality as central to the reality and theory of collective experience. To further characterise this important philosophical theme, section III expounds upon the key approaches to it. Section IV provides a brief overview of the chapters, while section V concludes by drawing a connecting thread between them and sharing reflections.

[1] Recent and relevant edited collections are M Garcia-Godinez, R Mellin and R Tuomela (eds), *Social Ontology, Normativity and Law* (Berlin and Boston, De Gruyter, 2020), and T Marques and C Valentini, *Collective Action, Philosophy and Law* (Oxon and New York, Routledge, 2022).

I. THE LANDSCAPE OF SOCIAL ONTOLOGY

Social ontology is a dynamic and rapidly evolving field of philosophical enquiry in which a wide range of questions about the social world converge.[2] Among its central themes are the nature and properties of social facts such as money, law, language, power, and norms. It also examines social groups, considering how they take shape, how their members cooperate, and whether certain groups, such as corporations, can be held responsible. In addition, it investigates categories like gender, sex, and race, and whether these are natural kinds or socially constructed.

Each of these topics connects to a longer list of questions and avenues for research that have been explored in various areas of the social sciences, as well as being reflected upon within thematic philosophical subfields such as the philosophy of economics and law. In this diversified landscape, contemporary social ontology has emerged as a unifying yet multifaceted research field in which philosophers apply their expertise to address a variety of cross-disciplinary questions.[3] Considered together, the answers to such questions can provide systematic analyses of the social world. The philosophical part of this volume embraces the challenge of applying socio-ontological theories to enhance the legal discourse on associational life and freedom.

Etymologically, 'ontology' derives from the Ancient Greek *ontos* (being, that which is) and *logos* (study, discourse). Social ontology is therefore the study of social reality, of what there is in society. The development of this field has taken various forms, leading to at least three different approaches to socio-ontological research. The *descriptive* approach aims to identify and classify the entities that populate the social world.[4] The *explanatory* approach investigates how social entities come into being and are maintained.[5] The *ameliorative* approach questions how things are, as well as how we interpret the social, considering what should be improved, reframed or dismantled.[6]

[2] A clear and comprehensive introduction to social ontology can be found in B Epstein, 'Social Ontology', *Stanford Encyclopaedia of Philosophy* (Fall edn 2024) plato.stanford.edu/entries/social-ontology/ accessed 7 July 2025. Also from the same author is the book published for the Cambridge Elements series, *Social Ontology* (Cambridge, Cambridge University Press, 2025). *The Oxford Handbook of Social Ontology*, edited by Stephanie Collins, Brian Epstein, Sally Haslanger, and Hans Bernhard Schmid is forthcoming. Introductory videos on various themes within the field are available in M Garcia-Godinez, R Mellin and the Social Ontology Research Group (SORG) (eds), *Social Ontology: The Video Series* (2022) isosonline.org/Social-Ontology-The-Video-Series.

[3] This introductory framework, which includes key questions and connections with the social sciences, draws inspiration from Epstein (n 2) and from his video contribution to Garcia-Godinez at al. (n 2).

[4] K Koslicki and O Massin, 'A Plea for Descriptive Social Ontology' (2023) 202(60) *Synthese* doi.org/10.1007/s11229-023-04263-7.

[5] B Epstein, *The Ant Trap: Rebuilding the Foundations of the Social Sciences* (New York, Oxford University Press, 2015).

[6] S Haslanger, 'Gender and Race: (What) Are They? (What) Do We Want Them to Be?' (2000) 34(1) *Nous* 31.

These approaches serve to examine a wide array of topics, with social groups being a central theme. As a matter of fact, social groups are highly diverse, ranging from spontaneous gatherings and sports teams to ethnic communities and religious minorities. If we accept that the legal concept 'association' generally refers to certain types of social groups – typically those that are voluntarily formed by agreement around a common purpose – the relevance of social ontology to the study of human association becomes clear. A descriptive approach would identify and categorise existing associations as types of social groups; an explanatory approach would examine how they are formed and sustained; and an ameliorative approach would consider what associations ought to be instead and how the concept should be used. As the chapters in this volume will showcase, the development of various ontological approaches is not purely speculative but closely linked to normative questions of moral, political and legal concern,[7] and thus related to the practical dimension of associational freedom.

The term 'association' is not commonly used in social ontology. 'Organised social group', 'society' and 'organisation' are used more often instead. These terms refer to social groups that differ from random aggregates (such as the set of people in a room) and from social categories such as gender minorities, ethnic groups, and social classes.[8] Unlike those cases, organised social groups – hereafter referred to as associations – are formed voluntarily by members with a shared interest and serve as sites of collective life and action. In social ontology, they have been approached from multiple angles, suggesting that the term 'organised social group' and, by extension, 'association' can be understood in at least three ways – as regarding social entities, subjects, and practices.

As social *entities*, associations are made up of members, whether individuals or sub-groups. Reductive approaches to social entities argue that associations only exist as pluralities of their members and are therefore reducible to them.[9] In contrast, non-reductive approaches argue that associations exist as social entities and are not identical to the plurality of members.[10] They can be included in an inventory of the social and gain the additional status of legal entities when recognised by the relevant authority.

Just as some legal entities are recognised as legal persons by law, social ontology has advanced views whereby some associations are considered not just objects, but *subjects* too.[11] Broadly speaking, philosophers have three main

[7] E Díaz-León, 'Descriptive vs. Ameliorative Projects: The Role of Normative Considerations' in A Burgess, H Cappelen and D Plunkett (eds), *Conceptual Engineering and Conceptual Ethics* (Oxford, Oxford University Press, 2020).

[8] B Epstein, 'What Are Social Groups? Their Metaphysics and How to Classify Them' (2019) 196(2) *Synthese* 4899.

[9] J Horden and D López de Sa, 'Groups as Pluralities' (2021) 198 *Synthese* 10237.

[10] K Ritchie, 'The Metaphysics of Social Groups' (2015) 10(5) *Philosophy Compass* 310.

[11] P Pettit, 'The Reality of Group Agents' in C Mantzavinos (ed), *Philosophy of the Social Sciences: Philosophical Theory and Scientific Practice* (Cambridge, Cambridge University Press, 2009).

interpretations of this. First, they argue that some groups are sufficiently cohesive and organised to possess their own rational perspective and agency, making them capable of and perhaps responsible for group action.[12] Second, associations are seen as social objects, but all agency and responsibility are attributed to their members.[13] Third, associations are neither objects nor subjects; strictly speaking, only individuals are taken to exist and act, with 'association' referring to patterns of interaction and role-playing.[14]

In a minimal sense, 'association' refers to *practice*, beginning with spontaneous bonds and connections. It then captures the lived experience of being with others by joining together, acting collectively, pursuing common goals, and sharing interests. This practical dimension – which will be discussed further below in relation to the notion of collective intentionality – makes it possible for associations to be formed and sustained as entities or agents.

Considering the various meanings of 'association' and socio-ontological approaches to it, it emerges how complex and subtle the study of human association can be. A sustained interdisciplinary dialogue between philosophy and law holds significant promise. For legal scholars, philosophical insights can illuminate hidden assumptions, draw attention to overlooked aspects of associational life, and reveal alternative frameworks for reinterpreting normative concepts. Conversely, law provides social ontology with examples of disputes, decisions, and prescriptive arguments that can serve as testing grounds for theoretical innovation and the development of normative discourse.

II. WHY COLLECTIVE INTENTIONALITY MATTERS

Among the basic concepts and theories developed in social ontology that can be applied to the study of associations, fundamental is the notion of collective intentionality. This concept is typically used to explain human collective experience, action and deliberation, and it is especially pertinent in cooperative contexts. It is therefore relevant for interrogating associations as entities, subjects, and practices and for illuminating some important ways in which these meanings of 'association' relate to one another and to the social world to which they belong. Moreover, understanding how people cooperate is crucial for grasping how freedom of association is exercised and manifested in associational life, as well as for informing the implementation and reflection upon legal protections for it.

[12] P Philip, 'Group Agents are Not Expressive, Pragmatic or Theoretical Fictions' (2014) 79 *Erkenntnis* 1641.

[13] R Tuomela, *The Philosophy of Sociality: The Shared Point of View* (Oxford, Oxford University Press, 2007) C 6 Appendix.

[14] K Ludwig, 'Do Corporations Have Minds of Their Own?' (2017) 30(3) *Philosophical Psychology* 269.

The first aspect to clarify is that collective intentionality indicates a psychological feature. It is a property of the mind that manifests in social contexts – that is, contexts involving at least two individuals. In its individual form, intentionality is the property of the mind of being about something. Individual intentionality means that one's beliefs are about facts of the world or personal moods, that one's desires are about possible or even unrealistic scenarios, and that one's attention is focused on a landscape view, a book paragraph, or a song. Individual intentionality is involved in planning individual actions and is important in sustaining and guiding behaviours that are consistent with one's plans.

Collective intentionality is the directionality of the mind in a social context.[15] It indicates that we share a desire, belief or plan; that our attention is directed towards the same song when we sing together at a concert; and that our dance is not merely seemingly coordinated, but that we are making a joint effort to perform a choreography. Collective intentionality is at play whenever we wait in an orderly queue, shake hands or give a standing ovation. Whenever several minds are in tune with one another, some form of collective intentionality is at play. Therefore, collective intentionality has a fundamental role in associational life: it marks the point where individuals stop being isolated and start interacting with others. It directs association as a collective action; it explains that associations as objects exist because people collectively recognise their existence and functions; it provides an account for how some associations act cohesively, as social units.

Although collective intentionality is widely recognised as a key element of the social world, it poses a significant challenge, and there is much debate about it.[16] Since intentionality is the capacity of the mind to be directed towards something – and since it is generally accepted that there is no such thing as a collective mind – the challenge lies in understanding how this mental capacity could be considered collective. The debate is divided into two main perspectives.[17] Reductive views maintain that collective intentionality is an articulation of individual intentionality and can therefore be understood using the same concepts and principles that are used to explain individual attitudes and behaviour. Conversely, non-reductive views argue that discussions of

[15] M Jankovic and K Ludwig, 'Introduction' in K Ludwig and M Jankovic (eds), *The Routledge Handbook of Collective Intentionality* (New York and Oxon, Routledge, 2018) *cf* 2.

[16] For detailed introductions to the notion and theories of collective intentionality, some of which are presented here, excellent sources are DP Schweikard and HB Schmid, 'Collective Intentionality', *The Stanford Encyclopaedia of Philosophy* (Fall edn, 2021) plato.stanford.edu/entries/collective-intentionality/ accessed 11 December 2024, and D Tollefsen, 'Collective Intentionality', *Internet Encyclopaedia of Philosophy* iep.utm.edu/collective-intentionality/ accessed 11 December 2024. A rich overview of the debates surrounding the concept of collective intentionality is provided by Jankovic and Ludwig (n 15). A brief video introduction to theories of collective intentionality and group agency, recorded by Giulia Lasagni, is available as part of Garcia-Godinez et al. (n 2).

[17] For an overview of the two perspectives, see FM Alonso, 'Reductive Views of Shared Intention' and R Tuomela, 'Non-Reductive Views of Shared Intention' in Ludwig and Jankovic (n 15).

collective beliefs, actions, and emotions highlight genuine collective phenomena that cannot be fully explained by referring to individual mental attitudes and behaviour and the theories used to account for them.[18] What follows unpacks this debate further.

III. THEORIES OF COLLECTIVE INTENTIONS AND ACTIONS

Emerging in the 1990s, the debate on collective intentionality was initially driven by seminal contributions from philosophers such as Michael Bratman, Margaret Gilbert, John Searle, and Raimo Tuomela. A useful and established way of presenting and classifying different theories relies on their respective interpretations of the collective element as being inherent in the content, mode, or subject of collective intentional attitudes.[19]

To clarify, as already mentioned, intentionality is a property of the mind, so it is instantiated in mental attitudes such as beliefs and desires. A mental attitude is held by a subject who is oriented towards a certain object represented in the attitude's content and experienced in a particular way or mode. Consider this example: Walking through your neighbourhood after a storm, you spot Peter outside his house repairing a damaged fence. Let's assume that Peter intends to repair it, and that his movements realise this intention. Peter is the subject, the intention to fix the damage is the attitude, and the mode is that of an individual practical resolution. The fact that Peter will repair his house's fence is the object represented in the content of the intention.

Insofar as Peter's action is guided by an individual intention, it is an individual action: Peter intentionally and individually brings it about. This remark is relevant because part of the interest in the concept of collective intentionality is precisely that, just as individual actions are guided by individual intentions, collective actions are guided by collective intentions. Therefore, understanding the collective element of intentionality provides the tools needed to examine collective actions and distinguish them from individual actions or the mere sum of several individual actions. Reflecting on our lived experience, collective actions – such as those involved in associational activities – often appear to be more than merely the juxtaposition of individual acts. They may be coordinated and experienced as collective in a meaningful way, and the notion of collective intentionality is important to grasp it.

[18] Non-reductive views, then, can be categorised as either distributive or non-distributive. As intended here, distributive approaches interpret collective intentions and actions as embodied in the participatory intentions and actions of several agents. In contrast, non-distributive approaches study collective attitudes and actions in terms of group rationality and agency as displayed and performed by one social system.

[19] This framework has been proposed and articulated by Schweikard and Schmid (n 16). As it has become a common approach for introducing theories of collective intentionality, this section will outline the debate by drawing on it.

Imagine that, as you continue strolling around the neighbourhood, you not only notice Peter, but also Mark and Clara fixing fences. If they are doing it together rather than individually and simultaneously by chance, there must be a connection between them. If this is not a coincidence, then perhaps they have joined forces intentionally to take care of the neighbourhood following last night's violent storm. This is where collective intentionality becomes relevant. When it is at play – and it is therefore meaningful to say that people do things together – something like this would be the case: Peter, Mark and Clara repair the fences together with the collective intention to do so. But how is their intention collective? Where does the collective psychological trait reside?

A. Collective Content

Some philosophers hold that what characterises intentionality in social contexts is that the content of the attitude that every individual has regards a collective matter, yet the intention itself remains an individual mental state. The approach to collective intentionality is therefore reductive, as it goes all the way back to individual attitudes. Here is an exemplification of this:

> Peter, Mark, and Clara each intends that *we (that is, the three of them) will fix the neighbourhood fences together*.

This sentence depicts a collective element, which is expressed after the 'that', spelling out the content that everyone has in mind. No collective mind is present, nor is any special mental state required. Individual capacities are sufficient to explain the collective psychological trait. However, this does not mean that collective intentions and actions merely involve individual minds representing collective contents.

Michael Bratman, one of the main proponents of the content view, has studied human cooperation, proposing a planning theory of shared agency.[20] In his account, the capacity to act together – whether in repairing fences or, to cite one of his paradigmatic examples, painting a house – is explained through interdependent individual attitudes. When individuals cooperate, they intend to do so believing that the others will do the same. Mutual beliefs allow people to think that their individual contribution is part of a joint effort: it helps to achieve a plan that everyone is working towards, with the belief that others will cooperate. The building blocks of this line of explanation relate to individual agency and rationality. However, collective intentionality and agency require interaction and mutual beliefs to be realised. Indeed, individuals can only act jointly through interdependent, interlocking plans that are oriented

[20] M Bratman, 'Shared Intention' (1993) 104(10) *Ethics* 97; *Faces of Intention: Selected Essays on Intention and Agency* (Cambridge, Cambridge University Press, 1999); *Shared Agency: A Planning Theory of Acting Together* (New York, Oxford University Press, 2014).

towards a common goal; that is the object of their shared intention. Therefore, despite ultimately being reducible to individualistic concepts and principles, an explanation that considered individuals in isolation as merely representing in their minds a collective agency situation would not account for how they act collectively, even in this 'modest' sense.

B. Collective Mode

An alternative account of collective intentionality proposes that the collective element does not reside (solely) in the content of mental attitudes, and that even considering mutual beliefs about interdependent contributions does not suffice to provide an exhaustive explanation. According to this view, collective intentions have a distinctive collective mode that cannot be fully captured using the conceptual tools employed for individual attitudes. This approach is therefore non-reductive. Returning to our example:

> Peter, Mark, and Clara *collectively* intend to repair the damaged fences in the neighbourhood.

The adverb qualifies everyone's intention. This intention is held by everyone in the we-mode, that is, from a perspective with a collective character. The collective element provided by the mode thus belongs to the psychology of individuals; it is found in their minds.

The philosopher Raimo Tuomela developed a sophisticated theory of we-mode cooperation.[21] For Tuomela, there are various ways in which people can approach collective contexts of action. He argued that, in weak scenarios, individuals may interact with one another under the belief that others will participate, but do so in the I-mode, that is, for their own purposes and self-interest. They contribute to collective action personally, as individuals. In robust cases, individuals participate in the we-mode, acting as part of a collective, for the sake of shared goals and in keeping with a set of shared values, namely the ethos. Acting in view of shared goals or values, and so for collective reasons, entails that those reasons have been collectively accepted by the members, and that a collective commitment is formed among them, binding everyone to one another and to the intention to attain their objectives jointly. In other words, acting in the we-mode means acting collectively, as group members – for example, as volunteers in a neighbourhood association working together for the benefit of the community. The we-mode is therefore a perspective: a way in which individuals hold mental attitudes in a genuinely collective manner that cannot be reduced to the I-mode. Although it belongs

[21] R Tuomela, 'Joint Intention, We-Mode and I-Mode' (2006) 30(1) *Midwest Studies in Philosophy* 35; *The Philosophy of Sociality*; *Social Ontology: Collective Intentionality and Group Agents* (New York, Oxford University Press, 2013).

to the psychology of individuals, it arises in collective contexts of interaction and is a collective mental posture.

John Searle proposed an alternative interpretation of the collective mode, characterising we-mode intentions ('we-intentions' in his terminology) as primitive.[22] These arise from our inherent capacity as human beings to think in the plural grammatical form and do not necessarily require meaningful interaction. In principle, one could be mistaken in a we-thought about others' engagement.

C. Collective Subject

Finally, there is a third, non-reductive approach to collective intentionality. In this approach, the collective element lies in the subject of attitudes. Although this may sound mysterious at first, the view is less extravagant than it seems, since the collective subject in question is not a fantasy creature. Rather, the view works with the idea that individuals think and act as one. Below is an illustration of it:

> *Peter, Mark, and Clara, as a group*, intend to repair the damaged fences in the neighbourhood.

Various explanations have been offered as to what it means to intend and act as a group. One of the most influential accounts is that of Margaret Gilbert.[23] Gilbert's theory of cooperation is based on a normative bond among the members, created through an act of joint commitment by those willing to join, and only rescindable by them jointly.[24] By committing to one another, individuals also commit to acting as a unit – from the group's perspective, which is a rational, unified perspective that they have all endorsed and are jointly committed to pursuingas as a plural subject. The collective intentionality that animates individuals' psychology when acting as a unit does not iron out individual preferences, but those attitudes remain in the intentional realm that informs individual rather than group behaviour.[25]

While Gilbert's view is still related to the psychology of intentional attitudes, other approaches to the subject have focused on the functioning of the group as a system.[26] As part of the system, individuals act together in organised ways, enacting decisions that result from group-level deliberation

[22] JR Searle, *Consciousness and Language* (Cambridge, Cambridge University Press, 2002) C 6.

[23] M Gilbert, 'Walking Together: A Paradigmatic Social Phenomenon' (1990) XV *Midwest Studies in Philosophy* 1; *Joint Commitment: How We Make the Social World* (New York, Oxford University Press, 2014).

[24] For a non-normativistic approach to the plural subject, see HB Schmid, 'The Subject of 'We Intend'' (2018) 17(2) *Phenomenology and the Cognitive Sciences* 231.

[25] M Gilbert, 'Shared Intention and Personal Intentions' (2009) 144 *Philosophical Studies* 167.

[26] See C List and P Pettit, *Group Agency: The Possibility Design, and Structure of Corporate Agents* (New York, Oxford University Press, 2011); DP Tollefsen, *Groups as Agents* (Cambridge, Polity Press, 2015).

processes, such as those of an organised neighbourhood association. No mysterious mind is posited. The internal decision-making mechanisms make the group function as if it had a mind, and the joint action of its members enacts those decisions as if the system were a single agent. It is a performative person with cognitive capacities, and it is debated whether it could have any moral standing.[27] This functionalist view suggests that group deliberation and action belong to the high-level system – the group is not, or not primarily, a psychological feature.[28]

D. Collective Intentionality and the Construction of the Social World

The various interpretations of collective intentionality demonstrate the complexity and theoretical subtlety of human cooperation as encompassing individual psychology, interpersonal relationships, and organisational behaviour. When people act collectively, they can achieve complex goals, pursue shared interests and fulfil their needs. Importantly, they can even create social objects that serve this purpose. Collective intentionality is in fact integral to the way human beings construct the social world.

A key argument proposed by John Searle in this respect is that brute facts acquire social meaning, that is, status function, by being collectively recognised as such in a certain context.[29] For example, within a community, a piece of paper may count as money, a river as a boundary, a person as president, or a ticked box as a vote. Once objects are assigned status functions, they gain the related deontic powers (for example, rights and duties) and begin to regulate life and action in relation to them. This applies to associations as well. They qualify as specific practices, subjects or objects, depending on whether the relevant collective recognises them as such. In this way, they exist socially and, through formal registration, legally too, gaining further deontic powers according to their ascribed legal status. This will further shape the relationships between associations and individuals, as well as other associations and the state, establishing the rights and duties of associations and of other parties in relation to them.[30]

[27] For an introduction to the debate, see M Smiley, 'Collective Responsibility', *The Stanford Encyclopaedia of Philosophy* (Fall edn, 2023) plato.stanford.edu/archives/fall2023/entries/collective-responsibility/ accessed 3 July 2025. For an extensive overview of related topics and discussions, see S Bazargan-Forward and D Tollefsen (eds), *The Routledge Handbook of Collective Responsibility* (New York and Oxon, Routledge, 2020).

[28] Any of the member-level theories of collective intentionality outlined above could, in principle, be combined with a functionalist approach to group agency.

[29] JR Searle, *The Construction of Social Reality* (New York, Free Press, 1995); 'Social Ontology: Some Basic Principles' (2006) 6(1) *Anthropological Theory* 12; *Making the Social World: The Structure of Human Civilization* (New York, Oxford University Press, 2010).

[30] For a theory that approaches social groups for the normative function that they play in structuring human life in society, see AL Thomasson, 'The Ontology of Social Groups' (2019) 196(12) *Synthese* 4829.

Philosophy suggests that associational life is deeply collective, with the power to generate, animate, and sustain social reality, as well as the lives of the individuals within it. Therefore, the right to this is the right to freely experience, develop, and exercise the collective dimension of human life. What the contours and limits of this freedom are will be considered in the chapters contained within this book.

IV. OVERVIEW OF THE PHILOSOPHICAL CHAPTERS

The insights from social ontology into associational life and freedom feed into an interdisciplinary conversation launched as part of the *Societās* project. The authors – Kirk Ludwig, Judith H Martens, Valeria Martino, Hans Bernhard Schmid, Michael Schmitz and myself – have all been involved in its activities since an initial online symposium in November 2023, followed by an interdisciplinary workshop held at the School of Law, University College Cork, on 25–26 April 2024. At this workshop, they presented the ideas that have now been expanded upon in the book chapters.[31] The workshop employed an innovative methodology, combining the simulation of legal disputes with philosophical reflections and legal presentations from specific jurisdictions. The chapters in this volume reflect this synergy: informed by the contextual variability of the jurisdictions, philosophical ideas are developed and applied to two fictional scenarios resembling common disputes relating to freedom of association. *Cairde ar son Cairde Soup Kitchen* tells the story of a group of friends engaged in voluntary activities who are now required to register as a charity – with all the implications this holds for an informal association. *Róisín's Golfing Ambitions* addresses the issue of exclusion, prompting reflection on its legitimacy depending on the circumstances and the opportunities available to the candidate.[32]

The interdisciplinary journey begins with a discussion of informal, interpersonal association as a practice, moving on to consider increasingly structured and articulated groups. The focus then shifts to the nature, complexity and rights of human associations, whether as the subjects or objects of associational life and freedom.

[31] The workshop *Exploring Associational Life: From Social Ontology to Law and Back Again* was organised by Professor Maria Cahill and Dr Giulia Lasagni as part of the *Societās* project. It was supported by the IRCLA/2022/3860 grant and a National University of Ireland grant for Early Career Academics 2023.

[32] The text of the Moot Scenarios are to be found in M Cahill, 'Introduction: Comparative and Interdisciplinary Interfaces of Associational Life and Freedom' in M Cahill and G Lasagni (eds), *Associational Life and Freedom: Insights from Philosophy and Law* (Oxford, Hart Publishing, 2026), 15–17.

In particular, chapter twelve, entitled '*Associating on Familiar Grounds: A Habitual Perspective on the Freedom of Association*', authored by Judith H Martens, presents an interpretation of associational life and freedom that is grounded in habits and the sense of familiarity they engender. These resistant yet malleable elements are posited here as underpinning a sense of belonging, an idea of appropriateness and normalcy of behaviour, and providing proxy-reasons to act in certain ways – ways that are typical of the group. Reflecting on associational freedom therefore involves considering the imphat and informal, along with the more explicit and formal, roots and fabric of associational life. In chapter thirteen, '*The Right to Be We: The Case of Associations*', Michael Schmitz applies his multi-layered approach to human experience and sociality to highlight and explain the increasing complexity of associational life. He refers to a stratification of linguistic representations, modes of self-understanding, and interactions that lead from the most spontaneous groupings to the formalisation found at the institutional level. This raises important questions about the different layers of being 'We' as well as the various levels of articulation and application that are involved in a right to associational freedom.

Chapter fourteen, '*Recognising Associations: A Social Ontology Perspective*', authored by Valeria Martino, examines what qualifies as an association by exploring both formal and informal cases through the lens of social ontology. Rather than offering a fixed definition, the chapter presents relevant philosophical perspectives on how associations might be identified and categorised. It also discusses insightful considerations for normative and legal frameworks that are tasked with navigating what is – or should be – protected by the right to freedom of association. In chapter fifteen, entitled '*The Good of Association and the Freedom that We Share*', Hans Bernhard Schmid elaborates on the idea that associations are plural subjects of associational life and freedom. This freedom is a package that encompasses both everyone's freedom to form groups and the freedom to act as such, together. Drawing on his theory of collective intentionality and action, Schmid invites us to overcome the opposition between individuals and groups, instead regarding associational life as a plural experience enjoyed by many jointly with others. Finally, Kirk Ludwig in '*The Nature, Ground, and Legal Expression of a Right to Freedom of Association*', chapter sixteen of this book, offers an account of freedom of association, understood not primarily as a legal construct but as a moral value. Building on his work on collective and institutional agency, he explores the structure of the moral right to associational freedom as an ensemble right, delineating its multifaceted nature and the conditional rights inherent in it. He then examines some of the complexities involved in its application and protection within legal contexts.

The result is an innovative and thought-provoking collection of essays that offers new perspectives for philosophical and legal audiences alike. It challenges preconceived notions and enriches the conceptual framework for understanding associational freedom, venturing into a field of research where social ontology has only recently begun to tread.

V. CONNECTING THREADS AND REFLECTIONS

The philosophical chapters in this volume disclose new conceptual pathways for understanding associational life and freedom. Drawing from vibrant debates in social ontology, they offer tools to clarify not only what associations are or should be taken to be, but also how they come into being, what sustains them, and therefore on what grounds they deserve protection. On one level, the chapters explore the nature of associations, from formally recognised entities to informal, spontaneous bonds that precede any explicit articulation or institutionalisation. Underlying this analysis is the dual – partly descriptive, partly normative – question of what counts as an association and what should be counted as such. On another level, they examine the foundations of associational life, from the most basic and familiar seeds of sociality to the more structured, reflective, and institutional grounds on which formal associations are built.

Each chapter develops an independent and unique perspective on the social ontology of associational life and freedom. Rather than providing an exhaustive summary that attempts to encapsulate the richness of the positions advanced by the contributing authors, the following reflections seek to trace a connecting thread through their diverse philosophical insights. The aim is to offer one perspective from which to approach this part of the book and the distinctive dimensions of associational life, as these are illuminated through the philosophical lens of social ontology.

Such a philosophical lens brings into focus a complex web of interconnected subjects, relationships, mental attitudes, habits, practices, interests, moral values, and degrees of organisation and formalisation that are so interwoven as to resist easy separation. These elements are in fact presented as interdependent in multiple ways. Firstly, they are inherently interdependent because associational life is life shared with others. It unfolds only in the presence of others; it is a joint experience, created, sustained and enjoyed in common. Secondly, this interdependence emerges as reflecting conditionality: associating with others can only succeed if they are willing to do so too. Thirdly, the elements of associational life are interdependent because they mutually constitute one another: individuals constitute the groups they form, while the group partly constitutes the individuals' self-conception, behaviour, and identity. Informal interactions constitute formal groups, and formal structures in turn influence the evolution of informal, intersubjective dynamics. Interdependence then can also be asymmetrical. Some elements are more fundamental than others, forming the basis upon which more complex layers emerge, with legal articulations sitting on top.

When it comes to considering the regulation and protection of such interdependent layers and parties, one aspect that seems to reconcile the various philosophical views is the idea that, despite formal and legal layers apparently sitting atop informal dynamics, they are not extrinsic to them. By regulating basic, lower-level interactions, law also constitutes and changes them.

Formal constraints make the members of a collective think of themselves differently, as a unit, as an incorporated person, as a social entity. The flux of actions based on unreflective, habitual, and familiar connections is turned into a reflective, designed, and disciplined way of doing things. Although this step is important and even necessary for complex groups, it can hinder the activities and growth of smaller, more informal groups. For collective intentionality to operate, the psychological atmosphere from which collective attitudes originate would need to manifest and develop freely to some extent. Compliance with formal requirements may in part reify collective agency by crystallising the fluidity of sociality and compelling individuals to shift from a natural way of doing things together to a reflective mode of operating within rigid grids and fixed parameters. When this level of reflection and organisation is introduced, it becomes part of the group's dynamics, which will then change accordingly.

This is not to suggest that interpersonal relationships are completely unregulated or non-normative, but rather that the norms they are subject to are not the ones imposed by law. Collective commitment to achieving common goals, mutual expectations regarding appropriate behaviours, and moral feelings towards social practices and values are all normative attitudes that form part of human association before and independently of legal norms and principles. Formal norms add further layers of normativity which are indispensable for regulating, protecting, and constraining associational life, especially when its impact and scale become larger and of public, if not political, interest. However, applying legal regulations to small and still very spontaneous contexts can partially endanger the associational freedom they are meant to safeguard. This is because regulations can, to a certain degree, reduce the spontaneity of social interaction and inhibit some activities that once flourished in the absence of formal rules. At a fundamental level, freedom of association seems to require attention to the freedom to develop and nurture interpersonal relationships spontaneously.

Safeguarding associational life therefore entails the challenging task of regulating and protecting collective experience, by supporting without stifling, and structuring without reifying it. Finding the right balance is challenging, and this interdisciplinary volume aims to offer fresh perspectives on it. Law provides frameworks to deal with concrete cases according to general principles, specific norms, and particular contexts. Social ontology provides conceptual tools for further analysing the nature of such particular contexts of collective human experience and suggests avenues for developing normative reflection.

12

Associating on Familiar Grounds: A Habitual Perspective on the Freedom of Association

JUDITH H MARTENS*

IN THIS CHAPTER, I will introduce the idea of habits, familiarity, and proxy-reasons as important underpinnings of our associational life. I will use my analysis to examine the moot court scenario of *Cairde ar son Cairdre Soup Kitchen* (presented in the Introduction of this book).[1] To gain insight into the framework, I will begin by outlining the results of applying my approach to the moot scenario. In this scenario, Cairde ar son Cairdre is an outdoor soup kitchen initiated by a group of friends. Over time, several shops become involved, and the outreach goes beyond offering a shared meal to those in need. The group views their activities as an expression of community support that transcends formal legal structure. The group of friends wants to maintain an unofficial status and informal character, partly because they aim for an atmosphere that is open and friendly to their guests. The volunteers at Cairde ar son Cairdre, led by Gráinne, formed an association through their shared values and collective actions. To its members, this association is not a legal or formal agreement, but an expression of shared identity and commitment to a social cause. This is even though they clearly commit to a structural way of organising regular activities and have clear role divisions. The Charity Regulators want the soup kitchen to register as a charity and act in accordance with the Charities Act. They ask the soup kitchen to conform to formal registration and financial oversight. The group objects to this formalisation based on their right

* This publication is a contribution to the *Societās: Exploring the Value of Freedom of Association* project, led by Professor Maria Cahill at the School of Law, University College Cork, and funded by the Irish Research Council (now Research Ireland) under grant IRCLA/2022/3860. The chapter builds on ideas discussed during the workshop *Exploring Associational Life: From Social Ontology to Law and Back Again*, held at University College Cork on 25–26 April 2024.

[1] M Cahill, 'Introduction: Comparative and Interdisciplinary Interfaces of Associational Life and Freedom' in M Cahill and G Lasagni (eds), *Associational Life and Freedom: Insights from Philosophy and Law* (Oxford, Hart Publishing, 2026), 15–16.

to freedom of association. How can my conceptual work on habits, familiarity, and proxy-reasons help the legal and ethical discourse surrounding the freedom of expression and association? I will argue that my framework allows us to see how the proxy-reasons (a proxy or interim for reasons) offered by the sense of familiarity give meaning to the actions of the soup kitchen. Their informal familiarity-based structure is both meaningful and essential.

Initiatives such as Gráinne's soup kitchen are deeply rooted in a sense of familiarity, both for the volunteers who run the charity and for the guests who rely on their services. The operation of this group is guided by shared habits and practices that have developed over more than a decade. Habitual actions, such as sourcing food from local suppliers, providing personal items discreetly, and serving meals in a warm, communal atmosphere, are not merely functional. They constitute a form of associational life that reflects the group's values and their vision of what a supportive community should look like. The absence of formal structures, such as a registered charity status or financial bookkeeping, is not a result of neglect but a deliberate choice to preserve the informal and personal nature of the association, as the group is convinced that moving to a more formal and explicit structure might interrupt the way they operate; that is, it would interrupt the existing habits. The decision to avoid formalisation could be seen through the lens of a sense of familiarity; it could be tied to a deeply embedded understanding that the value of their work lies in these familiar, habitual practices, which would be undermined by the imposition of external legal requirements.

In cognitive science, association is often linked to the realm of the implicit, implied, unspoken, and automatic. Think of associations between black and white, salt and pepper, or Tom and Jerry. Association, in cognitive science, is a descriptive rather than a normative notion. So, how can we connect this conception of association to the ideas of rights and freedom of expression, which are associated with the freedom of association? Should we even attempt this connection? This chapter argues that the conception of association in cognitive science provides a foundational framework for understanding the dynamics of freedom of association. I examine recent research on habits as a form of associations in the cognitive sense and examine its implications for our normative understanding of ourselves, as individuals and as part of a collective. Through an analysis of habits and the sense of familiarity they generate, I conceptualise how we associate ourselves with groups and organisations and how this can give rise to reasons to act – placing us back in the normative domain of rights and freedoms. In doing so, I argue that the associations that cognitive scientists study are indeed essential and fundamental to associational life and freedom of association.

In psychology, the term 'association' pertains to the relations or connections we lay between different objects, ideas, thoughts, emotions, and others. Further examples of association include: (a) implicit biases: most of us hold associations between certain types of names and positive or negative ascriptions of people; and (b) habits, understood as associations between certain (kinds of) situations with particular (kinds of) actions. In particular, this latter form of association is foundational to my account. These relations are nonlogical. By that I do not mean to say that they are illogical, but rather that they are alogical. They are not in accordance with logical reasoning (eg, deductive reasoning).

This notion of association seems far removed from the notion of association that we find in the discussion of freedom of association. Not in the least because on the surface these psychological kinds of associations seem implicit, automatic, and non-agentic. Those who argue for the importance of freedom of association will have associations in mind that involve memberships, registrations, an agenda, shared goals, and/or a shared ideology. Such associations are often formalised explicitly. Think of unions, members of a sports club, those working for charities, people engaged in protecting cultural heritage, and activists. Even associations, including the 'informal' soup kitchen of Cairde ar son Cairde, which I will discuss as a case study in section V.A, which do not wish for such formalisation and registration, typically have clear explicit goals and/or a shared ideology.

The aim of this chapter is not to argue that any or all associations in the psychological sense give rise to associations and freedom of association. Nor that any association necessarily relies on the kind of associations that I will conceptualise. However, I argue that associational life *can* be quite loosely constructed and that associations, as a sense of familiarity, underpin the way we shape and act in associations. Consider the following examples: groups of writers creating a certain genre, people objecting to the production process for palm oil that boycott a certain brand, or people in a certain neighbourhood that let their dog out and form some kind of community.[2] However, most accounts of collective intentionality are built on mentality, which is understood in terms of propositional attitudes. I argue that it is a mistake to think that association will be either explicit and structured, with goals, etc, or the opposite in all respects. Rather, following Martens and Roelofs, I suggest thinking about association and associational life as something that should be understood on a multidimensional scale defined by various characteristics such as rules, memberships, agendas, habits, and a sense of familiarity.

Consider a group that is working diligently to preserve its cultural heritage. Members of this group share a common objective – to protect a culture or specific practices and narratives associated with that culture – however, the culture itself is also their own, and they are intimately acquainted with it. There will be a multitude of associations (in the psychological sense) related to this culture which makes it theirs, which makes it familiar and valuable for them.

[2] For a discussion of these examples, see JH Martens and L Roelofs, 'Implicit Coordination: Acting Quasi-Jointly on Implicit Shared Intentions' (2018) 4 *Journal of Social Ontology* 93.

Habits and the sense of familiarity that comes with them are my means of connecting different notions of association.[3] Other philosophers have analysed habits in relation to familiarity and familiarisation.[4] I think this is useful for two reasons. First, habitual actions are important in daily life. They play a significant role in explaining our behaviour, both individually and collectively. Second, the work by Hornett has linked habits, through their sense of familiarity, to the space of reasons. In this chapter, I explore the extent to which these reasons are of interest to us when considering the right of association within the realm of legal and judicial discourse. I will do so by arguing that the sense of familiarity can function as a proxy-reason that must stand in the right relation to further justifications.

The remainder of this chapter is organised as follows. In section I, I will start by briefly giving my account of habits, allowing me to then explain how they can provide a sense of familiarity and proxy-reasons in section II. From this, we can see how justifications at the individual and group level connect to individuals' habits in section III. This will allow us to return with a deepened understanding of the relationship between habits and freedom of association in section IV. Finally, in section V, I will return to the moot court scenario of *Cairde ar son Cairdre Soup Kitchen* as a case study to illustrate the importance of association in terms of a sense of familiarity in more detail. Conceptually connecting the cognitive conception of association to the legal and ethical discourse surrounding freedom of expression and association provides a richer understanding of how groups such as Cairde ar son Cairdre operate and why their informal, familiarity-based structure is both meaningful and essential.

I. HABITS AS ACQUIRED AUTOMATICITIES

There are many different conceptions of habits, and different authors assign varying degrees of importance to habits in understanding human behaviour. Some argue that habits are crucial for our reasoning abilities, while others view them as obstacles to our reasoning. Following research in cognitive science, as well as the pragmatic tradition, I consider habitual behaviour as the default mode in which we respond.[5] I further assume that habits also play a

[3] It goes beyond this chapter to discuss to what extent we can also consider other associations as habits of mind/thought, but one could extend my argument in that direction too. In the pragmatist tradition, for example, many consider reasoning to be a habit too.

[4] C Carlisle, *On Habit* (New York, Routledge, 2014); W Hornett, 'The Force of Habit' (2023) 104 *Pacific Philosophical Quarterly* 1.

[5] H Aarts and A Dijksterhuis, 'Habits as Knowledge Structures: Automaticity in Goal-Directed Behavior' (2000) 78 *Journal of Personality and Social Psychology* 53; N Arpaly, 'On Acting Rationally against One's Best Judgment' (2000) 110 *Ethics* 488; JA Bargh and TL Chartrand, 'The Unbearable Automaticity of Being' (1999) 54 *American Psychologist* 462; W Wood and others, 'Habits in Dual Process Models' in JW Sherman, B Gawronski and Y Trope (eds), *Dual Process Theories of the Social Mind* (New York, Guilford Press, 2014).

role in our intelligent capacities rather than obstructing them. Although habits raise important questions concerning human rationality, relying on habitual responses is generally considered adaptive.[6] This holds true, even if habits sometimes obstruct rationality or reasoning. I will explore this idea further when discussing how habits and the sense of familiarity they give rise to can provide the agent with proxy-reasons. First, I will spell out my account of habits in more detail, including why I think they are important for our understanding of groups, collectives, and associations.

Habits have been described as our second nature, allowing us to understand the sociality of our nature.[7] This should be understood as a description of habits of individuals, but it also tells us something about shared habits. Of course, each person has their own peculiar, idiosyncratic habits, but many of the habits we have are shared, are socially learnt, and in that sense, they are not only mine or yours but ours as well.[8] It is not a coincidence that Hume used the terms 'habit' and 'custom' interchangeably. Habits are cultivated and part of our culture.

On the understanding of the underlying mechanism of habits on the individual level, I understand them as acquired automaticities.[9,10] Acquired automaticity refers to the phenomenon in which a behaviour that initially requires conscious effort and attention becomes automatic and can be performed with little or no conscious awareness after repeated practice. As repetition is involved, one of the results of acquiring automaticities is that they come with both a receptiveness and resistance to change. James famously argued that habits are highly receptive to formation through repetition and practice.[11] He likens the creation of habits to the engraving of a path in the brain, where each

[6] L Cosmides and J Tooby, 'Are Humans Good Intuitive Statisticians after All? Rethinking Some Conclusions from the Literature on Judgment under Uncertainty' (1996) 58 *Cognition* 1; G Gigerenzer and W Gaissmaier, 'Heuristic Decision Making' (2011) 62 *Annual Review of Psychology* 451; G Gigerenzer and PM Todd, 'Fast and Frugal Heuristics: The Adaptive Toolbox' in G Gigerenzer, PM Todd and The ABC Research Group (eds), *Simple Heuristics That Make us Smart* (New York, Oxford University Press, 1999); M Oaksford and N Chater, *Bayesian Rationality the Probabilistic Approach to Human Reasoning* (Oxford, Oxford University Press, 2007).

[7] R Bartlett and S Collins (eds), *Aristotle's Nicomachean Ethics* (London, University of Chicago Press, 2011); P Bourdieu, *Pascalian Meditations* (Stanford, Stanford University Press, 2000); J Dewey, *Human Nature and Conduct: An Introduction to Social Psychology* (New York, Henry Holt and Company, 1922); D Hume, *Enquiries Concerning Human Understanding and Concerning the Principles of Morals* (Oxford, Clarendon Press, 1975).

[8] See also B Pollard, 'Explaining Actions with Habits' (2006) 43 *American Philosophical Quarterly* 57.

[9] Automaticity is a complex notion that I will not spell out in full detail here. For this chapter it should suffice to say that I do not understand automaticity as the inverse of controlled or intentional. Automaticity has several characteristics, each of them not necessarily co-occurring and each coming on a spectrum, meaning that a process can be automatic to some extent. For a full discussion *cf* JH Martens, *Doing Things Together: A Theory of Skillful Joint Action* (Berlin, De Gruyter, 2020).

[10] E Fridland, 'Automatically Minded' (2017) 194 *Synthese* 4337; JH Martens, 'Habit and Skill in the Domain of Joint Action' (2021) 40 *Topoi* 663; V McGeer, 'Intelligent Capacities' (2018) 118 *Proceedings of the Aristotelian Society* 347.

[11] W James, *Principles of Psychology* (New York, Holt, 1890).

repetition of an action deepens the groove, making it easier for that behaviour to be repeated. These established habits make a difference to a being's constitution. The same process that makes the behaviour automatic also makes it difficult to alter it. Once a habit is formed, it becomes rather resistant to change. This emphasises the 'tyranny' of habits that can explain their bad reputation; habits can dominate our daily life, making it challenging to change. Habits are powerful forces in human life; they are readily formed and are difficult to break. This duality, both receptive and resistant to change, underscores their importance in shaping our daily lives. This also holds for the habits that we share. Many of the acquired automaticities that each individual has will be socially acquired. Our parents, educators, and the wider environment will shape our acquired automaticities, which in turn will shape our constitution. For a large part, this happens long before a child can deliberately do so. While we each go about our daily lives, we rely on these common ways of doing things, and these common ways will also be resistant to change. Together, these (shared) acquired automaticities give rise to familiarity.

II. FAMILIARITY, NORMALCY AND PROXY-REASONS

Through repetition we become familiar with doing a certain (kind of) thing in a certain (kind of) situation.[12] This altered constitution gives us a specific sensitivity and responsiveness to our environment. This responsiveness is based on what has worked in the past. Familiarity shapes relationships, habits, and the way we interpret our surroundings. Importantly, familiarity gives rise to a sense of familiarity. This provides us with a sense of belonging. Something which Carlisle has described as being 'insulated from the threat of the unknown'.[13]

Picking up the idea of shared habits, we can easily see how familiar ways of doing things also shape a normative domain. These habitual ways of going about are considered normal, as expected by others. That which is normal is often also seen as the norm. Therefore, we can also consider the sense of familiarity as a sense of normalcy when habits are shared. Our habitual ways coincide with what we perceive as normal and the norm, as that which we anticipate.

Although this sense of familiarity is helpful in many situations and motivates us to act, it is important to highlight that it is not necessarily or solely positively characterised. First, this sense of familiarity can also lead to complacency, potentially stifling growth and new experiences. Second, a sense of familiarity can take away the thrill or positive affect that originally belonged to a certain event. It can dull the experience, making it more neutral or even negative. For

[12] For extensive discussion see C Carlisle, 'Creatures of Habit: The Problem and the Practice of Liberation' (2005) 38 *Continental Philosophy Review* 19; Hornett (n 4).

[13] Carlisle (n 12) 23.

example, cooking can be an adventure. Exploring new recipes or techniques can make cooking an exciting experiment. However, over time, the daily necessity of cooking can strip away the novelty, especially when you find yourself preparing the same dishes repeatedly due to convenience. Simultaneously, it may be exactly this routine that we look for after a long day at work. Hence, independent of the positive, neutral, or even negative effect, the sense of familiarity – as insulation from the threat of the unknown – is understood as motivating us to act.

The sense of familiarity will make it the case that some action feels like the right thing to do in a certain situation, and to that extent, it can function as a reason to do that thing. Therefore, the sense of familiarity is a response to the Anscombian why-question; it gives a justification for action, rather than merely a causal explanation. Anscombe argues that what distinguishes actions that are intentional from those that are not is that intentional actions are those 'to which a certain sense of the question 'Why?' is given application'. This is the sense in which 'the answer, if positive, gives a reason for acting'.

Although this sense of familiarity can answer the Anscombian why-question, as justification, one might feel that it is lacking. The sense of familiarity is not as deeply embedded in a more consistent and coherent picture of reasons, desires, and intentions as other answers to the why-question. Thus, while a sense of familiarity can serve as a reason for action, it may be seen as lacking a comprehensive answer to this question.[14] A sense of familiarity primarily provides comfort and reduces the perceived risk associated with a situation or a decision. While this may explain why an action feels right, it does not necessarily engage with deeper rational or ethical considerations that justify an action. In that sense, the reason a sense of familiarity provides can also be understood as a surface-level justification. Taking this into consideration, I will understand them as *proxy*-reasons and discuss them as such when discussing deeper justifications in the rest of this text.[15]

So why argue that these proxy-reasons are important? Philosophers have struggled to see how habitual actions can be understood as actions, even when agreeing that they are not mere bodily movements.[16] The sense of familiarity, understood as proxy-reason, gives us a way to understand how habits appear as justifying explanations. Especially if we accept that we are creatures of habit, such a link is important. I think we need to accept this understanding

[14] GEM Anscombe, *Intention* (Oxford, Blackwell, 1957) 9. Anscombe's question 'Why?' applies in the relevant sense even in cases where the answer to the question is 'no particular reason.' As she says, 'the question is not refused application because the answer to it says that there is no reason, any more than the question how much money I have in my pocket is refused application by the answer 'None'' (ibid 25).

[15] Note that as soon as we would critically engage with our habits, we move out of the domain of the sense of familiarity. Therefore, we cannot guarantee consistency with our broader goals while the sense of familiarity is our guiding principle. Decisions based solely on familiarity may not align with an individual's broader goals, values, or principles.

[16] A Kalis and D Ometto, 'An Anscombean Perspective on Habitual Action' (2019) 40 *Topoi* 637; Pollard (n 8).

of ourselves, as we simply do not have the time or cognitive capacity to reflect on every decision, based on a comprehensive set of rational criteria. A sense of familiarity provides some level of justification. In cases where they do so in ways that are shared and normative or culturally endorsed, the sense of familiarity also provides a sense of normalcy and leads to contextually appropriate behaviour. Acting in accordance with what feels familiar often also means that the agent adheres to social norms or accepted practices. With these considerations already on the table, I will now explore the extent to which the sense of familiarity can be a proxy for more complex justifications and can be connected to a deeper level of justification.

A. Habit Development and Sources of Justification

To salvage the relation between the sense of familiarity and a deeper rationality, I think it is useful to make a distinction between the justifying reason, if any, why a certain habit is a part of someone's constitution and the sense of familiarity as a justifying reason. In other words, we can distinguish between the reasons for having a habit and the reasons for acting on that habit. These reasons provide answers to different why-questions: (1) why a person has a habit, and (2) why a person acts on this habit. The first why-question does not always have a justificatory answer; it can also have a mere causal answer. However, we often develop our habits while trying to attain certain goals, and habitual behaviour can be intentional or goal-directed in at least this indirect sense.[17] The second why-question is answered through the sense of familiarity.

Exploring the distinction between the justifying reason for habit constitution and acting on that habit as a justifying reason reveals different layers of motivation and rationality. Why does someone develop the habits they have? Not every habit someone develops has been a deliberate choice. Many habits are formed in early childhood, making it the case that we all have habits we can only later engage with reflexively. Therefore, it seems safe to say that minimally some habits are acquired inadvertently. But a person *can* develop or change their habits based on reflection. In such cases, I assume that this habit is connected to deeper justificatory reasons. These justifying reasons typically involve a reflective process in which the benefits, values, or needs of the habit are assessed.

By contrast, the sense of familiarity as a justifying reason operates at a more immediate level. Once a habit is formed, continued engagement in the behaviour is driven by the motivation flowing from its familiarity rather than a recall of the original justifying reason. This sense of familiarity does not require the

[17] JR Anderson, 'Acquisition of Cognitive Skill' (1982) 89 *Psychological Review* 369; Arpaly (n 5); W Wood and DT Neal, 'A New Look at Habits and the Habit-Goal Interface' (2007) 114 *Psychological Review* 843.

individual to revisit the initial rationalisation; rather, it functions as a more immediate guide for action. In such cases, the sense of familiarity has become a proxy for justification, signalling to the individual that the habitual action is appropriate, safe, or preferable, without necessitating deeper reflection. This distinction is crucial because it highlights the potential divergence between the initial reasons for habit formation and the ongoing reasons for habit maintenance. While the original justifying reasons may align with broader goals, values, or rational considerations, the sense of familiarity as a justifying reason will not reflect these deeper motivations (or does so only indirectly).

Individual justifications are those that emerge from personal reflection and reasoning. When a person engages in developing a habit, they may have a clear, articulated reason for doing so – rooted in their own beliefs, values, or goals. These justifications are often grounded in a conscious understanding of why the habit is beneficial or necessary. For example, a person might regularly exercise because they value physical health and have internalised the benefits of staying fit, or adhere to a vegan lifestyle and exchange animal produce with alternatives, as they deem this an important consequence of their moral considerations. Here, the habit is supported by a coherent rationale that aligns with the individual's broader life goals. The strength of individual justification lies in its personal relevance and alignment with a person's values, making the habit more resilient to change or challenge.

Relevant to collective cases and associations, I suggest that deeper justifications of our habits can originate from sources other than the individual. Besides an individual's own reasoning, the reasoning of a group can provide a connection between the sense of familiarity and deeper justifications. As many habits are instilled by others, it is worthwhile considering the responsibility of others and groups for the habits they instil in others. Educators, parents, and other caregivers can have justificatory reasons why they try to develop certain habits in others. But also on a collective level we have systems in place that create habits. School systems have been developed with a certain rationale for the education of children. These justifications are often absorbed implicitly through socialisation and may not be critically examined by the individual (or caregiver). For instance, a person might adhere to certain traditions, customs, or routines not because they have personally reflected on their value but because these practices are deeply embedded in their cultural context or social environment. Examples include habits we learn while learning to play an instrument or table manners. External justification can come from other individuals, or from a collective level, or a combination. Most likely, many of the habits our parents instil in us will be justified at the collective level. The power of the justifications of community-shared justifications for certain habits lies in their collective acceptance. At the same time, these actions justified by group norms or cultural practices can provide a sense of belonging and social validation – a sense of normalcy – reinforcing the habitual behaviour, even if the individual has not personally scrutinised the rationale behind it. These collective justifications often carry significant weight because they are tied to a sense of identity and community.

III. GROUP JUSTIFICATION

At both the individual and group level there can be explicit justifications underlying a habit. For this chapter, I am not so much interested in group-habits as in habits individuals have that are tied to group justification, which are explained by their membership of certain groups, associations, etc. A group might consciously endorse a certain norm and be fully aware of the reasons behind it. For example, a religious community may observe specific rituals with a clear understanding of their spiritual significance, or a professional group may adopt certain standards of conduct based on shared values of integrity and excellence. These habits are collectively justified, and the justification reinforces group identity and cohesion. However, groups can also adhere to norms or customs without a clear or shared justification. Such habits may emerge historically and gradually become entrenched without ongoing reflection on their relevance or purpose. In some cases, these group habits might originate from a context that is no longer applicable, yet the practices continue simply because of tradition or inertia. For instance, a workplace might maintain outdated protocols because 'this is how it has always been done', even if no one can articulate a current, valid reason for doing so. In these cases, the group level can be explanatory for the individual's habits without a justification in terms of reasons. How responsible is an individual for knowing the reasoning behind habit-justification at the group level?

The sense of normalcy that comes with a group-endorsed habit may make it appear not only normal in a descriptive sense, but also in a normative, reason-providing sense. Furthermore, group members might adopt certain habits that are 'of the group' out of a desire for conformity or fear of social sanction, rather than because they find personal or rational justification. This can lead to the perpetuation of norms or customs that may no longer serve the group's best interests, align with its current values, or serve individuals adhering to these norms. In such cases, the habit's justification is unexamined and has become inadequate due to changes in the circumstances, yet it continues to shape behaviour and social interaction. This means that some reflection on the reasons behind habits, whether personal or collective, is crucial for ensuring that actions continue to serve meaningful purposes and align with evolving goals and contexts.

From a prescriptive standpoint, especially in contexts such as education where habits are instilled in the next generation or when officials are creating or adjusting policies that affect many, it seems very important to keep a keen eye on the relation between our deeper justifications and the proxy-reasons in terms of the sense of familiarity they create in individuals. Given ever-changing circumstances, it is crucial to actively reflect on and justify the habits and norms that we are promoting. This involves critically assessing whether habits are supported by still valid reasons that align with, for example, contemporary educational goals and societal values. By maintaining an active link between proxy-reasons and actual reasons, we can ensure that the habits we instil are not only familiar, but also meaningful and beneficial. This ongoing process of reflection and justification is essential for developing habits that are resilient, relevant, and capable of meeting the challenges of an ever-changing world. I take it that we cannot expect every aspect of this reflection and justification to happen at the individual level, which means they are the responsibility of a group, collective, association, etc. However, this does not mean that these justifications are not valuable to the individual. Each individual will need to weave together and find a balance between the individual and group level of justification and ensure that we are not solely running on unjustified senses of familiarity.

IV. ASSOCIATIONAL LIFE, PROXY-REASONS, AND REASONS

Given the availability and applicability of group justifications to individuals belonging to or associating with certain groups, these justifications will cause similar or even identical habits in more than one individual. Hence, in some sense, we can speak of habits of the group. These shared habits – those cultivated within and across social groups – play a crucial role in shaping our collective lives. Shared habits contribute to a collective sense of familiarity, creating bonds that make us feel at home within a particular group, culture, or context, with particular ways of doing things together and particular ways of interacting. These habits form the backbone of what I have referred to as proxy-reasons, which guide our actions in a way that feels intuitively correct even if not always fully articulated or consciously justified.

The notion of proxy-reasons becomes particularly significant when considering the functioning of associations, especially those with longer histories of large memberships. In these contexts, the shared habits and the resulting sense of familiarity are not merely byproducts of individual interactions but are also deeply embedded in the collective practices and traditions of the group. Shared habits provide a sense of continuity and belonging, anchoring individuals to the group's identity and purpose and are the normal way of doing things in that particular group. They allow members to navigate the complexities of social life with a sense of security and cohesion, as actions that align with these shared habits often feel inherently right and appropriate.

However, as I have argued in this chapter, the mere presence of proxy-reasons is insufficient for a fully normative account. For these proxy-reasons to be robust and meaningful, they must be connected to deeper justificatory reasons. These deeper reasons provide a more comprehensive foundation for why certain habits exist, ensuring that the actions they motivate are not just reflexive or customary but also grounded in rational, ethical, or cultural considerations. Importantly, these deeper reasons need not always originate from the individual. In the context of associations, especially those that are large or long-standing, the justificatory reasons often belong to the group as a whole.

Group-level justificatory reasons for our shared habits are valuable because they connect what feels right – those actions supported by proxy-reasons – with a broader framework of meaning and purpose. In many cases, these reasons have been developed and refined over time, shaped by the collective experiences, values, and goals of the group. For instance, a labour union may have a long history of advocating for workers' rights, and its members may feel a strong sense of solidarity and purpose rooted in the group's shared habits and traditions. The justificatory reasons behind the union's actions – such as the pursuit of fair wages, safe working conditions, and social justice – are not merely individual concerns but are deeply embedded in the collective ethos of the group. These reasons provide a deeper layer of meaning to the proxy-reasons that guide the union's activities, ensuring that the group's actions are not just habitual, but also aligned with its broader mission.

This connection between proxy-reasons and deeper justificatory reasons is crucial for maintaining the integrity and coherence of an association. When proxy-reasons are grounded in the group's shared justificatory reasons, they help reinforce the group's identity and purpose, creating a strong sense of collective agency. Members are not just acting out of habit; they also participate in a shared project supported by a well-articulated rationale. This gives their actions greater significance and helps ensure that the association remains relevant and responsive to its members' needs, changing circumstances, and the challenges it might face.

Moreover, the presence of group-level justificatory reasons can help prevent ossification of habits and practices within the association. As mentioned earlier, habits can be resistant to change, and this resistance can sometimes lead to complacency or a lack of critical engagement with established norms. The group can periodically reassess its practices and beliefs, ensuring that they continue to serve the association's goals and are responsive to changing circumstances. Thus, we avoid ossification while not overburdening the individual members.

In conclusion, while shared habits and the resulting proxy-reasons play a vital role in the functioning of associations, it is the connection to deeper justificatory reasons that gives these habits their true strength. These deeper reasons, often rooted in the collective experiences and values of the group, provide a solid foundation for the association's activities and ensure that the actions motivated by proxy-reasons are not only familiar and comfortable, but also meaningful and purposeful. By maintaining this connection, associations can navigate the balance between tradition and innovation, thereby ensuring that they remain dynamic and relevant in an ever-changing world.

V. APPLYING THE CONCEPTUAL FRAMEWORK – SUSTAINABLE POLITICAL COMMUNITIES

As outlined in the Introduction to this collection, Maria Cahill argues that associations deserve to be taken seriously for their increasingly critical role in promoting sustainable political communities, fostering genuine pluralism, and guarding against social alienation.[18] In an era in which individuals and groups face growing pressures from social, economic, and political forces that can lead to fragmentation and isolation, associations offer a powerful counterbalance. They provide a framework for individuals to connect, share values, and work together towards common goals, thereby strengthening the fabric of society.

In this context, the right to freedom of association emerges not just as a legal or formal entitlement but also as a fundamental psychological mechanism for building and sustaining connections between people. In this chapter, I focused on shared habits and how associations are rooted in a shared sense of familiarity, which serves as a proxy-reason that guides our actions within these contexts. These shared habits create a sense of belonging and identity, helping individuals feel at home in their social environment. However, for associations to truly fulfil their potential in promoting sustainable communities and pluralism, I argued that these proxy-reasons must be connected to deeper justificatory reasons that resonate with the group's broader mission and values. I illustrate this using a case study that can also be found in the introduction of this book.[19]

A. Case Study – Cairde ar Son Cairdre

With the conceptual apparatus in place, we can return to the moot scenario *of Cairde ar son Cairdre Soup Kitchen*, the outdoor soup kitchen initiated by a group of friends. The group views their activities as an expression of community support that transcends formal legal structure. To its members, this association is not a legal or formal agreement, but an expression of shared identity and commitment to a social cause. Their informal familiarity-based structure is both meaningful and essential. The charities regulator wants the soup kitchen to conform to formal registration and financial oversight. The group objects to this formalisation based on their right to freedom of association.

I opened this chapter with the statement that initiatives such as Gráinne's soup kitchen are deeply rooted in a sense of familiarity, both for the volunteers who run the charity and for the guests who rely on their services. Shared habits and practices have been developed and altered for over a decade. Habitual

[18] Ibid, 2–6.
[19] Ibid, 15–16.

actions, including sourcing food from local suppliers, providing personal items discreetly, and serving meals in a warm, communal atmosphere, are not merely functional. They constitute a form of associational life that embodies the group's principles and their idea of what a nurturing community ought to be. The choice to forgo formal structures, like obtaining registered charity status or maintaining financial records, is intentional rather than accidental. This decision is made to retain the group's informal and personal character. Adopting a more formal framework could disrupt their current operational habits. This avoidance of formalisation can be understood as stemming from a sense of familiarity, rooted in the belief that the true value of their work is found in these established, routine practices, which might be compromised by adhering to external legal obligations.

Now, one might wonder whether formalising some aspects of the organisation could be done in line with the sense of familiarity that is currently allowing the group to operate smoothly and, therefore, without disrupting the flow of work. As I have argued throughout this chapter, proxy-reasons and further reasons can reinforce one another. In order to see how external legal requirements might interrupt the sense of familiarity, it is important to not only look at the outward operation of the soup kitchen – the warm welcoming atmosphere they create, the way they support people in need with supplies – but also look at the familiar ways of running the soup kitchen – the informal arrangement the group has with the butcher, the way in which donating materials without registration might make people more inclined to do so, and the looser financial organisation that leads to a certain way of coordinating – all these elements feed into running the soup kitchen in a familiar way. It is especially on that level that many aspects would change when becoming an official association. This change may affect the motivation of those involved in organising the soup kitchen in ways that are detrimental to their cause.

We can connect this to normative implications that the right to freedom of association could bring. The soup kitchen's challenge to the Charities Regulator is based on the argument that enforcing formal registration and financial oversight would disproportionately violate their right to freedom of association. This argument rests on the idea that the right to freely associate includes the right to define the character and structure of the association. For this group, maintaining an informal structure is not simply a preference but an essential aspect of how they express their shared values and commitment to their community. Here, we see how the current habits and the sense of familiarity that accompanies these habits, connect to further justification of their current way of organising their association. These habitual aspects underscore a normative dimension in which freedom of association is exercised not just as a legal right but as an expression of communal bonds and moral responsibility towards the disadvantaged. The court's decision suggests that this must be weighed against the need for legal compliance and public trust in charitable organisations. If the prioritisation of financial accountability and transparency in charitable activities emphasised by the Charities Regulator leads to the dissolution of the soup kitchen, the regulatory intervention seems to run against other norms that the regulators will most certainly hold in high regard, such as helping those in need. Hence, it seems to me that the desire to preserve the informal nature of the group is rooted in a genuine concern for maintaining the social and supportive atmosphere that their habits and familiarity create.

13

The Right to be We: The Case of Associations

MICHAEL SCHMITZ*

I. INTRODUCTION

WHY FREEDOM OF association? Why a right to be a We, and why a right to be the particular kind of We, the particular kind of group, that is an association? For surely the right to freely associate is not the only kind of right to form and be a We that we commonly recognise. For example, we also recognise rights to marry or partner and to form a family, and even though these are in some sense rights to associate with others, this is not what is usually meant when we talk about the right to freedom of association. We would rather think of these as fundamental human rights. On the other end of the spectrum, we also recognise a right for people or peoples to form states – though how this is to be understood is a matter of some controversy. This right is also generally thought to be a fundamental human right or political right, and in some sense it concerns the association of people. But again, this is not what people ordinarily think of when thinking of freedom of association.

In this chapter, I want to contribute to clarifying what associations in the relevant sense are, what role they do and should play in a state, particularly a democracy, and how the freedom to associate should be justified. I will argue that freedom of association should not only be justified with the positive role associations play for the well-functioning of a state – top-down, as it were. It can and should also be justified bottom-up: as an expression of a fundamental human need to form groups and co-operate with others. I will also argue that

* This publication is a contribution to the *Societās: Exploring the Value of Freedom of Association* project, led by Professor Maria Cahill at the School of Law, University College Cork, and funded by the Irish Research Council (now Research Ireland) under grant IRCLA/2022/3860. The chapter builds on ideas discussed during the workshop *Exploring Associational Life: From Social Ontology to Law and Back Again*, held at University College Cork on 25–26 April 2024. This research was funded in part by the Austrian Science Fund (FWF), Grant DOI 10.55776/PAT7660524. For open access purposes, the author has applied a CC BY public copyright licence to any author-accepted manuscript version arising from this submission.

to play the positive role that they can play for the well-functioning of the state, associations must not be too close to the state and its government but must keep a certain distance from it. They must neither compete with the government nor try to overthrow it, nor must they be dependent on it so that they are in danger of becoming a mere tool of it.

I will address these issues from a point of view inspired by recent debates about what philosophers call 'social ontology' and 'collective intentionality'[1] and the recently emerging field of a theory of law that addresses some of the traditional questions of philosophy of law – as well as some new ones – with the help of tools from social ontology and the theory of collective intentionality.[2] Social ontology undertakes to make a fresh start on the nature of social entities such as groups, social norms and institutions like money and the law. By 'collective intentionality' I mean the capacity of human (and possibly non-human) subjects to perceive, act, feel and think jointly with others – to represent the world together.

I favour an approach that addresses questions about the nature of groups, the law and other social and collective entities in the context of a theory of mental and linguistic intentionality or representation. So groups are to be understood in terms of subjects representing the world in modes of identification with others – such as the we-mode or role-mode as discussed below – and different kinds of groups can be distinguished in terms of the kinds of representational acts, states and artefacts essentially involved in jointly representing the world. For example, jointly attending to an object only requires sensory-motor-emotional experiences, while forming a state essentially involves written language and other forms of documentation.

To understand associations, what kind of groups they are, what roles they can and should play in society and the state, and why there should be a right to be them, I think we need to have some understanding of what groups are in general and what ties them together. In the following, I will first briefly sketch my own version of such an account – a layered account of groups and social and institutional reality.[3] I will then show how associations can be characterised in terms of such an account, and this will eventually lead to answers to the questions of which role associations should play in the state and why there should be a right to be them.

[1] For an overview of recent philosophical debates about collective intentionality, *cf* DP Schweikard and HB Schmid, 'Collective Intentionality' in EN Zalta (ed), *Stanford Encyclopedia of Philosophy* (Fall 2021 Edition) plato.stanford.edu/archives/fall2021/entries/collective-intentionality/ accessed 26 July 2025.

[2] For a recent collection of such work, *cf* M Garcia-Godinez, R Mellin and R Tuomela (eds), *Social Ontology, Normativity and Law* (Berlin, De Gruyter, 2020).

[3] For fuller statements, *cf* M Schmitz, 'Co-Subjective Consciousness Constitutes Collectives' (2018) 49 *Journal of Social Philosophy* 137 and M Schmitz, 'From We-Mode to Role-Mode' in M Garcia-Godinez and R Mellin (eds), *Tuomela on Sociality* (Cham, Springer, 2023).

II. A LAYERED VIEW OF GROUPS AND THE SOCIAL WORLD

The view I am about to present is based on three basic ideas. First, there is a difference between experiencing and representing others as mere objects of one's attitudes towards the world – as when, for example, one simply perceives what they are doing – and experiencing and representing others as co-subjects of such attitudes – as when one, for example, watches a movie with them, or shares a belief or intention with them in a mode of identification with one another. Second, to understand such co-subjectivity, we always have to take into account both theoretical attitudes like perceptual or sensory states and beliefs and practical attitudes like actional or motor states and intentions. When, for example, we are truly jointly watching a movie, we must also at least be disposed to joint action – eg, to protect our enterprise against disruption or to share our thoughts on what we are experiencing. It is not enough for us to be just mutually aware that the other is watching the same movie. Mutuality is not the same as jointness.[4] The third idea is that the social world is layered, that collectivity and co-subjectivity happen on different layers or levels and that higher levels depend on lower levels in ways which we will explore.

For purposes of a first orientation, it is helpful to roughly distinguish three levels of the social world and of collective intentionality. Think of the first level in terms of small groups – eg, a couple taking a walk together or dancing – attending to things and acting jointly, evolving patterns of (acceptable) behaviour through what I like to call 'sensory-motor-emotional' interactions. 'Acceptable behaviour' because these interactions always have a normative, or proto-normative dimension, which is centrally manifest in the emotional valence of the interaction. For example, we may evolve patterns of dancing together, which start to feel familiar and appropriate, so that deviations from these patterns may be experienced as jarring or erroneous, or even shocking and upsetting – but in some cases also as great fun or even genius. This level is characterised by sensory-motor-emotional experience whose content is non-conceptual and non-propositional and by corresponding dispositions.

The second level involves the adoption and negotiation of shared plans, beliefs, values and narratives. For example, the couple may start making plans for the future and construct a narrative of their shared life. This level essentially involves concepts. It may include concepts of what is right or wrong, good or bad, cruel or nice, and so on, as well as concepts of roles such as being a friend, a girlfriend or boyfriend, that bring their own standards and normative expectations with them. Shared concepts and a shared language make it possible for larger groups to adopt shared attitudes than the pure sensory-motor-emotional intentionality we find on the first level. And even if the group remains small like

[4] *cf* M Schmitz, 'Joint Attention: The PAIR Account' (2024) 43 *Topoi* 271 for an elaboration of this argument.

our couple, they typically use concepts drawn from the larger community. This level essentially involves propositionally structured and conceptually articulated thought and (spoken) language.

The third level essentially involves written language and various forms of documentation. For example, if our couple gets married, this will be documented and registered. Some of the rights and obligations that derive from marriage are codified in a legal system, and specialists in institutional roles such as judges enforce them. To develop such complex systems of institutions with a high degree of role differentiation, requires even larger groups – whole societies.

All levels are characterised through different forms of co-subjectivity: subjects experience and represent the world in modes of identification with others, who are not represented and experienced as mere objects, but as co-subjects. This means that there is at least a certain degree of agreement with them, including agreement or identification with their goals. That is, subjects become co-subjects and thus form groups or collectives of various kinds through sharing relations towards the world, such as perceptual, actional and emotional relations, as well as attitudes such as believing or intending.

On the first level of the mode of joint attending, acting and feeling that others are co-subjects is manifest in how they shape our experience of the world: how we are attuned to them, align with them, affirm them and imitate them; in how we experience the world in identifying with their interests and needs. For example, when running with my wife, I'm much more sensitive to the presence of dogs, experience them differently and respond to them differently, because she is afraid of them. This level is very deeply seated: infants start sharing pleasure and other emotions in joint attention from around 9–12 months or even earlier.[5]

At the we-mode level of jointly believing and intending, we form beliefs, intentions and other attitudes from the point of view of the relevant group. And as members and functionaries of organisations and institutions, individuals or groups adopt positions in role-mode, that is, in a mode of identification with their role, with the purposes and assumptions connected to it and to the larger collective in which it is embedded. For example, an individual may take a position as a judge, or a group may take positions as a committee. Those positions may deviate from the positions they take as private individuals or in other roles, because the roles are connected to certain purposes as well as to certain standards of evidence. For example, a judge may sentence somebody to a punishment, even though as a citizen or private individual they think that the relevant kind of conduct should not be illegal. Or they may let somebody go even though they are privately convinced that they are guilty, because they can't prove it according to the evidential standards required by law, because, for example, certain pieces

[5] For a recent overview and discussion *cf* H Moll, 'What We Do and Don't Know About Joint Attention' (2023) 43 *Topoi* 247.

of evidence were obtained in inadmissible ways and therefore can't be used in court.

As I mentioned, the distinction in terms of the three levels is for purposes of first orientation. It roughly aligns with different forms of mental and linguistic representation: 1) sensory-motor-emotional experience; 2) spoken language and corresponding thoughts; 3) written language and other forms of documentation. More fine-grained distinctions can be drawn in terms of criteria such as the following:[6]

a) richness of content from concrete to abstract: compare, for example, the richness of the sensory-motor experience of dancing together to the abstraction of legal concepts such as citizenship;
b) degree of context dependence: sensory-motor experience is dependent on the immediate context of face-to-face interaction, whereas other forms of representation are not;
c) density/differentiation of representational role: linguistic representation is more differentiated in terms of representational role, there are, for example, verbs, nouns and adjectives in language, but not in sensory-motor-emotional experience; written language is yet more grammatically complex than spoken language, and cultural traditions also develop elaborate distinctions between different sorts of texts, eg between different kinds of legal texts such as briefs, letters to the court, depositions, opinions, law review articles, and so on;
d) degree of durability/stability: sensory-motor-emotional experience is more volatile, while concepts, institutionalisation and documentation are all about making things more stable, durable and reliable, for example, about keeping durable and reliable records of marriages, births, and possessions;
e) this in turn is connected to the degree of externalisation/standardisation of representations: compare sensory-motor-emotional experiences to speech and writing. Again, the degree of externalisation and standardisation provided by writing and documentation is required for a legal order and for large groups, because only externalisation and standardisation make it possible that representations are accessible to large groups and across extended periods of time.

There is an important explanatory hypothesis that I cannot really substantiate or discuss adequately here,[7] but which I want to at least introduce because it is important for things to be discussed later. It is that these criteria cluster, that they are connected to one another and to certain broader developments. The broadest development I have in mind here is that of institutional differentiation, for example, in the sense of the differentiation into a religious and a secular

[6] For more, *cf* M Schmitz 'Of Layers and Lawyers' in M Garcia-Godinez, R Mellin and R Tuomela (eds), *Social Ontology, Normativity and Philosophy of Law* (Berlin, De Gruyter, 2020).
[7] But *cf* Schmitz (n 6).

sphere and the differentiation of law from morals. The idea is that this development is connected to and at least partially realised in the differentiation of institutional roles, which in turn is connected to the representational parameters we have discussed. That is, the emergence of certain spheres, institutions and organisations in society is grounded in the emergence of institutional roles, in which specialists create new ways of thinking and new representational devices, which are ever more elaborate in terms of the parameters we have described, and which could only be created by such specialists, because specialisation is necessary to devise such abstract, context-independent, role-differentiated, enduring and standardised forms of representation.

On the layered view then, different kinds of groups can be described and explained in terms of the content, structure and format of the relevant representations. Higher-level groups and the higher-level, more abstract, role-differentiated and externalised representations that constitute them, are based on and can only function, or at least only function well, against the background of lower-level groups and the lower-level representations that constitute them. For example, it is well-known that historically basic institutions have been kin-based. The idea of the layered view is that the family is primarily constituted as a sensory-motor-emotional unit of creatures moving together, feeding together, and so on. Then concepts of being a mother, father, child etc are introduced, which also bring with them rules and expectations concerning behaviour. Then ever more elaborate institutional structures are built on this foundation, which only gradually move away from being outright family or clan structures. But even modern states still remain dependent for functioning, or functioning well, on the functioning of families and other lower-level, informal groups.

III. WHAT IS AN ASSOCIATION?

Having introduced this basic layered framework for understanding groups, let us now move to the question of how to characterise associations. I will try to show that associations and their position in society can be fruitfully described and explained in the terms of this framework. Among other things, I will do so by showing that the framework allows us to give satisfactory and illuminating answers to certain questions that have historically been asked about what is and what is not an association and about the relation between the concept of association and related concepts such as the concept of an assembly. I will not, however, try to give an outright definition of an association.[8] One reason is that different cultures may draw the boundaries of the concept

[8] For a reflection on the concept of association, see V Martino, 'Recognising Associations: A Social Ontology Perspective' in M Cahill and G Lasagni (eds), *Associational Life and Freedom: Insights from Philosophy and Law* (Oxford, Hart Publishing, 2026) 245.

of an association somewhat differently and that it is not important to the main themes of this chapter how these boundaries should be drawn precisely. Another is that the law may often not really be concerned with defining the concept in the abstract, but will, so to speak, offer the status of an association to any group interested in registering as such and leave any further clarification, if it becomes necessary, to the courts.[9] And this makes perfect sense from a legal point of view, particularly if, as in French law, an association is defined as a contract and the content of a contract is considered to be a 'thing of the parties'.[10]

My point of departure will be the following characterisation of associations: 'the term 'association' presupposes a voluntary grouping for a common goal'.[11] My working hypothesis will be that in addition to the concepts of kinds of groups and representations we have introduced already, associations can be characterised through the following parameters:

a) Membership: who can be a member, and how can they become a member?
b) Shared goals or purposes, beliefs or convictions of the group.
c) Institutional sphere (as mentioned above), that is, public/private/economic.
d) Position in an institutional network.

I now want to look at some cases where it may be instructive that they are not/only in some contexts associations. First, let us consider organisations that are governmental or government-instituted: 'a university founded by an act of government' and 'professional regulatory bodies founded by legislation'.[12] Such organisations are not usually considered to be associations. Why not? In the latter kind of cases, one answer is that if there is a statutory obligation to be a member of an organisation, then this defeats voluntariness. Another, more general and deeper answer is that freedom of association legislation is meant to strengthen and regulate a non-governmental sphere of civic activity. Assuming that in the terms outlined earlier, government represents the highest level of institutionalisation, associations do not and should not belong to that level.

It is instructive in this context to consider recent political disputes about a well-known kind of association, namely so-called NGOs – that is, 'non-governmental organisations' – in Germany and other countries. In Germany, these were triggered by the fact that several NGOs organised demonstrations against parties of the opposition while at the same time receiving financial

[9] See, M Cahill, 'Introduction: Comparative and Interdisciplinary Interfaces of Associational Life and Freedom' in M Cahill and G Lasagni (eds), *Associational Life and Freedom: Insights from Philosophy and Law* (Oxford, Hart Publishing, 2026) 6–8.

[10] V Barbé, 'Freedom of Association in France' (2025) 12 *European Journal of Comparative Law and Governance* 322, 324.

[11] *cf Young, James and Webster v United Kingdom*; cited after M Cahill, 'Freedom of Association at the ECHR: A Right in Service of Democracy' (2025) 12 *European Journal of Comparative Law and Governance* 124, 127.

[12] Cahill (n 11) 127.

support from the government and, critics argue, being financially dependent on the government.[13] Of course the worry here is that if these associations are dependent on the government, they really cease to be non-governmental associations and instead become an extended arm of the government. They then cannot perform one of the essential functions anymore that associations can have in a well-functioning state: namely, to organise, bundle and articulate opinions as part of a vibrant civil society. Such associations can be a check on the government and a laboratory where new ideas, new goals and plans for a society of the future are created. Vanessa Barbé emphasises this essential function of associations in her description of the situation in France:

> Freedom of association is also a factor in political innovation because the administration seems to be slow to adapt to social demand. On the contrary, the spontaneity with which associations are created means that they are directly in line with the concerns of today's citizens. That's the reason why, very often, the action of an association precedes that of the public authorities: it drives innovation, expresses a new need and gradually makes the State take it into account.[14]

Associations cannot perform this function well anymore if they become too dependent on the government. Of course, since associations can be so vital for a well-functioning society and state, there are good reasons for the state to support them. In this spirit, some defenders of the NGOs have framed the criticisms, which mainly came from conservatives, as an attack on civil society.[15] But whether associations are still part of civil society when they are too dependent on the government and do its bidding is precisely what is at issue here. To what extent associations can be supported by the state without becoming too dependent on it, will, of course, be a matter of debate, a debate that we can't engage in here. The crucial point for present purposes is that there is such a thing as too much support here, that associations like NGOs can only perform their proper function in a society when they retain a certain degree of independence from the government.

IV. ASSEMBLIES, ASSOCIATIONS AND DEGREES OF INSTITUTIONALISATION

I now want to consider a feature of the Constitution of the United States of America and its historical background: the US Constitution only recognises a right of assembly, even though freedom of assembly and freedom of association

[13] For a brief journalistic account *cf* www.dw.com/en/german-conservative-party-questions-political-neutrality-of-non-governmental-organizations/a-71794579. See also LM O'Grady, 'Freedom of Association in Germany' in M Cahill and G Lasagni (eds), *Associational Life and Freedom: Insights from Philosophy and Law* (Oxford, Hart Publishing, 2026) 81.

[14] Barbé (n 10) 325.

[15] *cf* www.reuters.com/world/europe/german-conservatives-prompt-anger-with-questions-about-ngo-funding-2025-02-26/.

and expression are often grouped together. What's the difference between freedom of assembly and freedom of association? The answer is stability: a right to assembly is not yet a right for long-term association with a high degree of institutionalisation. Assemblies, we might say, are short-term, highly context-dependent kinds of associations with a low degree of institutionalisation, and so the right to assemble does not necessarily entail a right to more long-term forms of association.

The first President of the US, George Washington, held that 'permanent, politically active associations of citizens were inconsistent with a republican form of government'.[16] The idea is that citizens should only assemble to elect representatives, and that between elections the right to speak on behalf of the people should only belong to elected representatives. This can make sense in a fledgling republic: any standing association of citizens may be or become a rival to Parliament, so that as long as the power of parliament is not fully established, it may be legitimate or even necessary to suppress such standing associations. (Of course, the legitimacy of this will depend on whether the government itself is legitimate.)[17] However, once Parliament and the government of which it is a part are firmly established, it will become apparent that they function even better against the background of a lively civic society, where many individuals and standing associations articulate a diverse set of viewpoints, which can be input to and otherwise shape the deliberations of representatives. I take it that this is our contemporary sensibility, based on historical experience. President Washington's attitude has become quite foreign to us.

Associations, then, are more institutionalised than assemblies. They are more durable and stable, and this also at least typically means that they will have more of the other characteristics discussed above. That is, associations will often employ writing and documentation and often have complex organisational structures with a high degree of role differentiation. But different associations, of course, differ widely with regard to all these parameters and accordingly display different degrees of institutionalisation. The law in fact often distinguishes different kinds of groups with different degrees of institutionalisation (though not in these terms). For example, in France the very liberal statute of 1901 states that 'Associations of persons may be formed freely without prior authorisation or declaration.'[18] Such undeclared associations are also

[16] A Bhagwat, 'Why Association?' (2025) 12 *European Journal of Comparative Law and Governance* 209, 212.

[17] Two more historical examples for the pattern of curtailing or suppressing freedom of association to protect the government's power: 1) Nigeria: 'The advent of British colonial rule saw a severe erosion of freedom of association with the colonial administration implementing laws that restricted public gatherings and associations aimed at suppressing anti-colonial movements and nationalist activities.' F Amao, 'Freedom of Association in Nigeria' (2025) 12 *European Journal of Comparative Law and Governance* 304, 305; 2) France: 'The statute [regulating freedom of association of 1901] established a very liberal regime, in complete contrast to the secular tradition *of suspicion of any coalition outside the control of the public authorities*.' Barbé (n 10) 324 (emphasis added).

[18] For this and the following, see Barbé (n 10) 324–5.

called 'de facto groupings'. Declared associations must submit their declaration in writing. Only then do they obtain the status of legal persons. The next category is associations that are recognised as being of public utility. They have even broader legal capacities and can receive donations and legacies. Finally, accredited associations have even more rights, particularly with regard to legal proceedings.

The higher the status, the more paperwork and documentation an association has to submit to obtain and maintain its status, and I would hypothesise, though I don't have data to support this hypothesis, that higher-status organisations are likely to also have more complex organisational structures and higher degrees of role differentiation. A higher status also means a higher degree of integration with governmental institutions and therefore more legal rights – and obligations – while at the same time, as we have emphasised, the association remains itself non-governmental and thus below the highest degrees of institutionalisation found in government. Is a higher status and a higher degree of institutionalisation better? It is insofar as it brings more legal rights with it! But it also brings more obligations with it and has other drawbacks as well, as we will explore in the next part.

V. FRIENDS FOR FRIENDS VS. BUREAUCRATLANDIA OR THE LIMITS OF INSTITUTIONALISATION

So far the argument has been: lower levels should be able to flourish and provide input to higher-level institutions, at least once their power is firmly established. In our earlier discussion of recent debates about the role of NGOs, we have also already made the point that lower levels need a certain degree of independence from higher levels. In this part, I want to extend this argument.

The moot scenario #1 about *Cairde ar son Caidre* ('Friends for friends') soup kitchen, which is presented in the Introduction to this volume, raises the issues of limits to institutionalisation and of the dangers of overregulating and overstandardising lower levels through higher ones. Gráinne has been running the outdoor soup kitchen with some friends for more than ten years: 'She receives leftover food from local grocery shops and a local butcher's shop has an account that allows people to donate money indirectly.'[19] *Cairde ar son Cairde* is not a registered charity, and has neither a bank account, a bookkeeper, a formal organisational structure, nor a constitution. And they want to keep it that way, even though the Charities Regulator is pressuring them to register and has told the butcher that what he does is illegal:

> Gráinne has always wanted to keep a more informal feel to the organisation. The volunteers are all good friends, and she wants her guests to feel like they are being

[19] Cahill (n 9) 15–16.

invited to a dinner with people they know, rather than receiving an impersonal hand-out from people who don't care.[20]

Gráinne therefore challenges the actions of the Regulator as a violation of her freedom of association, but the Supreme Court of Bureaucratlandia finds in favour of the regulator.

For Gráinne and her friends, the spirit of charity is dependent on the context of face-to-face interactions and friendly exchanges and – even if they may not think about it in this way – on the involved sensory-motor-emotional mental states. They want to keep things at that level and therefore resist the institutionalisation and the attendant forms of documentation that the Charities Regulator wants to force on them.

How could this problem be avoided in a land friendlier to charitable friends than Bureaucratlandia? A possible solution: groups could be exempt from registration and documentation up to a certain size of members and amount of donations. In this way the government would recognise limits to institutionalisation. It would recognise that forcing certain forms of representation and documentation on lower-level groups is in grave danger of destroying the spirit of charity that the government should foster.

VI. BUSINESSES VS. ASSOCIATIONS: THE ECONOMIC SPHERE, DISCRIMINATION AND THE STATE

Another interesting case is businesses. Can businesses be associations? No! Why not? Here's an answer from Ashutosh Bhagwat:

> … commercial entities must be excluded from the association right. Associational rights are largely meaningless without the right to voluntarily choose one's associations. But to grant such a right to commercial entities would be the end of all modern antidiscrimination law …[21]

As noted earlier, the government represents the highest institutional level, at least within a given state. It represents the universal We of all of its citizens and must protect their equal rights against discrimination. This includes protection against discrimination in the economic sphere, which is essential to the well-being and flourishing of the citizenry. This is why it could not be tolerated if businesses had policies of only employing people of a certain sexual orientation or race, or of only offering their services to these groups.

Why then should we accept freedom of association, which essentially includes the right to voluntarily choose who one associates with and thus also the freedom to exclude individuals and even groups from one's association? The

[20] Cahill (n 9) 16.
[21] Bhagwat (n 16) 223.

most fundamental answer is that the self-determination and freedom of groups is essential to human flourishing, and that people have a desire to associate with people who are like them in various ways. The state must have the interest of all its citizens at heart and therefore has a duty to ensure that they have equal rights in certain respects and spheres, including the economic sphere. But this does not mean that it has a right to forbid a group just because it has a more particular membership and a more particularist agenda than the state. This would amount to a totalitarian interpretation of the state and its ethos. As long as all individuals and all groups have the same right to freely associate, this is not in conflict with the state's universalist ethos. In fact, it can be argued that this freedom has a positive effect on the state's functioning: as we noted earlier, a well-functioning state needs a vibrant civil society that provides particularist input from groups representing certain segments of the population to universalist deliberation. It is therefore desirable that we have groups that articulate and represent the interests of, say, footballers, homeowners, or the unemployed, so that they can be properly taken into account in the deliberations and actions of the state. In contrast, a legitimate reason for restricting the freedom of association is when people associate to actively work against a state's universalist ethos, particularly, of course, when it is enshrined in the state's constitution.

An interesting problem case for this argument is provided by moot scenario #2 described in the introduction to this volume:[22] Róisín owns a local restaurant and is an amateur golfer, who golfs four mornings a week in the Kilgallen golf club, which has an open membership policy. But she would like to join another local golf club, the Kilmartin club, to build her connections and contribute more to the local community. But while the Kilmartin club has no formal policy excluding women, it traditionally only admits members who have been nominated by an existing member, and no woman has ever been nominated. Is it a violation of Róisín's freedom of association that she is not able to participate in the Kilmartin Golf Club? Is her claim to the freedom to join the club stronger than the claim of the club members to the freedom to exclude her? It seems to me the strongest argument on behalf of Róisín's claim is that the club membership is necessary for her to have full access to the economic sphere because the economic sphere must be free of discrimination. There is a long tradition of sex segregation in sports and of sex-segregated sports clubs, and it seems hard to argue that there is something legally wrong with this per se.

But what kind of access to the economic sphere is relevant here? Róisín has full legal access to the economic sphere; there is no legal obstacle to her participation. What she is looking for are networking opportunities. But we do not ordinarily suppose there is a legal right to access networking opportunities. In response, it can of course be asked what a legal right for access is worth if she is blocked from participation by non-legal, informal means? Even

[22] Cahill (n 9) 16–17.

on the terms of the example, though, she is not really blocked; she already owns a restaurant after all. It may still be true that the men exclude her from further opportunities in a way that is at least morally wrong. Even then the best – in the sense of the most effective – way to respond may be in kind, in the sense that one should first respond to an actual or perceived injustice at the level that it is committed at. Since the club does not even have a formal policy against the inclusion of women, the best course of action may be to first talk to one or several of the members. Perhaps one will nominate her after all. Or, failing that, Raisin may found a new club and put out word that the Kilmartin club is rather fuddy-duddy. Legal action may only be appropriate as a last resort and if there is evidence that there is a concerted and systematic effort to limit women's participation in the economic sphere. From the point of view of the state, there's also a danger of legal action being perceived to be too heavy-handed and meddlesome, similarly to how forcing Cairdre ar son Cairdre to register as a charity, or treating it like a registered one, is too heavy-handed and meddlesome in moot scenario #1. Educational campaigns may be a more appropriate form of government action here.

VII. CONCLUSION

What has been accomplished concerning the nature of groups in general and associations in particular, and what does this mean for how freedom of association should be justified?

I have argued that collectives in general should be understood in terms of people mutually representing themselves as co-subjects of perceptual, actional and affective relations and of positions such as believing and intending that they take towards the world in modes of identifying with their co-subjects and of occupying certain roles within an organisation. Such representation connects different kinds of groups, from joint attention dyads over we-subjects of intentions to take walks and cook meals to associations and nation states. Different groups can also be found on different layers or levels of society or collectivity, and the difference between these layers can be described and explained in terms of the kinds and formats of representations – both mental and linguistic – that are involved. These can be distinguished in terms of such properties as their degree of context-dependence, representational role differentiation and concreteness or abstractness. For example, the representational states shared in a joint attention situation are dependent on that context, have a low degree of representational role differentiation, and are comparatively concrete, while the shared representations of a state, as, for example, written down in its constitution, are highly context-independent and abstract and have a high degree of representational role differentiation. Another central claim of the layered view is that higher layers can only work, or at least work well, against the background of lower layers. For example, the state, which represents the highest institutional level, can only work well on the basis of a vibrant civil society and a well-functioning public sphere.

What is the place of associations in this picture? To begin answering this question and to try to demonstrate the descriptive and explanatory power of the picture, I addressed certain traditional issues about associations and related entities. What is the relation between assemblies and associations? Assemblies are more momentary entities, and the positions taken in them are therefore more context-dependent. Allowing freedom of assembly only and forbidding long-term associations with a high degree of institutionalisation, as advocated by President George Washington, may be understandable and even appropriate if these organisations threaten the functioning of the government. This is a possibly legitimate reason to restrict freedom of association. However, once the government is firmly established, restricting freedom of association in this way becomes counterproductive. Articulating and justifying the attitudes and interests of groups within the population is vital for a well-functioning democracy, because these more particular viewpoints are crucial input for the universalist deliberations of the government.

To be able to flourish and fulfil their functions in society, some low-level forms of associations should also be exempted from mandatory institutionalisation and the corresponding oversight. I used moot scenario #1 of the *Cairdre ar son Caidre* Soup Kitchen to make this point. For Gráinne and her friends, the charitable spirit is dependent on the context of their friendship and face-to-face interactions with the people they help. To force them to formally register as a charity and document their funds and how they use them through a bookkeeper would be to extinguish that spirit. I suggested a solution to this may be to exempt groups from a duty to register and the corresponding regulations and forms of oversight up to a certain number of members and amount of donations.

In contrast, businesses cannot be associations because they cannot be exempted from certain regulations, particularly antidiscrimination law, while the right to freely associate entails the right, for example, to exclude non-Muslims from a Muslim association. Moot scenario #2 raises a problem about this freedom: Róisín argues that her exclusion from the Kilmartin golf club because she is a woman unjustly restricts her freedom of association. I tried to show that her strongest argument for this is that her exclusion impedes her access to the economic sphere, because many business owners frequent the club, but that this argument is still not compelling: we don't normally suppose that people have a legal right to networking opportunities, and informal or educational responses should be preferred over legal means, which will often be too heavy-handed, similarly to the behaviour of the charities regulator in moot scenario #1.

What does this all mean then for the justification of the right to be the certain kind of We that is an association? First, we have found support for the view that associations may be crucial for the proper, healthy or good functioning of democracy, because they can articulate and justify particularist group viewpoints which may be essential input to the more universalist deliberations of Parliament and other government institutions. But, second, we have also emphasised that the co-operative, we-seeking and we-forming nature of humans goes much deeper than this and is present on the many layers of collective intentionality, starting very early from about 9–12 months, if not earlier. In light of this, it seems to me that freedom of association should not only be justified instrumentally through the beneficial effects it has on democracy. It should also be justified through the inherent desire of humans to perceive, act, feel and think with others, and it may therefore also be justified to think of it as a human right. Third, we have also noted two justifications for restricting freedom of association. The state may sometimes be justified in defending its own institutions against associations that try to undermine or overthrow them, and the freedom of association of one group or individual may be restricted through that of another one, as in moot scenario #2, where Róisín's freedom to join an association was in conflict with that of the association to exclude her.

14

Recognising Associations: A Social Ontology Perspective

VALERIA MARTINO*

I. INTRODUCTION

IN THIS CHAPTER, I adopt the perspective of social ontology, specifically its ontological posture – the philosophical inquiry into the nature of things and the cataloguing of what exists[1] – and apply it to the central subject of this book: associations. This approach prompts us to ask what qualifies as an association and whether its existence should necessarily depend on formal recognition. In the following pages, I will elaborate on the distinction between formally recognised and informal associations, drawing on the analysis of groups in social ontology and their possible intersections with social kinds,[2] exploring various paths to shed light on the issue. Indeed, the question 'What is an association?' invites a nuanced exploration of both formal and informal groupings of individuals. The tension between the two is clearly shown by one of the scenarios described in the introduction of this edited book.[3]

To summarise it briefly, it concerns Gráinne, who has been running an informal outdoor soup kitchen, *Cairde ar son Cairde*, for over a decade with the help of volunteers. The initiative, which provides food and essential supplies to those

* This publication is a contribution to the *Societās: Exploring the Value of Freedom of Association* project, led by Professor Maria Cahill at the School of Law, University College Cork, and funded by the Irish Research Council (now Research Ireland) under grant IRCLA/2022/3860. The chapter builds on ideas discussed during the workshop *Exploring Associational Life: From Social Ontology to Law and Back Again*, held at University College Cork on 25–26 April 2024.

[1] Sometimes philosophers distinguish between metaphysics and ontology. According to Achille Varzi, for instance, ontology concerns the classification and organisation of entities, asking *what exists*, while metaphysics addresses broader questions about the nature and fundamental structure of reality. A Varzi, 'On Doing Ontology without Metaphysics' (2011) 25 *Philosophical Perspectives* 407.

[2] I will use 'social kind' broadly to refer to all categories related to social entities – specifically, those kinds that designate things recognised as existing in the social realm.

[3] M Cahill, 'Introduction: Comparative and Interdisciplinary Interfaces of Associational Life and Freedom' in M Cahill and G Lasagni (eds), *Associational Life and Freedom: Insights from Philosophy and Law* (Oxford, Hart Publishing, 2026), 15–17.

in need, operates without formal registration, financial records, or a governing structure. *Cairde ar son Cairde* contravenes the Charities Act in the jurisdiction in which it is alleged to operate because it does not keep proper accounts and is not registered as a charity. Despite multiple warnings, Gráinne refuses to register as a charity, valuing the informal, community-driven nature of the group. The Charities Regulator deems the operation unlawful, leading to potential prosecution, and defends its actions on the grounds that all charities must be subject to the same legal standards, so that members of the public can be assured that charities are operating with financial integrity as they pursue their charitable purposes. Gráinne challenges the actions of the Charities Regulator for being a disproportionate violation of her right to freedom of association.

This case examines the tension between freedom of association – understood as the right of individuals to form, join and leave groups, and decide their rules – and the competing needs of protecting informal associations, on the one hand, and ensuring shared standards and regulated services, on the other. This tension reflects a classic struggle in political philosophy: the balance between freedom and security. These two principles often appear to be in conflict, and one of the fundamental goals of politics is to navigate and reconcile this opposition.[4]

With the aim of offering insight into this topic, this chapter will introduce elements from key debates in social ontology. Hopefully, this will provide legal scholars with valuable philosophical perspectives on the concept of group while also demonstrating to philosophers how social ontology can be applied to concrete legal issues. The chapter is organised as follows. Section I will introduce key discussions on social groups within social ontology, with a particular focus on the distinction between formal and informal groups. Section II will present the debate between realist and antirealist perspectives. Section III will apply these debates to the case of marriage to illuminate the philosophical distinctions at play. Reflecting on marriage helps highlight a potential discrepancy between philosophical classifications and the legal frameworks needed to safeguard distinct – and sometimes conflicting – rights. Finally, section IV will draw conclusions by considering the potential of applying the previously discussed elements to the legal understanding of associations and related freedoms.

II. SOCIAL ONTOLOGY DISCUSSES SOCIAL GROUPS

Social ontology, in its ontological posture, has extensively explored the conceptualisation of groups and their consequent categorisation. In the literature, a wide

[4] Just to mention a famous case, consider T Hobbes, *Leviathan* (Oxford, Oxford University Press, 2014), in which the need to limit individual freedom in order to obtain social security and avoid chaos is explicitly stated.

variety of groups have been considered and discussed, ranging from informal gatherings, such as a couple of friends deciding to take a walk[5] or to paint the house together,[6] to more structured entities like chess clubs, orchestras, nations, and corporations.[7] However, associations as a distinct category have not been thoroughly analysed. In the legal field as well, there is no universal definition of 'association': distinct approaches and definitions can be found across different jurisdictions, or even within the same jurisdiction depending on the type of association.[8] At first glance, this appears to support the idea that identifying instances of associations is merely an empirical matter. It has been argued, seemingly, that because group categorisation is largely shaped by cultural factors, it is primarily a task for the social sciences rather than for ontology or philosophy more broadly.[9] Nevertheless, there are important theoretical considerations that warrant philosophical analysis, which can help clarify common features or reveal how we use (or wish to use) the term 'association' in various contexts.

The categorisation of groups has been a central concern of so-called 'standard social ontology',[10] that focused on defining coordinated actions and, as a consequence, groups of people as subjects of those same actions, through the concepts of reflexivity, collective intentionality, and performativity.[11] To briefly illustrate the concepts, 'reflexivity' refers to the phenomenon where beliefs shape reality, often through so-called 'self-fulfilling prophecies'. Robert Merton illustrates this phenomenon, for example, by considering the case of twentieth-century Black workers in the US, labelled 'scabs' because they were excluded from unions. Their exclusion forced them to avoid strikes, reinforcing the label and justifying further exclusion.[12] In this sense, labelling some categories of people can directly influence their behaviour, ultimately causing the predictions to come true. 'Collective intentionality' is a central concept in social ontology and refers to the shared mental states, intentions, or beliefs that enable individuals to act together as a group.[13] It underlies social phenomena, allowing

[5] M Gilbert, 'Walking Together. A Paradigmatic Social Phenomenon' (1990) 15 *Midwest Studies in Philosophy* 1.

[6] M Bratman, 'Shared Intention' (1993) 104 *Ethics* 97.

[7] See, for instance, JR Searle, *The Construction of Social Reality* (New York, Free Press, 1995); C List and P Pettit, *Group Agency. The possibility, Design, and Status of Corporate Agents* (Oxford, Oxford University Press, 2011).

[8] The legal chapters of this book illustrate a useful range of cases.

[9] So, for instance, K Ritchie, 'Social Structures and the Ontology of Social Groups' (2020) 100 *Philosophy and Phenomenological Research* 402; J Horden and D López De Sa, 'Groups as Pluralities' (2021) 198 *Synthese* 10237.

[10] F Guala, 'The Philosophy of Social Science. Metaphysical and Empirical' (2007) 2 *Philosophy Compass* 954.

[11] Å Burman, *Nonideal Social Ontology. The Power View* (Oxford, Oxford University Press, 2023). For a survey on the idea that groups can be agents, *cf* D Tollefsen, *Groups as Agents* (Cambridge, Polity Press, 2015).

[12] R Merton, *Social Theory and Social Structure* (Glencoe, Free Press, 1957).

[13] Its centrality is clearly shown, for instance, by its synonymity with 'social ontology' itself, as explicitly done by Margaret Gilbert. The quotation goes: 'In the realm of contemporary

people to coordinate actions, establish institutions, and create shared meanings. John Searle, one of the founding figures of social ontology, argued that collective intentionality is fundamental to the existence of institutional facts, as opposed to brute facts. This means that collective intentionality – the capacity of people to think as a 'we' rather than as many 'I's – is what allows a paper sheet (a brute or natural fact) to be a dollar bill (an institution).[14] Finally, 'performativity' means that language does not merely describe reality but actively shapes and creates it. As elaborated by John Searle on the basis of John Austin's work, we create social objects by the formula 'X counts as Y in C'.[15] The classic example is 'I now pronounce you husband and wife', which does not merely describe a married couple but actually creates one – provided it is spoken by the appropriate authority in the right context.

According to standard theories in social ontology, namely those based on the three concepts just explained, there is a meaningful distinction between different types of groups based in particular on collective intentionality. Specifically, only some collections of individuals attain the status of proper social groups, while others remain mere aggregations or categories of people. This distinction depends, at least in part, on the presence and use of collective intentionality.[16] The philosopher who has explored this distinction most extensively is Margaret Gilbert. In her work, she differentiates between 'plural subjects' and 'populations'. Plural subjects function as cohesive units, making joint commitments and acting as a single body, whereas populations are simply groups of people who share certain characteristics, such as eye colour, a common name, or a specific location in time and space, without any deeper social bond or shared purpose.[17] Another possible distinction is made by Katherine Ritchie, who deals with two types of groups, named 'Type 1' and 'Type 2': the former are groups with collective intentionality; the latter are racial, gender, ethnic, and sexual orientation groups. They share common features and are difficult for an individual to voluntarily join or leave; moreover, membership does not require collective intentionality among the members.[18] Associations can be understood as plural subjects rather than mere populations, following Gilbert's distinction, insofar as they involve a form of

philosophical social theory, sometimes referred to as *social ontology*, or, again, *collective intentionality* […]'. M Gilbert, 'A Real Unity of Them All' (2009) 92 *The Monist* 268, 269.

[14] For the sake of completeness, collective intentionality is not the only necessary condition for deriving institutional facts from brute facts. Searle also introduced the distinction between regulative and constitutive rules, as well as the concept of assignment of function. *cf* Searle (n 7) C 1.

[15] Searle (n 7) 28.

[16] I explored this distinction in V Martino, 'Attaching Value to Membership. A Criterion?' (2023) 82 *Rivista di Estetica* 79 and V Martino, 'Redesigning Social Groups. Understanding the Young-Elder Divide' (2024) 27 *Phenomenology and Mind* 1.

[17] *cf* M Gilbert, *Joint Commitment. How We Make the Social World* (Oxford, Oxford University Press, 2013) 59.

[18] K Ritchie, 'The Metaphysics of Social Groups' (2015) 10 *Philosophical Studies* 310, 315. Ritchie considers the view that 'Type 2' groups require collective intentionality in virtue of being social kinds but also presents an alternative perspective in which collective intentionality is not indispensable. In

agreement regarding their objectives, as well as the rules for joining and leaving. In this sense, the requirements of plural subjecthood are relevant, such as the need for the individuals involved to have common knowledge that they are all part of the same group and are committed to acting as such. Moreover, it entails a social bond[19] rather than a legal one and can therefore only partially explain the case we started with.[20]

This standard distinction in social ontology is helpful in distinguishing between different kinds of groups and thus provides a framework for thinking of associations as one of them. However, since associations themselves can be of different kinds, depending, for example, on whether they are formal or informal, some further specification is needed. Indeed, groups based on collective intentionality and characterised by plural subjecthood can be of either type. A useful reference in this direction is Kirk Ludwig's work, in which he maintains this contraposition, with the aim of discussing a group's identity and its dependence on the groups' structure.[21] The distinction is examined in the context of the persistence of groups over time when their members change – a classic metaphysical problem, also known as the paradox of the Supreme Court.[22] In informal groups, a change in membership results in the formation of a new group, whereas institutional groups, such as football teams, retain their identity despite member changes. Crowds occupy an intermediate position: although they lack predefined roles like informal groups, they can change members without becoming a new group.

Again, this distinction alone does not seem sufficient to differentiate between formal and informal associations, as these characteristics can also apply to associations that are not legally registered. However, it remains a valuable distinction because it provides a way to approach the formal/informal divide and highlights the need to refine our theoretical considerations further. Thus, they only partially contribute to our understanding of freedom of association and, in particular, of the kinds of groups that it protects. However, the characteristics that define a social group in social ontology – namely collective intentionality, common

distinguishing the two types, she explicitly states that collective intentionality is not required in the latter case.

[19] Gilbert is very clear about the social nature of the relationship among individuals in a plural subject. It is not even a moral bond, though she explains how one can rebuke others when they change their minds and leave the plural subject without justifying their actions or seeking agreement from others. *cf* M Gilbert, 'Modelling Collective Belief' (1987) 73 *Synthese* 185, 192.

[20] However, Gilbert tried to explain more formal groupings too by using the same distinction. M Gilbert, *A Theory of Political Obligation. Membership, Commitment, and the Bonds of Society* (Oxford, Oxford University Press, 2006).

[21] K Ludwig, *From Plural to Institutional Agency. Collective Action II* (Oxford, Oxford University Press, 2017) 160ff.

[22] R Sharvy, 'Why a Class Can't Change Its Members' (1968) 2 *Noûs* 303; G Uzquiano, 'The Supreme Court and the Supreme Court Justices. A Metaphysical Puzzle' (2004) 38 *Noûs* 135. Sharvy highlighted the problem that a class can never change its members, whereas entities we typically consider as classes – such as the Supreme Court – must, by definition, be able to change their members, as they do in practice.

knowledge, and a social bond – can help identify key features of associations in contrast to other kinds of groupings, while also highlighting potential challenges in directly applying social ontology categorisations to legal distinctions. Let us now turn to the perspectives offered by the debate on realism and antirealism, which will provide key elements to enrich our discussion and move forward in a fruitful direction.

III. ANTIREALIST AND REALIST PERSPECTIVES

The distinction between antirealist and realist perspectives in social ontology is a crucial point for our analysis. According to the former, social entities exist because of our mental attitudes towards them, whereas the latter posits that such entities possess some form of independence from us. Applying this debate to the concept of groups allows us to delve deeper into the analysis of associations qua groups and sets the stage for illuminating the case of marriage discussed in the next section.

Firstly, the debate has been applied to discussions of social objects and social kinds. Social objects are usually understood as what is part of the social realm and, as such, are contraposed to natural objects. For instance, John Searle, as we saw referring to the elements of standard social ontology, states that natural objects can exist independently of human knowledge (mountains or molecules exist even though no human being knows about them), whereas social objects (a dollar bill, a party, a war) require human knowledge.[23]

Social kinds are categories used in the social sciences to explain and make sense of social phenomena.[24] Instances of social kinds are woman, money, intellectual property, and citizen. Indeed, they refer to categories or types of things that exist because of human social practices, conventions, and institutions. Some common social kinds analysed in philosophy are exactly money and social roles, but also race and gender. They are not just abstract classifications; when applied to human beings, they also represent traits that individuals share, which can lead to the formation of social groups or at least classes of people who are perceived as belonging together because of those traits.[25] Although almost everyone in social ontology agrees that social kinds are mind-dependent,[26] philosophical

[23] Searle (n 7) 9ff.

[24] A definition of social kinds, also in contrast with natural kinds, can be found here: A Bird and E Tobin, 'Natural Kinds' in EN Zalta and U Nodelman (eds), *The Stanford Encyclopedia of Philosophy* (Spring 2024 Edition) plato.stanford.edu/archives/spr2024/entries/natural-kinds/ accessed 26 July 2025.

[25] Scholarly discussions on social kinds are usually separate from those on social groups. Researchers often focus either on how to define and understand social groups or on the epistemology or political implications of social kinds. However, it is possible to combine them to enrich our discussion.

[26] Some examples can be found in M Gilbert, *On Social Facts* (London, Routledge, 1989); I Hacking, *The Social Construction of What?* (Cambridge MA, Harvard University Press, 1999);

approaches can be distinguished according to whether they are antirealist or realist. Many versions of the two positions exist, as well as very distinct meanings of realism and its opposite. We will focus only on a few that are exemplary and useful for our analysis.

Briefly, according to a widely accepted view, antirealism holds that the existence of certain social entities depends on human conceptual schemes, practices, and collective acceptance.[27] As a consequence, they are not real, as far as ontological realism entails that things exist independently of human beings and their dispositions towards things. According to this view, social kinds do not exist independently of our beliefs and language but are brought into being through our recognition and use of them. Antirealism aligns with constructivism, and as such is a very popular position in social ontology. For instance, Amie Thomasson's constructivism builds on her broader artifactualist approach to metaphysics.[28] She argues that many social and institutional entities are dependent on human practices, conceptual schemes, and collective recognition and that these collective attitudes are constitutive of social kinds. From her standpoint, social entities are not independent realities, but practices sustained by conceptual and linguistic commitments.[29] Antirealism is also related to infallibilism, namely the theory according to which, because social kinds are our product, we cannot be wrong about them.[30] However, scholars usually set some limitations to infallibilism, arguing that it applies only to some social kinds but not all. In this context, we can refer to 'opaque phenomena', namely those that are not immediately evident to human beings, even though they depend on them (at least in the sense that they do not exist in nature independently of human society).[31] A classic example of this phenomenon is racism: a society or an individual can exhibit racist behaviour without acknowledging it. Another example is a recession, which occurs independently of any single individual's beliefs about economic systems or trends. 'Opaque' thus refers to the fact that these phenomena are not evident to the people involved.

Accordingly, Ali Khalidi classifies social kinds into three categories based on their dependence on collective acceptance, naming them first, second, and

MA Khalidi, 'Interactive Kinds' (2010) 61 *British Journal for the Philosophy of Science* 335; R Tuomela, *The Philosophy of Sociality. The Shared Point of View* (Oxford, Oxford University Press, 2007).

[27] See, for instance, A Thomasson, 'Foundations for a Social Ontology' (2003) 18–19 *ProtoSociology* 269 and 'Realism and Human Kinds' (2003) 67 *Philosophy and Phenomenological Research* 580.

[28] *cf* A Thomasson, *Ordinary Objects* (Oxford, Oxford University Press, 2007) and *Ontology Made Easy* (Oxford, Oxford University Press, 2015).

[29] About social groups she emphasises the normative component of their creation and persistence. The function that a group performs is in turn recognisable through the internal and external rules that regulate it. A Thomasson, 'The Ontology of Social Groups' (2019) 196 *Synthese* 4829.

[30] F Guala, 'Infallibilism and Human Kinds' (2010) 40 *Philosophy of the Social Sciences* 244.

[31] Thomasson, 'Realism and Human Kinds' (n 27).

third kinds of social kinds.[32] The first kind of social kinds does not depend on our representations, either at the type (general category) or token (specific instance) level.[33] Opaque phenomena are part of this kind. The second kind of social kinds depends on our representations at the type level but not at the token level (eg, war, money). In other words, while the concept itself is socially constructed, specific instances exist independently of our recognition and dispositions towards them. Finally, the third kind of social kinds depends on our representations at both the type and token levels (eg, prime minister, permanent resident). Their existence and identity rely entirely on collective recognition and institutional frameworks.

Applied to associations, a generic antirealist account would suggest that an association exists only when individuals intentionally conceive of themselves as part of it. Its existence is therefore contingent on shared intentions and beliefs, meaning that without collective recognition and commitment, the association would not exist as a distinct entity. From an antirealist perspective, an association does not have an independent ontological status apart from the practices and shared understandings of its members. It exists only because people recognise it as such and act accordingly. Without this collective intentionality, the association ceases to exist as a meaningful entity. In relation to the example discussed at the beginning, the antirealist view would imply that the soup kitchen association exists because it is recognised by people.

In contrast, the realist perspective in social ontology holds that certain social entities exist independently of collective intentionality, meaning that their existence is not solely dependent on shared beliefs or recognition. Instead, these entities are seen as grounded in external structures, functions, or institutional frameworks. Within this broader realist framework, I will focus on two specific accounts – those of Maurizio Ferraris and Francesco Guala – to illustrate different ways in which social entities, including associations, can be understood as objectively existing.

Maurizio Ferraris develops a realist account of social ontology grounded in his theory of documentality, which emphasises the role of written records in

[32] MA Khalidi 'Three Kinds of Social Kinds' (2015) 90 *Philosophy and Phenomenological Research* 90. The distinction between the second and the third kinds had already been emphasised by Searle. According to the latter, in fact, the formula that produces institutional facts can work either for a category of social facts or for the single fact, depending on the customs we have in our cultures. In particular, the point is exemplified through the different way we conceive of a single dollar bill and a cocktail party. In the former case, the rule for the constitution of institutional facts applies to the type, while in the latter to the token. Indeed, any piece of paper that satisfies the conditions to be a dollar bill is a dollar bill, regardless of the use we make of it. In contrast, in the case of the cocktail party, collective intentionality applies to the specific event: if the participants do not believe that what they are taking part in is a cocktail party, then that is not a cocktail party. *cf* Searle (n 7) 31ff.

[33] For the sake of clarity, 'type' refers to a general category, such as the species 'cat', while its corresponding token is an individual instance, like Sylvester the cat. Again 'book' is the type, the copy of *Light in August* on my shelf is a token.

the existence of social objects.[34] He classifies objects into three categories: natural objects, which exist in time and space independently of human intervention (for example, mountains and planets); ideal objects, which exist independently of the physical world but depend on human thought (for example, mathematical entities); and social objects, which exist in time and space but depend on human intervention, at least for their inception (for example, laws, money, and contracts). Once they come into existence, however, they no longer require human intervention to persist, much like artefacts.

The key distinction between natural and social objects lies in their ontological dependence – while natural objects exist regardless of human beliefs, social objects are brought into being through documents, rules, and institutions that establish their existence. However, this does not imply an antirealist position – quite the opposite. The fundamental principle governing social objects is 'Object = Inscribed Act', meaning that it is precisely the trace left by documentation, with its objective epistemological value, that gives social objects their meaning.[35] As a result, Ferraris adapts Jacques Derrida's well-known adage 'there is nothing outside the text' into 'nothing social exists outside the text', shifting from a constructivist (or postmodern) perspective to a realist one.[36]

Applying this to associations, Ferraris could argue that an association exists when it is formally registered, meaning its existence is tied to documentation and legal recognition. This formalist perspective aligns with legal definitions, where an association is not merely a group of individuals acting together but a recognised entity with rights, obligations, and institutional standing. Under this view, informal groups or gatherings lack ontological status as associations unless they are officially documented, reinforcing the idea that social reality is shaped by formal records rather than collective intention.

What we can add here, however, is that Ferraris advocates for a very broad concept of document, leveraging the notion of trace. For instance, he argues that even a verbally made promise can count as a social object if we consider the mnestic trace (the memory of the promise) as the necessary document to record the act as a social one.[37] From this perspective, what truly matters is the distinction between what is private – occurring solely in an individual's mind – and what is public, meaning it is shared by more than one person to varying degrees of institutionalisation. These different forms of public recognition are then classified within an ontology of social objects, based on how these objects

[34] M Ferraris, *Documentality. Why It is Necessary to Leave Traces* (New York, Suny Press, 2013).

[35] Ferraris (n 34) 120ff.

[36] To better grasp his analysis, see M Ferraris, 'Collective Intentionality or Documentality?' (2015) 41 *Philosophy and Social Criticism* 423; M Ferraris and G Torrengo, 'Documentality: A Theory of Social Reality' (2014) 57 *Rivista di Estetica* 11.

[37] Ferraris (n 34) 142.

are created and the type of document that supports them – whether strong or weak, for example.[38]

Francesco Guala develops a functionalist approach to social ontology, which focuses on the roles and behaviours of social entities rather than their formal definitions or institutional recognition.[39] His account is influenced by the rules-in-equilibrium framework, which draws from game theory and economics to explain the persistence of social institutions. According to this view, social entities exist insofar as they fulfil a function involving stable expectations and interactions within a system. Rather than being defined solely by legal recognition or collective intentionality, social entities persist because individuals behave in ways that reinforce their existence, responding to incentives and constraints within a given social structure. This framework can also account for ineffective rules, namely norms that are legally at work but not followed by anyone.[40]

Applying this kind of account to associations, we could argue that an association exists as long as it functions as one, regardless of whether it is formally recognised. A group of individuals who regularly meet, coordinate activities, and achieve shared goals may count as an association in practice, even if it lacks legal status. This perspective contrasts with Ferraris' documentality-based account by suggesting that associations are not defined by registration or official recognition, but by the roles they play and the stability of their social interactions. Within this functionalist framework, an informal collective can be considered an association provided that it operates with a certain degree of structure and continuity, albeit without any legal documentation.

The key difference between Ferraris' and Guala's accounts, thus, lies in how they define the existence and persistence of social entities. Ferraris' documentality-based approach argues that social objects come into being through written records and institutional recognition. For Ferraris, the act of documentation itself would grant an association ontological status, meaning that without formal registration, a group does not technically exist as an association. This view aligns with a legalistic and institutional perspective, where

[38] For the sake of clarity, a 'weak document' indicates something that is not produced with the intention of creating a document but can be used as such at a later time. For example, a murderer does not leave a trace for the purpose of creating a document, but the police, trying to identify them, can use their traces (fingerprints, ie, a weak document) as evidence (and therefore as a strong document). The strong document, indeed, has very clear and precise rules. Although these rules may be different in relation to the case (if it is a testament or a degree certificate) and in relation to the culture in which the document is produced (in temporally and spatially terms), they have one thing in common: they are codified by the society. To get married, we have to sign an act done in a particular way, have witnesses, and do a whole series of acts identified by the law of the community. However, this does not imply that these rules are subjective: even if they are not natural, but dependent on the subjects, once they are put down in words, they become objectively valid. To change them we will need to proceed by following other social and legal rules. Ferraris (n 34) 267–8.

[39] F Guala, *Understanding Institutions. The Science and Philosophy of Living Together* (Princeton, Princeton University Press, 2016).

[40] Guala's example is the law in France that prohibited women from wearing trousers, which remained technically valid until it was repealed in 2010. Guala (n 39) 41ff.

social reality is shaped by objective, external records rather than informal practices or intentions. Although, as we have already mentioned, 'document' can be understood in a very broad sense, the standard case is based on the written component.

In contrast, Guala's functionalist approach would define associations not by their formal registration but by their function and persistence within a system of interactions. According to Guala, a group that regularly coordinates activities and has a shared purpose qualifies as an association, even without legal recognition. His account is grounded in a rules-in-equilibrium framework, which emphasises stability, expectations, and behaviours rather than formal documentation. These contrasting views reflect a broader debate in social ontology between some forms of realism[41] and functionalism.

IV. THE CASE OF MARRIAGE: RECOGNITION VS. REALITY

One useful case for investigating the nature of associations is the institution of marriage. Indeed, marriage, like association, presents a case where legal recognition and social reality do not always align. There are instances where individuals consider themselves married despite lacking formal recognition by the state. Historically, this has been the case for same-sex couples, polygamous unions, and other non-traditional relationships that have sought legal recognition. Moreover, some individuals who are legally eligible to marry choose not to, often to avoid the legal consequences that come with marriage. Similarly, some associations opt not to register because they lack the seriousness or commitment required to seek legal recognition. In this way, both associations and marriages can reflect comparable dynamics. The underlying issue is that social ontology and jurisprudence may categorise social entities differently, leading to potential conflicts in recognition and protection.

In chapter 14 of *Understanding Institutions*, Francesco Guala explores whether one can simultaneously be a realist and a reformist regarding social institutions. He argues that institutions can be modified without fundamentally changing their nature, balancing externalist realism – where the meaning of institutional terms is determined by the world – with the need for institutional evolution to fit normative goals.[42] Instead, he suggests that institutions should

[41] Consider that Ferraris is among the founders of so-called 'New Realism'. *cf* M Ferraris, *Manifesto of New Realism* (New York, Suny Press, 2014).

[42] Guala critiques Sally Haslanger's 'ameliorative' approach, which challenges traditional views on normative rather than descriptive grounds. Haslanger's ameliorative approach is a method in philosophy, particularly in social ontology and feminist theory, that seeks to redefine concepts based on their practical and political usefulness rather than merely their common usage or underlying essence. Haslanger argues that instead of asking 'What do our concepts mean?' (conceptual analysis) or 'What is their underlying nature?' (metaphysical inquiry), we should ask 'What should our concepts do?'. This means redefining terms in a way that helps achieve social justice and addresses

be analysed as types and tokens: a token institution (for example, marriage in a specific culture and time) is an instance of a broader institutional type. Using marriage as a case study, Guala highlights how past social arrangements do not necessarily dictate the institution's essential nature. He applies insights from scientifically-informed ontology, arguing that determining what marriage (or any institution) is requires examining the coordination problems it solves rather than simply generalising from historical cases. While courts and lawmakers shape institutions, they do not define their ontological nature qua social kinds. Indeed, this constitutes social scientists' goal. In this sense, he supports a descriptive, scientific approach to institutional reform, separating what an institution is from what it ought to be in legal and political debates. Therefore, rather than being inherently heterosexual or bound to a specific legal framework, marriage is a flexible institution that can take multiple forms while still serving similar coordination functions.

According to Maurizio Ferraris, marriage is both a promise and a social object, meaning it exists within the framework of his documentality theory. As a social object, marriage depends on written records, legal recognition, and institutional structures that formalise and sustain its existence. In a specific context, it does not depend on our intentions or volitions but rather on performing specific actions, following established procedures, and signing written documents. At the same time, Ferraris views marriage as a promise – a commitment between individuals that carries social and legal obligations. However, unlike informal promises, marriage as a documented social object gains permanence and enforceability through institutional backing. In this sense, Ferraris' view contrasts with functional or historical definitions, emphasising instead the role of legal formalisation in constituting marriage as a social act.

We could say that the case of associations, particularly in relation to freedom of association, raises the opposite concern. While some individuals may seek formal recognition for their associations, others may wish to operate without formal registration. This could be due to legal restrictions, political concerns, or personal preferences. The challenge, then, is ensuring that unregistered groups pursuing common interests are not compelled to formalise in ways that might undermine their autonomy or expose them to regulatory burdens, as highlighted in the soup kitchen scenario.

The tension between descriptive and normative social ontology becomes evident when considering how legal systems define and regulate associations. A descriptive approach seeks to categorise associations based on observable social patterns, while a normative approach considers what the law ought to recognise and protect. This distinction is crucial for ensuring that legal frameworks do

systemic inequalities. *cf* S Haslanger, *Resisting Reality. Social Construction and Social Critique* (Oxford, Oxford University Press, 2012).

not inadvertently exclude certain groups or impose unnecessary restrictions on informal associations.

For instance, if a legal system adheres strictly to a formalist view, it may fail to protect informal associations that function as cohesive units but lack official recognition. Conversely, a rigid functionalist approach might force legal recognition upon groups that do not wish to be categorised as formal associations. A balanced approach must acknowledge both perspectives, ensuring that legal definitions align with social realities while safeguarding individual and collective rights.

V. CONCLUDING REMARKS

The question of what constitutes an association is not merely a theoretical concern but has significant legal and social implications. By examining a definition of group, antirealist and realist perspectives, and the institution of marriage, this chapter has highlighted the complexities of recognition in social ontology. The key challenge lies in ensuring that legal categorisations are flexible enough to accommodate diverse forms of association while protecting fundamental rights. The interplay between social ontology and jurisprudence must be navigated carefully to reconcile philosophical categorisations with the practical needs of governance and social organisation.

This chapter aimed at introducing scholars working on freedom of association to key elements of social ontology. To do so, it first examined the categorisation of social groups in standard social ontology, addressing theoretical distinctions such as aggregates vs collectives and formal vs informal groups. While these distinctions alone do not fully explain the nature of formal and informal associations, the concept of collective intentionality proves useful in understanding how people come together and how shared goals and rules contribute to the formation of social groups, associations included.

Secondly, the discussion moved to the realism and antirealism of social kinds, raising questions about whether social objects can be grounded solely in collective intentionality. This led to a consideration of different levels of social reality, precisely because our collective dispositions can refer to distinct levels – either the type or the token level. This distinction allows us to ask whether associations should be understood more like dollar bills or cocktail parties, following Searle's examples – namely, whether they depend on collective behaviour as a category or as individual associations – and what, instead, depends on the legal definition of associations.

To further develop this analysis, we applied two realist perspectives to the case of marriage, using it as a concrete example to contrast a positive realist[43]

[43] The reference is to M Ferraris, *Positive Realism* (London, Zer0 Books, 2015).

account with a functionalist one. This approach helped clarify the theoretical advantages of both positions in explaining historical institutions. Hopefully, the philosophical distinctions explored in this chapter may provide legal theorists working on freedom of association with useful insights and conceptual tools for refining their definitions and approaches.

15

The Good of Association and the Freedom that We Share

HANS BERNHARD SCHMID*

IN THE INTRODUCTION to this collection, Maria Cahill writes that the 'right to freedom of association protects individuals in their sociality, in the collaborative context of their relationships with others'.[1] As the good that is protected by the right to freedom of association, sociality here appears as a value. Although existing rationales for freedom of association focus on its protection of the individual's right to live their life as they see fit or on the ways in which it serves a healthy democracy, and even on the ways that associations support self-development and flourishing,[2] none of those defences focuses on the dimension of sociality that is inherent to associations.[3]

This picks up on earlier observations made in the philosophical literature on freedom of association, but marks an interesting contrast, too. It aligns with Amy Gutman's diagnosis in the introductory essay of her influential 1998 collected volume.[4] 'Associational freedom', Gutman says here, 'is not merely a

* This publication is a contribution to the *Societās: Exploring the Value of Freedom of Association* project, directed by Professor Maria Cahill at the School of Law, University College Cork, and funded by the Irish Research Council (now Research Ireland) under grant IRCLA/2022/3860. The chapter builds on ideas discussed during the workshop *Exploring Associational Life: From Social Ontology to Law and Back Again*, held at University College Cork on 25–26 April 2024. I wish to thank the participants in this webinar and the main workshop, and especially Giulia Lasagni and Maria Cahill for detailed and very insightful criticism and comments!

[1] M Cahill, 'Comparative and Interdisciplinary Interfaces of Associational Life and Freedom' in M Cahill and G Lasagni (eds), *Associational Life and Freedom* (Oxford, Hart Publishing, 2026) 1, 1.

[2] ibid 2–7.

[3] The invitation to consider the importance of sociality within associational contexts was made by Maria Cahill and Giulia Lasagni under the auspices of the *Societās* project in the context of an invitation to dialogue between social ontologists and legal theorists (See www.associationalfreedom.org/post/webinarnovember2023, last accessed 29 August 2025), which led to the *Exploring Associational Life* workshop referenced above. This chapter considers the dimension of sociality within associations from a philosophical perspective and is offered as a contribution to that dialogue, sensitive to the fact that no settled position has yet been articulated on the same theme by legal scholars.

[4] A Gutman, 'Freedom of Association: an Introductory Essay' in A Gutman (ed), *Freedom of Association* (Princeton, Princeton University Press, 1998).

means to other valuable ends'.[5] However, Gutman does not focus on sociality, but locates the value of associational freedom in its connection to individual freedom, on the one hand, and liberal democracy, on the other hand: 'associational freedom [...] is essential for [...] individuals to live a good life and for constituting a just society'.[6]

In her project of elucidating freedom of association, Gutman gathered philosophers and social scientists, and the spirit of the discipline at the time shortly before the turn of the millennium was communitarian – with a renewed emphasis on the importance of social bonds and belonging, directed against the perceived individualism of the 'liberal' tradition.

Cahill's initiative is distinctive in that it aims to bring together legal scholars and social ontologists, and the task is to articulate the specific value of associational freedom.

As a rapidly evolving and diverse field that came to be established only in the decades after Gutman's publication, social ontology is certainly not a unified position, or method, or stock of knowledge. But it is not entirely without recognisable contours either. One view on which, although in different versions, many (although certainly not all) early twenty-first-century social ontologists agree is this: agency is not only instantiated by individuals, but also by (some) groups, too. As freedom arguably centrally involves agency, and as associations are often defined as forms of joint action, the issue of collective or group agency is obviously relevant to the question of the value protected by the right to freedom of association. It is thus reasonable to expect substantial insight from enlisting social ontologists for the task of discussing the value of freedom of association.

This chapter thus approaches the issue from a joint action-focused view of Social Ontology.[7] The question is how the value protected by the right to freedom of association involves associations *as subjects* rather than just as objects – as belonging to those who *have* the right and whose *own* good is thereby protected rather than just as an object (or good) *to which* there is a right.

Cahill suggests that the right to freedom of association protects *individuals* in their sociality, which might perhaps be taken to suggest that individuality and sociality relate in the way of a subject (or substance) and a property thereof (or accidents). This chapter explores challenges to any such reading. Might 'individuals in their sociality', as protected by the right to freedom of association, be just that – *groups as agents* whose *own* good is thereby protected rather than just them in turn being protected as the good of other agents, the individuals?

Tackling this question, of course, involves the ontology of groups, the theory of 'group rights', as well as considerations of the many ways in which 'the good' (or 'value') is relational. The chapter has two main parts. Section I approaches

[5] ibid 4.
[6] ibid 5.
[7] HB Schmid, *We, Together – The Social Ontology of Us* (New York, Oxford University Press, 2023).

the question of how sociality figures in the right to freedom of association with some considerations on how the right to freedom of association might be an individual *and* a collective right. It is argued in this section that this distinction, drawn in terms of individual and collective rights-holders, collapses. It is not the case that the right to freedom of association is an individual right to associate or disassociate (with individuals as rights-holders), and a collective right to organisational autonomy (with associations as rights-holders), as the 'individual' right extends to associations, too, and the 'collective' right is also the participating individuals', in terms of rights-holders. Section II engages critically with a prominent (and influential) proposal of a group rights perspective (and underlying conception of group agency) in early twenty-first-century social ontology – Christian List's and Philip Pettit's. A significant feature of this view is its firm commitment to (normative) individualism, and the way in which the ontological view and normative commitment interrelate in this theory is instructive. It is argued in this section that considering the case of freedom of association might reveal both a flaw in the conception of group agency and, correspondingly, a somewhat limited conception of political freedom (Pettit's 'Republicanism') in that conception.

A concluding section III applies the plural action view of the ontology of associations to one of the moot court cases depicted in the introduction to this volume. In matters of the relevant jurisdiction, the emerging view of the status of organisation and incorporation seems practically relevant when it comes to the question of whether 'unregistered' or formally non-incorporated plural agencies (such as a group of people running a non-profit soup kitchen together) should count as protected by the right to freedom of association. The social ontology of association that emerges in this chapter tends to give a positive answer even in cases where no informal 'governance' structure (or distribution of roles) has been established – such cases are paradigmatic instantiations of the right to associational freedom; imposing organisation and registration on them may be harmful to them and constitute an infringement on their right to freedom of association. However, it is argued that incorporation (and registration) may reasonably be demanded of larger-scale plural activities.

I. FREEDOM TO ASSOCIATE AND ORGANISATIONAL AUTONOMY

In early twenty-first-century social ontology, there is a widely shared view (perhaps even one of the core claims) that agency can be properly instantiated not only by individuals, but by groups, too. Constituent features of agency are identified in the literature, and different degrees of agency are distinguished – just that something is an agent does not imply that it is a *person* capable of moral action – and it is argued on that basis that not only individuals but also groups can be agents. Christian List's and Philip Pettit's uniquely influential account makes the further case that some groups can be of the kind of agents that make them suitable for the role as *holders of rights*.[8] The kind of agent that can be a holder of rights is, they argue, a person, and a person is – to paraphrase the view – a suitable target of normative expectations, that is, an agent who can act for normative reasons. Although List and Pettit argue that some groups are indeed of that kind and thus may (or should) have rights, they should not, they say, have 'equal rights' – the rights that they may (or should) have are not 'on a par with individuals'.[9] In List's and Pettit's view, groups should only be given rights that are compatible with 'normative individualism', defined as the view that 'something is good only if it is good for individual human or, more generally, sentient beings'.[10]

Are associations potential cases in point, and might it perhaps even be that the right to freedom of association is – in part – just that, a group right? List and Pettit do not discuss the issue of freedom of association, and neither do they discuss associations in particular. Indeed, it seems rather obvious that associations of the 'intimate' (or 'primary') kind, such as married couples – do not qualify as groups (and thus potential group agents or even holders of group rights) in their sense. List's and Pettit's concept of a group assumes an entity that persists through the exchange of their members, which is not the case in marriage or friendship, where the death of one of the participants necessarily terminates the association. This conception of a group, however, might very well be associations of the 'collective' (as defined by Brownlee and Jenkins),[11] 'secondary' or 'third' kind (as defined in Gutman)[12] – the 'groups of people organised for a joint purpose' as which the Oxford English Dictionary defines associations. 'Collective' associations (on which the focus will be in the following) do seem, in principle, to be fit candidates for List/Pettitean groups, and thus for holders of group (or collective) rights, too.

Might freedom of association, in part at least, be just that – a group right in the sense of a right that some groups (the groups that are associations) have? Before investigating this further, one should not forget, however, that classical formulations of the right to freedom of association do themselves address the question of who its subjects are. 'Everyone has the right to freedom of peaceful assembly and association', the Universal Declaration of Human Rights famously states in Article 20. This answers – with some authority at least – the question of whose *right* freedom of association is. But who is everyone? The Universal Declaration does *not* say 'every individual', or 'every natural person'. And it seems quite easy to spell out the right to freedom of association as an individual *and* a collective right in a way that the two are not simply

[8] C List and P Pettit, *Group Agency. The Possibility, Design, and Status of Corporate Agents* (New York, Oxford University Press, 2011) C 8.

[9] ibid 170.

[10] ibid 182.

[11] K Brownlee and D Jenkins, 'Freedom of Association' in EN Zalta and U Nodelman (eds), *The Stanford Encyclopedia of Philosophy* (Fall 2024 Edition) plato.stanford.edu/archives/fall2024/entries/freedom-association/ accessed 26 July 2025.

[12] Gutman (n 4).

(and perhaps implausibly) on a par (with individuals and associations having *equal* rights).

That freedom of association is an *individual* right seems obvious enough. Freedom of association obviously protects the agency *of individuals* from state interference; in this regard, the right to freedom of association can be characterised as each individual's right to team up with other individuals in the formation of an association (which is, one might think, something that *individuals* can do), or the right of each individual to join any existing organisation that is willing to accept them as a member. In particular, it protects individuals against states preventing them from joining up or joining in (organised) team action. Viewed in this way and based on an understanding of association as shared activity, it does indeed seem quite basic: it is the individual's right to engage (with others) in joint action.

There is yet another regard in which the right to freedom of association seems to be focused on the protection of *individuals*. It is, as it seems, characterised as an *individual* right as the right to *leave* any association, too – this point is stated separately in Article 20 of the Universal Declaration of Human Rights, right after the above: 'no one may be compelled to belong to an association'. Why should one think that this does not exhaust the right to freedom of association, and that it is a collective right (or group right), too? One way to approach this is as follows. Associations, it seems, are not just spontaneous team acts. They are organisations. Although this of course involves individual participants, organising associational activity is in an important way the association's *own* business – its role in the act is that of an agent rather than that of an object acted upon. As a collective or group right, freedom of association is recognition of associational agency; it is every (legal) association's right to pursue its purpose as it, the organisation that it is, sees fit (within the limits of the law).

It thus seems that freedom of association *cannot* just be the freedom to (not) join up or join in but needs to extend to the freedom to do (at least) that for which the association has been founded and for which it is kept running by its members. This is the association's business, it seems, and pursuing it should be recognised as a freedom that is, in this sense, really *the association's*, as the collective or group that it is. Freedom of association is the association's freedom to pursue its goals, and to do so in the way it sees fit, within the limits of the law.

The law might certainly distinguish between different types of association, and place requirements on their organisational structure accordingly, but the state cannot prescribe a pursuit, goal, or purpose to it, or infringe on associational self-organisation by determining the way it pursues its goal (or else the association would cease to be an association, and turn into a de facto state organ). In order to see this collective aspect of freedom of association, it is necessary to recognise that associations exist, that they exist as agents, and that in an important sense, the right that is freedom of association is the associations' own freedom, which makes them holders of the right to freedom of association of their own.

Most controversially perhaps, the collective dimension of freedom of association comes to the fore when thinking about the *right to exclude*, which is arguably part of freedom of association, too,[13] and which obviously attaches to associations rather than to any individuals as the relevant subjects (rights-holders); *you* (singular, as an individual) cannot enrol me or throw me out of the History of Ontology Association, unless the association has, in virtue of its organisation, authorised you to do so, so that what you do is what the association does.

It is not difficult to make the case that the right to freedom of association implies the right to exclude. For associations to be able to pursue their business in a modally robust way, they need to be able to not accept (or to exclude) members who are obviously inimical to or unfit for the purpose that is the association's. To mention some clear cases, no fringe political party can be required to accept members who apply only to subvert or take over the association (the right to exclude allows an association to defend itself against what is known in the literature as 'entryism', the strategic infiltration of an association with the aim to repurpose rather than support it).

Is the answer to the above question – who is everyone? – thus perhaps simply this: each and every individual, *and* each and every (legal) association, so that associations are included in a full list of rights-holders – although plausibly not 'on a par' with individuals, since it is the *collective* right of which they are the holders? Is the answer that there are really two separate rights to freedom of associations, an individual right and a collective right, with two kinds of rights-holders to consider?

If associations are indeed to be counted as subjects of the right to freedom of associations *alongside* individuals (on one and the same list of who is included in 'everybody', although in different categories), one should expect individuals and associations to be sufficiently similar (analogous) in the way in which they 'have' their respective (individual or collective) right to freedom of association (or in how it is that the right to freedom of association is 'theirs').

Although it is notoriously difficult to determine what's 'sufficiently similar' for something to be an analogy rather than a disanalogy, one might think that this is not supported by the description of how the right is individual and collective so far.

An apparently clear disanalogy is that for individuals, the right to freedom of association includes, besides the right to form or join an association, the right *not* to participate. Not joining – or leaving – are protected options; they are exertions of individual freedom of association. There seems to be no correspondent to this in the collective case, considered so far. One might perhaps think that an association's freedom extends not only to being in charge of

[13] M Walzer, 'On Involuntary Association' in A Gutman (ed), *Freedom of Association* (Princeton, Princeton University Press, 1998).

(and going about) its own business without undue interference, but also to 'change its mind' and do *something else entirely* (for example, by changing its statutes) or to close down shop altogether, too. Or one might think that the correspondent to the individual 'stay out' or 'exit-option', in the collective case, is the exertion of the right to exclude (with the exclusion of *every* member perhaps being a way of deciding to close down shop).

It seems obvious, however, that – ontologically speaking – that which is protected by the right to freedom of associations relates to associations in a much more fundamental way than how it attaches to individuals (at least if one takes associations to be *voluntary*). Take away individual freedom of association, and you end up in a world where individual lives are lived in isolation except for state-ordained venues; the existence of the individual right-holders does not depend on the right. Take away collective freedom of associations, and you end up in a world in which there *are no voluntary associations*, but perhaps only state agencies of sorts. A traditional distinction that might be apt to capture the difference is this: freedom of association is *regulative* as an individual right, but it is *constitutive* as a collective right.

The thought experiment – if it works – even gives a reason for doubt concerning the distinction between an individual and a collective right to freedom of association that is not affected by the vagueness of analogy. The world without individual freedom of association and the world without collective freedom of association are *one and the same* world: a world without associations. This suggests that individual and collective rights to freedom of association may not be different rights (the respective rights of different kinds of rights-holders) after all. If they come and go together, perhaps one is either *reducible* to the other, or they are non-reducibly *identical* in some way after all? Might it be that the 'individual' right to freedom of association *is* (in some sense of identity) a 'collective' right, and/or vice versa?

One might think that joining up with others freely (or joining in an association – the exertion of the individual right to freedom of association) is a very different thing from the associations' not being unduly interfered with in the running of their business (the exertion of the collective right to freedom of association). But the thought experiment (if it does indeed have the stated result) perhaps supports a different view. One could perhaps imagine a non-revolutionary anti-liberal regime change where the existing associations are left in charge of running their business as they see fit, but where people are not free to set up new associations, or join any existing association without special state permission (arguably, this would be a scenario with collective freedom of association without individual freedom of association). This would likely result in the persistence of exactly those 'associations' (if they can still be called such) which the state regime would have permitted to exist had it chosen the opposite route by abolishing the 'collective' right to freedom of association while maintaining the 'individual' right to freedom of association.

Of course, this does not prove identity – sometimes, very different things can have the same result. But this perhaps still supports the intuition that the right to freedom of association is not two rights with two different types of rights-holders but, in some way, one package.

A further complication with the (apparently) neat and clean housekeeping solution to expand the list of rights-holders to include associations while keeping them distinct as different kinds of holders of a different kind (or perhaps just 'aspect') of the right to freedom of association is this: it does not seem absurd to think that the individual right to freedom of association, as depicted so far, applies *to associations*, too. The actual legal facts are certainly difficult to see from a philosopher's armchair (even with an internet connection), but it is not obvious at all why, besides 'natural persons', associations should not have, in virtue of freedom of association, a right to associate, too. Associations, too, are free to team up, to associate with each other, to form partnerships, coalitions, federations or some such that are, in fact, associations of associations.

It is perhaps not obvious why the associations' right to associate with other associations (assuming that it is part and parcel of the right to freedom of association) should be regarded as similarly 'basic' or 'essential' as the right of 'natural persons' to associate.

One could perhaps imagine a world in which the individual right to freedom of association is realised for 'natural persons', but not for associations (in this scenario, if an association felt that its purpose required strengthening another association's activity, it would have to disband itself and encourage its members to join in the other association that could then perhaps decide whether it deems it fit to organise itself in such a way as to allow those members to form one of its 'organs', such as a regional chapter). An association's *individual* right to freedom of association is perhaps not tied to the right to freedom of association *as such* (or *sans phrase*) quite in the way the individual right to freedom of association is tied to the collective right to freedom of association (where it seems that the one stands and falls with the other). But it seems plausible enough to assume that the distinction between the individual and the collective right that is freedom of association (according to the above characterisation thereof) may not coincide with the distinction between 'natural persons' and associations as rights-holders. The individuals that 'have' the right to freedom of association include, it seems, associations.

Is the converse true, too – might a point be made that among those who have the 'collective' right that is freedom of association are not only associations, but individuals, too? Here is a reason why this may indeed be the case. Whatever exactly it may be which individuals have a right to do freely, in virtue of the right to freedom of association – the process of teaming up with each other in founding an association (arguably the conceptual core of the right to freedom of association) – already involves (to some degree at least) an exercise of that which the *collective* right to freedom of association is to protect: the exercise of the sort of joint self-organisation that is the core of associational autonomy. Associating with each other, or founding an association together, is joint action, and we usually can't just do it spontaneously if it is to be about more than just enjoying our company while it lasts. If you and I do it, it is something that we, together, do, and arguably on an agreed-upon plan that involves *some* degree of organisation. Although you may have proposed the plan, it becomes real only by me accepting it, with your proposing it to me and my accepting it being our respective individual contribution to a token act that is *ours*, collectively: our founding an association.

The legal picture may or may not align perfectly with this ontological claim. The French 1901 association law (according to the currently valid amendment of the law) requires at least two signatories in order to come into existence through registration (although significantly, the 1901 original version of the law did not require registration). If it should turn out that some legislation does allow for single individuals to formally found (via registration) an association all by themselves, a point could perhaps be made that what registration constitutes here is an *initiative* for an association rather than the association itself. However, if – as the French case suggests – registration is needed for the association to exist as a *legally recognised* entity, it seems that our above picture is incomplete. It is not just any bunch of individuals who can associate by any means – they need to show up, in some form, in front of some government teller and hand in the paperwork – and wait for state confirmation of recognition.[14]

However, it seems rather clear that restricting the concept of association to associations of the *legally registered* kind is way too restrictive for the spirit of the right to freedom of association, and indeed, in a very important sense, it would interfere so heavily in the process of founding an association that doing so would become very cumbersome if not outright impossible. The nineteenth-century fight over the legal right to freedom of association was for legal *toleration, acceptance*, or *recognition* of what people were already doing: gathering up in clubs and other circles to promote their shared interest. And even a legalistic view of association presupposes some way in which (proto-)associations can exist prior to legal recognition. People already need to associate with each other and act together in an organised way, as it were, even if it is just to register their association with the government. Arguably the right to do so is itself a collective right after all, or rather, not to be neatly distinguished from, but identical with the right to 'team up'.

'Founding and organisation' (a part of freedom of association as an individual right) and associational self-organisation (a part of freedom of association as a collective right) might not really be separable in the way assumed by the initial description. Even people's meeting up and discussing an issue of shared

[14] I vividly recall doing this together with Alessandro Salice with the Austrian *Vereinspolizei* – literally, the association police – in the process of founding the International Social Ontology Society (ISOS).

interest is already a joint activity. It is not simply a distribution of actions (you saying something, I saying something etc), it is a token action that involves a plurality of participants, and it involves them together. It is done *collectively*.

The conversation and self-organisation that result in the founding of an association are certainly not *the association's* action in a sense that is distinct from what the participating 'natural persons' are doing. And it does not seem to be a matter of the right to freedom of association, but rather a matter of the right to *freedom of assembly*. A cursory look at the literature in legal theory and legal philosophy suggests that the two are indeed (seen as) being tightly interrelated. It seems that as far as the right to found an association is concerned at least, freedom of association *presupposes* freedom of assembly, and it is difficult to even imagine an associational life without any opportunities for assembly – and of course, assembly is hard to imagine without *freedom of expression*, which explains why so much of the literature seems to be discussing them together. 'Assembling', as an action type, seems to be plural – it is a token action with a plurality of agents.

It thus seems that the proposed distinction between the 'individual' and 'collective' aspects of the right to freedom of association not only fails to distinguish between individuals and collectives as rights-holders. It seems to collapse altogether. The right to team up and form an association *is* the right to joint activity, and the right to self-organisation that is identified as the collective aspect of the right to freedom of association is essential already for the formation-story.

If you and I fail to organise ourselves in the pursuit of a shared goal, it is *us*, *together*, who fail, not just you, me (and whoever else is involved) severally. Self-organisation is not an individual task, but a joint task. Achieving self-organisation is something we, the participants, should do *together* (and setting up some 'aggregation procedure' with extra insurance of collective rationality in virtue of which we constitute a formal extra group agent are just ways of tackling this). Organisation is not a *prerequisite* for a bunch of individuals to be a collective agent – rather, organisation – in terms of self-organisation – is something *we* do, and we do it together.

II. TOWARDS A PLURALIST ONTOLOGY OF GROUP AGENCY

The most successful theory of group agency in recent social ontology – List's and Pettit's – suggests that group agency comes to be and exists as an *extra agent* (that is, as an addition to the full list of agents), an entity that ensures the collective rationality of the group's attitudes to such a degree that one can plausibly speak of an agent, and potentially a group person with rights of its own. But the view that a group can only be an agent (or indeed a group person that is a rights-holder of its own) if it is sufficiently organised misses an important point that neatly comes to the fore when thinking about assembly and association (rather than corporation): coming together, setting up a joint venture, and establishing an organisational structure is itself something in which the participants are involved collectively rather than severally.

If I am not mistaken, it is this pre-corporate 'jointness' of agency that seems to be at the core of what the right to freedom of association protects. It is neither 'just' individual agency (or freedom), nor some corporate agency (or freedom), but perhaps better adequately described as *plural agency*, and thus a freedom that is neither distributive (anyone's own individual freedom) nor collective (the freedom of some 'group agent'), but the freedom that agents *share*, or *have together*.

Association crucially involves a plurality of individuals participating in one token activity, and the self-organisation thereof over time. That activity is *neither* just individual activity, nor is it some group agent's own. If this is right, exploring the specific value that is protected by freedom of association will hardly profit from the group agency idea as developed in early twenty-first-century social ontology; to the contrary, thinking about freedom of association could perhaps better serve as a starting point for rethinking the ontological commitments involved in established group action theory. But how could this help further in elucidating the value protected by the right to freedom of association?

It is worth noting that (conceptions of) values are closely tied up with ontological commitment. Values are openly declared in List's and Pettit's conception of group rights, where they argue that group rights should be compatible with what they call normative individualism. To recall, normative individualism is described as the view that 'something is good only if it is for individual human or, more generally, sentient beings'.[15] In a footnote to this sentence, they explain further that they 'take it as a working assumption that group persons do not have whatever functional characteristic it is that makes individual human beings distinctively valuable, such as sentience of the right kind or other distinctively human qualities',[16] but this seems confusing, because the footnote thus shifts from the subject of value (that for whom something has value) to the object of value (that which is valued). A reference is given in the text for the concept of 'normative individualism', and it is to a monograph[17] on John Rawl's *Theory of Justice*[18] where 'moral individualism' is ascribed to Rawls as the plausible view that the good that is a socio-political arrangement is to be judged according to the good it is *for* individuals. In an instructive discussion, this 'doctrine' of moral individualism is distinguished from three other versions of individualism about the good.

The first 'doctrine' that they reject as distinct from the 'good for individuals' doctrine of normative individualism is the 'good by individuals' doctrine, as the

[15] List and Pettit (n 8) 182.

[16] ibid 85.

[17] C Kukathas and P Pettit, *Rawls: A Theory of Justice and its Critics* (Cambridge and Stanford, Polity Press and Stanford University Press, 1990).

[18] J Rawls, *A Theory of Justice* (Cambridge MA, Harvard University Press, 1971).

authors call it, a view according to which the good is to be understood according to the individuals' own conception thereof (rejecting this view leaves room for the possibility that individuals might not recognise what is good for them). Second, the authors distinguish the 'good for individuals' doctrine from what they describe as the 'good of individuals' doctrine, which is best explained in the authors' own words:

> The *of* doctrine decrees that the only goods in virtue of which a state can be praised are items that belong to individual people: items like their liberty, their happiness, their equality. It rules out the approval of a socio-political arrangement for the production of goods which, though they affect people, belong in the first place to aggregate-level entities. Examples of such aggregate goods might be the solidarity of a community, the continuity of a culture, or the harmony of relations between racial groups.[19]

'Aggregate goods' – the term introduced here – need not be disregarded by moral individualists of the advertised doctrine. And even more decidedly, the 'good for' doctrine is distinguished from the 'good in individuals'-doctrine, according to which 'proper' good takes into account only what individuals can 'have for themselves', in separation from each other.[20]

In this normative discussion, it is easy to recognise a distinction that Pettit contributed to social ontology in work published shortly after the Rawls book. This discussion pre-empts, one might think, the influential distinction between the atomism-holism controversy on the one hand, and the individualism-collectivism controversy on the other hand, as presented by Pettit in his *Common Mind*.[21] The individualism vs collectivism issue is basically over whether or not social facts (or collective entities) compromise the picture of intentional agency (the collectivist view for which Durkheim is taken to be the paradigm gives a positive answer). The atomism vs holism issue is over whether or not agential capacities can be understood as being non-causally dependent on social relations (Hobbes, with his assumption of pre-socially constituted individual agents. serves as the paradigm for the atomistic view here). Pettit argues that these two controversies are independent of each other, leading to a 2 × 2 matrix of potential positions (with Pettit arguing for the combination of individualism and holism, and against both atomism and collectivism).

Certainly, one should not forget that the descriptive issues surrounding individualism (or atomism) are not exactly the same as the normative question,[22] but as Kukathas' and Pettit's discussion shows, any normative position depends, in what it is understood to be, on a view of what it is, descriptively, that it is

[19] Kukathas and Pettit (n 17) 15.
[20] ibid 11–16.
[21] P Pettit, *The Common Mind: An Essay on Psychology, Society and Politics* (New York, Oxford University Press, 1993) P 2.
[22] S Lukes, *Individualism* (New York, Harper & Row Publishers, 1973).

about. In particular, the point made that focusing on the good *for* people does not commit to limiting one's view of what's good in, by, or of people is congenial to the view that people are who they are not just in, by, and of themselves. As Pettit himself puts it in a much later paper that looks back on the issues, a commitment to individualism and holism, in terms of a position in social ontology, has normative 'corresponding implications': individualism commits to prioritising the interests of individuals, and holism commits to including the good that comes from social relations.[23]

The discussion of associations in the previous section, with its emphasis on plural action, however, casts doubt on the attempt to capture the good of association as merely an 'aggregate good', with the producers thereof understood as 'aggregate entities'. It is not obvious, to say the least, that the concept of an aggregate good captures the distinction between what is produced as a non-intended consequence of a complex individual action (such as a market equilibrium), and a feature of intentionally acting together (such as, arguably, a convention – unless one thinks that a conventional equilibrium account thereof works, and that a joint action account thereof is unnecessary).

Focussing on association (and the good thereof) thus nourishes the suspicion that there might be something important missing in the influential 2 × 2 matrix of the distinction between atomism and holism and the distinction between individualism and collectivism, and it concerns a form of 'sociality' that is not just a precondition of individuality (that the holist view holds), but sociality of the *active* kind: the joint pursuit of living together.

To conform to Kukathas' and Pettit's labelling method of 'doctrines', we should perhaps identify as separate from the other 'doctrines', and as mistaken, the 'good out of individuals' view. It is the view that the good that is anybody's acting well (admittedly, a rather Aristotelian conception of the good) is realised only in the actions of single individuals. Normative or moral individualism, if it is to be a plausible position, should be compatible with the contrary view, that is, the view that part of the good that is in acting well is realised in plural action, in activities that jointly involve several individuals as agents (just the sort of activity that is associational life, if we disregard associations of the 'tertiary' kind, that are basically corporations with little contact to their 'members').

The ontological correspondent to this normative issue is the distinction between singularism and pluralism, that is, between the view that any action has *one* agent, and the view that there are plural actions, too – that is, token actions with a plurality of agents. This issue is, as it seems, independent of both the atomism/holism and individualism/collectivism issues: one need not *necessarily* be committed to any view concerning whether or not human agential capacities

[23] P Pettit, 'Three Issues in Social Ontology' in J Zahle and F Collins (eds), *Rethinking the Individualism-Holism Debate. Essays in the Philosophy of Social Science* (Cham, Springer, 2014).

non-causally depend on social relations or concerning whether or not social-structural regularities override intentional regularities to choose one's position in the singularism versus pluralism controversy.

Pettit calls the controversy between atomists and holists the 'horizontal issue', and the controversy between collectivists and individualists the 'vertical issue'.[24] In his important 2014 paper on *Three issues in Social Ontology*, Pettit – based on his and Christian List's recent work on group agency – does indeed add a third issue to this – the *depth issue*, one might think, although Pettit does not use this obvious way to place it as a third dimension in the geometry of his previous two ontological distinctions. Pettit labels it the controversy over singularism and anti-singularism. Singularism is the view that only agents of the kind, some of which are 'natural persons' ('individuals', one might be tempted to call them), can instantiate agency; anti-singularism is the view that groups can instantiate agency, too. Based on his previous work, Pettit, of course, argues for the 'anti-singularist' view.

Why, one may ask, resort to the label 'anti-singularism' rather than choosing the natural antonym 'pluralism'? After all, the other controversies are not over 'individualism' versus 'anti-individualism' and 'atomism' versus 'anti-atomism' either – Pettit has no issue with choosing the proper antonym there. Whence does the reservation against pluralism come from?

The straightforward answer is, I submit, this: Pettit's position, his group agency view, is *not pluralist*. He does not conceive of the agencies that meet his criteria for group agents as plural, but rather as collectively singular – an often-made mistake in the history of thought – the misconception of 'us' as a collective 'me'. As to the issue of how agency might be realised cooperatively, he follows down the Platonic line rather than heeding Aristotle's sage advice. Plato famously argued (throughout the *Republic*)[25] that for the city to be a proper agent, it needs to have the same form of unity as the properly active soul – to which Aristotle objected (most convincingly, I tend to think) in the *Politics* that this misconceives of the city, which is a unity of *many* rather than just one.[26] In the depth-issue, List and Pettit's position thus seems thoroughly singularist.[27] The groups which they discuss as agents are singular agents (they instantiate agency in the same way as individual persons), and from a pluralist perspective, they thus mistake the plural for a collective singular.

Thinking about the value of the right to freedom of association invites a pluralist view. Freedom of association is insufficiently conceived of as a right that attaches to associations, as corporate agents, qua collective right, and that attaches to individuals as an individual right. Freedom of association undercuts the view that wherever there is action, it needs to be a singular agent's (individual

[24] Pettit (n 21) 111.
[25] Plato, *The Republic* (Cambridge, Cambridge University Press, 2000).
[26] Aristotle, *The Politics* (Chicago, University of Chicago Press, 1984).
[27] List and Pettit (n 8).

or collective). It is the freedom to action that is many agents', and perhaps this is (part of) its specific value.

To return to the normative issue: the good of associations, thus conceived, might be inadequately captured by normative individualism in (List's and) Pettit's sense. The good of a particular association may indeed be the 'good for' its individual members, in Pettit's sense, and this is certainly the case if it is the *purpose* of the association, and if it is successful in its purpose. But many associations are not about promoting what is 'good for' their members but about what is good for other people, or about the common good, or about values that may not easily be reducible to what's 'good for' anybody in particular or indeed everybody, such as the pursuit of knowledge, or ecocentric concerns, or transcendent religious belief. As a socio-political arrangement, the right to freedom of association may be about the protection of the 'good out of' pluralities rather than just the 'good out of' singular activities, about the protection of the 'pursuit of the good' (happiness, or whatever else it might be after) that is done *together* rather than just alone.

The suggestion is that social ontology might learn from thinking about the right to freedom of association. It invites us to reconceive of Pettit's 'singularism/anti-singularism issue' as the singularism-pluralism issue that it really is.

This has normative ramifications in thinking about the good, as an important part of the good that is associational life is inadequately captured as a good 'for' individuals; it involves individuals not just as *beneficiaries*, but as *sources* of the good, but it involves them *plurally*, or together, rather than severally. This is an issue that Pettit has sadly missed in his turn towards group agency, which remains thoroughly singularist in what we might call the 'depth' issue in social ontology.

From the earliest pre-history of the label in the nineteenth century, 'social ontology' tended to come with political commitments (of a wide range of orientations).[28] It seems that this history continues with Pettit. Towards the end of his seminal *Common Mind*, Pettit observes that how we view the make-up of the 'social world' is 'bound to have an impact on the way we see political values'.[29] His anti-atomist anti-collectivism, he argues further, is related in this way to republicanism as a normative view. Pettit's book on *Republicanism* picks up on this, and it centrally involves a theory of freedom as non-domination, that one might perhaps legitimately call *republican* rather than democratic in that it features public *contestability* of government action rather than government by popular consent.[30] The ideal of freedom around which this thinking revolves is of none of us being *subordinated* to anybody else, every one of us being able

[28] HB Schmid, ''Social Ontology'-Pre-Histories of a Label' in S Collins, B Epstein, S Haslanger and HB Schmid (eds), The *Oxford Handbook of Social Ontology* (New York, Oxford University Press, forthcoming).

[29] Pettit (n 21) 285.

[30] P Pettit, *Republicanism. A Theory of Freedom and Government* (New York, Oxford University Press, 1997).

to look anybody else in the eye without having to resort to 'fawn or toady or flatter'.[31] The concern is with the relation between agents – it is not, however, so much with our potential to act bottom-up together. Joint agency involves an additional dimension of freedom: a freedom that we *share*.

With his republican conception of freedom, Pettit is heavily invested in political agendas, as is manifested by his special relation to the Spanish socialist Prime Minister José Luis Zapatero.[32] Pettit has established himself as a thinker of considerable political influence on social democracy at a time of vacuum after the 'third way' phase in the last decade of the twentieth century.

Some of Pettit's remarks seem to suggest that the order of inspiration goes from social ontology to politics – perhaps the order might appear to be reversed in hindsight. In their 1990 book, Kukathas and Pettit say of John Rawls' *Theory of Justice* that it is 'more than the reconstruction of political prejudice' because it relies on consideration and on a back and forth between principles and particular judgments,[33] and this is certainly true of Pettit's venture, too. If I am right, Pettit's later concerns with issues concerning joint action could (or should?) perhaps have had the potential – if developed – to give his thinking about sociality a more decidedly democratic direction by taking a *pluralist* stance rather than just extending singularism to the collective level.

Considering the question of how the right to freedom of association attaches to agency supports a decidedly pluralist view – a view that does not subscribe to the doctrine that the only practical source of the good is singular activity. It involves a conception of freedom that goes beyond non-domination; it is freedom that is shared. The value protected by the right to freedom of association is the good that comes out of the source of acting together.

III. APPLICATION TO THE PROBLEM OF LEGAL RECOGNITION

How does pluralism in social ontology, along the lines developed in this chapter, matter for legal issues surrounding the right to freedom of association? Let us see whether (and perhaps how) this applies to the scenarios of legal dispute that the editors of this volume have proposed for the contributors to consider (see Introduction).

I have suggested that the fundamental ontology of associations is plural action, rather than formal organisation, constitution, or incorporation as a 'group agent'. This may make a difference concerning the question of registration as it comes up in one of the moot scenarios proposed by the editors.[34]

[31] Pettit (n 21) 5.

[32] JL Martí and P Pettit, *A Political Philosophy in Public Life. Civic Republicanism in Zapatero's Spain* (Princeton, Princeton University Press, 2010).

[33] Kukathas and Pettit (n 17) 7.

[34] M Cahill, 'Introduction: Comparative and Interdisciplinary Interfaces of Associational Life and Freedom' in M Cahill and G Lasagni (eds), *Associational Life and Freedom: Insights from Philosophy and Law* (Oxford, Hart Publishing, 2026), 15–16.

This seems obviously relevant to the type of legal dispute, such as that captured by the 'soup kitchen' moot scenario presented at the beginning of this volume.[35] The case is a number of friends and family running a non-profit soup kitchen together. They are faced with the accusation of not complying with the Charities Act by failing to register. Against mandatory registration, they invoke the right to freedom of association.

The reasons for the soup kitchen's resistance against registration (as mentioned in the moot scenario) are, first, that registration (and the organisational structure that it imposes) is costly (the case description suggests that they might have to pay for a bookkeeper once they open a bank account) – money that would then have to be diverted from the charitable work. A second (and perhaps even more weighty) reason is that the soup kitchen people understand what they are doing as a joint activity of friends who offer their service to people they know personally as their guests; they feel that formal organisation (or incorporation), as demanded by registration, would make what they are doing somewhat 'impersonal' (a charity providing services to customers).

From a plural action view as suggested in this chapter, the soup kitchen people's argument receives much sympathy and support. Being the plural agency that they are, they do not want to turn what they, together, are doing (and how they, together, thereby relate to their guests) into something else. They do not want to turn it into something 'the association', as a corporate agency, is doing. They do not want to establish, among themselves, a supervenient collective group agent entity to which they then basically relate third-personally ('the association', 'the charity') rather than just being who they are in acting together ('we, together').

The philosophically relevant point here is that a joint activity changes its nature once it is incorporated as group agency – a fact to which much of conventional social ontology seems rather blind, but which seems rather obvious from a plural action perspective.

The scenario has the soup kitchen run as informally organised in some way, with established roles, but they may not wish to establish formal decision procedures or officer roles (such as 'the treasurer', etc), as they may be demanded by their national association laws. In a more radical version of the case than the one assumed in the description, they may even want to keep things in flux rather than settle on one established division of roles. And all of this may not only be because of how they themselves see what they are doing – it may also be that this is not how they want their joint effort to relate to the people they serve. They may want to relate *directly* and *personally* to their soup kitchen's guests rather than having a corporate third party ('the association') mediate between them, as would happen if the guests became the association's clients, and the soup kitchen members the association's role bearers.

[35] Cahill (n 34) 15–16.

A plural action ontology may thus be taken to support the line of argument of the soup kitchen volunteers in this case. It is, from this perspective, good news that, according to the narrative in the case description, they won in court.

And yet, even from the armchair of a social ontologist who recognises plural action as fundamental, it is not difficult to fathom potential reasons for legal impositions of registration on joint activities of certain kinds. By requiring people who are jointly engaged in charity work on a regular basis to register as a charity, the law aims at making sure that what's going on is indeed charity work – to protect the donor's and stakeholder's interest, to protect the public interest by making sure that tax-exemption is indeed deserved, and to prevent fraud and misuse of funds, which serves to promote public trust in the entire charity sector. It is comprehensible, from a legal perspective, that joint action, if it is happening at some scale and with some regularity, not only be charitable, but *accountably* so. This requires self-organisation of the sort that requires the plural activity to incorporate and register; it is not enough for the participants to actually solve their task through shifting and more or less spontaneous divisions of work, as this can easily lead to a lack of transparency and knowledge of who is doing what exactly in the joint action, which may already become problematic for any joint venture, in and by itself; they also need to be solving it in a way in which the government knows whom to ask about what when it comes to core functions. In order to fulfil these demands, plural agency needs to be constituted at an organisational level.

From this perspective, the case at hand is thus expressive of a general feature of acting together; it is not in virtue of 'constitution' or incorporation that people act together, but in order to know properly what it is they are doing and how – in order to act *accountably* together – constitution and incorporation come into play.[36] And yet, constitution and incorporation do change the nature of what is being done and how, and here, the soup kitchen activist's complaint is relevant.

As a general matter, this issue is characteristic of living together. In the specific case at hand, this is perhaps best seen as a case of balancing of interest or proportionality assessment. Here is an armchair philosopher's recommendation to lawmakers, administrators, and judges: leave plural activities such as the soup kitchen people alone; people such as these know well enough what it is they are doing together and how, even without the sort of formalisation that comes with registration. But do require formal registration, incorporation, and organisation of larger-scale associations, where the issue of accountability becomes more pressing.

[36] Schmid (n 7).

16

The Nature, Ground, and Legal Expression of a Right to Freedom of Association

KIRK LUDWIG*

> … from this liberty of each individual, follows the … freedom to unite, for any purpose not involving harm to others: the persons combining being supposed to be of full age, and not forced or deceived.
>
> John Stuart Mill, *On Liberty*, Chapter 1.

I. INTRODUCTION

What is a right to freedom of association? In asking this, I am not asking what the various *legally* codified rights regarding freedom of association are in one or another jurisdiction or what they may have in common. My project is not descriptive. That is, it is not an investigation into extant legal practices.[1] I intend to be asking a more general, extra-legal question. I am interested, specifically, in connection with thinking about freedom of association as a fundamental human value, in the grounding and logical form of a *moral* right to freedom of association. I take the content of the moral right to freedom of association to have some bearing on how we should think about

* My thinking on this topic has been aided by participation in the interdisciplinary workshop *Exploring Associational Life: From Social Ontology to Law and Back Again* at University College Cork, Ireland, 25–26 April 2024, and the online Symposium held on 30 January 2025, organised as part of the *Societās: Exploring the Value of Freedom of Association* project, directed by Professor Maria Cahill at the School of Law, University College Cork, and funded by the Irish Research Council (now Research Ireland) under grant IRCLA/2022/3860.

[1] This contribution takes a step back from questions about how a legal right to freedom of association is implemented in various legal jurisdictions to consider the more abstract question of freedom of association as a fundamental human value, and then what guidance that may provide in thinking about how to construct a legal right to freedom of association.

designing a legal right to freedom of association – though, as I will argue, it is not entirely straightforward how to work out its implications. My method will be analytical. What are the elements that go into the concept of freedom of association? How do they interact? What is the source of the moral value of freedom of association? In accordance with this, I structure the investigation around three more specific interconnected questions.

(1) What do we mean by *freedom* in this context? What is its structure and limits?
(2) What kinds of association do we have in mind?
(3) What can ground a moral right to freedom of association?

I will sketch a foundational theory of a moral right to freedom of association by way of preliminary answers to these three questions. I do so from the field-specific standpoint of the theory of collective and institutional agency. By collective agency I mean any instance of our doing things together, especially our doing things together intentionally. By institutional agency, I mean any instance of our doing things together when we act in institutional or organisational roles. Each of these has a role to play in the following. The overarching goal is to provide a structural and normative account of a moral right to freedom of association and to explore some of the complexities in its application to the conditions of legality.[2]

II. THE LOGICAL FORM OF A RIGHT TO FREEDOM OF ASSOCIATION

An association implies at least two individuals interacting with each other (see the Introduction to this book for further discussion).[3] A right to freedom of association, then, constitutively involves reference to others. It has a negative and a positive component. It is a right not to associate with others if one so chooses (negative) and a right to associate with others (certain conditions being met) if one chooses to (positive). Each is necessary for the other. The negative component of the right can be exercised individually. However, the positive right to freedom of association can only be exercised in and by an ensemble of individual agents. By an ensemble I mean a collection or group of agents, whether or not they share any purpose or are engaged in any joint activities or interacting with one another, but who nonetheless have the potential to do so. An association, in contrast, implies a shared purpose among those involved. So 'ensemble' picks out a group that may form an association without implying that it has. While the right to freedom of association is a right

[2] I borrow this phrase from S Shapiro, *Legality* (Cambridge MA, Harvard University Press, 2011).
[3] M Cahill, 'Introduction: Comparative and Interdisciplinary Interfaces of Associational Life and Freedom' in M Cahill and G Lasagni (eds), *Associational Life and Freedom: Insights from Philosophy and Law* (Oxford, Hart Publishing, 2026), 1.

of an individual, rather than of a group, the other agents with whom one may wish to associate have the same right, including the right not to associate with others if they so choose. A consequence is that for any member of an ensemble to exercise their positive right to associate with others, the others must correspondingly exercise their positive rights to associate with everyone else in the ensemble. Thus, the positive right to freedom of association is exercised *by* individuals but only if and when the others with whom they would associate likewise exercise their rights to associate with the others. More precisely, let G be an ensemble of agents, and let G/x be the group consisting of all and only members of G except for x. Then:

> For any group G, for any member x of G, x can exercise a right to associate with the members of G/x
>
> if and only if
>
> for every y in G $\neq$ x, y exercises y's right to associate with the members of G/y.

This generates a network of the mutual exercise of individual rights binding each of the members to each of the others. This is illustrated in Figure 16.1 for an ensemble of six.

Figure 16.1 Each arrow represents an expression of willingness on the part of one to associate with the other conditional on their willingness to associate with her. When the entire structure is in place, they jointly exercise their rights to associate with one another

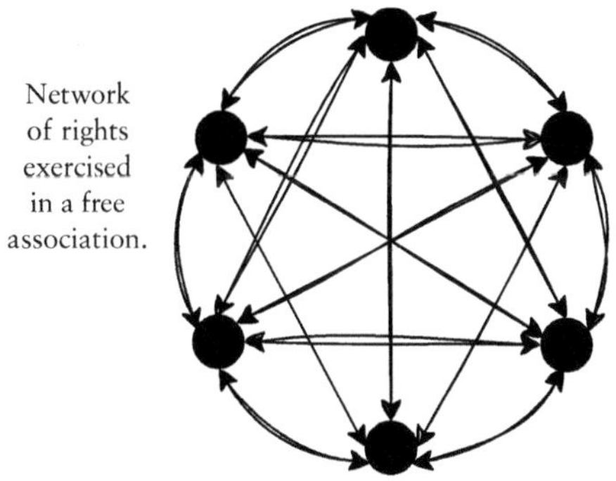

I will call a right with this structure an *ensemble right*. This is not the same as a group right because a group right is held by the group as such. While *we* have a right to associate with one another if we want to, the right is distributed over members of the group. Since an individual's proper exercise of the positive component of an ensemble right requires the reciprocal exercise of the right by all members of the ensemble, the positive right to freedom of association is a conditional right. It is a right to associate with others conditional on their (all each individually) freely choosing to do so. A corollary is that the exercise of an ensemble right requires transparency in the sense that the members of the ensemble must be in a position to be reasonably assured that the other members of the ensemble willingly enter into the association. In contrast, the negative right, absent other moral constraints (such as promissory duties), is an unconditional right. It does not depend on whether or not others wish or do not wish to associate with you.

III. ASSOCIATING AND ASSOCIATIONS

The *content* of a moral right to freedom of association depends on what we understand by 'association'. The word 'association' is used in several related senses. It can mean the *act* of associating or a *result* of associating, namely, *an* association. Associating as an act is conceptually basic. A right to associate with others for various purposes is prior to the right to form associations. Associating with one or more others implies a shared purpose. Associating with others for a shared purpose entails a commitment on the part of each participant to their engaging in a shared intentional activity for promoting the purpose together. The purpose may be transitory (a pickup basketball game, a conversation while waiting for a train) or longer term (a friendship, a marriage, a club or political party).

While not every act of associating with others for a shared purpose (like a casual conversation) is an association, a right to associate implies a right to participate in associations. An association must have some stability and involve recurrent jointly intentional activities or the shared intention to engage in recurrent activities for some shared purpose. A shared intention is constituted by the participatory intentions of the members of a group directed toward their doing things together. I will call these participatory intentions, which are individual intentions, 'we-intentions'. On the account of we-intentions I favour, for each of us to we-intend that we move a bench (and so for us to share an intention) is for each of us to intend to make a contribution to there being a collective action plan in accordance with which we move the bench.[4] For example, I lift the left side and you lift the right side

[4] K Ludwig, 'Collective Intentional Behavior from the Standpoint of Semantics' (2007) 41 *Nous* 355; K Ludwig, *From Individual to Plural Agency: Collective Action 1* (Oxford, Oxford University Press, 2016). Other accounts include M Bratman, *Faces of Intention: Selected Essays on Intention and Agency* (Cambridge, Cambridge University Press, 1999) C 8; M Bratman, *Shared Agency: A Planning Theory of Acting Together* (Oxford, Oxford University Press, 2014); R Tuomela, 'We-Intentions Revisited' (2005) 125 *Philosophical Studies* 327; R Tuomela, *Social Ontology: Collective Intentionality and Group Agents* (Oxford, Oxford University Press, 2013); M Gilbert, 'Walking Together: A Paradigmatic Social Phenomenon' (1990) 15 *Midwest Studies in Philosophy* 1; M Gilbert, *A Theory of Political Obligation* (Oxford, Clarendon Press, 2006); R Tuomela and K Miller, 'We-Intentions' (1988) 53 *Philosophical Studies* 367. For an overview, *cf* Ludwig, *From Individual to Plural Agency*, C 16. Differences in detail won't be relevant to the points I wish to make, excepting Gilbert, for whom joint action constitutively involves sui generis directed

at the same time, and we each then move in the direction of the foyer, etc. I call this the shared plan account of we-intending. A shared intention may be generalised. We may intend to meet in the library every Friday evening to play chess. In this case, the members of the group have generalised we-intentions: each intends to contribute to there being a plan in accordance with which we meet in the library every Friday night. An association is underwritten by a generalised shared intention of its members to engage with other members on appropriate occasions in the kinds of activities that forward the association's purposes. These are implemented in more detailed plans on particular occasions.

Associations may be informal or formal. Informal associations are part of the fabric of everyday life. A group of friends who get together regularly are an informal association whose purpose is companionship, emotional support, a sense of belonging, the enjoyment of one another's company, and so on. The shared purpose need not be stated explicitly, and the goals and purposes of the informal association may change over time. Formal associations are distinguished from informal associations not just by having a division of labour, but by virtue of the assignment of status roles to members of the group. A status role is a function assigned to an agent in social interactions defined in terms of how the agent in the role interacts with others in virtue of their status roles.[5] Hence, status roles are defined in terms of their position in a network of status roles. Examples are being a president, treasurer, university professor, student, policeman, judge, citizen, employee, club member, and so on. A status role is a special type of status function, like being a ten-dollar bill, or the black queen in chess.[6] Something can function as a ten-dollar bill in an economic transaction only if those party to it collectively accept it for that role. In practice, this is expressed in our we-intentions being directed at the same things for the same roles. Thus, collective acceptance is constituted by the appropriate coordination of our we-intentions on items for the roles defined by the activity type we wish to engage in. On a train trip we may press bottle caps and a checkered tablecloth into service as chess pieces and a board. As long as our we-intentions coordinate on the same things for the roles of the various pieces, they can play those roles; otherwise not.

A status role is a status function assigned to an agent in which the agent is expected to express her agency in fulfilling its function. These can include command roles, compliance roles, decision-making roles, and so on. For example, a private in an army has a compliance role. His role is defined in part by the role-based duty to obey lawful orders issued by those of higher rank in his

obligations on the part of members of a group acting together to other members of the group to do their parts. *cf* Bratman, *Faces of Intention*, C 7; Ludwig, *From Individual to Plural Agency*, C 16.5 for responses.

[5] K Ludwig, *From Plural to Institutional Agency: Collective Action 2* (Oxford, Oxford University Press, 2017) C 10.

[6] J Searle, *The Construction of Social Reality* (New York, Free Press, 1995); Ludwig (n 5) C 8–9.

chain of command. A sergeant occupies a command role with respect to the private and a compliance role with respect to a first lieutenant. The club treasurer is responsible for collecting and depositing dues, signing cheques, managing the books, and so on. All institutions in the organisational sense are groups of agents realising a network of interdefined status roles designed for the purpose of carrying out collective action. All formal associations are institutions in this sense. Formal associations, as defined, need not have a legal status, but *any organisation that has a legal status will be a formal association*. Some features of formal associations are important to how they interface with a general moral right to freedom of association. In particular, three hallmarks of formal associations are:

(1) Their roles have entry and exit conditions. Meeting the entry conditions, someone has the role until the exit conditions are satisfied. Although it is presumed that the person occupying the role is party to the collective acceptance by which he has it, provisions are typically in place for what to do if he does not adhere to the requirements.
(2) In virtue of this, roles are time-indexed; that is, an agent can have the role at one time but not at another.
(3) Thus, they can be potentially occupied successively by different agents, and the number of roles may both expand and contract over time. This is how organisations (understood as realised patterns of status roles) can persist through changes in membership and what gives rise to the possibility of perpetual existence. This, together with the formal division of labour, gives organisations their power.

Given that the positive right to associate with others cannot be exercised individually but only in concert with others, it is not per se a restriction of the right to freedom of association that a formal association has membership conditions that not everyone meets.

Formal associations raise a prima facie difficulty for the requirement of reciprocal exercise of positive rights of association. Someone voluntarily joins a large-scale formal association by meeting the entry conditions, for example, paying dues for a club membership, or accepting an offer of employment at a university. But in large organisations this is typically done without most members of the organisation knowing it. How is the requirement that the other members exercise their right to associate with the new member satisfied? It is satisfied because when they joined the organisation, they also accepted the conditions for membership. Thus, they are committed to accepting as a member anyone now or in the future who meets the appropriate entry conditions. Thus, when a new member joins, they meet the condition the others have already accepted as appropriate for associating with them, and the new member accepts all those who have already satisfied the membership conditions.

IV. THE MORAL RIGHT TO FREEDOM OF ASSOCIATION

We can ground a moral right to freedom of association on two considerations.[7] The first lies in the fact that acting with others in pursuit of shared purposes is a fundamental value for social beings, for it is only in the context of joint intentional activities that we can express what most fundamentally defines the kinds of beings we are. This is not to say that just any form of joint intentional action answers to our most fundamental needs for social interaction, but that only social interaction meets those needs. It is only in finding our place in a social world that we can reach full self-realisation. The second is a general duty to respect the autonomy of other agents, constrained only by the requirement that the exercise of that autonomy be consonant with the exercise by others of a comparable degree of autonomy and that it otherwise not be in conflict with the requirements of morality. Autonomy is a central value in the Kantian tradition.[8] It is also given a central role by Mill in his utilitarian liberalism, 'one of the elements of well-being'.[9] Autonomy, as I understand it, is the ability to govern oneself in accordance with one's own goals, values, and interests[10] rather than being manipulated, guided, or governed by forces or constraints external to the self or by psychological compulsions or addictions that are not reflective of one's basic values and interests.[11] Autonomy is expressed in both thought and action. It is expressed in thought in thinking for oneself. It is expressed in action through choosing for oneself what to do, especially in connection with life-shaping projects. Autonomy is expressed both in choosing what to do and in what not to do. Autonomy is a fundamental value for self-conscious agents capable of thinking of themselves as the authors of their own lives. Part of what gives a human life the value it has for its protagonist is that from among the range of recognisably human goods and excellences, which cannot all be realised in any one individual, the ones

[7] One argument for a legal right to freedom of association goes through a moral right to freedom of association. There are other grounds as well, namely, that it is required as a precondition for the proper maintenance of a liberal democracy, which must presuppose certain civic virtues of its citizens which are cultivated through associational life. In addition, freedom of association is essential for the voices of multiple persons to be properly heard in the public sphere, for it is typically only by collectivising their voices and speaking as a group that their views can effectively enter public debate. My concern, however, is to identify a fundamental moral ground for a legal right to freedom of association.

[8] I Kant, *Groundwork for the Metaphysics of Morals* (New Haven, Yale University Press, 2018).

[9] JS Mill, *On Liberty* (London, J. W. Parker and Son, 1859).

[10] A common view is that one's own values, desires, and interests are those that one would reflectively endorse. This traces back to HG Frankfurt, 'Freedom of the Will and the Concept of a Person' (1971) 68 *Journal of Philosophy* 5. For present purposes it is not necessary to take a position on what makes desires, interests, and values one's own.

[11] G Dworkin, *The Theory and Practice of Autonomy* (Cambridge, Cambridge University Press, 1988).

realised in a life are chosen by the agent whose life it is; that is, the life is one authored by the one who lives it.[12]

Kant's Formula of Humanity enjoins us to 'So act that you treat humanity, whether in your own person or in the person of any other, always at the same time as an end, never merely as a means.'[13] Having identified engagement with social life and autonomy as two fundamental values for the kind of agents we are, it follows that treating others as ends in themselves requires minimally not restricting the expression of their autonomy in their decisions about what social arrangements they enter into, provided those decisions are compatible with the simultaneous exercise by others of their autonomy and not otherwise in conflict with the moral law. This grounds a duty of non-interference when there are no countervailing moral considerations and, correspondingly, a right to choose what social arrangements one enters into. The right is unrestricted except by the requirement of consistency with the moral law. This subsumes all forms of association – transitory, private, public, stable, informal and formal. As we observed above, when autonomy is expressed positively in the choice of who to associate with, given that it must be consistent with everyone else's right to make their own choices, it can only be expressed appropriately as a member of an ensemble of agents exercising their positive right to associate with the others.

The qualification about giving equal status to the autonomous choices of others and the moral law generally is important. Autonomy is not an absolute value. There can be considerations in favour of an abridgement of autonomy. These can go beyond mere consistency with others exercising their autonomy freely. The proper exercise of autonomy presupposes competence in identifying one's own most important values, determining means to ends, and executing decisions effectively. We restrict the autonomy of children not because it is not a value for children but because they are still forming their values and outlook on life, and their emotional, moral, and cognitive abilities are still under development. Similarly, we do not let someone suffering from dementia choose to cross the road when there is heavy traffic. And even when competence is not in question, in particular cases intervention may be appropriate because of the knowledge we possess which others do not that puts us in a position to see that without intervention their autonomous actions would result in significant unanticipated harm to them (or others), or the frustration of their goals, which could

[12] Authoring a life is a matter of degree and depends to some extent on the range of opportunities open to one and the extent of harms and deprivations to which one is subject, but in most any life there are many decisions that shape the kind of life it is that are made by the agent who lives that life, minimally in shaping and expressing the character of its subject and her relations to others.

[13] Kant (n 8) AK 4:429. For a discussion of the Formula of Humanity and its relation to the other formulas of the moral law in Kant *cf* A Wood, *Formulas of the Moral Law* (Cambridge, Cambridge University Press, 2017).

be achieved in some alternative way. This would be an intervention that the agent herself would recognise as in her best interest and which she would have chosen herself with the additional knowledge we possess. Nonetheless, even in cases in which someone insists on doing something which we are well justified in thinking is not optimal for her, she has a (defeasible) right to choose the less optimal path. For there is value in it being her choice, and disvalue in restricting it. And the value it derives from it being her choice, together with the disvalue attendant on not being given a free choice, can weigh more heavily than the difference in overall well-being as measured independently of whether the path was chosen by the agent.

V. FROM A MORAL TO A LEGAL RIGHT

I assume here that the law is socially constructed, and, hence, an invention.[14] On this assumption, the law is not constitutively moral: unjust laws are still laws. Consequently, legal rights and duties are not per se moral rights and duties. Even on this assumption, however, insofar as the law provides a framework for a society and for large-scale social organisation, and insofar as we have an interest in the moral law, we have an interest in shaping positivist law so that it does not violate the moral rights of those it governs. While the moral law does not dictate every aspect of the design of a legal system, it may be thought of as scaffolding within which the details for the circumstances of a particular society are worked out. In light of this, the question arises of how to implement a moral right to freedom of association in a legal system, that is, as a legal right.[15] I think we can identify two very general principles. The first is motivated by the fact that autonomy is a fundamental moral value and that social relations are a basic source of value for us. The second is motivated by the fact that autonomy is a fundamental value and by the potential for abuse of the enormous power of the state to suppress associations it disfavours.

(1) A right to freedom of association should be encoded at the level of constitutional law, that is, a part of the basic framework for a legal system.

[14] I argue for this assumption, from the standpoint of the field of social ontology and institutional agency, in K Ludwig, 'The Social Construction of Legal Norms' in M Garcia-Godinez, R Mellin and R Tuomela (eds), *Social Ontology, Normativity and Law* (Berlin, De Gruyter, 2020). See the related arguments of: Shapiro (n 2); JL Coleman, *The Practice of Principle: In Defence of a Pragmatist Approach to Legal Theory* (Oxford, Oxford University Press, 2001); C Kutz, 'The Judicial Community' (2001) 11 *Philosophical Issues* 442. The interest in assuming it here lies in showing that even so there is room for the question of how moral law should shape positive law without making it definitional of law as a human invention that is in harmony with morality.

[15] The practical issues are the same whether one adopts positivism or the natural law theory.

(2) A right to freedom of association should be presumptively unrestricted in the sense that unless there are specific and weighty countervailing considerations grounded in the moral law or in the practicalities of maintaining a stable legal system, the right to freedom of association cannot be abridged.

It is in the 'unless' clause of the second general principle that all the complexities of a legal right to freedom of association must be worked out. These complexities combine, on the one hand, the complexities of the application of general moral principles to particular circumstances and the balancing of competing moral values and, on the other, the complexities of crafting laws whose conditions of application are clear, which can be supported by a broad consensus among citizens, which are practically enforceable, and which are not liable to abuse. A legal system must be stable to fulfil its function. It must be compatible with a plurality of views about the best forms of life. It must balance the freedom of individuals against the common good. It must take account of the actual contingent historical state of society and of the fact that the social conditions it governs are non-ideal.

VI. SOURCES OF LIMITATIONS ON A LEGAL RIGHT TO FREEDOM OF ASSOCIATION

While a moral right to freedom of association is grounded in a fundamental moral right to autonomy, like the moral right to autonomy from which it derives, it is a pro tanto right. It may be overridden by other moral considerations in particular circumstances. Thus, we can expect that a legal right to freedom of association may be restricted in light of other moral and social exigencies. I consider four important kinds of limitation in this section without suggesting that these are exhaustive.

First, there may be restrictions on the formation of associations with certain purposes.

Second, there may be restrictions on the form that associations with certain purposes must take, for example, formal versus informal, and if formal, then on how they are structured given their purposes.

Third, especially in the case of formal associations of certain sorts, there may be restrictions on who may be excluded, that is, on the form of the entry conditions.

Fourth, there may be prima facie restrictions on the negative component of the right to freedom of association; that is, citizens may be required to participate in certain kinds of formal associations.

The discussion here can only touch, in a fairly abstract way, on some of the issues that arise in each case.

(1) Limitations based on purpose. An association may be legally banned or restricted on the basis of *certain* purposes. Some cases are relatively straightforward. An association whose purpose is to overthrow the state may be legally prohibited as a formal condition on the coherence of a (presumptively just) system of laws, namely, that they should be allowed to defend their own sovereignty. In addition, an association whose purposes are themselves immoral may be legitimately declared illegal, for example, criminal gangs, the mafia, a company of assassins for hire, organisations involved in human trafficking, or organisations devoted to political violence.

A more difficult case is that of creedal and expressive associations, that is, those organised around an ideology or set of beliefs (creedal) or for the purpose of expressing shared views (expressive). Many of these will be relatively innocuous, such as the Flat Earth Society, the Boy Scouts of America, many, if not all, political parties, and so on. The difficulties arise when the association's ideology is not innocuous but harmful. Take the white supremacist ideology of the KKK as an example. Racism is a disease, not of the individual, but of the social order. If it becomes too widespread, it leads to widespread discrimination and the enactment of laws that underwrite racial bias. But there are dangers and costs to banning associations based on racist or other harmful ideologies, as opposed to criminal action. First, banning them drives them underground without treating the source of the disease. Second, it puts us on a slippery slope. Where do we draw the line, and who decides what is pernicious enough to ban? For example, the Catholic Church's patriarchal structure is explicitly sexist. Why should it get special treatment? Third, a governmental power to ban associations on the basis of their ideology is a recipe for abuse. Fourth, by allowing the public expression of pernicious views, as Mill noted, we keep ourselves alive to the reasons against them and deepen our appreciation and understanding of the principles of liberty. Finally, there are alternatives that arguably treat the disease more effectively: namely: (i) openly challenging the racist ideology through education, social media, entertainment, advertisements, the news, and so on, and (ii) promulgating policies that integrate racial minorities into the economic and civic life of a nation so that their socio-economic status matches that of the general population. Even so, there is no single answer to the question of whether a creedal or expressive organisation organised around pernicious views can legitimately be banned. For it depends on the degree of risk in not doing so, which is sensitive to the actual conditions of a society and its history, and on whether there are alternatives which can effectively mitigate the risks.

(2) Restrictions on the form that associations take. There are at least two dimensions to this. The first concerns what forms associations must have given their purposes. Business laws, for example, govern how businesses are formed, operate, and are governed. The second concerns when an association is required to become formal by becoming legally registered. For the right to freedom of association extends not only to the association's purposes and members, but

also to how it is organised, that is, *how* the members choose to associate with one another. I focus on the second case here.

For specificity, consider the following case.[16] A group of friends organise informally to run an outdoor soup kitchen. They receive leftover food from local grocery shops. A local butcher shop has an account that allows people to contribute money indirectly. They provide sleeping bags and clothing when possible. They are not a registered charity, have no bank account or bookkeeper, and no formal organisation – they are an informal organisation in the sense of not realising a network of status roles. The members are friends. They want those who use the soup kitchen to feel like they have been invited to a dinner with people they know. It is important for their understanding of what they are doing that it be an informal association. Let us say that there is a law requiring charitable organisations to register. Though they have been maintaining the informal association for some years, they are now charged with violating the law. Let us say that the justification given is that all charities should be subject to the same legal standards so the public is assured they operate with financial integrity. Can there be an adequate ground for requiring them to register as a legal charity, that is, become a legal entity, open a bank account and hire a bookkeeper? My concern is not with the correct legal judgment given the actual content of the law. It is with whether there can be an adequate normative justification for the law if it requires the informal charitable association to legally register. Our second basic principle above says that their right to freedom of association, which subsumes freedom to choose its form, should be abridged only if

> there are a specific and weighty countervailing considerations grounded in the moral law or in the practicalities of maintaining a stable legal system.

The question then is what harms result from allowing informal charitable organisations of this sort. In our case, the group of friends have been running the soup kitchen without causing anyone harm for some years. If there is a ground for requiring them to register, it will have to lie in the risks of harm if associations of the same sort were generally allowed to remain unregistered. The risk of harm would have to outweigh both the good done by such associations and the costs in general of requiring every such organisation to register.

We can accept that large charitable associations which solicit donations from the public should be regulated, and, hence, required to become a legal entity, to ensure financial integrity and that the funds donated go toward the charitable purposes of the organisation. This is important for securing the public trust that all such charities rely upon. These requirements are in the interest of the associations themselves. However, the association in the present

[16] This is closely modelled on a moot scenario discussed at the *Exploring Associational Life* Workshop at University College, 25–26 April 2024. Cahill (n 3) 15–16.

case does not solicit donations from the public and does not maintain a bank account. An *individual* who shares food with those who are hungry should not be required to register as a legal entity. There is no question about a need to assure *the public* of the individual's financial integrity. No more should a small group of friends who pool resources to do the same be required to register as a legal entity merely because they work together to promote a common interest. If a local grocery shop provides an individual with leftover food to be distributed, this introduces no significant new factor, and it would not do so when it is a group of friends who work together to distribute food. Perhaps a wrinkle in the present case is that the butcher has an account so that others can contribute indirectly. But is it only the friends in the group or those closely associated with them who contribute? Are there any solicitations of the public generally for contributions? Plausibly, the key question is who contributes. If only friends and neighbours are involved, and there is no solicitation of money from the general public, then they are a private association. The public does not have an interest in whether private individuals handle *their* money with integrity. The provision for an account they contribute to should not here be a significant factor. They could alternatively put cash in a canister and use it to buy meat for the soup kitchen. The principle that can be applied in this case then is that a private charitable association need not be regulated, but that a public one may. It suffices to be a public charitable association that solicits support from the general public. In this case, the public has an interest in the financial integrity of the charitable association, as it touches their interest, and it is reasonable to require legal registration. The case then illustrates two things of interest. The first is that a dimension of the right to freedom of association is whether to engage in a formal as opposed to informal association. The second is that the distinction between a private and public association is relevant to whether it may be reasonable to require an association to become a legal entity.

(3) Restrictions on who may be excluded. Since the basic structure of the right to freedom of association requires for the proper exercise of the positive right that those with whom one associates agree to the association, the basic presumption is in favour of a group excluding anyone who they do not want to join. For informal associations in the private realm, there should be no abridgements of this right of exclusion. For formal associations which are in the public realm, there is a presumption in favour of a right of exclusion, especially when it is tied to the association's character and purposes. For example, a church may require members to be adherents to its creed. Creedal and expressive associations should in general be protected from having to accept anyone who does not accept their core doctrines. To abridge this right would be tantamount to banning such associations, for they cannot fulfil their purposes without the restriction.

What would count as a consideration weighty enough to overrule a formal association's conditions on membership when they are not integral to its character and purpose? A state formed for the good of its citizenry will treat each of them as having an equal stake in the goods of society. I will assume that this minimally requires affording them equal access to those goods. If the way public associations regulate their membership undermines access to the goods of society for some subset of citizens on the basis of a salient common property, such as sex or race, then the state has an interest in regulating their membership. There are two subcases to consider.

The first is explicit discrimination. If a grocery co-op offers any member of the public the option to buy shares, except for Blacks, it has an explicitly discriminatory membership policy. Any rule that if universalised would undermine access to public goods for any portion of the public on the basis of some non-morally relevant feature of them would violate the obligation of the state to provide citizens with equal access to the goods of society. This provides a ground for prohibiting restrictions on membership in public associations on the basis of sex, race, religion or any other common feature irrelevant to the character and purposes of the association.

The second case is one in which the membership condition itself is neutral with respect to, for example, race or sex, but the association still intentionally discriminates. Let's consider a particular, somewhat tricky, case.[17] A golf club of long standing is formed initially by a group of businessmen in part for informal networking. It has been highly successful. The club requires that new members be nominated by current members. There is no rule against nominating a woman. Thus, it is open formally to any businessperson, and it counts as a public association. But in fact the members of the club do not want women to join, and the formal conditions of membership provide an effective means of remaining a male-only club. A local businesswoman who is an avid golfer wishes to build her business connections by joining the club. There are other places to golf close by, and she is a member of another golf club, but it does not provide the same opportunities for business networking.

Is it a violation of *her moral right to freedom of association* not to be able to participate in the male-only golfing club? The answer is a straightforward 'no'. Exercising the positive right to freedom of association presupposes that those with whom one associates exercise the positive rights reciprocally (section II). The right question to ask is whether the state has an interest in restricting the pro tanto right of the members of the male-only golf club to intentionally exclude members on the basis of sex.[18] More specifically, the question is whether there

[17] This case is also modelled on a moot scenario discussed at the Exploring Associational Life Workshop at University College, 25–26 April 2024. Cahill (n 3) 16–17.

[18] Suppose that they accede to the requirement to admit women but only because of a legal order to do so. Does it follow that the conditions for the local businesswoman to exercise her right to join them are not met because they are not willing to associate with her? For example,

are weighty considerations in favour of abridging that right in this case. First, does the exclusion of businesswomen from membership undermine their access to public goods on the basis of features irrelevant to the purpose of the club? Second, does it matter that the exclusion is not written into the entry conditions?

Suppose that the club explicitly required that members be male. Then it would formally discriminate on the basis of sex when that is not integral to the kind of club it is. If this is permitted, then we must permit it potentially by every professional organisation whose membership is de facto male. Suppose most businessmen are in fact male. Since networking is an important resource for businessmen and women, allowing professional organisations formally to exclude businesspeople on the basis of being female would permit a significant restriction on the access to a resource on the basis of sex. Thus, it would be disallowed. Keeping everything else fixed, is it relevant whether the formal conditions of membership allow women to join but club members conspire to exclude women? In the case in which the formal conditions exclude women, the conditions are in place as a result of the members sharing an intention to exclude women. In the second case, the members also share the intention to exclude women. The only difference is that it is not expressed as a formal condition on membership. There is no moral distinction between the cases. The intention and the effect are the same. Whether the means involves a formal membership condition that explicitly excludes women is not relevant to why it is wrong. Therefore, it is not just when the formal conditions exclude women that the state has an interest in restricting the exclusion of women from membership in organisations that afford professional benefits to them.

Consider now a case in which a group of women organise a golf club that is *formally* restricted to women. This would not violate the right of local businessmen to join because that right is conditional on the willingness of the others to associate with them. But can the women-only club members' right to exclude men be restricted on the same grounds as I argued the right of the male-only golf club to admit only men could be restricted? First, it may make a difference what the purpose of the association is. If it is to provide a space for networking for women in particular against the backdrop of a

when someone is coerced into a marriage, their right to freedom of association is violated, and the conditions for the other party to the marriage to exercise a positive right to associate are not met. But it is not as clear in the case of a legal ruling about membership in a public association. We sometimes do things we are pressured to do without that entailing that we do not do it voluntarily. In particular, if we accept the legitimacy of the authority of the law, even if we disagree with it or its application, then in acting in accordance with it, we do not act under coercion. In this case, following the legal order, the members of the club do accept women as members willingly in the sense that is relevant. In the same sense, if we participate in a decision procedure, we accept the outcome, whether or not the outcome is the one we thought was best or the one we hoped for.

somewhat hostile male business community, then it is integral to its purpose that members be women. There is no such justification for the exclusion of women in the case above. Second, even putting this aside, a restriction on their right to exclude men would be justified only if it restricted access to a public good that would not otherwise be available to men. But if we assume, as above, that most businesspeople in the community are men, and that there is a club to which they can belong which affords them ample opportunities for networking, then there is no corresponding ground for restricting the right of the women-only club to exclude male members.

As a final wrinkle, consider a golf club that decides to exclude businesspeople on the grounds that it doesn't want the club to become a spillover chamber of commerce. The question should be approached by focusing on whether allowing this in general may permit a circumstance in which a class of citizens is excluded from access to certain public goods. In this case, it is clear that it would, and so the restriction should not be permitted. But that does not entail that a club cannot have rules of conduct for their members that include no discussion of business on the club premises, and so there is plausibly another remedy for the need for a social space which is not an extension of the business sphere.

(4) Restrictions on the negative component of freedom of association. Common examples of restrictions on the negative component of freedom of association are being drafted into the armed forces and being called up for jury duty. But the case for these being restrictions on the negative right to freedom of association is not clear. Why? Let us suppose that we are thinking of a legitimate state, by which I understand one that has the consent of those it governs. This does not mean that all citizens believe that all of the state's institutions and laws are just, but that they accept that the state adequately, even if imperfectly, represents the interests of its citizens as a whole. In a representative democracy, this is expressed in citizens accepting the procedures by which representatives are chosen. In accepting the procedures, they accept the results as legitimate, even if the candidates that they voted for do not win. The legislature then acts as a proxy agent for them. In this way, ideally, the laws have internal authority over the citizens, that is, authority that is endorsed by those they govern.[19] Citizens who accept their roles as citizens, then, have authorised indirectly the legal requirements to participate in jury duty when called. Thus, it is not a violation of their negative right to freedom of association because they are already willing to serve if called to do so. That leaves citizens who are not willing to fulfil their duties as citizens under the law. But this is simply a case of the moral legitimacy of the law in general for citizens. If the laws are justifiable, then no all-in moral rights are

[19] Ludwig (n 14).

violated, when someone otherwise not disposed to follow them does so only because there are enforcement mechanisms.

VII. CONCLUSION

An assumption of this project is that moral rights and duties provide a scaffold for the design of a legal system. Given this, the focus has been on how the ground and logical form of a *moral* right to freedom of association may inform our thinking about how to design a legal right to freedom of association.

Since a right to freedom of association involves others in its exercise, the negative (not to associate with others) and positive (to associate with others) rights have different implications. The negative right can be exercised individually. The positive right, given the negative right of others, can only be exercised when those with whom one would associate likewise exercise their positive rights with respect to the same group. The positive right then is a conditional right, and this gives rise to a right of exclusion for any group that has formed an association. It follows that the exercise of a right to exclusion is not a violation of anyone's moral right to freedom of association.

The moral right to freedom of association and its importance is grounded in a moral right to autonomy, a right to make one's own decisions about the shape of one's life, together with social interactions being a fundamental source of value for us. The moral right is distinct from the legal right. But even on a positivist view of law, to the extent that we have an interest in respecting moral rights in the design of positive law, we should seek to find an appropriate legal expression of a right to freedom of association. Given its importance, it should be encoded at the level of constitutional law and be treated as presumptively unrestricted, if not absolute. Restrictions should be based on countervailing moral considerations that are weightier or justified by the practical necessities of maintaining a stable legal system.

Significant issues that come up in implementing a moral right to freedom of association in a legal code are: (i) under what conditions the purpose or content of especially a formal association constitutes a ground for banning it, (ii) when an informal association may be required to become a legally recognised and hence formal association, (iii) when an association's right to exclusion may be abridged, and (iv) when the negative right not to associate may be overridden. There can't be a general algorithm because decisions depend on balancing considerations in light of empirical facts. The open texture of the law in this connection is not a flaw but a virtue: it ensures that the precise shape of a right to freedom of association will be worked out in part through case law when confronted with circumstances that could not have been anticipated ahead of time.

Figure 16.2 summarises some of the themes of the discussion.

Figure 16.2 An analysis of the moral right to freedom of association and notes on its application to the conditions of legality

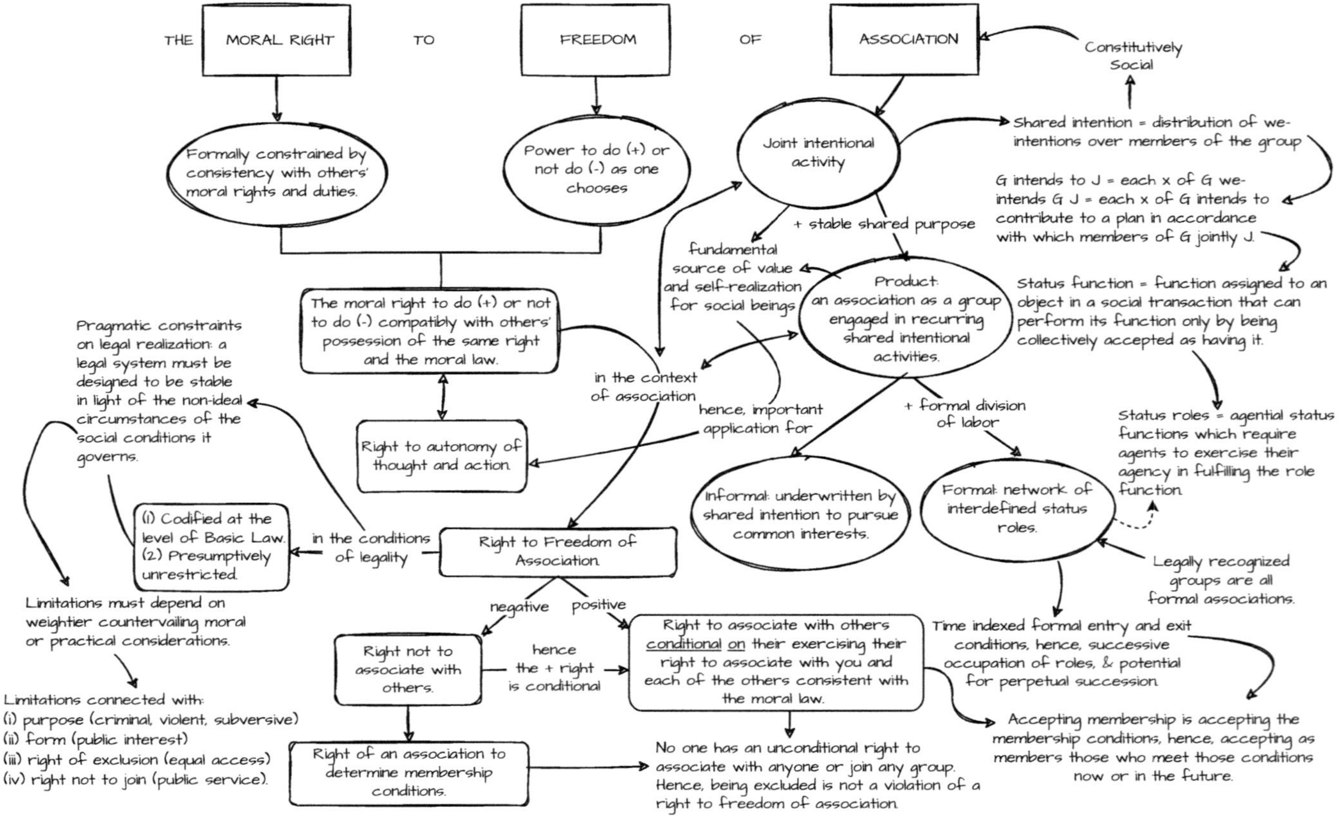

Index

Aarhus Convention, 78
abortion, 42, 56–8
adoption, 38
African Charter on Human and Peoples' Rights, 140, 150
agency *see* **group agency**
Allende, Salvador, 45
Amanwinata, Rukmana, 116
Amao, Femi, 13
American Convention on Human Rights, 49
Amnesty International for Indonesia, 125, 126
Amunátegui, Miguel Luis, 44
Anscombe, GEM, 219
antirealism, 250–5
Anzures Gurría, José Juan, 11, 14, 151–66, 179
Argentina, 42–3, 57
Aristotle, 61, 79, 271, 272
Asfinawati Ayub, 128
association agreements:
  applicable law, 152–4
  judicial review, 151–66
    types of agreements, 162–6
  legality, 153, 163–4
  punitive agreements, 164–5
associational life:
  forms, 287–8
  importance, 2–6
  individual protection, 3–4
  interdependence, 210
  legal protection landscape, 6–11
  liberal justification, 3–6
  meaning, 280–2
  moral value, 209, 277–94
  participatory democracy and, 4–5
  plural experience, 209, 268–74
  value, 259–60
Atalay, Şerafettin Can, 113
Atmadja, Dewa Gede, 119
Austin, John, 248
autonomy of associations:
  Chile, 51–6
  exclusion right, 264
  Germany, 90–3, 152, 154
  group agency, 261–3, 268–74, 278
  individual and collective right, 261–8
  Indonesia, 122–3, 124
  internal disputes, 151–6
  meaning, 283–4
  recognition and, 274–6
  Slovenia, 66–8
  Spain, 152
Aylwin, Patricio, 46

Barbé, Vanessa, 236
Bascuñán, Silva, 45
Bello, Andrés, 49
Bhagwat, Ashutosh, 239
Bilbao Ubillos, JM, 159
Blair, Tony, 33
Bolivia, 43
book clubs, 184–5
Boy Scouts of America, 287
Bratman, Michael, 203, 204
Brazil, 43
Brownlee, K, 262
Bulgaria: religious disputes, 171–5, 177–8
bureaucracy, 108, 149, 238–9
businesses, 96, 239–41, 242

Cahill, Maria, 1–17, 169, 225, 259, 260
Cairdè ar son Caidre Soup Kitchen, 14, 15–16, 208, 213–14, 225–7, 238–9, 242, 245–6, 275
Canada: secularism, 105
Catholic Church, 38, 44, 58, 85, 287
child abuse, 168
Chile:
  abortion, 42, 56–8
  association autonomy, 51–6
  Catholic Church, 44, 58
  constitutionalism, 42–8
  formation of association, 49–50
  freedom of association, 9, 41–59
    19th century, 43–4
    20th century, 44–7

21st century, 47–8
history, 42–8
rights, 48–52
freedom of education, 55
issues, 52–8
legal personality, 49–50
modernisation, 53
non-association right, 50–1
political parties, 54
professional associations, 51
religious beliefs, 57
subsidiarity principle, 52–4
trade unions, 50
Cifuentes, Abdón, 44
Clarendon Code, 23
collective intentionality:
approaches, 202–8
collective content, 204–5
collective mode, 205–6
collective subject, 206–7
construction of social world and, 207–8
importance, 201–3
meaning, 230, 247–8
plural experience, 209, 268–74
right to be We, 230, 248, 280–1
types of social groups, 246–50
Colombia, 43, 57
commercial entities, 96, 239–41, 242
constructivism, 251, 253
conventicles, 23
Costa Rica, 126
Court of Justice of the European Union (CJEU), 101
Covid-19, 9, 63, 76–7

democracy: participatory democracy, 4–5, 62, 139, 148
Derrida, Jacques, 253
Dicey, Albert Venn, 22–4, 28
discrimination:
economic sphere, 239–41, 242
gender, 16–17, 287, 290–2
Germany, 91, 96, 177
Kenya, 146
prohibition, 290–2
racism, 247, 251, 287
religious beliefs, 34
United Kingdom, 36–9
Dobrindt, Alexander, 99–100
Dominican Republic, 43
Elfudlatsani, B, 115–16
Epping, Volker, 89, 95
Ernst, R, 153
European Convention on Human Rights (ECHR):
freedom of association (Article 11), 33–6, 170–1
freedom of religion (Article 9), 170–1
Germany and, 101
internal religious disputes, 167–79
jurisdiction, 169–71
proportionality, 170, 173
Türkiye and, 111, 112, 113
UK HRA (1998) and, 33–6
European Union:
Germany and, 96
Slovenia and, 80
Turkish law and, 104
exclusion right, 35, 91, 93, 139, 239–40, 264, 289–92, 293
see also **discrimination**

Ferdian Andi, 132, 133
Ferraris, Maurizio, 252–3, 254–5, 256
Ferrer Riba, Josep, 159
Flat Earth Society, 287
formal associations, 281–2
formalism, 253, 257
France:
freedom of association, 237
legal model for Türkiye, 114
meaning of association, 236
registration of associations, 267
religious disputes, 175
secularism, 105
freedom of association
see also individual countries
bureaucracy, 238–9
businesses, 239–41, 242
exclusion right, 264
human need, 229
institutionalisation, 236–9, 242
layered view of groups, 231–4
legal right, 6–11
from moral to legal right, 285–6
restrictions, 286–93
logical form, 278–80
meaning of association, 234–6
moral right, 209, 277–8, 283–5, 293
diagram, 294
from moral to legal right, 285–6

non-participation right, 50–1, 64, 66, 68–9, 264–5, 278
plural experience, 209, 268–74
pressure points, 12–15
restrictions *see* **restrictions**
right to be We, 209, 229–43, 248, 280–1

freedom of conscience, 3–4

freedom of expression:
Chile, 55
freedom of association and, 4, 5, 69, 214, 216, 268
Germany, 86–7, 98, 99, 101–2
hate speech, 101–2
Indonesia, 118, 126
Kenya, 136, 146–7, 150
Slovenia, 62, 75
Türkiye, 10, 111, 112–13
United Kingdom, 22, 34
United States, 237

functionalism, 254, 257

game theory, 254

Gargarella, R, 42

gender discrimination:
Catholic Church, 287
exclusions, 290–2
Kilmartin Golf Club, 14, 16–17, 158–9, 162–3, 165, 208, 240–1, 242–3

genital mutilation, 168

Germany:
Article 9 (1), 84, 86–8
association agreements, 162–3
punitive agreements, 164
autonomy of associations, 90–3, 152, 154
Basic Law, 81–3
collective agreements, 95, 100
definition of association, 87–8, 96
economic entities, 96
ECtHR and, 101
employers' organisations, 88
EU law and, 96, 101
Federal Constitutional Court, 83
forced labour prohibition, 94
freedom of association, 9, 81–102
beneficiaries, 96
contemporary culture, 84–6
debate, 101
negative right, 94–5, 101
special cases, 88–90
freedom of expression, 86–7, 98, 99, 101–2
fundamental rights
non-discrimination, 96
status, 82–3
internal disputes, 155, 161, 165–6
legal model for Türkiye, 104
monopolistic associations, 91–2
national security, 97–100
Nazi legacy, 81–2
NGOs, 235–6
Palestinian solidarity movements and, 101
political parties, 85, 89–90
Communist Party, 97
public law associations, 95
registered associations, 84
religious freedom, 85–6, 90, 94
restrictions on associations, 96–100, 101–2
secularism, 105
trade unions, 86, 88, 93

Gilbert, Margaret, 203, 206, 248–9

golf clubs *see* **Kilmartin Golf Club**

group agency:
concept, 261–3, 278
pluralism, 268–74

Guala, Francesco, 252, 254–5, 255–6

Guatemala, 43

Guerra, José Guillermo, 45

Gümüş, M, 108

Gutman, Amy, 259–60

habits:
acquired automaticities, 216–18
associating on familiar grounds, 209, 213–27
Cairdè ar son Caidre Soup Kitchen, 213–14, 225–7
development, 220
freedom of association and, 223–4
group justification, 222–3, 224
proxy-reasons, 218–24, 226
sources of justification, 220–2
sustainable political communities and, 225–7

Haiti, 43

Hamid, Usman, 126

Harrington, Glenda, 14

Hatta, Mohammad, 118

Hepple, Bob, 36

Hesse, Konrad, 88

Hornett, W, 216

human flourishing, 3, 5–6, 240, 259

hunting, 30

İmamoğlu, Ekrem, 113
Indonesia:
civil society organisations
2013 Act, 117, 119–25
autonomy, 122–3, 124
bans, 127–8, 134
definition, 115–16, 120, 123
empowerment, 123–4
entitlements, 120–1
internal disputes, 124
prohibitions, 124–5
corruption, 132–3
fair trial, 129, 134
freedom of association, 10, 115–34
assessment, 133–4
constitutional right, 117–19
restrictions, 125–33
scope, 119–25
Human Rights Act (1999), 119–25, 129
mining projects, 130–2, 133
National Revival Period, 118
national security, 127–8
Pancasila, 127, 128
religious organisations, 130–2, 133
Indra, Radhiyya, 131
informal associations *see* **Cairdè ar son Caidre Soup Kitchen**
institutionalisation, 236–9
internal disputes:
applicable law, 152–4
autonomy, 151–2
divided communities or internal dissent, 177–9
formal judicial control, 154–5
judicial review, 11, 151–66
guidelines, 159–66
property disputes, 175–7
type of agreements, 162–6
type of association, 159–62
material judicial control, 155–6
pressure points, 12–13
property disputes, 175–7
reasonable ground criterion, 156–9
religious associations, 11, 172–5, 175–7
International Center for Not-for-Profit Law (ICNL), 148
International Covenant on Civil and Political Rights (1966):
Indonesia and, 116–17, 133
Kenya and, 139–40
International Criminal Court, 138
International Labour Organization (ILO), 111
interviews, 11, 181–93
Ireland:
Cairdè ar son Caidre Soup Kitchen, 14, 15–16, 208, 213–14, 225–7, 238–9, 242, 245–6, 275
charity regulation, 16, 238–9, 246
Kilmartin Golf Club, 14, 16–17, 158–9, 162–3, 165, 208, 240–1, 242–3
pilot study, 182–3
religious laws, 188
Italy: legal model for Türkiye, 104

Jackson, Erin, 11, 181–93
Jamaica, 43
James, William, 217–18
Jenkins, D, 262
Jokowi (Joko Widoko), 130, 132, 134
judicial review:
applicable law, 152–4
guidelines, 159–66
internal disputes, 11, 151–66
reasonable ground criterion, 156–9
type of agreements, 162–6
type of associations, 159–62
Junaenah, Inna, 10, 115–34

Kant, Immanuel, 283, 284
Kenya:
2010 Constitution, 138, 139–40
bureaucracy, 149
customary law, 135
freedom of association, 10, 135–50
assessment, 148–50
case law, 144–7
constitutional right, 139–40
history, 136–9
legislative regulation, 140–4
freedom of expression, 136, 146–7, 150
fundamental rights, 141–2
international law and, 138, 139–40
legal history, 135–6
national security, 143
political parties, 142, 144–6, 147
protests, 149, 150
religious expression, 146
sexual orientation, 145, 146
social media and, 149
trade unions, 142–3

Khalidi, Ali, 251–2
Khan, Irene, 101, 192
Kharsi, Aoife Nazneen, 11
Kilmartin Golf Club, 14, 16–17, 158–9, 162–3, 165, 208, 240–1, 242–3
KKK, 287
Kukathas, C, 167–8, 178, 179, 270–1, 274

Lagos, Ricardo, 47, 53
Lahera Forteza, J, 165
Lasagni, Giulia, 2, 197–211
Latifulhayat, Atip, 128–9
Lauterbach, Karl, 99
LGBT groups, 190–1
List, Christian, 261–2, 268–9, 272
List, R, 115
Loasana, Nina A, 131
locus standi: **Slovenia,** 77–9
Ludwig, Krk, 208, 209, 249, 277–94

MacCormick, Neil, 7
McIntyre, Ruari, 13
McMurry, Nicholas, 11, 13, 167–79
Maitland, FW, 24–5
Manssen, Gerrit, 98
Marín, TV, 152
Marín López, JJ, 157
marriage, 246, 248, 255–7
Martens, Judith, 209, 213–27
Martino, Valeria, 208, 209, 245–58
Marzuki, Suparman, 129
Mboce, Njoki, 10, 135–50
Merten, Detlef, 88, 98
Merton, Robert, 247
Mill, John Stuart, 277, 283, 287
Moi, Daniel, 137
moot scenarios:
  Cairdè ar son Caidre Soup Kitchen, 14, 15–16, 208, 213–14, 225–7, 238–9, 242, 245–6, 275
  Kilmartin Golf Club, 14, 16–17, 158–9, 162–3, 165, 208, 240–1, 242–3
Muqoddas, Busyro, 131
murder, 168

Nankan, Sahara, 13
national security, 49, 97–100, 127–8, 143
Nicaragua, 43
non-participation right, 50–1, 64, 66, 68–9, 264–5, 278

Ó Conaill, Seán, 13
O'Grady, Leannán Martan, 9, 81–102
opaque phenomenon, 251–2
Organised Crime and Corruption Reporting Project, 132–3
Öztürk, Fatih, 9–10, 103–14

Palestinian solidarity movements, 101
participatory democracy, 4–5, 62, 139, 148
personal narratives:
  dataset, 182–3
  faith-based communities, 188–9
  fighting for change, 188
  frustration, 189–91
  fulfilment, 187–9
  leaving, 189–90
  legacy in one's life, 191–2
  motivations, 184–7
    coaching children, 186
    keeping home connections, 184–5
    loneliness, 187
    new place connections, 185–6
  professional communities, 189
  themes, 11, 181–93
Peru, 43
Pettit, Philip, 168, 178, 179, 261–2, 268–9, 270–4
Pinochet, Augusto, 46–7, 53
Plato, 272
Prabowo Subianto, 133, 134
pressure points, 12–15
privacy rights, 3–4
professional associations:
  Chile, 51
  compulsory association, 43, 47, 50–1, 57
  personal narratives, 189
property disputes, 175–7

racism, 247, 251, 287
Rawls, John, 269, 274
Raz, Joseph, 120
realism, 250–5
recognition:
  Cairdè ar son Caidre Soup Kitchen, 14, 15–16, 208, 213–14, 225–7, 238–9, 242, 245–6, 275
  categories of social groups, 246–50
  France, 267
  informal associations, 246, 247, 287–9
  marriage, 246, 248, 255–7
  pluralism and, 274–6
  realism and antirealism, 250–5

registration and, 267, 275
restrictions, 286–93
social ontology, 209, 245–58
reflexivity, 247
religious associations:
discrimination, 34
Indonesia, 130–2, 133
internal disputes, 171–5
divided communities, 177–9
property disputes, 175–7
liberalism and, 167–9, 178
pernicious beliefs, 287
personal narratives, 188–9
republican tradition, 168–9
Slovenia, 67
United Kingdom, 37–8
republicanism, 168–9, 237, 261, 273–4
Research Ireland, 1
restrictions:
exclusion rights, 289–92
Germany, 96–100, 101–2
harm, 287
Indonesia, 125–33
informal associations, 287–9
negative rights, 292–3
pressure points, 12
purpose, 287
Slovenia, 76–9
sources of limitations, 286–93
Türkiye, 108
United Kingdom, 29–33
Ritchie, Katherine, 248
Rivers, Julian, 8–9, 21–39
Riwanto, Agus, 120, 129
Rome Statute, 138
Russia: invasion of Ukraine, 102

Salamon, LM, 115
Salvador Coderch, Pablo, 159
same-sex couples, 38, 255
Schmid, Hans Bernhard, 208, 209, 259–76
Schmitz, Michael, 208, 209, 229–43
Scholz, Olaf, 85
Searle, John, 203, 206, 207, 248, 250
Seehofer, Horst, 99
Setiawan, Putra, 120
sexual orientation, 36, 38, 145, 239, 248
Siregar, Adil, 116
slavery, 178
Slovenia:
Article 42, 61–70
children's autonomy, 67–8
Covid-19, 9, 63, 76–7
environmental protection, 78–9
foundations, 65–6
freedom of association, 9, 61–80
case law, 64–70
forms and features, 63–70
restrictions, 76–9
independence, 70–1
individual autonomy, 66
languages, 69–70
locus standi of associations, 77–9
minority groups, 69–70
political parties, 71–6
private-law associations, 68
religious communities, 67
right not to associate, 64, 66, 68–9
right to strike, 62
types of association, 62, 65–6
social democracy, 53, 74, 75, 274
social ontology:
autonomy *see* **autonomy of associations**
categories of social groups, 246–50
collective intentionality *see* **collective intentionality**
etymology, 199
habits *see* **habits**
landscape, 199–201
meaning, 199
meaning of association, 234–6
moral value, 209, 277–94
overview, 208–9
perspective, 197–211
plural experience of association, 209, 268–74
realism and antirealism, 250–5
recognition of associations *see* **recognition**
right to be We, 209, 229–43, 248, 280–1
Societās project, 1–2, 8, 11, 13–14, 181–2, 208
Soekarno, 118
Sokolowski, SW, 115
Soto, Sebastian, 9, 41–59
soup kitchen *see* **Cairdè ar son Caidre Soup Kitchen**
Spain:
association agreements: legality, 153
autonomy of associations, 152
charities, 153, 160
internal disputes
reasonable ground for judicial control, 156–9
type of agreement, 165
type of association and, 161

political parties, 160
social democracy, 274
trade unions, 160–1
status roles, 281–2
Stöber, K, 155
Sudan, 149–50
suicide, 168
Supomo, 118
Switzerland, 104, 126

Thomasson, Amie, 251
Thoolen, Hans, 125
Tocqueville, Alexis de, 5–6
torture, 168, 178
trade unions:
Chile, 50
Germany, 86, 88, 93
Kenya, 142–3
Spain, 160–1
Türkiye, 107, 111–12
UK history, 23–4
United Kingdom, 32
United States, 247
Tuomela, Raimo, 203, 205
Türkiye:
Article 33, 103, 106–10
bureaucracy, 108
Constitutional Court
case law, 110–13
powers, 105–6
courts, 105–6
definition of association, 107
elitism, 114
freedom of association, 9–10, 103–14
assessment, 114
case law, 109–13
restrictions, 108
freedom of expression, 10, 111, 112–13
Hatay Tombs and Shrines, 109
hunger strikes, 109–10
Law No 5253, 103, 106–10
legal models, 104, 113
legal system, 104–6
political parties, 112–13
secularism, 104–5
trade unions, 107, 111–12

Ukraine, 102
Umar, ARM, 131
United Kingdom:
charities, 24–5, 32, 38
Clarendon Code, 23
constitution, 22–5
conventicles, 23
counterterrorism, 31
freedom of association, 8–9, 21–39
Equality Act (2010), 36–9
Human Rights Act (1998), 23
negative and positive right, 21–5
restrictions, 29–33
freedom of expression, 22, 34
friendly societies, 31–2
fundamental rights, 22–3
Human Rights Act (1998), 33–6
hunting, 30
law and liberty in association, 26–9
legal personality, 24
parliamentary supremacy, 33
political parties, 30–1
quasi-military organisations, 30
religious associations, 37–8
religious conformity, 23
religious disputes, 171, 175
Royal Assent, 21
secularism and, 105
single-characteristic associations, 37–8
single-sex services, 37
trade unions, 23–4, 32
United Nations: Germany and, 101
United States:
Constitutional Court powers, 106
constitutional right of association, 236–7
Indonesia and, 126
NAACP v Alabama, 69
racism, 247
secularism and, 105
trade unions, 247
Universal Declaration of Human Rights, 262, 263
Uruguay, 43, 57
USAID, 118–19
utilitarianism, 283

Valenzuela, Arturo, 52–3
Vatovec, Katarina, 9, 61–80
Vosskuhle, Andreas, 102

Wahyu Agung Perdana, 132
Washington, George, 237, 242

Yamin, Mohammad, 118

Zapatero, José Luis, 274
Zhu, Shaoming, 13

9 781509 986699

Printed by Libri Plureos GmbH in Hamburg,
Germany